# THE
# BUTTERFLIES
## OF
# BRITAIN
# & IRELAND

THE NATIONAL TRUST

PUBLISHED IN ASSOCIATION  WITH THE NATIONAL TRUST

# THE BUTTERFLIES OF BRITAIN & IRELAND

JEREMY THOMAS
RICHARD LEWINGTON

DK

DORLING KINDERSLEY
London • New York • Stuttgart

A DORLING KINDERSLEY BOOK

*For our daughters, Emily and Anna Thomas
and Alexandra Lewington*

Edited and designed for Dorling Kindersley
by DAVID BURNIE and PHILIP LORD

SENIOR EDITOR Krystyna Mayer
MANAGING ART EDITOR Derek Coombes
MANAGING EDITOR Jemima Dunne

First published in Great Britain in 1991
by Dorling Kindersley Limited,
9 Henrietta Street, London WC2E 8PS.

A CIP catalogue record for this book is available from the
British Library.

ISBN 0–86318–591–6

Typeset by Suripace Limited, Milton Keynes
Reproduced by Pica, Singapore
Printed and bound in Italy by Graphicom

# CONTENTS

# INTRODUCTION

THE AIM OF this book is to share some of the pleasure that British butterflies have given us during the course of our careers. Its origin goes back to 1983, when Richard Lewington found a wild chrysalis of a Red Admiral, and realized that no book past or present did justice to its subtle beauty. This feeling grew as he collected the eggs, caterpillars, and chrysalises of other species, and kept them in his Oxfordshire garden until they became adults. With it came the ambition to rear and illustrate every stage in the life-cycle of all the British butterflies, emulating the great work of F. W. Frohawk earlier this century.

Frohawk was both the author and the illustrator of his books. Although most species of butterfly were more abundant in his day, major excursions were needed to reach many of their remoter sites, and he took 24 years to complete this task. The illustrations in this book took just seven years, a testimony both to the ease with which one can visit all the British species in the age of the car, and to the generosity of other butterfly enthusiasts who so kindly sent livestock whenever ours failed.

Many excellent books on butterflies have been written since Frohawk's *Natural History of British Butterflies* was published in 1924, including some that are works of scholarship. However, the growing concern about the future of British and Irish species has led to a great deal of recent research into their behaviour, ecology, and distribution, and the results of this are less readily available. Most, if published, have appeared only in obscure journals or in books written primarily for fellow academics. In this volume, we have tried to present this new information in a more digestible form, by combining it with many personal observations and by drawing upon the wealth of anecdotes left by Victorian and earlier naturalists.

## THE SCOPE OF THIS BOOK

This book provides detailed coverage of every species that currently lives in the British Isles, as well as of three common immigrants that arrive every spring, but which are unable to survive our winters. In addition to these 60 species, a concluding section describes a number of rare vagrants that occasionally reach our shores, together with two extinct species.

For each species, the upperside and underside of the male and female adult butterflies are illustrated, except in the few cases where the sexes look the same. Some species vary in appearance with the time of year, or in different parts of the British Isles,

and these forms are shown as well. Also included are some of the many strange varieties or aberrations that periodically crop up in a number of species.

It should be remembered that, in the wild, butterflies only rarely rest with their wings held wide open. So, complementing the formal diagnostic portraits are one or more pictures of the living butterfly shown sitting in a typical position.

All the paintings of adult butterflies are life-size, but the eggs, caterpillars, and chrysalises are enlarged to display the full beauty of their shapes and markings. To give an idea of scale, a life-sized outline of these stages appears beside each enlargement. In general, only the fully grown caterpillar has been painted, exceptions being where the young caterpillar looks markedly different from the older one.

## THE LIFE OF A BUTTERFLY

Every butterfly goes through four very different phases in its life: egg, caterpillar, chrysalis, and adult. In many species, the first three of these stages can be just as interesting as the last, and they are often quite easy to find in the wild.

Most butterflies take one year to complete their life-cycle, although certain species fit in two, three, or even four generations between spring and autumn. A chart at the head of each species illustration shows the typical dates when each stage can be found. In some cases, this varies slightly with the warmth of the season, or in different parts of the butterfly's range. In general, emergence dates are later, and there may be fewer generations, in the north.

In many of the texts that follow, one or more aspects of the behaviour or ecology of butterflies is described in particular detail. Taken together, these give a fairly full account of the current knowledge about British and Irish species. The caterpillar is perhaps the most interesting of the three immature stages. It is the only period in the life-cycle in which growth occurs, and the necessity to expose itself while feeding makes a caterpillar extremely vulnerable to enemies. Much of the behaviour and appearance of the caterpillars of different species is due to their different ways of avoiding predators.

Most caterpillars live singly, and are beautifully camouflaged against their foodplants. All are tiny when they emerge from the egg, but grow rapidly, shedding their skin several times before pupating (forming a chrysalis).

# BUTTERFLY FAMILIES

The 60 species of butterfly that regularly occur in Britain belong to seven separate families of closely related Lepidoptera. The individual members in each group possess similar family characteristics, which are briefly summarized here.

## Family HESPERIIDAE: The Skippers

These are the most moth-like and primitive of the families of butterflies. All are small, lively insects, with broad, hairy bodies and wide-set heads, and an unusually large gap between the bases of the two antennae. There are eight resident species in Britain, and a ninth species on Jersey. Five of these – the "golden" Skippers – sit in a highly characteristic pose with the fore- and hindwings held at different angles.

FAMILY HESPERIIDAE
*The heads of Skipper butterflies have a large gap between the bases of the antennae.*

## Family PAPILIONIDAE: The Swallowtails

This magnificent family of butterflies includes the Swallowtails, Apollos, and the wonderful Birdwings of Australasia and the Far East. The family has just one representative in the British Isles, the Swallowtail. Like most of its relatives, this is a large, striking insect with distinctive, long wing-tails.

## Family PIERIDAE: The Whites and Yellows

These are pale, medium-sized butterflies, with predominantly white or yellow wings. Most species roam widely through the countryside, rather than living in identifiable colonies. Their eggs are invariably tall and cylindrical, a characteristic most easily seen in those familiar pests of vegetable gardens, the Large and Small ("Cabbage") Whites.

## Family LYCAENIDAE: The Coppers, Hairstreaks, and Blues

About a third of the world's butterfly species belong to this family. They are small, active butterflies with a metallic sheen to their wings. There are 16 species in the British Isles. During their development, many have an intimate relationship with ants. These provide protection for the caterpillar or chrysalis in return for a nutritious, sugary secretion. Lycaenid butterflies have small, bun-shaped eggs, slug-like caterpillars, and short, stumpy chrysalises.

FAMILY LYCAENIDAE
*Adonis Blue caterpillars attended by ants. Ants play a role in the development of many Lycaenids.*

## Family RIODINIDAE: The Metalmarks

This beautiful family of butterflies reaches its greatest magnificence and diversity in central America. There is just one European species – the Duke of Burgundy – which is one of the family's less distinguished members. Some consider the Riodinidae to be a subfamily of the Lycaenidae.

## Family NYMPHALIDAE: The "Aristocrats" – Vanessids, Emperors, and Fritillaries

This large family of butterflies contains some of the biggest and gaudiest species in the world. There are 16 species in the British Isles, all with caterpillars that are protected by sharp spines. One diagnostic feature of the adult is that the first pair of legs is vestigial, the butterfly walking on two pairs alone.

FAMILY NYMPHALIDAE
*The body of a Red Admiral. Nymphalids have only two pairs of functional legs.*

FAMILY SATYRIDAE
*The wing of a Satyrid butterfly with eye-spots, a typical feature of this family. In a number of species, these provide protection by diverting the attacks of birds away from the otherwise vulnerable body.*

## Family SATYRIDAE: The Browns

Although considered by some to be a subfamily of the Nymphalidae, we regard this group of 11 British species as belonging to a family in its own right. These are medium-sized or small butterflies, with small, gleaming eye-spots towards the outer margins of the wings. Most species have a brown coloration.

In many respects, the chrysalis is the most beautiful stage in the life-cycle, and the detailed paintings of these are one of the features of this book. Apart from those Lycaenid chrysalises that are found in ant nests, all exhibit some form of camouflage. This ranges from dead, dew-spangled leaves in the case of the Fritillaries, to living leaves in many Browns, and to bird-droppings in the case of the Black Hairstreak.

## THE ADULT BUTTERFLY

It is easy to imagine that an adult butterfly is a purposeless creature that lives out its short life by flitting aimlessly between flowers. Nothing could be further from the truth. Almost every action has a function, and it adds considerably to the enjoyment of watching these insects to understand what they are doing.

Having emerged from the chrysalis and inflated its wings, the main goal in a male butterfly's life is to pair with as many females as possible. The female, on the other hand, usually mates shortly after emergence, and spends the rest of her life avoiding males and searching for places to lay eggs. But before they can do anything, both sexes must raise their body temperatures to well over 30°C (86°F).

Butterflies have the reputation of being cold-blooded animals that are active only in sunshine. In fact, they regulate their body temperatures within remarkably narrow limits by using their wings to absorb or reflect the sun's heat. Temperature regulation occurs throughout the day, often at the same time as other activities. However, it dominates a butterfly's behaviour in marginal weather, such as first thing in the morning and late afternoon, and these are the only times when many species fully open their wings, in order to warm up.

## COURTSHIP AND MATING

Once warm, the males search for mates. Many fly to a particular place where virgin females also gather. This may simply be around a certain part of the site, as in the case of the Small Heath, or it may be some distance away. A good example of the latter is shown by the Purple Emperor, which breeds at very low densities over considerable areas of countryside. If the sexes are to have any chance of meeting, it is necessary for them to gather at the highest point in the neighbourhood, a phenomenon known as "hilltopping".

Having arrived in a suitable area, most male butterflies hunt their mates in one of two ways. Some, such as the Duke of Burgundy, merely perch in a prominent place, and launch themselves after any insect flying by. Others, such as the Wood White, fly ceaselessly through their sites, searching every nook and cranny for hidden females. Some species behave in both ways, depending on the time of day or the habitat.

Once an unmated female is discovered, there follows a courtship ritual which is prolonged and complicated in species such as the Grayling and Silver-washed Fritillary, but brief and simple in others. The act of mating usually lasts about 30 minutes. During this time, a packet of sperm is transferred from the male to the female's body, usually sufficient to fertilize every egg as it is laid. Few females mate more than once.

## FOODPLANTS, HABITATS, AND DISTRIBUTION

The females of most species take enormous care during egg-laying, placing their offspring in situations where they are best adapted to survive. We describe this in detail for most species, because it is usually the key to why certain species are rare and restricted, whereas others are widespread and common. In most cases the eggs are laid on a particular growth form of the one (or few) species of plants that are eaten by the caterpillar. Many, such as the Adonis Blue and Lulworth Skipper, restrict breeding to extremely warm parts of their sites. Colonies occur only where these specific breeding conditions exist, and if there are many plants that are suitable for egg-laying present, then the odds are that the colony of that butterfly will also be large.

Many species of butterfly are exceedingly sedentary, and live in small, discrete areas from which they almost never stray. Others have no fixed abode, but roam through the countryside, selecting different places for different activities. A few species, such as the Painted Lady, even migrate across continents, breeding in the British Isles during the summer, with their offspring dying, or migrating south, in autumn.

The distribution of British butterflies has been recorded with great precision in recent years, although there are still gaps to be filled in Ireland. We include a map showing the current range of every species. In the case of migrants, a distinction is made between those regions in which most sightings are made, and others with few or occasional records. Unless otherwise stated, a cross indicates a site where a species is now extinct. A question mark indicates that its presence has not been confirmed.

Many species of butterfly have declined enormously in recent years, and some now depend wholly on conservation bodies for their survival. The main causes of decline are described in detail in this book, in the hope that this will help the owners and managers of breeding areas to rectify some of these changes. Gardens can often be improved for butterflies, but unfortunately they attract only the most common and mobile species. The most effective way to help the survival of our butterflies is to join voluntary conservation bodies. Foremost among these are the National Trust, the Woodland Trust, the many County Trusts for Nature Conservation, and the British Butterfly Conservation Society.

# CHEQUERED SKIPPER

*Carterocephalus palaemon*

THIS BEAUTIFUL dappled Skipper is almost certainly now restricted to Scotland, having disappeared mysteriously from its last English sites in about 1975. Although always considered a rarity, its loss in England came as a severe jolt to conservationists, for in the 1960s there had been fine colonies on at least four east Midland nature reserves. This extinction is particularly lamentable, because the Chequered Skipper was the most attractive of the English Skippers, seen at its best in late spring, darting around bugle flowers in sunny woodland rides.

Like all the Skippers, the Chequered Skipper flies in rapid dashes, zig-zagging a few centimetres above the ground and changing direction – even reversing – at the slightest obstacle. It can be difficult to follow in full flight, when the wing markings blur into an orange-brown haze. Hopeful beginners sometimes misidentify the Duke of Burgundy *(see p.111)* for this rarity, but there is no mistaking the real thing. At rest, the Chequered Skipper's wings are much more angular than those of the "Duke". Also, It has no spots along the base of its lower forewings, and the pale patches on the undersides form a jumbled mosaic with the darker areas, rather than occurring as two neat bands.

*Distribution In England, last seen in the east Midlands in 1976; still locally common in Argyllshire and Inverness-shire.*

## REGIONAL VARIATIONS

It is often claimed that English and Scottish Chequered Skippers belong to distinctly different races, with the former being slightly larger and lighter, and possessing underwings that are more yellow-brown with creamier yellow spots. We depict specimens from both England and Scotland, but in truth this is a somewhat variable butterfly and any regional distinction is slight.

The Chequered Skipper is a handsome insect in all its forms. It emerges in one generation a year, peaking in late May or early June, depending on the weather. If anything, the Scottish butterflies emerge slightly earlier, but they can be extremely frustrating to find, due to the wind and rain that frequently lashes western Scotland in late spring.

## DEFENDING A TERRITORY

The behaviour of this charming butterfly has been well studied by Neil Ravenscroft, of the University of Aberdeen, and Ray Collier, of the Nature Conservancy Council. English Chequered Skippers were highly colonial, with the adults restricted to small areas of a ride or woodside for the whole flight period. In Scotland they are slightly more free-ranging. There is one famous colony that occurs more or less continuously along an 8-km. (5-mile) stretch of roadside, and another that extends even further beside a loch. This is not to say that all populations are large. Although Neil Ravenscroft has found colonies consisting of hundreds of adults, others contain no more than a few dozen, at least in poor years for the species.

The male is the easier sex to find, for he establishes a territory in the sunshine, perched on prominent vegetation, with wings draped back and open, waiting to buzz every passing intruder. Males have favourite places for perching, such as sunny nooks beside sheltered wood edges, particularly in south facing dips in undulating terrain. Almost every naturalist familiar with the butterfly has noted how it loves to visit flowers, concentrating on blue species like bluebell *(Endymion non-scriptus)* and bugle *(Ajuga reptans),* which were far and away the favourite nectar source of butterflies in the English colonies of old.

## A SLOW DEVELOPMENT

The Chequered Skipper's egg is a large pale sphere, laid singly on the underside of tall, coarse grassblades. Before they died out, the butterflies in English colonies bred mainly on wood false brome *(Brachypodium sylvaticum)* in woodland rides and glades, with tor grass *(B. pinnatum)* sometimes being used in adjoining grassland. Things are rather different in Scotland.

Although Ray Collier saw eggs on brome on one site, the plant is absent in most localities and there was growing evidence that purple moor grass *(Molinia caerulea)* was used instead. This was confirmed by Neil Ravenscroft, who is also some way towards solving the mystery of why the butterfly is so rare and localized when vast tracts of Scotland are infested with purple moor grass. It seems, as with so many species, that female Chequered Skippers are particular over egg-laying, choosing only a certain type of purple moor grass tussock for their offspring. The attributes of these have not been fully analysed, but may consist of a need for some shelter and shade, a warm local climate, an absence of stagnant water, and the existence of high nitrogen concentrations in the leaves. What is clear, however, is that few sites in Scotland meet these requirements.

Like those of related Skippers, the caterpillar has sluggish movements, and lives in a tube of grass made by folding a blade double, with the edges secured by little cords of silk. It emerges to feed both above and below the tube, first making characteristic, V-shaped notches, then eating more of the blade until the tube is left isolated on the midrib.

The caterpillar of the Chequered Skipper is one of the slowest-growing of any British butterfly. Not until October, after a hundred days of feeding, is it fully grown. It then changes from being a rather undistinguished pale green grub, to a straw colour, which blends with the hibernation nest that it constructs from dead grass and silk. There the caterpillar remains until the following spring, oblivious to the ferocity of the Scottish winter. It reappears in mid-April and, after about a week without feeding, spins another nest of dead leaves, where it forms an chrysalis, which also looks very much like a withered grassblade.

## DISCOVERY AND DECLINE

It seems probable that, like their Scottish counterparts, English Chequered Skippers also had very particular breeding requirements, although their exact habitat may never now be known. The species was always scarce, and there is much uncertainty about the earliest recorded sightings, as they are often confused through misidentifications and fraud.

A Rev. Dr. Abbott is usually credited with the first genuine report, in 1798 in Clapham Park Wood, Bedfordshire, and he found another colony at Gamlingay, near Cambridge, a few years later. However, there must be a slight doubt even about these records. In his delightful reminiscences, published in 1943, P. B. M. Allen showed that there was a lively trade in false English rarities in the late eighteenth century, and Dr. Abbott himself was duped on at least one occasion. Moreover, he had a reputation for introducing rarities and aliens to Clapham Park Wood only to "discover" them soon after.

Whatever the original range of Chequered Skippers, English colonies were confined for most of the nineteenth century to a band of woods and associated limestone grassland that stretched from Oxford to south Lincolnshire, with another group of colonies to the north, in Lincolnshire. Most were fairly wet sites, some more or less waterlogged. The Chequered Skipper lived mainly in ridings and glades, and one by one these colonies disappeared until by 1950 the butterfly was largely restricted to Lincolnshire, and to the woods of Rockingham Forest in Northamptonshire and Rutland.

There then followed a brief re-expansion when the Chequered Skipper recolonized some former sites, including Monks Wood and Woodwalton Fen in Cambridgeshire. It remained plentiful enough on the best of its sites, and as recently as 1961, R. E. M. Pilcher wrote: "Castor Hanglands [near Peterborough] has always been the metropolis of this insect. It is still very common [there] but no longer enjoys its former abundance. An insect in no apparent danger of extinction but well worth some trouble to maintain in good numbers".

It was, alas, to become extinct on that nature reserve exactly 10 years later, having already disappeared from almost every other English site in the decade.

## A FUTURE IN THE NORTH

In England, there has been no accepted sighting of the Chequered Skipper since 1975, despite many surveys of former sites. There remains a glimmer of hope that a colony may yet turn up in the east Midlands, but this becomes increasingly unlikely with every year that passes.

The situation in Scotland is much more encouraging. The butterfly was unknown there until 1942, when Lt.-Col. Mackworth-Praed astonished the entomological world by announcing that he had found specimens near Fort William, roughly 480 km. (300 miles) north of the nearest known colony. In fact a Miss Evans had discovered the butterfly nearby three years earlier, but this remained secret for a while.

These two sites held the only known Scottish colonies for 30 years, until an amateur naturalist, J. E. H. Blackie, informed Monks Wood that he had found some in Argyll. Surveys were quickly organized, notably by the Scottish Wildlife Trust, and soon about 40 colonies had been found.

Despite these recent discoveries, no one thinks that the butterfly has spread, but merely that it had been overlooked in a region that few entomologists visited. It is, however, a most heartening chapter in the history of this beautiful Skipper.

# CHEQUERED SKIPPER · *Carterocephalus palaemon*

### LIFE-CYCLE

| | JAN | FEB | MAR | APR | MAY | JUN | JUL | AUG | SEP | OCT | NOV | DEC |
|---|---|---|---|---|---|---|---|---|---|---|---|---|
| EGG | | | | | | | | | | | | |
| CATERPILLAR | | | | | | | | | | | | |
| CHRYSALIS | | | | | | | | | | | | |
| ADULT | | | | | | | | | | | | |

**Male**
English specimen from former colony in Northamptonshire; sexes are very similar.

**Female**
Northamptonshire specimen; females are generally slightly larger than males.

**Feeding male**
Adult feeding at flowers of bluebell – a favourite nectar source.

**Male**
Rare aberrant form from Brigstock, Northamptonshire. Collected 1933.

**Male**
Typical specimen from Scottish colonies.

**Resting adult**
English female at rest on grassblade.

SIDE VIEW        VIEW FROM ABOVE

**Egg** [*x15*]
Laid singly on underside of a grassblade.

**Chrysalis** [*x1½*]
Formed inside a nest of dead leaves; camouflaged to resemble a dead grassblade.

**Spring caterpillar**
Straw-coloured caterpillar in spring, prior to forming chrysalis.

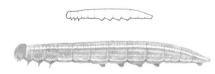

**Summer/autumn caterpillar** [*x2¼*]
Caterpillar remains green until hibernation.

# LULWORTH SKIPPER

## *Thymelicus acteon*

THIS TINY SKIPPER is found only on sheltered downs, cliff-tops, and crumbling under-cliffs in the extreme south of England. Fewer than a hundred breeding sites are known, but some support vast numbers of the butterfly. Indeed, there is good reason to believe that the species is now more abundant here than at any time since its discovery, by J. C. Dale, at Durdle Door in Dorset in 1832.

Any increase by a British butterfly is encouraging these days, but it is particularly pleasing in this case, for the Lulworth Skipper is a local and declining species in northern Europe, and is already extinct in the Netherlands.

This is both the smallest and darkest of our five "golden" Skippers. It is also one of the latest Skippers to emerge. Apart from its smaller size, the male Lulworth Skipper can be distinguished from other "golden" Skippers by its dark, dun-coloured wings that are tinged with olive-brown. The tiny female has one distinctive circle of golden marks on each forewing, a pattern that has been aptly likened to the rays around the eye of a peacock's feather. The same marks are sometimes faintly visible on males.

**Distribution** *Almost entirely confined to south-facing chalk hills, cliffs, and undercliffs between Weymouth and Swanage.*

### RESEARCH IN THE WILD

The young stages of this attractive Skipper were painstakingly studied by F.W. Frohawk at the turn of the century but, until recently, little was known of the natural history of the butterfly in the wild. In 1978, I had the pleasure of filling some of the gaps when, with the help of Robert Smith, David Simcox, and Chris Thomas, I surveyed all but a handful of the colonies in Britain.

During the course of this study, we analysed the habitat of each colony to see why some contained hundreds of thousands of adults whereas others supported fewer than 50. We spent long summer days catching the adults in order to paint different combinations of coloured spots on their wings, so that every individual could be distinguished at a later date. By doing this, it was possible to determine the numbers present, the lifespan of the adults, and whether they migrated between breeding sites along the coast, or remained in self-contained colonies – all information that is vital for the conservation of any butterfly.

By marking over 400 butterflies, we found that Lulworth Skippers live in discrete colonies, with little or no interchange between neighbouring sites. Adults fly only in sunshine, but are then extremely active, darting and weaving just above the grassheads, or making rapid hops from one flower to the next. Marjoram *(Origanum vulgare)* is a great favourite, and so small is this Skipper that five or six individuals can often be seen jostling together at the same nectar-rich flowerhead.

### DEVELOPMENT AND FEEDING

Typical adults live just seven to ten days – a normal lifespan for any butterfly that does not hibernate at this stage. No elaborate courtship has been reported. Indeed, their behaviour is unremarkable in all aspects except when egg-laying, over which the females take immense care.

The egg-laying female Lulworth Skipper fusses around tall grass clumps like a broody hen. She invariably selects tor grass *(Brachypodium pinnatum)*, but lays only on large, flowering tussocks that are growing in sunny, sheltered nooks. I have never found eggs or caterpillars on any clump that was under 10 cm. (4 in.) high, and their preferred grasses are 30 to 50 cm. (12 to 20 in.) tall.

Having found a suitable tussock, the female crawls backwards down a flower sheath, probing the crease in the same way as the Small Skipper *(see p.19)*. She inserts a row of up to 15 eggs within the sheath. The eggs hatch after about three weeks, and immediately hibernate, each spinning a little cocoon around both itself and the remnants of the eggshell. These white silken beads can be found by splitting open the old brown stalks on suitable plants at any time in autumn and winter.

In spring, the little caterpillar bores through both cocoon and flower sheath to feed on the tender young grassblades. Each

# LULWORTH SKIPPER · *Thymelicus acteon*

## LIFE-CYCLE

| | JAN | FEB | MAR | APR | MAY | JUN | JUL | AUG | SEP | OCT | NOV | DEC |
|---|---|---|---|---|---|---|---|---|---|---|---|---|
| EGG | | | | | | | | ▨ | ▨ | | | |
| CATERPILLAR | ▨ | ▨ | ▨ | ▨ | ▨ | | | | ▨ | ▨ | ▨ | ▨ |
| CHRYSALIS | | | | | | ▨ | ▨ | | | | | |
| ADULT | | | | | | ▨ | ▨ | ▨ | ▨ | | | |

**Male upperside**
This is the smallest and darkest of the "golden" Skippers.

**Male underside**
Male's underwings are tinged with olive-brown.

**Female upperside**
Each forewing has a characteristic circle of golden marks.

**Female underside**
Female's underwings are less green than those of the male.

**Colour variant**
Female *alba* form – a rare example of variation.

**Resting male**
Male resting on grass, with wings held together.

**Perching adults**
When perching, the fore- and hindwings lie at different angles, as in other "golden" Skippers

SIDE VIEW  VIEW FROM ABOVE

**Egg** [x22]
Laid in rows in flower sheaths of tor grass; hatching takes place after three weeks.

**Chrysalis** [x1½]
Concealed deep in a tussock of grass; has a long and pointed "beak".

HEAD CAPSULE [x4½]

**Caterpillar** [x2¼]
Feeds only on tor grass, retreating to the safety of a grassblade tube when not eating.

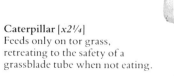

**Caterpillar tube**
Constructed by fastening the edges of grassblades together with silk; fresh tubes are made as the caterpillar grows.

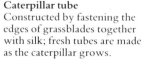

lives separately within a tube made by fastening two edges of a blade together with stout cords of silk. These are quite easy to find in May and June on good sites. They can be spotted by feeding damage both above and below the tube, starting as V-shaped notches in the blade and ending up with an isolated tube on the midrib. The caterpillar constructs fresh tubes as it grows larger, but often rests exposed along a blade in its final days.

The chrysalis is very much harder to find, being formed inside a loose nest of grass and silk spun deep within a tussock of tor grass. It lasts for about a fortnight.

### A COASTAL TOEHOLD

The Lulworth Skipper reaches the northern limit of its range in England, and can live only in the warmest and most sheltered places near the southern coast. Most of its sites are steep, south-facing downland or cliffs, and all contain tor grass in great abundance. However, the Skipper is by no means ubiquitous in places where the turf is dominated by tor grass, even in its stronghold of the Isle of Purbeck. Colonies are restricted to stretches where the grass is left to grow into the tall clumps needed for egg-laying. Small colonies exist where there is just a scattering of suitable plants, but vast numbers develop if the vegetation becomes overgrown or dense. One colony that I studied increased by 20 times in just four years after the farmer reduced grazing on it.

It is changes in grazing that are probably responsible for the welcome increase of this Skipper. In the eighteenth century, most known colonies bred on unfarmed undercliffs, where

**WARMTH AND SHELTER**
*The temperature in a grass clump is coolest near the ground, and warmest halfway up, below the windswept tips. Lulworth Skipper caterpillars live in the warmest zone.*

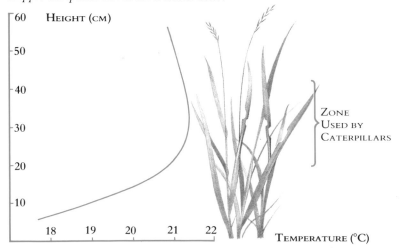

HEIGHT (CM)

ZONE USED BY CATERPILLARS

TEMPERATURE (°C)

periodic falls created a moonscape overgrown by giant tussocks of tor grass among a mosaic of scrub and shorter plants. These slumps still support huge numbers of Lulworth Skippers right down to the shore. However, little of the downland that adjoins the Dorset coast contained colonies in the past, almost certainly because most of it was heavily stocked with sheep.

Much of Dorset's sheepwalk was abandoned in the present century, for it was generally unprofitable to "improve" the pasture on these steep slopes by ploughing or spraying. Nevertheless, in many areas large numbers of rabbits kept the turf closely cropped, to the great advantage of most butterflies and plants, but to the distinct disadvantage of the Lulworth Skipper.

A dramatic shift in fortunes occurred in the 1950s when the rabbits were all but eliminated by myxomatosis. Not only did tor grass spread unchecked at the expense of less vigorous grasses and herbs, but it was also free to grow into the large tussocks that are ideal for egg-laying. From then on, the Lulworth Skipper both increased in numbers, and spread to adjoining land. However, it is not known to have colonized any new region of Britain where tall tor grass is abundant, probably because it is too poor a migrant to reach distant sites. For example, large stretches of the North Downs near the Kent coast now look highly suitable and it would be interesting to see the outcome if a few Lulworth Skippers were introduced.

### THE DORSET COLONIES

There are today about 90 colonies of the Lulworth Skipper, whereas fewer than 40 were known before the last war. As is clear from the map *(see p.12)*, the vast majority are in southeast Dorset, confined to uncultivated stretches of chalk and limestone. During our survey, we found three apparent exceptions – on acid heathland and heavy clays. However, these all proved to be butterflies that were breeding on narrow strips of chalk rubble that had been laid as ballast for the small quarry railways that once crisscrossed these soils.

The finest colonies of Lulworth Skipper can be found on or very near to the coast between Weymouth and Swanage. Much the largest of these are just east of Lulworth Cove itself, where vast acreages of ideal grassland have developed on the extensive army ranges. Nearly 400,000 adults emerge annually on Bindon Hill, with perhaps a million individuals on the ranges as a whole. They make a beautiful sight in high summer, monopolizing every marjoram bloom that is available.

A second string of colonies runs parallel to the Purbeck coast, but a few kilometres inland. Most lie on the southern scarp of the Purbeck Hills, and most contain under a thousand adults. Elsewhere in Britain there are two colonies near Burton Bradstock, west of Weymouth, and a very few on the Devonshire coast.

# ESSEX SKIPPER

## *Thymelicus lineola*

THIS COMPARATIVELY common southern Skipper was discovered in Germany as long ago as 1808, but was overlooked by British naturalists, who mistook it for the Small Skipper. Another 80 years were to pass before Mr. F. W. Hawes of Essex realized that three specimens in his collection were in fact members of a different species. So it was that the last of our resident butterflies was added to the British list. Little ceremony attended the event. In a letter to *The Entomologist,* Hawes announced his discovery and astutely predicted that "if all collections in this country were carefully examined, I have little doubt that other *T. lineola* would be found hidden away in some unexpected corners." And so, indeed, they were.

Even today, many experienced lepidopterists are unable to distinguish between Essex and Small Skippers. This is surprising, for it is relatively simple to make the distinction, even in the field, and requires no more than persistence and reasonable eyesight.

### POINTS OF IDENTIFICATION

The trick in identifying the Essex Skipper is to examine the curved ends of the antennae, in order to look at the colour of their undersurfaces. This is best done in the early evening, when the Skippers bask or roost communally, but it is also perfectly possible during the heat of the day.

Adults frequently settle on grassheads or stems with their bodies pointing upwards at 45 degrees. All that is necessary is to creep up to them on all fours, until you are head-on and close enough to look upwards at the antennae. The difference then becomes obvious: the Small Skipper has antennae that are dull orange or brown underneath the tips, whereas those of the Essex Skipper are glossy black, looking rather as if the tips have been pressed into a black ink pad to take their prints.

Many naturalists prefer to net these two species for identification. This is perfectly harmless, for both are tough little insects. The trapped butterfly is extracted from the net and

*Distribution Common in grassland in the eastern half of its range; much more local elsewhere, but expanding and probably much overlooked.*

gently held by the thorax, between thumb and forefinger, with the wings pressed firmly enough to prevent them from flapping. Some people find that they can also distinguish the two species by the slightly more pointed wings of the Essex Skipper and, in the case of males, from the black sex marks in the middle of the golden forewings. These are very fine and run parallel to the leading edge of the wing on the Essex Skipper, whereas they are bolder and at a slight angle on the Small Skipper. The differences are, however, slight and variable, and are difficult for a beginner to spot.

### PATCHWORK OF KNOWLEDGE

It is worth describing these differences at length, for our knowledge of the behaviour and distribution of the Essex Skipper is very poor, simply because few entomologists bother to distinguish between these species. We can confidently state, though, that the Essex Skipper lives in sedentary colonies, with the annual emergence of adults occurring throughout July, and peaking a good week later than that of the Small Skipper. There is considerable overlap, however, in both flight period and habitat of the two species, which can be seen flying together in many places at the height of summer.

Their behaviour is similar too, although those who know the Essex Skipper claim that its flight is the slower and more purposeful of the two, and that it generally flies even closer to the ground. The only exception is with courting males, which make a series of steep ascents and dives before pairing with a female back-to-back on a grassblade.

Essex Skipper colonies range enormously in size from a few individuals that breed on small, rough banksides to the many thousands found on large embankments, certain road-cuttings and dykes. They gather by the score in late afternoon on good sites, to bask gregariously in the fading sunlight before settling down to roost in groups of four or five per grass-stem. Next morning they separate to lead solitary lives, the females flying slowly just above ground level through a tall, sparse sward of wild grasses as they prepare to lay their burden of eggs.

## A HIBERNATING EGG

Each female is as particular as the Small Skipper in choosing her egg-laying sites. She takes great care to select a firm, tightly furled sheath or hard, dead stem, usually of cock's-foot (*Dactylis glomerata*), or creeping soft grass (*Holcus mollis*). Timothy (*Phleum pratense*), tor grass (*Brachypodium pinnatum*), and wood false brome (*B. sylvaticum*) are also occasionally used, but Essex Skippers invariably avoid the Small Skipper's favourite grass – Yorkshire fog (*Holcus lanatus*) – probably because its sheaths are insufficiently compact.

The egg has a thick, flattened shell, well designed both for insertion into a tight grass sheath and for survival through the winter. The fully formed caterpillar remains in the shell for eight months, unlike the Small Skipper, which hatches after two or three weeks. Essex Skipper eggs are laid in strings of four or five, and are primrose-yellow at first but gradually clear to a pearly opaqueness.

The thick, protective shells of the eggs of all butterflies that hibernate are far too tough to provide food for their occupants, so the emerging caterpillar merely nibbles a neat exit hole in one end and immediately starts feeding on grassblades. It eats only the tenderest spring growth, and soon spins the two edges of a blade around itself, forming the characteristic tube of a grass-feeding Skipper.

These tubes, the distinctive V-shaped feeding damage on leaf-blades, and the caterpillar itself, can be found by patiently examining cock's-foot on good sites in June. Apart from having different foodplants, Essex and Small Skipper caterpillars can be distinguished by the colour of their heads. This species is yellowish with three brown lines, whereas the Small Skipper has a pale green head capsule. Essex Skipper chrysalises last about three weeks.

## A VARIETY OF HABITATS

No one really knows which habitat this golden Skipper prefers. I usually find it in well-drained, wild grassland that has been left to grow quite tall, but which is not so lush or dense as that occupied by Small Skippers. Typical sites are grassy sea walls, dyke sides, and embankments, especially, but not exclusively, on chalky or sandy soils.

Despite this preference for dryness, the Essex Skipper's overwintering eggs can withstand prolonged submersion, as occurs regularly on the coastal marshes of East Anglia and north Kent where it abounds. It was, indeed, originally thought to be confined to these habitats, but more recent surveys have revealed that it is very much more widespread once you begin to look for colonies. These can be found in tall chalk grassland, on grassy banks, in woodland rides, rough corners, and even on strips of road verge throughout most of the southeast quarter of England, extending as far north as the Wash. Colonies are undoubtedly much more localized in the southwest quarter of England, but I suspect that they are much overlooked. It is always worth checking what appear to be Small Skippers anywhere in the southern half of the country.

## SPREADING BY ROAD

There is a considerable body of evidence to suggest that the Essex Skipper is also spreading in many places where it was formerly absent or scarce. This certainly appears to be the case in Sussex and Hampshire, where it was perhaps aided by the development of tall, sparse grass on chalk downland and verges following the disappearance of rabbits after the mid-1950s.

This Skipper also benefits from the steep embankments and cuttings that border many of our new motorways and trunk roads. For example, in Dorset, where there are but 15 known colonies, the County Council was persuaded in 1982 to seed the Bere Regis bypass – a deep, long cutting through "improved" arable land – with a mixture of fine grasses and wild vetches. Cock's-foot and other plants arrived unaided and, after five years, an enormous population of Essex Skippers had developed. Today these dart in their thousands right up to the verge of this exceptionally busy trunk road.

It is likely, indeed, that our modern road system has been responsible for the spread of this little Skipper. This is certainly the case in North America, where it was introduced and is known as the European Skipper. It was first recorded at London, Ontario, in 1910, just 21 years after its discovery in Britain. Over the decades it has become widespread and common, so much so that it is now regarded as a pest of Timothy grass. Although rather sedentary as an adult, the most likely cause of its spread is through the transportion of hay crops to distant states. In one study, about 5,000 hibernating eggs were found per bale of hay.

It is very likely that the same thing happens in Britain. As farms increasingly become more specialized, the transportation of hay has become commonplace, often over considerable distances. This happened on a large scale in the drought years of 1975 and 1976, when convoys of hay were transported from the heart of the Essex Skipper's domain – East Anglia – to the parched dairy farms of the southwest. As the hay lorries rumbled down southern bypasses, it is easy to imagine the butterfly's eggs being scattered along the grass verges, establishing new colonies along the way.

# ESSEX SKIPPER · *Thymelicus lineola*

## LIFE-CYCLE

| | JAN | FEB | MAR | APR | MAY | JUN | JUL | AUG | SEP | OCT | NOV | DEC |
|---|---|---|---|---|---|---|---|---|---|---|---|---|
| EGG | | | | | | | | | | | | |
| CATERPILLAR | | | | | | | | | | | | |
| CHRYSALIS | | | | | | | | | | | | |
| ADULT | | | | | | | | | | | | |

**Male**
The scent patches (sex-brands) on the forewings are shorter and straighter than those on the Small Skipper.

**Female**
Slightly smaller than the Small Skipper; ground-colour more dull, with darker veins.

**Colour variant**
Adult male, rare *fulva* form.

**Antenna**
Underside of antennal tip is glossy black.

**Perching male**
Similar to Small and Lulworth Skippers; black antennal tips can just be seen at close range.

NEWLY LAID EGG

**Egg** [*x15*]
Pearly white when laid; the tiny caterpillar develops within the egg, hatching in spring.

OVERWINTERING EGG

**Chrysalis** [*x1½*]
Formed at the base of the foodplant; head of chrysalis is long, with a rounded tip.

**Feeding female**
Adults visit a wide variety of flowers, including thistles.

HEAD CAPSULE [*x3*]

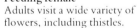

**Caterpillar** [*x2¼*]
The striped head capsule of the caterpillar is the easiest means of identification.

17

# SMALL SKIPPER

## *Thymelicus sylvestris*

A T LEAST four British Skippers are smaller than this species, whose unimaginative name was intended simply to distinguish it from the only other Skipper – the Large – that is really common in the south. It would have been far better, in my opinion, to have stuck by their original names of "Spotless Hog" and "Cloudy Hog" respectively, but these became defunct early in the nineteenth century, and a revival seems highly unlikely.

Although diminutive, this is a creature of considerable charm, that weaves between grass-heads, flashing gold in the sunshine of high summer. July is the main month to see it, but emergence starts in mid-June in a warm year, and old, faded individuals last well into August in a cool one. There is one generation each year.

Small Skippers live in self-contained colonies, seldom wandering far from the patches of tall grassland that serve as breeding grounds. They are, nonetheless, seen quite often in southern country gardens, for a colony can be supported by a few square metres of rough grass nearby. Typical colonies contain a few dozen adults, but this can rise to thousands given extensive areas of Yorkshire fog *(Holcus lanatus)*, the favoured foodplant.

*Distribution A common Skipper of rough grassland and woods throughout its range. A slight expansion occurred in the north in the 1980s.*

The female chooses tall, sheltered clumps of Yorkshire fog on which to lay. She shuffles backwards down each stem, revolving and probing the furled grass sheath with an abdomen swollen with eggs, yet somehow bent double. As she descends, her ovipositor slips inside the sheath then, after a short adjustment to find the perfect position, she lowers both antennae, stiffens, and pumps three to five eggs into the sheath.

The egg is white, turning primrose-yellow, and much rounder and less robust than the otherwise similar egg of the Essex Skipper *(see p.17)*. It hatches in August. The caterpillar eats most of its shell and then spins a tiny silk cocoon around itself, still inside the grass sheath. Each row of cocooned caterpillars remains in its stem until April, before emerging to nibble the tender new growth of leaves. From then on they live singly, each constructing progressively larger tubes by spinning a Yorkshire fog leaf double. By mid-June, each caterpillar is fully fed, and descends to the base of its grass clump to spin a loose tent of leaves in which the chrysalis is formed. This lasts for about a fortnight.

## MASTER OF THE AIR

Small Skippers tend to be secretive, but when they do take to the air, their golden wings glint conspicuously in the sunlight. The male is the more active sex, and his powers of manoeuvre are remarkable. At one moment he will weave slowly between tall grass-stems, then zip away sideways only to stop almost instantaneously in mid-air to hover above another clump.

Females, by contrast, are sedentary, and perch for long hours among the tussocks, sitting with the two forewings pointing upwards in a V, while the hindwings are held parallel to the ground. Hunger and a need to lay eventually force them out into the open. They can fly fast, but their egg-laying flights are slow, deliberate, and quite easy to spot.

## SURVIVING IN A CHANGING LANDSCAPE

Yorkshire fog is abundant on all types of soil, and Small Skipper colonies occur almost everywhere in southern Britain where this grass is regularly left to grow as tall clumps. On the whole, the Small Skipper is found in taller, lusher grassland than the Essex Skipper, and in more open places than the Large Skipper. It is, nonetheless, common within its range in woodland glades and sunny rides, as well as in a host of other grassy habitats, ranging from overgrown downlands and grassy heaths to cliffs and undercliffs. There is little doubt that this species has suffered through the elimination of wild grasses on most agricultural land. Nonetheless, it remains one of the commoner butterflies throughout the south, although there is an abrupt cut-off in its occurrence as one travels north.

# SMALL SKIPPER · *Thymelicus sylvestris*

## LIFE-CYCLE

| | JAN | FEB | MAR | APR | MAY | JUN | JUL | AUG | SEP | OCT | NOV | DEC |
|---|---|---|---|---|---|---|---|---|---|---|---|---|
| EGG | | | | | | | | | | | | |
| CATERPILLAR | | | | | | | | | | | | |
| CHRYSALIS | | | | | | | | | | | | |
| ADULT | | | | | | | | | | | | |

**Male**
Males have a black curve (sex-brand) on each forewing; markings of both sexes are similar throughout their range.

**Female**
Black sex-brand is absent from the fore-wings; inconspicuous, spending much time on the ground.

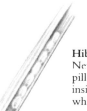

**Hibernating cocoons**
Newly hatched cater-pillars spin cocoons inside grass sheaths, in which they hibernate.

**Antenna**
Underside of antenna tip is orange, distinguishing it from the Essex Skipper *(p.17)*.

**Egg-laying**
Female inserts her abdomen into a grass sheath and lays her eggs in a row with a pumping action.

**Egg [*x15*]**
Laid in groups of 3 to 5. Initially white it then becomes yellow.

SIDE VIEW    VIEW FROM ABOVE

**Chrysalis [*x1½*]**
Formed near the ground. Head of the chrysalis has a short, blunt point.

**Feeding male**
Male drinking nectar at a favourite foodplant, greater knapweed.

**Caterpillar [*x2¼*]**
After emerging from hibernation, caterpillar lives within a tube formed out of a single grassblade.

# SILVER-SPOTTED SKIPPER

*Hesperia comma*

THIS HANDSOME SKIPPER is common on lime-stone throughout central southern Europe, but is rare in Britain, where it maintains a toehold on about 20 of the warmest southern downs. Yet, where it does occur, it can be abundant. The adults make a charming sight in high summer, darting between flowers above the sparse, springy turf, or basking in the August sunshine upon crumbly chalk screes.

This is one of our latest butterflies to emerge. The first adults are seen during the last days of July following a warm summer, but more often appear in the second week of August. They reach a peak towards the end of the month and then rapidly decline, although a few tattered individuals may last late into September.

### A RELUCTANT TRAVELLER

Working with my brother Chris Thomas and David Simcox, I have marked adults in a number of colonies over the years, in an effort to establish more about this butterfly's habits. Our results showed that although Silver-spotted Skippers seldom emigrate far from isolated downs, there is considerable mixing between nearby sites on the same escarpment, as along the North Downs west of Dorking. The species is thus significantly more mobile than the Black Hair-streak, Silver-studded Blue, or Adonis Blue, yet still has great difficulty in colonizing new sites if this means flying over intensively farmed land.

This reluctance to cross farmland has been a particular problem for the species in the last decade. Many sites lost their colonies of Silver-spotted Skippers in the 1950s to 1970s, but became suitable in the 1980s, as rabbits returned *(see p.100)* and conservation measures became more widespread. However, to date, only those sites that were within a few kilometres of an existing population have been recolonized. An extreme example involved the fine Hampshire reserve of Old Winchester Hill, where a suitable habitat was restored as long ago as 1960. It took 17 years for the Skipper to cross the Meon Valley – a distance of

**Distribution** *A rare and declining species, now confined to about 50 warm downs in the centre and east of England's chalk regions.*

just 3 km. (2 miles) – which separates this down from Beacon Hill, where more than a thousand adults fly every year.

### FEEDING AND COURTSHIP

Adult Silver-spotted Skippers live about six days on average, and are inactive in cloudy weather, or when the air temperature falls below 20°C (68°F). They require warmer conditions than any other British butterfly and, even on hot days, spend most of their lives basking in hoof-prints, along paths, or on patches of scree – in fact anywhere where the sun can bake the ground. Like all "golden" Skippers, they sit with the fore- and hindwings held at different planes, as shown opposite.

Their flight is rapid and buzzing, with the ability of all Skippers to dart forwards, side-ways, or backwards at high speed. They make numerous visits to late summer flowers, especially concentrating on stemless thistle *(Carlina acaulis)*, knapweeds *(Centaurea* spp.*)*, yellow members of the daisy family, and felwort *(Gentianella amarella)*. They also fly during courtship and egg-laying, although males do not actively seek the females, but instead perch in sunlit spots, waiting for a mate to pass by. There is then a rapid, tumbling aerial courtship before the male drives his hen to the ground. He crash-lands beside her, and for a minute or two there is a curious scene when the two butterflies stand alongside each other, the male twitching and slightly to the rear before mating takes place.

### THE ROLE OF GRAZING

Once mated, the female makes slow, investigative flights a few centimetres above the turf as she searches for places to lay. She deposits her eggs singly on sheep's fescue grass *(Festuca ovina)*, the caterpillar's only foodplant, but she is extremely fussy in her choice of plants. First she alights in a warm patch of bare ground then, after waiting a few seconds, starts a jerky walk that takes her around or just into the surrounding vegetation, where she

# SILVER-SPOTTED SKIPPER · *Hesperia comma*

## LIFE-CYCLE

| | JAN | FEB | MAR | APR | MAY | JUN | JUL | AUG | SEP | OCT | NOV | DEC |
|---|---|---|---|---|---|---|---|---|---|---|---|---|
| EGG | | | | | | | | | | | | |
| CATERPILLAR | | | | | | | | | | | | |
| CHRYSALIS | | | | | | | | | | | | |
| ADULT | | | | | | | | | | | | |

**Male**
Each forewing has a black bar (sex-brand) made up of scent scales.

**Female**
The forewings lack the black sex-brand, otherwise similar to male.

**Hibernating egg**
Egg attached to blade of sheep's fescue.

**Colour variant**
Undersides are deeper green in some adults.

**Resting female**
Female on leaf of salad burnet, a typical plant of the butterfly's downland habitat.

**Egg [*x15*]**
Laid singly on a blade of sheep's fescue; no other grass is used.

**Chrysalis [*x1½*]**
Formed at ground level in a grass tussock; emerges after about 2 weeks.

**Caterpillar [*x1½*]**
Lives within a nest of silk and grassblades, protruding its head to feed, and retreating if disturbed.

**Basking adults**
Male and female warming their bodies by basking in sunshine on a chalk scree.

lays her curious pudding-basin of an egg. My colleagues and I have analysed the exact position of over 800 Silver-spotted Skipper eggs. We found that the females reject the vast majority of sheep's fescue plants on nearly every site, restricting themselves to the minority that grow as vigorous fine tufts, ideally no more than 2.5 cm. (1 in.) in diameter, and with about three-quarters of their edges abutting onto bare ground or scree. These conditions prevail on sites that have been very heavily grazed in the recent past. But the females also avoid any hummock of sheep's fescue that is under 1 cm. (about ½ in.) tall and that has had its nutritious growing tips nibbled off, choosing only those plants that have been left to grow up without grazing during the summer months.

This butterfly's idea of heaven is thus a thin-soiled, south-facing southern down that has a shortish, sparse sward in which about 40 per cent of the ground is bare, 45 per cent consists of little sheep's fescue plants, and the remaining 15 per cent is composed of flowers. This, almost certainly, reflects its need for the warmth of exposed ground, because in southern France colonies are common in much more overgrown turf. British sites, however, need regular heavy grazing, and there was a spate of extinctions from the mid-1950s onwards after rabbits largely disappeared through myxomatosis. Ironically, sheep's fescue increased on many sites, but without the rabbits, the small, sparse plants grew into dense clumps that were totally unsuitable for egg-laying.

## EGGS AND CATERPILLARS

The eggs of the Silver-spotted Skipper are very easy to find once you know which type of sheep's fescue the butterfly prefers. They are large, off-white, and conspicuous, and are attached to the fine, wiry leaves of the grass. Up to 10 eggs can often be found on the same little tuft on the best sites, but it is best to search in the early autumn, for many eggs drop off to complete their hibernation on the ground.

The caterpillar bores out through the tough eggshell in March, and immediately constructs a small nest of silk and tender fescue leaves. It lives in this and similar nests for the next 14 weeks, usually alone, but sometimes with up to three other caterpillars. Nests are not particularly easy to spot, and are disappointing when found, for they contain one of the ugliest caterpillars of all – a brown-green wrinkled maggot that stretches out of its nest to browse on the surrounding leaf-tips. When gently blown upon, the caterpillar darts back into its nest to press against the bare ground – an invaluable escape mechanism for a creature whose habitat is subject to heavy grazing.

When fully grown, the caterpillar abandons its nest and starts wandering in search of a denser tussock in which to pupate. It spins a coarse cocoon at ground level in a grass tussock, and it lives as a chrysalis for about a fortnight.

## DECLINE AND RECOVERY

The status of this Skipper has given great cause for concern in recent years. It appears always to have been scarce, although Richard South, a leading lepidopterist at the turn of the century, considered that colonies bred "on most of our chalk hills" at that time. Earlier entomologists – who knew it as the "Pearl Skipper" or "August Skipper" – list rather few sites, and there is doubt over some of these for then, as now, it was frequently confused with the Large Skipper.

Despite problems with identification, there is no doubt that this butterfly was much more widely distributed in the past. Occasional colonies were known from as far north as Yorkshire, whereas the Chilterns today mark its northern limit. The species has been declining for most of this century, but when Chris Thomas and David Simcox surveyed all known British localities in 1982, it became apparent that few had changed in any fundamental way. The turf on most former sites was still dominated by sheep's fescue.

From the butterfly's point of view, the problem with most sites was that they had been abandoned for farming and received little or no grazing after the mid-1950s. The situation has reversed in the past decade as rabbits have returned to many areas, and farmers have also restocked downs. However, as already described, only those sites close to an existing colony have been recolonized.

## THE SILVER-SPOTTED SKIPPER TODAY

Today there are roughly 55 colonies of Silver-spotted Skipper in Britain. About half were very small when measured in 1982, but some have increased greatly since then due to the return of rabbits as the effects of myxomatosis have abated. There were, in any case, 10 very large colonies containing over 1,500 adults each. These still appear to be prospering.

Apart from a curious colony breeding on limestone ballast on an abandoned railway in Somerset, Silver-spotted Skippers are confined mainly to the centre and east of the southern chalk downland. The main strongholds are in the Chilterns, with seven colonies (including the largest), Hampshire, with eight colonies, and the North Downs of Surrey, where the butterfly breeds in a string of 28 more or less self-contained clusters along the escarpment between Guildford and Reigate. Many of these are on land owned by the National Trust, as are some of the largest colonies elsewhere. In addition to these there are two colonies in East Sussex, a small group in Kent, and one each further west in Dorset and Wiltshire.

# LARGE SKIPPER

## Ochlodes venata

THE LARGE SKIPPER is a common butterfly in England and Wales, to be found in almost any sheltered patch of grassland that contains tall clumps of native coarse grasses. But it soon becomes a rarity as one travels north, extending no further than to Durham in the northeast and to the Scottish Lowlands in the northwest. It has never reliably been recorded in Ireland.

Like all our "golden" Skippers, the adult adopts a characteristic basking stance, with the forewings and hindwings held apart at different angles. It is easy to identify, being the only common Skipper to have mottled rather than clear golden wings, and the markings are more or less constant throughout the butterfly's range. Hopeful beginners sometimes mistake old, faded adults for the Silver-spotted Skipper (see p.21), or even for the Lulworth Skipper (see p.13), but both these have different colours or patterns, and both are restricted to a very few sites in southern England. If in doubt, it is always safest to assume that any golden Skipper belongs to this species.

***Distribution*** *Common in rough grassland and woods throughout its range. Scarcer in the north, and absent from most islands.*

### A GARDEN VISITOR

There is one generation of Large Skippers a year, which lasts for most of the summer. Given a warm spring, the first males emerge in the last days of May, building up to a peak in late June and flying throughout July. Small numbers usually survive into August, and a few battered individuals linger on until mid-September, but these are pale and hardly recognizable from their scaleless wings.

The Large Skipper is one of the few butterflies that is regularly seen in gardens. This generally means that there is a colony in an adjoining field or verge, for the adults seldom fly far from their self-contained breeding sites and rarely breed in gardens. Typical colonies contain just a few dozen adults. However, much larger numbers can develop under ideal conditions, such as during the first five years after a large area of woodland has been cleared, replanted, and left to grow wild.

For many naturalists, the image of this Skipper is of a burly little butterfly, darting in golden flashes around shrubs and tall grassheads in the summer sunshine. A more scientific account is provided by Roger Dennis, who made an excellent study of a colony in Cheshire. Dennis confirmed that the males were active only in hot weather, and showed that they divided their time between feeding and locating females, which they found either by patrolling back and forth through their habitat or, at other times, by perching close to the ground, waiting for virgin females to fly past.

### PATROLS AND COMBAT

The males patrol mainly from 10 a.m. to noon, although it is possible to find the odd one doing this at any time of day. A patrol involves slow extended flights, hovering just above the ground, or weaving around grass clumps, scanning each for the presence of a female. The final detection is apparently by scent. Dennis watched one male persistently circling around a tussock in which a female was blowing up her wings after emerging from her chrysalis, and saw another spend 15 minutes weaving in and out of the branches of a seedling tree before it eventually located the female that this contained. These slow patrolling flights are punctuated by swifter dashes, covering several metres a second, as the male abandons one small area to search in another further off.

Patrolling flights give way to perching from noon until about 4 p.m. Each male selects a position in the sun, usually where shrubs, a wood edge, or a hedgerow form some sort of boundary along which females like to fly. Open junctions in sunny woods are particular favourites, and are much fought over, for every male tries to exclude rivals from his territory.

Having selected a suitable place, a male then chooses a flat leaf that is sturdy enough to act as a launching pad for his many forays. This is usually just above ground level and is invariably in the sun. Here he sits with wings apart, basking and waiting.

He challenges any passing insect with what seems like quite unnecessary force, while rival males are attacked and pursued in violent aerial conflicts. These are so rapid that the combatants are hard to see, but so fierce that you can clearly hear the clashing of their wings. The intruder is usually banished, whereupon the victor returns to the same leaf in his territory.

If a female Large Skipper flies by, she triggers a rapid courtship flight, culminating in both insects landing 3 to 4 m. (10 to 13 ft.) up in a tree or bush top. An intricate courtship ensues before mating begins.

## LIFE AMONG THE GRASSBLADES

Once mated, a typical female spends most of the day basking or resting, interrupted by short periods of egg-laying or feeding. The egg-laying flight is gentle and investigative, like that of a patrolling male. She circles around and between tall tussocks, examining each before laying single white eggs on the under-surfaces of suitable blades. On most soils, egg-laying is restricted to cock's-foot *(Dactylis glomerata)*, large clumps growing in open ground being particular favourites. However, purple moor grass *(Molinia caerulea)* is usually the main foodplant on wet, acid soils, and there are also reliable records of egg-laying on wood false brome *(Brachypodium sylvaticum)*, tor grass *(B. pinnatum)*, and the wood small reed *(Calamagrostis epigejos)*. The last three are unusual choices, and perhaps never support a colony in isolation.

Eggs are easy to find on good sites, for each is comparatively large and lies exposed on its leaf-blade. It hatches after about two weeks. The caterpillar immediately constructs a grass tube, drawing the two edges of a leaf-blade together around it with silk cords. It lives inside this tube, periodically emerging to nibble the edges of its leaf. The grass tube is similar to that inhabited by other "golden" Skippers, and would be highly unsanitary but for an ingenious comb-like device that enables these Skippers to flick their droppings a good metre (3 ft.) away from the tube.

The caterpillar hibernates after its skin has been shed for the fourth time, and resumes feeding in the spring. It moults twice more before forming a chrysalis. The ugly grub-like caterpillar is quite easy to find in its grass tube in early May, and can be distinguished from other Skippers by its blue-green body and

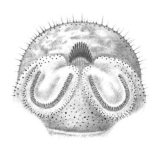

**KEEPING CLEAN**
*Those Skippers that live in grass tubes have a comb-like device that is used to keep the tube clean. It springs upwards, flicking the caterpillar's droppings up to 1 m. (3 ft.) away from the tube.*

black head. The chrysalis is also hidden in grass, in a nest of blades spun in the heart of a tussock. It lasts for about three weeks before the adult emerges.

## A TWENTIETH-CENTURY SURVIVOR

The Large Skipper tends to be found in wetter and more wooded places than our other "golden" Skippers, although there is a considerable overlap in habitats. Typical sites are sunny areas of grassland where cock's-foot or purple moor grass grow in large, ungrazed clumps. Very small patches of land, including road verges, hedge banks, and rough corners, can support a colony. Most sites are sheltered by scattered shrubs or wood edges and, indeed, there can be few southern woodland glades that do not contain a colony.

Numerous Large Skipper colonies have been destroyed in recent years because of the intensification of agriculture and the general tidying up of the countryside. Nevertheless, this species remains one of the commonest butterflies in lowland Wales, the Midlands, and southern England. It is even common in East Anglia, where a high proportion of other butterflies have disappeared. Colonies are distinctly scarcer further north, and are confined to warm, sheltered, low-lying sites. Yet it is still locally common where it survives, even in Scotland, where there was a decline in the mid-nineteenth century but few losses since then. The main Scottish colonies are now around Dumfries and Galloway.

The Large Skipper is absent from virtually all the smaller British islands, apart from Anglesey and the Isle of Wight. This suggests that it was either a late or slow colonizer as the glaciers of the last Ice Age retreated. This would also account for its surprising absence from Ireland, where there exist innumerable places in which one might expect it to thrive.

# LARGE SKIPPER · *Ochlodes venata*

HESPERIIDAE · Large Skipper

### LIFE-CYCLE

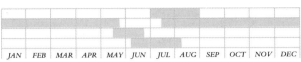

| | JAN | FEB | MAR | APR | MAY | JUN | JUL | AUG | SEP | OCT | NOV | DEC |
|---|---|---|---|---|---|---|---|---|---|---|---|---|
| EGG | | | | | | | | | | | | |
| CATERPILLAR | | | | | | | | | | | | |
| CHRYSALIS | | | | | | | | | | | | |
| ADULT | | | | | | | | | | | | |

**Male**
Male has a prominent black line (sex-brand) on each forewing.

**Female**
Markings, like those of the male, are constant throughout range.

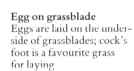

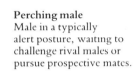

**Egg [*x15*]**
Laid singly, hatching after about 2 weeks.

**Egg on grassblade**
Eggs are laid on the underside of grassblades; cock's foot is a favourite grass for laying

**Perching male**
Male in a typically alert posture, waiting to challenge rival males or pursue prospective mates.

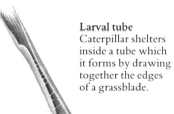

**Larval tube**
Caterpillar shelters inside a tube which it forms by drawing together the edges of a grassblade.

**Chrysalis [*x1½*]**
When formed, covered in a white, waxy powder.

**Basking adults**
A male and female basking in characteristic Skipper stance, with wings angled and body positioned for rapid take-off.

HEAD CAPSULE [*x3*]

**Caterpillar [*x1½*]**
Normally enclosed within larval tube; head capsule is clearly striped with cream.

# GRIZZLED SKIPPER

## *Pyrgus malvae*

THE GRIZZLED SKIPPER is a butterfly that appeals more, perhaps, to the specialist than to the general naturalist. Its small size and moth-like appearance seldom invite a second look, which is a pity, for this is a highly attractive species when newly emerged, and an insect of considerable character. It is best seen on a hot spring day when the males bask nervously in sunlit spots, forever on the alert for rivals that have entered their domains. The dogfights that follow are remarkable for their ferocity. The males circle, dive, and soar, each trying to outmanoeuvre the other and flying so fast that the blurred wings become impossible to follow. Few butterflies can match these spectacular aeronautics.

Although a grey blur in flight, the black-and-white wings and fringes are distinctive when the adults do settle. Indeed, the chequered pattern has led to the butterfly being given a variety of names over the years, for the species was once much more common than today, and was familiar to all early entomologists. The first, coined by James Petiver in 1696, were "Our Marsh Fritillary" and "Mr. Dandridge's Dark Fritillary", a reminder that in those days any chequered animal or plant was called a fritillary, after the Latin for a chequer board. It then passed through several titles, including the "Spotted Skipper" and my favourite, the "Grizzle".

**Distribution** *Declining and now rare through most of its range, although common on a few southern downs that have escaped intensive agriculture.*

### COLONIES AND EGG-LAYING

Adult Grizzled Skippers live in self-contained colonies, of which even the largest seldom comprise more than 150 individuals. The males gather at the bases of hills, in sheltered hollows, and along tracks, where they sit twitching on dead leaves or bare patches of ground, with their backs to the sun and wings fully expanded to absorb maximum warmth. Every so often they dart into the sky, circling at high speed to court a female or fend off a rival. Females are seen less often, but are conspicuous enough when egg-laying, during which they flutter back and forth, investigating every nook and cranny.

The small, bun-shaped eggs are laid singly, for the most part on wild strawberry *(Fragaria vesca)*, although creeping cinquefoil *(Potentilla repens)*, tormentil *(P. erecta)*, agrimony *(Agrimonia eupatoria)*, and short suckers of blackberry *(Rubus fruticosus)* may also be used and can even support an entire colony in isolation.

The egg hatches after about 10 days, and at first the solitary caterpillar lives under a film of silk which it spins along the midrib on the top of its leaf. It emerges to nibble the leaf around the edges of its shelter, leaving distinctive blotches that are quite easy to find. After the first skin moult, a more substantial shelter is made by folding and spinning the edges of its leaf together to form a tent. The caterpillar constructs fresh shelters over the next two months as it grows larger. It finally descends to the rough vegetation to spin a neat netting of silk in which the remarkably beautiful chrysalis is formed.

### A RANGE OF HABITATS

Grizzled Skippers live in a variety of places where their food-plants occur as lush, bushy growths. Typical sites include the sunny edges of scrub on chalk and limestone downs, crumbling south-facing banks supporting sparse, scrambling vegetation, and sheltered but unshaded woodland rides and glades. They are also quite frequently found in cuttings and on the edges of railway tracks, where wild strawberries encroach onto the ballast as straggly runners that bake among the chippings.

Despite this range of habitats, the Grizzled Skipper is far from common. Scattered colonies occur as far north as Yorkshire, but a great many have disappeared in recent years and the species is now rare outside central southern England. However, it is still a butterfly that one half expects to find in any suitable habitat from the Cotswolds and Chilterns southwards, especially in large, sunny woods and on unfertilized chalk and limestone downs. Dorset is perhaps the current stronghold, with more than 200 known colonies in the one county.

# GRIZZLED SKIPPER · *Pyrgus malvae*

## LIFE-CYCLE

| | JAN | FEB | MAR | APR | MAY | JUN | JUL | AUG | SEP | OCT | NOV | DEC |
|---|---|---|---|---|---|---|---|---|---|---|---|---|
| EGG | | | | | | | | | | | | |
| CATERPILLAR | | | | | | | | | | | | |
| CHRYSALIS | | | | | | | | | | | | |
| ADULT | | | | | | | | | | | | |

**Male**
Distinctive patterning is blurred when in flight; spotting on wings in both sexes is variable.

**Female**
Patterning is very similar to male's; less conspicuous than male, except on egg-laying flights.

**Male**
Rare aberrant form *taras*, seen regularly on a few sites.

**Hair pencil**
Hindlegs have a tuft of black hairs that can be extended to release an aphrodisiac scent during courtship.

**Roosting adults**
Grizzled Skippers may congregate on dead flowerheads in order to roost.

**Egg** [*x15*]
Laid singly on a variety of plants, hatching after about 10 days.

**Chrysalis** [*x2¼*]
The hibernating stage of the life-cycle, formed near ground level.

**Basking male**
Males perch for long periods on bare ground, absorbing the warmth of the sun.

**Caterpillar** [*x2¼*]
Lives within a tent made of leaves, bound together with silk, and emerges to feed.

# DINGY SKIPPER
*Erynnis tages*

THE DINGY SKIPPER was regarded as a common butterfly in much of England and Wales before the last war, and as a rather local species in Scotland and Ireland. Nowadays it is distinctly scarce throughout its range, although nothing like the rarity it has become in the Netherlands, where perhaps two colonies survive. Here it simply belongs to that large group of butterflies which one hopes – rather than expects – to find when exploring new, suitable-looking ground.

Beginners usually find the adult difficult to identify in flight, for its wings beat so quickly that they become a grey-brown blur, resembling those of many other butterflies or day-flying moths. It is much easier to distinguish at rest, although some people find the Grizzled Skipper *(see p.27)* confusingly similar. The latter has a clear-cut pattern of small black-and-white squares on its wings, the fringes of which are also chequered. The Dingy Skipper, by comparison, has much browner wings, which can be quite variegated when fresh.

Some Dingy Skippers also have an oily, iridescent sheen for the first few days of life. However, with age, they lose many of the scales on their wings, and increasingly live up to their name by becoming pale and drab.

### AN EARLY EMERGENCE
The Dingy Skipper is essentially a springtime butterfly. The first males can be seen in late April in warm years, but the main emergence occurs throughout May, reaching a peak in the first week of June. It is over by the end of the month, except perhaps for a few faded stragglers that last for a week or two into July. There may then be a small second brood in August, but this occurs only after hot summers on the warmest southern sites.

A typical Dingy Skipper colony is quite small – indeed, there are probably few that contain more than 50 adults even in their better years. My brother Chris Thomas measured the size of one of the largest known colonies in 1978, a hazardous under-

***Distribution*** *A declining species that is rare through most of its range, but locally common on southern downs and coasts.*

taking since the butterfly is a rapid and agile flier, and the site consisted of about 3 ha. (7 acres) of crumbling undercliff perched near the top of a high cliff-face. By marking the adults with minute, coloured ink-spots, he was able to study individual movements and the size of the colony. He found that there were about 300 butterflies present when emergence had reached its annual peak. This probably represented a total flight of about 900 adults that spring, for these butterflies are short-lived and, as a rough rule of thumb, no more than a third of the individuals that emerge in a year are alive on the peak day.

### FLIGHT AND DEVELOPMENT
Marking the adults also confirmed that Dingy Skippers live in close-knit colonies, with butterflies breeding and flying on the same small sites year after year. They spend long periods of the day basking, with their wings held wide open and their bodies pressed hard against bare patches of ground in order to obtain the maximum warmth from the spring sunshine. Males tend to gather towards the bases of hillsides, in gullies, or in any small depression, where they settle on the ground and wait for females to chase.

The flight of both sexes is extremely fast. They dart back and forth just above the short, sparse vegetation that typifies their sites, and then climb at high speed into the sky, like aircraft "peeling off" from a formation.

Females fly widely over their breeding sites, but in late afternoon both sexes gather to roost in tall vegetation. They sit on grassheads or on brown, dead flowers, heads uppermost and with their backs pointing towards the evening sun. All Skippers have a moth-like appearance, but roosting Dingy Skippers look more like moths than most, as they drape their wings tightly around a flowerhead, with the upper surfaces exposed.

On the great majority of sites, the females lay their eggs on bird's-foot trefoil *(Lotus corniculatus)*, although on warm downs they prefer horseshoe vetch *(Hippocrepis comosa)*, if it is available.

# DINGY SKIPPER · *Erynnis tages*

## LIFE-CYCLE

| | JAN | FEB | MAR | APR | MAY | JUN | JUL | AUG | SEP | OCT | NOV | DEC |
|---|---|---|---|---|---|---|---|---|---|---|---|---|
| EGG | | | | | | | | | | | | |
| CATERPILLAR | | | | | | | | | | | | |
| CHRYSALIS | | | | | | | | | | | | |
| ADULT | | | | | | | | | | | | |

**Male upperside**
Front margin of forewing contains scent scales, shown unfolded on the right wing.

**Male underside**
Wings of both sexes become more pale and drab as they age and lose scales.

**Female upperside**
Female lacks scent scales; coloration of both sexes is otherwise similar.

**Female underside**
Underwings are slightly brighter than those of the male.

**Female, Irish form**
This is the only Skipper found in Ireland.

**Resting adult**
At night, adults rest on grasses or flowerheads, adopting a characteristic, moth-like pose.

**Egg** [*x22*]
Laid singly, on bird's-foot trefoil. Initially green, becoming a conspicuous orange after five days.

**Chrysalis** [*x2¼*]
Formed in spring; butterfly emerges after about a month.

**Basking female**
Adults often bask with their bodies pressed against bare ground between rapid bursts of flight.

**HEAD CAPSULE** [*x3*]

**Caterpillar** [*x2¼*]
Hibernates when fully grown in a nest of vetch leaves.

On heavier soils, entire colonies breed on the taller, hairier leaves of greater bird's-foot trefoil *(Lotus uliginosus).*

The eggs are quite easy to find on good sites. To see them, search small plants growing in warm, sheltered nooks, partly hidden by other vegetation or spreading over bare soil. Although each egg is laid singly, several may be found together on more suitable plants. Most will be on the youngest leaflets or, more often, in the groove where the stalk joins the leaves. Although yellow when laid, they soon turn bright orange, making them especially conspicuous.

Each egg hatches after about a fortnight, and the young caterpillar immediately spins two or three vetch leaflets together with silk threads, forming a tiny tent in which it then lives. It feeds on these vetch leaves, periodically spinning a larger tent as it grows. This nest can be found with practice, but the effort is not well rewarded. The caterpillar concealed within is a rather unattractive, grey-green grub with a purplish-black, shiny head. It is unlikely to be confused with any other in Britain.

The caterpillar is fully grown by August, when it spins and twists vetch leaves to make a more substantial nest. It lives in this for a further eight months, hibernating as a caterpillar then forming a chrysalis the following April. Another month passes before the adult butterfly emerges.

## THE THREAT OF AGRICULTURAL "IMPROVEMENT"
Colonies of Dingy Skipper can be found in a wide range of habitats and on all soils. Most live on warm, south-facing downland, particularly where the turf has been disturbed by grazing stock, yet is not cropped too short. The species is also common on dunes, cliffs, and undercliffs along much of the coast, for bird's-foot trefoil flourishes wherever there is a regular supply of bare soil. These sites are also often sheltered and warm, which is probably why – together with abandoned quarries – they support the highest densities of Dingy Skippers known in the British Isles.

Smaller numbers can be found in the grassier areas of heathland, on embankments, and on wasteland. Many woods also contain small colonies, which breed either along the broad, rutted access rides or, in wetter areas, along ditches, where they feed on greater bird's-foot trefoil.

Unfortunately, many colonies have been lost in recent years, making this one of our most rapidly declining butterflies. The principle cause has been the "improvement" of most of our ancient grassland for agriculture, which eliminates the butterfly's foodplants. In addition, much of the grassland that has escaped improvement has still become unsuitable because it is seldom grazed. Both bird's-foot trefoil and horseshoe vetch are soon shaded out by the tall grasses that grow unchecked when grazing stops. In woods, coppicing once played a vital role in maintaining breeding grounds. Now that the practice has virtually ceased, many of these sites have also been eliminated. Finally, many colonies have disappeared due to the development of wasteland and the neatening of the countryside.

## STRONGHOLDS IN THE SOUTH
Despite these losses, this species remains our most widely distributed Skipper. It is the only Skipper in Ireland, but is not particularly common, being restricted to areas of limestone outcrop, such as the Burren. These western Irish butterflies have a slightly different appearance to other Dingy Skippers.

For some reason, virtually no colonies are to be found on the Irish coast or on the smaller British islands, except for Anglesey and the Isle of Wight, even though bird's-foot trefoil is abundant in most of these places. In Scotland, colonies occur even further north than those of the Chequered Skipper, but again the butterfly is not particularly common. It is restricted to two main areas: around Ross, Banff, Aberdeen, and Inverness in the north and, less surprisingly, in the warm southwest lowlands.

Fine Dingy Skipper populations survive in most northern English counties, but they are few and far between. The butterfly becomes considerably more common further south, with many colonies along the coasts of Wales and southern England. Inland, this species has become much more localized. It was never abundant in East Anglia, and the declines there have been severe, leaving it restricted to one or two colonies per county. Its current strongholds are the central southern counties of England, particularly Wiltshire, Hampshire, and Dorset, where scattered colonies survive on all soils. In Dorset alone there are perhaps 200 colonies, making the region internationally important for this declining European butterfly.

# SWALLOWTAIL
## *Papilio machaon*

THIS IS ONE of the rarest and most magnificent of our resident butterflies. Colonies, nowadays, are confined to the Norfolk Broads, although they once occurred in ancient fenlands. Occasional sightings are also made in a very different habitat – the chalk downs from Kent to Dorset – but these are of a continental subspecies that occasionally migrates to Britain and briefly establishes itself here.

### A RACE APART

Resident British Swallowtails belong to a unique subspecies, *P. m. britannicus,* which differs in several ways from the continental form, *P. m. gorganus.* Although superficially similar, our Swallowtails are slightly smaller than their continental counterparts, and have more extensive dark markings. They also behave differently: *britannicus* Swallowtails live in self-contained colonies and breed almost exclusively on milk parsley *(Peucedanum palustre),* whereas *gorganus* Swallowtails roam widely through the countryside, laying eggs on a range of Umbellifers, including wild carrot *(Daucus carota)* and fennel *(Foeniculum vulgare).* Furthermore, British Swallowtails have one main generation a year in late May and June, and no more than a partial second emergence in warm years, during August. The continental subspecies has two full broods.

The British Swallowtail is seen at its best skimming over open water from one Broad to the next. Although non-migratory, it is still a powerful flier that wanders between all the Broads adjoining the rivers Ant, Thurne, and Bure. There is evidence that it used to roam more widely before its vast former breeding grounds were drained, for the Swallowtails from a century ago were larger, more robust insects.

Adult Swallowtails feed mainly in the morning and late afternoon. They drink nectar from red campion *(Silene dioica)* and other fenland flowers, slowly flapping their wings to support their heavy bodies while they feed. Males spend the rest of the day patrolling around prominent shrubs among the

***Distribution*** *The English subspecies is resident only in the Norfolk Broads; occasional continental immigrants are seen on southern downs.*

reedbeds, and virgin females fly to these for mating. Their encounters with females are spectacular. Both partners hover a little in the breeze before soaring high into the air and then descending to mate in a reedbed or on a shrub. They may remain several hours together before the female departs in search of egg-sites.

A good deal is known about the natural history of this butterfly, thanks to the researches of Jack Dempster and Marney Hall of the Institute of Terrestrial Ecology. They noted how each female was highly selective when egg-laying, skimming a few centimetres above the vegetation to lay on large, prominent milk parsley plants, or on those regenerating in freshly mown areas. The shining, spherical egg is laid singly on the tenderest leaflets of milk parsley, and is easy to find once one knows the type of plant the butterfly chooses.

### PREDATORS AND DEFENCES

Swallowtail eggs hatch after a week or two, and the tiny caterpillars begin nibbling the upper surfaces of leaves. They show a remarkable mimicry in the period up to their third moult, resembling small bird-droppings encrusted on the milk parsley. This camouflage, however, does not fool spiders, and up to 65 per cent of the caterpillars may be killed before they undergo their first skin change. As the caterpillars grow larger, fewer are killed by spiders but instead they become the prey of birds, which eat about two-thirds of the population. Reed buntings seem to be the main culprits, with sedge warblers and bearded tits taking appreciable quantities.

It is curious that the caterpillar should be so vulnerable to birds, for it has a strange, scented organ on its head, the osmeterium, that is designed to deter enemies. Barrett, the Victorian entomologist, noted in the nineteenth century how "Fenmen always assert that they know by the scent when a large specimen… has fallen among the mown herbage, and this assists them to find it." But even the undisturbed caterpillar is easily

**REPELLING PREDATORS**
*Looking like a bright orange snake's tongue, the osmeterium is flicked out for a few seconds whenever the caterpillar is alarmed. It emits an acrid smell reminiscent of rotting pineapple.*

found, for it advertises this deterrent by having conspicuous stripes on its body and by sitting high on a foodplant.

After feeding for roughly a month, the caterpillars desert the milk parsley to pupate on the stems of reeds and other fenland plants. The Swallowtail chrysalis has two colour forms, yellow-green and brown.

## THE EFFECTS OF DRAINAGE

It is impossible to say just how widespread Swallowtails used to be in British wetlands, for many breeding sites would have been inaccessible to early butterfly collectors, and most of the vast drainage schemes were completed before systematic records began. The butterfly clearly occurred in several southern marsh-lands, including the Thames Valley, where one of the first authentic specimens was caught at St. James's Palace in the seventeenth century. This was given to James Pettiver, who christened it the "Royal William". Perhaps this was a stray from then undeveloped areas around London for, years later, Barrett reports that its caterpillars were taken "year after year in Osier beds in Battersea Fields".

But the true home of the Swallowtail was in the vast undrained fenlands around the Wash. The butterfly was reported to be abundant at Whittlesea Mere, Yaxley, and Burwell in Cambridgeshire before the great drains were dug, but as the swamps were reclaimed, it became increasingly confined to isolated fragments. The last of these colonies was at Wicken Fen, near Cambridge, where it remained common until the 1940s. This relic then received a severe blow during the last war, when a substantial area was ploughed for potatoes. To make matters worse, the traditional cutting of sedges often lapsed, smothering the butterfly's foodplants. The Swallowtail lingered on for a further decade at Wicken before becoming extinct through lack of food.

Similar problems afflicted colonies in the Broads, at least until recently. An important factor here was the decline of fen management, especially in the areas of sedge and mixed fenland vegetation, where milk parsley grows at its greatest abundance. The former areas were traditionally cut on a three-year rotation to provide sedge to crown the ridges of thatched houses; the latter as an annual crop to provide bedding for domestic animals. Reed-cutting, too, was in decline, but this was less serious for the Swallowtail, because comparatively few milk parsleys grow in the very wet areas where reeds proliferated. The worst period of neglect occurred during the Second World War, when there was no cutting at all for four years. Some management resumed in the post-war years, but on such a small and patchy scale that the butterfly declined considerably, and its position was causing great concern in the mid-1970s.

Since then, there has been a revival in the Swallowtail's fortunes. The restoration of derelict cottages throughout England has ensured that fine Norfolk sedge and reed has never been in greater demand. Large areas of overgrown fen have been opened up by the Broads Authority, and are again being cut on a commercial basis. In addition, several surviving fens are managed by conservation bodies, which also mow much of the mixed fenland vegetation. As a result, there has been a re-surgence of vigorous milk parsley plants, and the Swallowtail is now more abundant in the Broads than for at least 20 years.

## CROSS-CHANNEL VISITORS

The future of the butterfly now seems reasonably secure. There is also the chance, if our climate does indeed become warmer, that the continental subspecies, *P.m. gorganus,* will establish itself in the south. It is a far commoner immigrant than is generally thought, although records are bedevilled by introductions and fraud.

There is no doubt, however, that the subspecies was well established on a few downs in Dorset and Kent in the early nineteenth century, only to disappear during the cold summer of 1816. Caterpillars have regularly been found eating wild carrot on southern chalk during the last century, and even more often in gardens, again feeding on carrot-tops as well as parsnip and rue. The entomologist J. M. Chalmers Hunt calculates that there has been, on average, at least one sighting of a continental Swallowtail in Kent every three years since 1850. The butterfly established itself again in the south in prolonged warm periods, for example near Deal in 1857-69, near Hythe in 1918-26, and during the mid-1940s in Dorset, Kent, south Hampshire, and the Isle of Wight.

Although slightly less beautiful, in my opinion, than our native subspecies, the permanent presence of continental Swallow-tails on southern downland would offer some recompense for our own Swallowtail's sad decline.

# SWALLOWTAIL · *Papilio machaon*

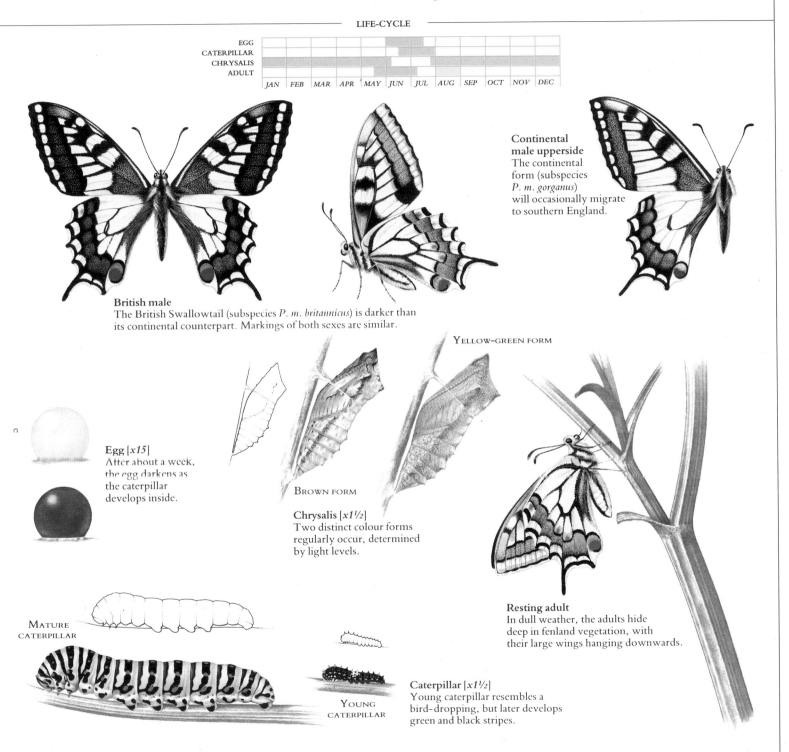

LIFE-CYCLE

| | JAN | FEB | MAR | APR | MAY | JUN | JUL | AUG | SEP | OCT | NOV | DEC |
|---|---|---|---|---|---|---|---|---|---|---|---|---|
| EGG | | | | | | | | | | | | |
| CATERPILLAR | | | | | | | | | | | | |
| CHRYSALIS | | | | | | | | | | | | |
| ADULT | | | | | | | | | | | | |

**Continental male upperside**
The continental form (subspecies *P. m. gorganus*) will occasionally migrate to southern England.

**British male**
The British Swallowtail (subspecies *P. m. britannicus*) is darker than its continental counterpart. Markings of both sexes are similar.

YELLOW-GREEN FORM

**Egg** [*x15*]
After about a week, the egg darkens as the caterpillar develops inside.

BROWN FORM

**Chrysalis** [*x1½*]
Two distinct colour forms regularly occur, determined by light levels.

**Resting adult**
In dull weather, the adults hide deep in fenland vegetation, with their large wings hanging downwards.

MATURE CATERPILLAR

YOUNG CATERPILLAR

**Caterpillar** [*x1½*]
Young caterpillar resembles a bird-dropping, but later develops green and black stripes.

# WOOD WHITE

## *Leptidea sinapis*

**Distribution** *Locally common, and possibly increasing, throughout Ireland, but a declining rarity in English and Welsh woods.*

THE WOOD WHITE is the smallest, daintiest, and by far the rarest of our British Whites. It is quite easy to recognize even in flight, for it flaps its slender wings so slowly that their distinctive outlines are clearly visible, as are the male's black tips. Sometimes a Green-veined White fluttering weakly on a cool spring day may be mistaken for the female, but at rest there should be no confusion. The delicacy of the wings, their oval shape, and the long, slender body, all distinguish this from other Whites. It differs, too, in that it always sits with closed wings, so that only the undersides are visible.

Unlike other Pierid butterflies, Wood Whites live in self-contained colonies, although males have occasionally been found several kilometres from their breeding sites. Typical colonies contain only a few dozen adults, but there are still places where it is the commonest springtime butterfly. Several thousand emerge each year in Salcey Forest near Northampton, adding immense charm to an ancient woodland that has been hideously disfigured by planted conifers.

### ADULT BEHAVIOUR

The first adults are generally seen in mid-May. Numbers reach a peak around the second week of June, then the population dwindles, with very few surviving into July. There may also be a small second brood in the south, especially after a warm summer. These emerge in mid-August and look slightly different, the males having smaller, but darker, black wingtips.

Working in England and Sweden respectively, Martin Warren and Christer Wiklund have revealed much about the life-cycle of this butterfly. Given reasonable weather, the males spend most of their lives flying 50 to 100 cm. (about 1½ to 3 ft.) above ground level, slowly patrolling woodland rides and shrub edges in a continuous search for mates. They swerve to investigate any white object, and if this proves to be a female, begin the curious head-to-head courtship shown on p.36. Female Wood Whites fly only half as frequently as the males, and hence are seen less often. When spotted, most will be feeding from flowers; bugle *(Ajuga reptans)*, ragged robin *(Lychnis floscuculi)*, and taller bird's-foot trefoils *(Lotus* spp.*)* are favourites, although almost any springtime flower may be used. Males spend less time feeding on nectar, but supplement their diet with mineral salts by drinking from the muddy edges of puddles. "Puddling" generally occurs in hot, dry weather, and is more often seen further south in Europe. It is well worth looking for: often many males will be grouped together, so pre-occupied that they can be approached very closely before they gracefully flutter up and away in a white cloud of wings.

### EGG-LAYING

An adult can live for two to three weeks, but most die of old age after a fortnight, and the average lifespan is eight to ten days. By then, a typical female will have laid between 30 and 60 eggs, the total being largest if the weather stays fine. Eggs are laid singly, on – in descending order of preference – yellow meadow vetchling *(Lathyrus pratensis)*, bitter vetch *(L. montanus)*, tufted vetch *(Vicia cracca)*, marsh or greater bird's-foot trefoil *(Lotus uliginosus)*, and on bird's-foot trefoil *(L. corniculatus)*.

These are all quite common plants but, like so many butterflies, female Wood Whites are distinctly careful over which particular specimen they choose. In the first place, they prefer to lay on sheltered plants growing along ride edges that are shaded for at least a fifth, but not more than half, of the day. They also choose rather prominent vetches, that have clambered above the surrounding vegetation. Once typical plants are known, the pale, bottle-shaped egg is quite easy to find on good sites during June. The female is very precise in the way she lays her eggs. When searching meadow vetchling, look especially beneath the first and second pair of leaflets down from the tip and under the youngest bracts. On bitter vetch, nearly all eggs will be found beneath the second to fourth pair of leaflets from the tip.

# WOOD WHITE · *Leptidea sinapis*

LIFE-CYCLE

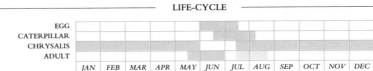

| | JAN | FEB | MAR | APR | MAY | JUN | JUL | AUG | SEP | OCT | NOV | DEC |
|---|---|---|---|---|---|---|---|---|---|---|---|---|
| EGG | | | | | | | | | | | | |
| CATERPILLAR | | | | | | | | | | | | |
| CHRYSALIS | | | | | | | | | | | | |
| ADULT | | | | | | | | | | | | |

**English male, first brood**
Springtime male with larger wings,
greyer than those of second brood.

**English female, first brood**
Wings of females are more rounded than
those of males, and black tips less intense.

**English male, second brood**
Smaller and less numerous than
males of the first brood.

**English female, second brood**
Smaller and less numerous than
first-brood counterparts.

**Subspecies *L. s. juvernica***
Irish specimens have greener
undersides than those in
England.

**Egg [x15]**
Laid singly on a variety
of vetches and trefoils.

**Chrysalis [x2¼]**
Formed in dense clumps
of grass away from the
foodplant.

**Feeding adult**
English female on
marsh thistle, with
wings closed.

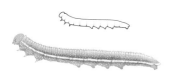

**Caterpillar [x2¼]**
Perfect camouflage conceals the
caterpillar when resting on the
stem of its foodplant.

**Resting adult**
English male, second
brood, in a typical
resting position.

## LOSSES TO PREDATORS

The eggs hatch after 10 to 20 days, but by then up to half may have been killed by predators or by tiny, parasitic *Trichogramma* wasps. The solitary caterpillar eats the vetch leaves during summer, starting at the tip of a shoot and gradually working its way down. This, too, is a vulnerable time of life. Many caterpillars are killed, mainly by birds. Although beautifully camouflaged, the caterpillar can be found, with practice, on suitable vetches in early August.

The chrysalis is the prettiest stage in the life-cycle, with the veins and edges picked out in pink on a translucent green background. Unfortunately, it is very difficult to find, for the caterpillar leaves its vetch to pupate among dense clumps of grass. For most people, the only realistic chance of seeing this chrysalis is to rear the butterfly in captivity, which is quite easy.

## DECLINING FORTUNES

The number of Wood Whites in any colony fluctuates considerably from one year to the next, depending chiefly on whether the females had sufficient sunshine the year before to lay large quantities of eggs. Over a longer period, numbers also drift up or down in response to the amount of suitable foodplant

### COURTSHIP AND MATING

**THE ONSET OF COURTSHIP**
*At first, the male (left) sits opposite the female, and slowly uncoils his proboscis.*

**SIGNALLING**
*The male then waves his proboscis and the conspicuous, white-tipped antennae back and forth.*

**THE FEMALE RESPONDS**
*Stimulated by the male's signals, the female bends her abdomen towards the swaying male.*

**PAIRING**
*The two butterflies couple, and remain together for 30 minutes, until fertilization is complete.*

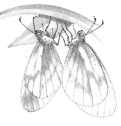

on the site; the largest colonies are not necessarily found where vetches and vetchling are most abundant, but rather where they are growing in ideal situations for egg-laying.

Suitable conditions were quite common in earlier centuries, when most British woods were coppiced. In those days Wood Whites bred abundantly in the shrubby regrowth, thriving in most counties south of Cumberland. The butterfly's great decline occurred around the turn of the century, when coppicing was largely abandoned. By the early 1900s, it had disappeared altogether from Cumbria, East Anglia, Kent, the New Forest, and the Isle of Wight, and by 1920 it had been lost from Nottinghamshire, North Wales, and Yorkshire.

## A RECENT RECOVERY

Since the first quarter of this century, the story has been a happier one. With the widespread planting of conifers, suitable breeding conditions often exist along the bushy edges of access rides, about 20 to 40 years after the plantation was established. Many British plantations are at that stage now, and the Wood White has increased in several woods. It has even spread to new sites, often helped by the deliberate introduction of a few females. Another bonus was the abandonment of railway lines during the cuts of the 1960s; the scrubby regrowth in sheltered cuttings currently offers ideal breeding conditions in several places, and some support very large colonies indeed.

Today there may be as many as 90 Wood White colonies in England and Wales. There are four main strongholds. The finest populations occur in conifer plantations in the east Midlands and along some railway tracks on heavy clays in Northamptonshire and Oxfordshire. A second centre is on the highly wooded Wealden clays of West Sussex and Surrey, especially around Haslemere and Chiddingfold. Wood Whites are also locally common in the Forests of Dean and Wyre, and in woods in Herefordshire and Worcestershire. The fourth stronghold is in south Somerset and east Devon, where some of the finest colonies breed on scrubby undercliffs, west of Lyme Regis.

## THE WOOD WHITE IN IRELAND

Fortunately, the Wood White is much less of a rarity in Ireland, where it exists as a separate subspecies, *L. s. juvernica*, a particularly beautiful form, with a distinct green tinge to the underwings. Irish Wood White colonies have spread considerably in recent years, and it is not unusual to find the butterfly in any suitable-looking habitat. As on the Continent, they live in more open places than in England, and can be found in scrubland, old quarries, and even along road verges. They are particularly common among the hazel scrub and limestone grassland of the Burren.

# CLOUDED YELLOW

## Colias croceus

ALTHOUGH THE Clouded Yellow is seen every year in Britain, it is one of three butterflies that cannot survive our cool and damp winters. Its existence this far north depends on the arrival of fresh immigrants from southern Europe each spring. But unlike the Painted Lady and Red Admiral, this species arrives in irregular numbers. On average, it is scarce in nine years out of ten, making the occasional great "Clouded Yellow years" all the more memorable.

This is one of the great migratory insects of Europe. Permanent populations occur in the southern half of Europe and north Africa, where the butterflies breed continuously on lucerne (*Medicago sativa*), clovers (*Trifolium* spp.), and other leguminous plants. These populations give rise to large migrations every spring, with Clouded Yellows teeming in strong purposeful flights northwards through Europe. It is very much a one-way flight at this time of year, and the sea is clearly no obstacle. Indeed, Britain receives a great many more Clouded Yellows than Holland, and this is one of only six species of European butterfly to have colonized the Azores, 1,450 km. (900 miles) from the nearest colonies on the Spanish coast.

*Distribution Seen every year on southern coasts; occasionally abundant, spreading in diminishing numbers north to central Scotland.*

### JOURNEY'S END

In Britain, the first bands of immigrants usually reach the south coast in May and June, although there is some evidence of occasional arrivals from as early as February. The number to reach us varies greatly each year. Although normally seen in ones and twos, the major immigrations can be astounding. F. W. Frohawk quotes one famous account from the nineteenth century by the Rev. D. Percy Harrison:

"My greatest experience was in Cornwall as far back as 1868, when I was only 11, and sat on a cliff near Marazion, and saw a yellow patch out at sea, which as it came nearer showed itself to be composed of thousands of Clouded Yellows, which approached flying close over the water, and rising and falling over every wave till they reached the cliffs, when I was surrounded by clouds of *C.(=croceus) edusa,* which settled on every flower... They swarmed in the district for a space of some three weeks and were good specimens when they arrived."

E. B. Ford, in his famous book, *Butterflies,* makes the same point that immigrant butterflies often arrive in mint condition, having perhaps flown hundreds of kilometres. This is my experience too. It is when butterflies pursue, court, or reject mates among tangled vegetation, or when females scrabble around for egg-laying sites, that the scales fly, and the butterflies lose the pristine appearance of the new arrivals.

### BREEDING IN BRITAIN

In Dorset, which along with Devon receives more Clouded Yellows than any other county, the adults immediately strike inland on arrival and then fan out through the county, settling particularly in clover fields and on chalk downs. They lay their eggs mainly on the leaves of clovers, lucerne and, less often, on bird's-foot trefoil (*Lotus corniculatus*) and other native vetches. There is therefore no shortage of habitat, and it is interesting that this is the only species of butterfly in the British Isles capable of breeding on modern improved grasslands, in which sown clover often forms an important component.

The bottle-shaped eggs are laid openly on the tops of leaves, and are easy to find in Clouded Yellow years. Initially they are white, but soon turn pinkish-orange, hatching after about a week. The caterpillar greedily devours the leaves of its food-plant and may be fully grown within a month. The chrysalis, which I have yet to find in the wild, lasts a further two or three weeks. It is believed that both caterpillars and chrysalises die in cold, wet weather, and that is the reason why this butterfly is unable to survive permanently in northern Europe.

The offspring of the first batch of immigrants generally emerge in mid-August. These are far more plentiful than their parents, and their numbers may also be boosted by fresh arrivals from the Continent. I saw this for myself when I made weekly counts of butterflies on the downs near Swanage during the Clouded Yellow year of 1983. In the first half of June, only three Clouded Yellows occurred within the narrow boundaries of my survey lines (transects), although odd adults could be seen egg-laying throughout the area. But in August there was a magnificent emergence, and I counted 109 Clouded Yellows along the transects, and 20 or 30 individuals were always visible elsewhere on the down at any one time. There is often a further brood that can produce enormous numbers in September and October, but this failed to materialize in 1983 due, it is believed, to unseasonably bad weather.

## MASS IMMIGRATIONS

There is probably no year in which a few Clouded Yellows do not reach Britain, but immigrants are generally few and far between, and seldom penetrate beyond the southern English counties. Indeed, they usually breed near the coast, especially that of the Isle of Wight, Dorset, Devon, and Cornwall. Here one can expect to see the odd individual in August every year, and about half-a-dozen or so on a coastal walk every five years or so. But, about ten times a century, there is an immigration on an altogether grander scale.

Clouded Yellow years do not come regularly once a decade, but are erratic and unpredictable. Thus there were six in the period between 1941 and 1950, followed by a lean period of 33 years before the next in 1983. The 1983 immigration came as a complete surprise to a generation of entomologists – myself included – who had never experienced one of these years. It had, indeed, been suspected that these mass immigrations might be a thing of the past, on the grounds that vast migratory swarms were unlikely to build up nowadays due to the modernization of agriculture in the Clouded Yellow's permanent breeding grounds. However, long gaps between Clouded Yellow years are not new. In the nineteenth century, there were three periods from 15 to 22 years between the major immigrations.

These mass immigrations make a wonderful spectacle, particularly on southern downs and coasts, where Clouded Yellows reach an extraordinary abundance. In my own county of Dorset, one encountered a Clouded Yellow every few hundred metres in August 1983, and every clover field had at least a dozen fluttering above the sward. On the southern downs, 20 or 30 could always be seen at a glance.

In 1983, Clouded Yellows spread northwards in diminishing numbers as far as the southern half of Scotland. During that summer, they were more common than Brimstones in many parts of southern England. The Clouded Yellow and Brimstone

(*see p.41*) do have a superficial similarity, but these two butterflies are easy to distinguish because their tones are entirely different. The Clouded Yellow is a rich, sulphurous colour, which led to the early English name of the "Saffron Butterfly", while the Brimstone has a paler, clearer, almost luminous tint. It is well to note, however, that the full colours of both species are apparent only when they fly, for both settle and bask with their wings firmly closed, so that only the pale undersides are visible.

Many naturalists are unaware that there is a beautiful, pale-coloured form of the female Clouded Yellow, *helice*. These account for up to a tenth of all females – and appear in various tones, ranging from white to grey. Some are easily confused with the much rarer Pale or Berger's Clouded Yellows (*see p.199*). They look almost white on the wing, and in Clouded Yellow years, can be more common than Small, Large, or Green-veined Whites on the southern English downs.

Clouded Yellow years often coincide with large immigrations of those two other great travellers, the Red Admiral and Painted Lady. They should be enjoyed when they occur, for it is just as likely that after the spectacle is over, an exceptionally poor year will follow. This was the case after 1947, which was by far the greatest Clouded Yellow year of the century, with 36,000 sightings of the butterfly, which out-numbered every other species along the southern coast in high summer. Although contemporary accounts are peppered with superlatives, this immigration had, in fact, been surpassed 70 years earlier, in 1877. However, as there were fewer entomologists in those days, an exact comparison is impossible.

## DEPARTURE FOR THE SOUTH

Clouded Yellow years end as quickly as they begin. A few individuals may survive the mildest southern winters, but the vast majority either die or migrate south. Southern migrations occur regularly throughout Europe in the autumn, and the butterflies can be seen making their way through passes in the Pyrenees. Although Clouded Yellow migrations are not often observed from Britain, they can be spectacular. In the book *Insect Migration,* C. B. Williams recounts the experience of J. Blake, who witnessed the end of the *annus mirabilis* 1947, aboard a steamer sailing up the English Channel between Ushant and Start Point on 14 October:

"For many miles he saw Clouded Yellows over the sea moving steadily to the S.S.W. He considered that the flight was on a front of about fifty miles and that there must have been well over a hundred thousand butterflies taking part."

Where they made a landfall, nobody knows. Perhaps they simply pressed on into the Atlantic and perished for 1948 was one of the poorer years on record.

# CLOUDED YELLOW · *Colias croceus*

## LIFE-CYCLE

| | JAN | FEB | MAR | APR | MAY | JUN | JUL | AUG | SEP | OCT | NOV | DEC |
|---|---|---|---|---|---|---|---|---|---|---|---|---|
| EGG | | | | | | | | | | | | |
| CATERPILLAR | | | | | | | | | | | | |
| CHRYSALIS | | | | | | | | | | | | |
| ADULT | | | | | | | | | | | | |

**Male**
Markings are fairly constant throughout their range; male upperwing margins are solid black.

**Female**
Normal colour form; black margins of wings are broken by ragged yellow spots, unlike those of male.

**Female**
Pale coloured form *helice*; colour ranges from white to grey. There is no male equivalent of this form.

**Feeding adult**
Clovers and lucerne are both caterpillar foodplants and nectar sources for the adults.

**Egg [*x15*]**
Laid singly, quickly changing from white to pinkish orange.

**Chrysalis [*x1½*]**
Head slightly upturned; attached to foodplant by a silk girdle.

**Caterpillar [*x1½*]**
Very similar to Pale Clouded Yellow caterpillar, but less heavily speckled on back.

**INDIVIDUAL SEGMENT**

# BRIMSTONE

## *Gonepteryx rhamni*

THE BRIMSTONE is a conspicuous nomadic butterfly that will be familiar to every naturalist who lives within a few kilometres of its foodplants, the purging buckthorn *(Rhamnus catharticus)* and alder buckthorn *(Frangula alnus)*. As one of our longest-lived species, it can be seen in almost every month of the year. However, there are two distinct peaks: one on the first warm days of spring, when the butterfly flutters along hedgerows and around woods, and the other in high summer, when it gorges on nectar anywhere it can, laying down reserves before its winter rest.

### FLOWERS AND FOODPLANTS

Brimstones fly during the heat of the day but tend to roost early, usually disappearing between 3 p.m. and 4 p.m. to settle upside-down beneath leaves in shrubs. There is one generation a year, which emerges over several weeks from early July onwards. Newly emerged adults spend much of the day feeding, concentrating on purple, nectar-rich flowers like teasel *(Dipsacus fullonum)*, buddleia *(Buddleia spp.)*, purple loosestrife *(Lythrum salicaria)*, and thistles.

The Brimstone selects these flowers for anatomical reasons, a fact borne out by a butterfly count that I undertook at Monks Wood in Cambridgeshire. Walking down a 250-m. (800-ft.) ride one August day, I noted the butterflies that were attracted to various flowers. Of the 110 Brimstones I saw, 105 were feeding on teasels, as were all but seven of the 346 Peacocks counted. By contrast, 68 of the 74 Gatekeepers were on ragwort *(Senecio jacobaea)*, with none drinking at teasel. Puzzled by this, I later measured the lengths both of the probosces of these butterflies and the flower-tubes. As can be seen on p.42, Brimstones, like Peacocks, have exceptionally long tongues enabling them to feed on teasel, whereas Gatekeepers must make do with ragwort.

Freshly emerged Brimstones remain around their breeding grounds for two or three weeks, but in some regions then

*Distribution A nomadic butterfly that is common throughout the southern half of England, but occurs at low densities in Ireland and Wales.*

migrate to feed and hibernate in flower-rich woods. They hibernate after a few weeks' feeding, probably beneath evergreen leaves, such as those of ivy *(Hedera helix)* and holly *(Ilex aquifolium)*, although they sometimes also use clumps of bramble *(Rubus fruticosus)* on downland. Although nomadic at a regional level, the Brimstone is not a true migrant. Its distribution in the British Isles matches that of its foodplants very closely. Thus the butterfly is largely absent from the uplands and west of Wales, and from most of northern England apart from the Lake District; no more than six individuals are reported to have strayed over the border into Scotland. Its distribution can be patchy even within a county. It is common, for example, in most districts of Dorset, yet few sightings are made south of the Purbeck Hills, where both species of buckthorn are rare.

### BREEDING ON BUCKTHORN

The last Brimstones that emerge in summer feed late into October, and occasionally re-emerge on warm winter days. Mating is always delayed until spring. The males awake first and begin patrolling wood edges, sunny glades, and hedgerows in their search for females. There is then a spectacular courtship, with male and female spiralling high into the air. The female is seemingly reluctant to mate, but finally she descends into a bush where she sits with wings half-open, quivering as the male pairs with her. It is possible that she releases an aphrodisiac at this stage, for it has been noted that a pair of Brimstones may attract a number of other males, even though they may be hidden from sight among the leaves.

Once mated, females search for either of the two buckthorns, flying along hedges, and in woods and scrub. Although alder buckthorn can be abundant on acid soils, both foodplants grow extremely sparsely in many areas, and it is remarkable how seldom a suitable specimen is missed. However, Brimstones do not lay indiscriminately. At Monks Wood, it was discovered

# BRIMSTONE · *Gonepteryx rhamni*

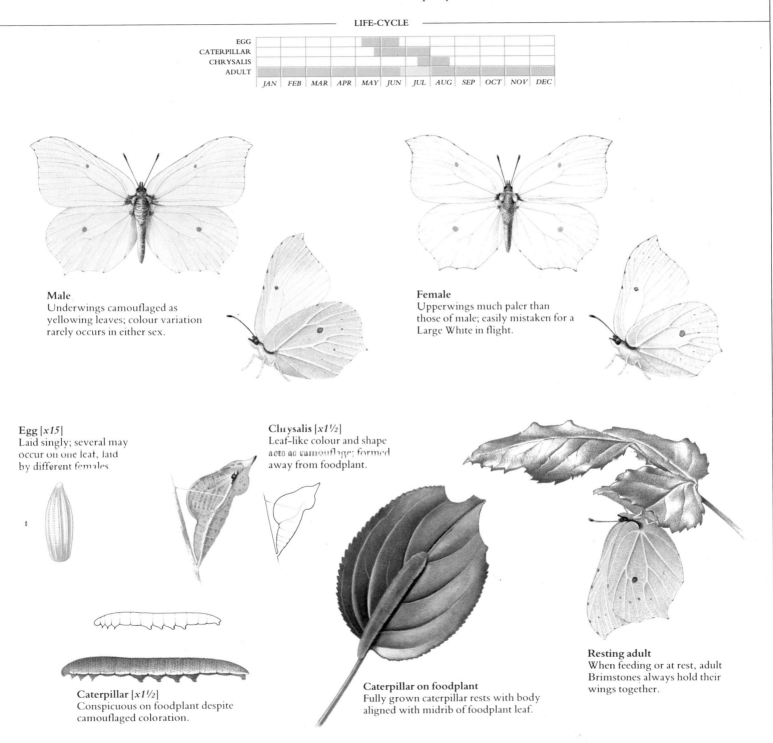

## LIFE-CYCLE

| | JAN | FEB | MAR | APR | MAY | JUN | JUL | AUG | SEP | OCT | NOV | DEC |
|---|---|---|---|---|---|---|---|---|---|---|---|---|
| EGG | | | | | | | | | | | | |
| CATERPILLAR | | | | | | | | | | | | |
| CHRYSALIS | | | | | | | | | | | | |
| ADULT | | | | | | | | | | | | |

**Male**
Underwings camouflaged as yellowing leaves; colour variation rarely occurs in either sex.

**Female**
Upperwings much paler than those of male; easily mistaken for a Large White in flight.

**Egg** [*x15*]
Laid singly; several may occur on one leaf, laid by different females

**Chrysalis** [*x1½*]
Leaf-like colour and shape acts as camouflage; formed away from foodplant.

**Caterpillar** [*x1½*]
Conspicuous on foodplant despite camouflaged coloration.

**Caterpillar on foodplant**
Fully grown caterpillar rests with body aligned with midrib of foodplant leaf.

**Resting adult**
When feeding or at rest, adult Brimstones always hold their wings together.

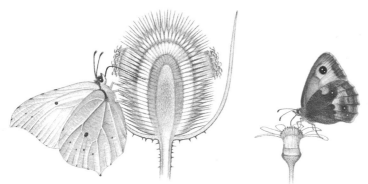

LONG-TONGUED AND SHORT-TONGUED FEEDERS
*The Brimstone (left) has an unusually long proboscis, about 15 mm. (½ in.) in extent. It can reach the nectaries at the bottom of teasel flowers. In contrast the Gatekeeper's proboscis (right) is only 6 mm. (¼ in.) long. It can feed only on flat flowers.*

that just two of the 12 buckthorn bushes that grew in the 150-ha. (370-acre) wood held 94 per cent of the Brimstone eggs, and that plants that were not both in the sunshine and sheltered from the wind had few or none. The butterflies laid their eggs at all heights on these bushes, but particularly on crowns protruding into sheltered sunshine. Elsewhere, however, they prefer stumpy bushes in more open situations, choosing young buckthorns between 60 cm. and 1 m. (2 and 3 ft.) high, and largely ignoring mature shrubs.

Brimstone eggs are easy to find once you learn where to look. Females choose the sunny sides of bushes and lay on unfurling leaflets. Although they lay just one egg at a time, many are eventually placed on the undersides of the tender tips, leaving them protruding like a cluster of tiny, pale bottles. Brimstones are sometimes ready to lay before the buckthorns come into leaf. If forced to, they will place the eggs on the twigs beside unopened buds.

The eggs hatch after one to two weeks, and the small caterpillar starts feeding on the upper surface of the leaf, biting holes in the tender tissue below. This makes irregular perforations which expand and distort as the leaf grows, and which are very easy to spot. Slightly older caterpillars eat entire leaves, and are also easy to find, despite a near-perfect camouflage. Each rests on top of a leaf, aligned head outwards along the midrib, raising the front half of its body slightly above the leaf surface at the slightest disturbance.

Many caterpillars fail to complete their development. Although I have not made exact counts, I have the impression that a large number disappear during the final period of growth.

Warblers, almost certainly, are the main predators, although some caterpillars are killed by wasps, and tachinid flies (*see p.123*) parasitize many others. The survivors nearly always leave their foodplants to pupate. Only once have I found a chrysalis on buckthorn, low down beneath a leaf, although I have searched scores that had held full-grown caterpillars. The chrysalis hatches after about a fortnight.

## A WIDESPREAD DISTRIBUTION

Brimstone butterflies are common throughout the entire southern two-thirds of England, particularly on calcareous soils where purging buckthorn grows and on moist acid soils where alder buckthorn is the foodplant. Although attracted to flowers in summer, adult Brimstones congregate near buckthorns in spring. It is well worth growing two or three bushes in a sunny, sheltered corner of any southern garden, not only to attract this lovely insect in spring, but also for the pleasure of seeing the eggs and caterpillars. Elsewhere in England there are strong concentrations of the Brimstone in the Lake District, and the butterfly is common in southeast Wales. It also occurs over wide areas of Ireland, but is often uncommon due to the shortage of buckthorns. Only in the Burren are Brimstones plentiful, flying among the scrub on the limestone pavement.

It is difficult to say whether the number of Brimstones has changed much in recent years, although it is likely that the species was more common before the widespread grubbing-up of hedgerows, and also when hedge-cutting was carried out by hand. Woods, too, were probably much more suitable when coppicing was common, for this produced sunny, sheltered conditions and a succession of vigorous shrub regrowth. The species was certainly well-known to early butterfly collectors, and there are some people who maintain that the word "butterfly" is nothing more than a diminutive for its old name of "butter-coloured fly".

Whether this is true or not, the Brimstone has a unique place in the early history of British butterflies through being the first species known to be the subject of fraud. A. Maitland Emmet has recently given a fascinating account of the "Piltdown Butterfly". James Petiver, one of the fathers of British entomology, illustrated this in 1702, writing that it "exactly resembles our English Brimstone... were it not for those black spots and apparent blue moons on the lower Wings. This is the only one I have yet seen". This specimen was even given its own species name by the great natural historian Linnaeus, but in fact, it proved to be a normal Brimstone with the spots painted on its wings by a dealer.

# LARGE WHITE

## *Pieris brassicae*

THIS IS THE larger and more pernicious of the two Cabbage White butterflies that infest kitchen gardens and farms from the Channel Isles to the Shetlands. Its caterpillars are vastly destructive. They roam over Brassica crops in bands, reducing each plant to a skeleton of ribs, and leaving it enveloped in the acrid smell of mustard oil. Little wonder, therefore, that this is the least loved of all native butterflies, and that many people who are prepared to encourage the Peacock and Small Tortoiseshell by growing nettles in their gardens will think nothing of killing the Large White's caterpillars, or of squashing its yellow eggs.

It would be unfortunate, however, if this were to blind us to the Large White's more attractive features. It is a handsome insect by any standards, and the eggs that so disgust gardeners are as delightful as those of the Orange Tip *(see p.53)* when viewed close up. From a naturalist's point of view, this is also one of the most interesting of all European butterflies, due to the protective use it makes of mustard oils, and to its remarkable migratory flights.

***Distribution*** *A very common migrant to be seen anywhere except on high mountain-tops. Large swarms sometimes arrive from continental Europe.*

became highly popular, and every settlement in Europe contributed towards creating one vast continental breeding ground for this butterfly. The populations that developed were awesome: numbers have diminished in recent years, but even today some can be measured in millions rather than thousands of adults. These develop principally in southern Scandinavia, the Baltic Islands and northern Europe, and sweep southwards every year to breed in central Europe, although many other migrations occur. Our own populations undoubtedly reside in the British Isles, with hibernating chrysalises being reported from as far north as the Orkneys. But they, too, are regularly reinforced by immigrants, and home-grown individuals often reach the Continent.

British Large Whites have a tendency to fly north in spring, and there is scarcely a cabbage-patch in the land that is not colonized in some years. There is a strong sense of purpose to these migratory flights, very different from the erratic flutterings that one sees once adults have settled in a district. The wings are beaten in short, powerful flits as the butterflies press onwards, flying 1 to 2 m. (3 to 6 ft.) above ground level. Large Whites fly at up to 16 km/h (10 mph) given a following breeze, but it is not known how far each can travel without resting. They can certainly cross hundreds of kilometres of ocean, but may be assisted by resting on ships. There is one description of a great swarm that once settled on the sea. Many were resting with their wings erect, and others lay flat on the water, but all flew off easily when disturbed.

The main bands of immigrants reach Britain in high summer, as offshoots from the regular southerly flights of central Europe. Some are of extraordinary size. In his classic book on insect migration, C. B. Williams recounts the earliest record of a swarm, on the northern coast of France:

"1508, the 23rd year of Henry the 7, the 9 of July, being relyke Sonday, there was sene at Calleys [*Calais*] an innumerable swarme of whit buttarflyes cominge out of the north

## MIGRATION PAST AND PRESENT

The Large White has two or three generations a year, although adults can be seen at any time from February to November. The first brood emerges mainly in late April and May, and remains on the wing well into June. As can be seen from the illustrations overleaf, springtime adults differ slightly from later ones in having grey rather than black tips to their wings, and were once considered to be of a different species. Butterflies from the second emergence are usually three to ten times more numerous than those from the first, and are on the wing from July to September. A third brood often follows in autumn.

Like many pests, it seems likely that the Large White was scarce before Neolithic man first tilled the land, and started domesticating the wild cabbage *(Brassica oleracea)*. In the centuries that followed, various forms of cultivated Brassica

este and flyinge south-eastwards, so thicke as flakes of snowe, that men beinge a shutynge in St. Petars fields without the town of Calleys could not see the towne at foure of the clock in the aftarnone, they flew so highe and so thicke."

Later observers were often to use the same analogy. Barrett, the Victorian entomologist, wrote that there were "many cases of... vast flights at sea, sometimes so as to form clouds like a snow-storm, or to cover a vessel and its sails when alighted".

The number of butterflies involved in these swarms is usually impossible to gauge. One serious estimate was of 400 million adults in a front almost 5 km. (3 miles) wide, while a more accurate figure was obtained from a freak disaster on an island in Sutton Broad, in Norfolk. Here, in an area of just under 1 ha. (2.5 acres), 6 million butterflies were caught in the sticky leaves of insectivorous sundews (*Drosera* spp.).

There are more conventional attacks, too, on these swarms. Williams describes how flycatchers, sparrows, and other birds homed in on one flight through Harpenden, and how the ground became littered with white wings.

## CHEMICAL PROTECTION

The immigrants disperse once they have settled in a region, and may be seen in ones and twos in any flowery habitat. Favourite sites include meadows, downs, hedgerows, and wasteland, but they especially gather in gardens, where the cocktail of sulphurous scents that wafts up from mixed rows of Brassicas is a far stronger lure than any open field of cabbages. The female first detects these through her antennae, but having homed in and settled on a Brassica, she taps the leaves of successive plants with her feet, tasting each to select those with the strongest concentrations of sinigrin, which is the mustard oil she prefers. She then bends her abdomen, and pumps out from 40 to 100 eggs, at a rate of about four a minute. At the same time, she deposits a chemical marker on the eggs, which deters other females from laying on the plant.

The eggs of the Large White will be all too familiar to gardeners. They stand in small, erect groups on either side of a leaf, pale yellow at first but gradually ripening to a rich orange. Each one contains a small dose of mustard oil, which is presumed to deter enemies. Eggs are found on a whole range of Brassicas, including cabbages, kale, and Brussels sprouts. Wild mignonette (*Reseda lutea*) is also occasionally used, as are the leaves of garden nasturtium (*Tropaeoleum majus*).

Large White eggs hatch after one to two weeks, and the little caterpillars remain in a band until their fourth and final skin change. At first, they concentrate on the outer leaves, cutting holes between the veins until only a skeleton of ribs remains. All rest and feed together in synchrony, and are indeed stimulated to eat by the oily fumes that escape from the damaged leaves. They spin grubby, grey webs of silk over the plant, and between feeds the caterpillars bask on these, in the multi-coloured groups so detested by gardeners.

One might think that these clusters would be vulnerable to any passing bird or mammal, but the caterpillars have a highly effective defence. While feeding on the leaves, poisonous oils are accumulated in their bodies in sufficient concentrations to deter most vertebrates. For, as has long been known to the military, mustard oil – or gas – is a burning irritant in low doses and a lethal nerve poison when concentrated.

## PARASITES AND PUPATION

One group of enemies is not deterred by these chemicals. Stinging wasps and flies often lay eggs in the bodies of the caterpillars, and their grubs feed as parasites on the caterpillars' tissues. One species, in particular, concentrates on the Large White – a wasp called *Apanteles glomeratus*, which is so tiny that up to 80 grubs can emerge from one fully grown caterpillar. The female wasp injects eggs into a layer of fat that lies just beneath the caterpillar's skin, and the maggots grow within this, avoiding the vital organs. Then, just as the caterpillar has spun a web on which to pupate, they kill it by piercing through the skin, and form rows of yellow silk cocoons along both sides of the flabby body. Vast numbers of caterpillars are killed in some years, accounting for more than four-fifths of the population.

Both doomed and healthy caterpillars wander some distance to pupate. They often settle beneath the eaves of a building, under a fence, or on tree-trunks, where the cocoon-lined corpses or pretty, speckled chrysalises are quite easy to find. The latter have various colour patterns, the exact tone being partly determined by the intensity of light surrounding the caterpillar, as with the Swallowtail (*see p.33*). This gives the chrysalis some camouflage against its background. It also contains sufficient mustard oils to burn the mouth of any bird that is foolish enough to peck it.

Enough caterpillars survive their enemies for the Large White to remain one of the most common and pestilential butterflies in Europe. It is seldom, however, that the really large swarms of yesteryear develop. This reduction is often attributed to another mass-killer of caterpillars, a granulosis virus which reached the British Large White populations from the Continent in 1955. Thus, while it is still common for caterpillars to strip an entire kitchen garden of Brassicas, there has been nothing in recent years to approach one outbreak in 1884 when, as John Feltwell relates, "a train in the Russian town of Kiev was held up by thousands of larvae wandering over the line. The larvae were crushed 'like pâté' in front of the locomotive."

# LARGE WHITE · *Pieris brassicae*

## LIFE-CYCLE

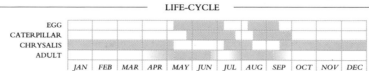

| | JAN | FEB | MAR | APR | MAY | JUN | JUL | AUG | SEP | OCT | NOV | DEC |
|---|---|---|---|---|---|---|---|---|---|---|---|---|
| EGG | | | | | | | | | | | | |
| CATERPILLAR | | | | | | | | | | | | |
| CHRYSALIS | | | | | | | | | | | | |
| ADULT | | | | | | | | | | | | |

**Male, first brood**
Springtime males have slightly greyer wingtips than second-brood males.

**Male underside**
Both sexes have a similar underside in both first and second broods.

**Female, first brood**
Springtime females are generally lighter in colour than their offspring.

**Egg** [*x15*]
Initially pale yellow, becoming orange; hatches after one to two weeks.

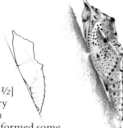

**Chrysalis** [*x1½*]
Markings vary depending on background; formed some distance from the foodplant.

**Female, second brood**
Females of the second, summer brood are often heavily marked with black and grey.

**Egg batch**
Clusters of eggs are usually laid on the undersurfaces of Brassica leaves.

**Parasites**
Tiny *Apanteles* wasps kill many caterpillars. Their larvae live in the caterpillar's body, and then they pupate beside the corpse.

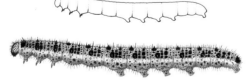

**Caterpillar** [*x1½*]
The caterpillars live communally until their fourth moult, feeding or resting at the same time.

**Basking adult**
Adults sit with their wings half-open to regulate their temperature.

# SMALL WHITE

## *Pieris rapae*

THE SMALL WHITE is a plain, medium-sized butterfly that will be familiar to every naturalist and gardener. It appears, in most respects, to be a less spectacular version of the Large White *(see p.45)*. Adults have the same basic wing pattern, but are generally smaller and duller. Its migratory swarms are rarely so vast, and although it, too, can be a serious pest of Brassica crops, the damage in Europe is seldom as devastating as that caused by major infestations of Large Whites.

These two species of Cabbage White can usually be distinguished by size, although this is by no means an infallible guide. Quite small specimens of the Large White sometimes emerge, especially in years when the caterpillars exhaust their foodplants. However, the male Small White usually has a black spot in the centre of each forewing, a feature missing on the male Large White. Furthermore, in both sexes, the dark tips on the upperwings are confined to the wings' extremities and do not extend down the outer edges, as is the case with both the Large White and the Green-veined White *(see p.51)*. These dark tips are much fainter in the first, spring brood of Small Whites, and are almost non-existent on some males.

### MIGRATIONS AND DISPERSAL

The Small White is a butterfly that lives in loose, open populations – a roamer through the countryside that reaches every sheltered habitat in its search for nectar and egg-sites. It hibernates, like the Large White, as a chrysalis. After a mild winter, the first adults are seen as early as February, although late April is more usual. Numbers then build up to a peak by mid-May, and gradually fall off during June. A second brood emerges towards the end of the month, and continues throughout July. There may also be a third emergence in late summer.

Small White numbers fluctuate considerably between years. The second brood is always the more abundant, sometimes by a factor of several hundred-fold, but whether this is due to

***Distribution*** *A very common nomad, absent only from the Orkneys, Shetlands, and high mountain-tops.*

breeding success or to massive reinforcements from the Continent is unknown. Large migratory flights undoubtedly occur from time to time, occasionally in the company of Large Whites. Some of their swarms are immense. A spectacular example is quoted by The Rev. F. O. Morris, from an account in the *Canterbury Journal* of 5 July 1846:

"Such was the density and extent of the cloud, that it completely obscured the sun from the people on board the continental steamers on their passage, for many hundreds of yards, while the insects strewed the deep in all directions. The flight reached England about twelve o'clock at noon, and dispersed themselves inland and along the shore, darkening the air as they went... gardens suffered from the ravages of their larvae, even at a distance of ten miles from Dover."

There has, however, been considerable debate over the regularity of the Small White's migrations. Some people maintain that these occur every year, and that British populations instinctively fly northwards in spring, with their offspring returning south in late summer. Robin Baker, an authority on insect migration, estimates that they can fly over 160 km. (100 miles) in a lifetime. He cites the spread of this butterfly in Australia, after it was foolishly introduced to Melbourne in 1939, as evidence of its mobility. Within three years, and no more than 25 generations, it had reached the west coast, a distance of 3,000 km. (1,850 miles) and has been a pest throughout the continent ever since. The butterfly was also exceedingly quick to colonize North America after an introduction in the nineteenth century, and regular migratory patterns have developed there as the species has spread to exploit this new region. In addition, definite migrations are regularly recorded passing north, and later south, through the Pyrenees. On the whole, it seems likely that this is a regular, rather than a casual, migrant, although there seems little doubt that some individuals travel no more than a kilometre or two during their lives.

# SMALL WHITE · *Pieris rapae*

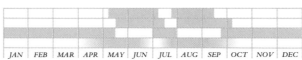

## LIFE-CYCLE

| | JAN | FEB | MAR | APR | MAY | JUN | JUL | AUG | SEP | OCT | NOV | DEC |
|---|---|---|---|---|---|---|---|---|---|---|---|---|
| EGG | | | | | | | | | | | | |
| CATERPILLAR | | | | | | | | | | | | |
| CHRYSALIS | | | | | | | | | | | | |
| ADULT | | | | | | | | | | | | |

**Male, first brood**
The black spots and wing margins of
first brood males can be very faint.

**Female, first brood**
Markings bolder than on the male; all
females have two spots on the forewings.

**Male, second brood**
Summer males are larger,
with blacker markings.

**Female, second brood**
As in the first brood, females
are darker than males.

**Basking adult**
Adult male, basking in the
sun on a cabbage leaf.

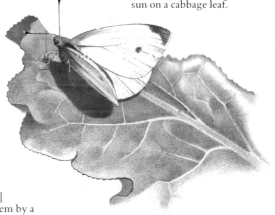

**Green form**

**Chrysalis [x1½]**
Attached to a stem by a
silk girdle; two main
colour forms.

**Brown form**

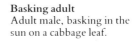

**Resting adult**
In dull weather, Small Whites
rest inconspicuously in
vegetation.

**Egg [x15]**
Laid singly on
a Brassica leaf.

**Single
segment**

**Caterpillar [x1½]**
Slightly furry; green colour
camouflages the caterpillar.

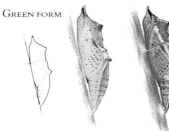

What is not in doubt is that the Small White is sufficiently mobile to reach every suitable breeding site in the country. This unfortunately includes even town gardens, where it is a familiar visitor to both flowers and vegetables. Small Whites have a penchant for white or pale blossoms, and visit a different range of flowers from the Vanessid butterflies. I have, for example, seen scores on my hedge of pale lavender, while the Small Tortoiseshell, Peacocks, and Commas gorge on the nectar of *Buddleia* just a metre or so away. Small Whites often roost, too, on white blooms, where they can be difficult to spot.

## EARLY DEVELOPMENT

Small Whites become ready for egg-laying no more than two or three days after mating. They then flutter around kitchen gardens in a tireless search for cabbage *(Brassica oleracea)* and its relatives. The pale, tubular egg is laid singly on the underside of a leaf, and young plants growing in warm nooks often receive large quantities. Every variety of cultivated Brassica is infested, and the female also lays on wild members of the cabbage family, such as garlic mustard *(Alliaria petiolata),* and charlock *(Sinapis arvensis).* They are partial, too, to the garden nasturtium *(Tropaeoleum majus).*

Individual females continue laying until they die, although at nothing like the rate that they do when young. Egg-laying occurs only in warm weather, but the occasional rainy day is no deterrent, for they store ripe eggs inside their bodies and merely lay at twice the rate when conditions improve. Female Small Whites have a strong preference for laying in warm, sheltered situations, and it is seldom that large fields of Brassicas are affected beyond the first few rows in from a hedge. A small, sunny kitchen garden, on the other hand, is tailor-made for their requirements, and attracts large numbers of butterflies.

It may take less than a week for the egg to hatch, by which time it has gone through a succession of colour changes, from almost white to bright yellow to grey. The solitary caterpillar then eats a small hole in its leaf, and bores inwards towards the heart of its plant. There it remains hidden for a week or two, eating a series of ever larger holes in the tender tissue. It finally lives in the open, resting lengthways along the midrib of a leaf, where the slightly furry green body is exquisitely camouflaged.

## THE SMALL WHITE'S NATURAL ENEMIES

There has been many a study of the predators and parasites of these caterpillars, much of it prompted by the enormous damage Small Whites can inflict on Brassica crops. That by Jack Dempster is especially interesting. He found that between half and nearly two-thirds of the caterpillars were eaten by other invertebrates, mainly in the first few days after hatching. Harvestmen and beetles were the chief predators; both are ground-dwellers, which scale the crops to hunt by night. He found, too, that there is a strong case for maintaining an untidy garden. For the weedier the bed, the greater the number of harvestmen and beetles that can live there, and a higher proportion of caterpillars is killed before they can damage the crop. Equally at risk is the farmer who sprays insecticides on his crops. These certainly destroy many caterpillars, but they also kill the caterpillar's natural enemies, and these take much longer to recover than this very mobile butterfly.

Many Small Whites are also eaten by birds. Sparrows take eggs and young hatchlings, and tits and warblers kill large numbers of older caterpillars. Thrushes inflict a final blow as the caterpillars search for somewhere to pupate. The chrysalis, too, is often attacked. Like the caterpillar, it contains few of the poisons that give such effective protection to the Large White.

Viruses are another killer, especially in cold, wet summers and when caterpillar densities are high. One further enemy is the pernicious *Apanteles* wasp. The Small White is mainly afflicted by *Apanteles rubecula* – a different species to that which attacks Large Whites, but the effect can be no less devastating. It was found in one study that caterpillar and parasite numbers oscillate together, but out of synchrony: high numbers of caterpillars led to large emergences of wasps, but these in turn killed so many caterpillars that the butterfly's numbers temporarily slumped.

None of these enemies is sufficient to pose a real threat to the Small White, which remains one of our commonest butterflies. It is one of the few species that shows little sign of having declined in recent years, and can be seen in almost every habitat in England, Wales, and Ireland. Large populations also abound through the southern half of Scotland, but it is scarce further north. Thus the Highlands are largely free of this insect, as are the outer islands such as the Hebrides, Orkneys, and Shetlands.

# GREEN-VEINED WHITE

## *Pieris napi*

ALTHOUGH OFTEN overlooked as a Cabbage White, this petite and attractive Pierid is a much more delicate creature which well repays closer examination. It is an inhabitant of moist, sheltered places, and possesses a weak fluttering flight that seems perfectly attuned to its peaceful surroundings. The underwings are especially beautiful, with the edges of every vein picked out by a dusting of dark scales, giving the illusion of a green stripe along either side.

### REGIONAL VARIATIONS

There is much variation in the markings of individual Green-veined Whites, and these also differ between the sexes and at different times of year. Springtime adults of both sexes tend to have darker veins than those of the summer brood, but there is usually less black on their upper-wings. This is particularly apparent in males, which can be almost pure white in the first generation and also extremely small. They are frequently mistaken for the rare Wood White *(see p.35)* when seen fluttering slowly down a woodland ride.

There is also some variation in their appearance throughout the British Isles. The ground-colour is brighter yellow and the veining considerably darker in parts of Ireland and Scotland. These handsome insects are sometimes described as distinct subspecies, and have much in common with the Green-veined Whites of Scandinavia. It has even been suggested that they are the modern descendants of Scandinavian stock, which colonized the British Isles during the ebbs and flows of tundra as the last great Ice Age receded. I suspect, however, that this colour form is part of the natural variation of this widespread and successful butterfly, which has been described as countless subspecies throughout Europe, Asia, and North America.

The existence of so much local variation suggests that the Green-veined White is a fairly sedentary butterfly, which is confined to isolated breeding groups throughout its range. Adults are certainly quite colonial in the north of the British Isles, but

*Distribution A common species in damp pasture and woods, absent only from the Shetlands and high mountain-tops.*

wander more freely in the south, at least on a relatively local scale.

Although many of its flowery breeding sites have been destroyed in recent years, the Green-veined White remains a common butterfly of damp grassland and woodland rides throughout the British Isles, and one that is especially abundant in Ireland and the west of Britain. Colonies are much more localized in the extreme north, and are not found at all in the Shetlands or at altitude in the Highlands. Nor do they often occur in dry, open habitats such as chalk downs. However, there may be small populations among patches of scrub and in copses, particularly on northern slopes, or on pockets of deeper soil, or, indeed, in any warm, sheltered place where the humidity is high.

### SEASONAL CHANGES

Green-veined Whites can be abundant where they do occur. Populations of thousands, if not tens of thousands, of adults are common in a good year, but numbers also fluctuate greatly between the generations. They often crash after a hot, dry summer, reflecting the need for a humid habitat. The drought of 1976 was particularly devastating, although it took no more than two fairly wet years for numbers to stage a rapid recovery.

There are consistent differences, too, in the abundance of the two main broods. Throughout most of the Green-veined White's British range, adults emerge from hibernating chrysalises in late April and May, and are on the wing almost to the end of June. Egg-laying occurs during this period and, provided the weather is warm, the caterpillars develop quite quickly to form thin-shelled chrysalises, which produce a second, very much more numerous, brood of adults in July and August. They, in turn, lay eggs, but in this case the caterpillars develop into chrysalises that have thick, waxy skins. These hibernate and produce the next brood of adults the following spring.

There is not, however, an all-or-nothing alternation between thin-skinned and hibernating generations of chrysalises. Scientists in Japan and also Scandinavia have shown that every caterpillar can develop into either form, depending on the temperature and the hours of daylight it receives. Caterpillars that live in regions or at times of year when the days are short invariably produce hibernation chrysalises, whereas those that experience 12 or more hours of light a day go on to produce the thin-shelled form which hatches into adults two or three weeks later.

### A SCENTED COURTSHIP

The natural history of this attractive White is well known, thanks mainly to the excellent studies by Johan Fosberg in Sweden. Male Green-veined Whites start emerging a few days earlier than the females, and soon begin to patrol back and forth in the sunshine, fluttering in weak, zig-zag flights to investigate the edges of shrubs, woodland rides, and any tussock that might house a mate. Females remain perched among leaves, but are fairly conspicuous. On sighting one, the male flutters around and lands nearby, showering her with a "love dust" so potent that even we can smell its scent of lemon verbena. Very few females succumb without a chase though, and the two fly off together before she lands and signals acceptance by folding her wings. They promptly pair, and the male then drags her on a short nuptial flight before they settle, locked in tandem.

The female is also smeared with an anti-aphrodisiac during mating, which deters other males from trying to court her. However, its effects are short-lived, and the most attractive females are frequently harassed by suitors. Like most Whites, females signify their rejection by opening their wings wide and holding their abdomens upright at 90 degrees, making it impossible for a male to mate. But, unusually for a European butterfly, the females frequently succumb, and many are mated four or five times during their lives. This is unnecessary for the fertilization of the eggs, and they mate merely to receive a fresh dose of the males' scent. This keeps suitors at bay for a few more days, leaving the females free to lay their eggs in peace.

FENDING OFF MALES
*The female rejects unwelcome suitors by sitting with her wings open and abdomen raised.*

### FEEDING AND EGG-LAYING

Both sexes of Green-veined White are avid feeders on flowers, and the males sometimes supplement their diet of nectar by mud-puddling. The males of several species of butterfly do this, probably because they need sodium and other salts to replace the minerals lost when they mate. Nectar is an excellent source of energy-rich sugars, but it has a low mineral content – hence the attraction of salts from the soil.

The female Green-veined White makes do with nectar alone, and spends much of her adult life fluttering a few centimetres above the ground, constantly landing to tap leaves with her feet. It is a slow, topsy-turvy kind of flight, almost as if she were injured and making desperate attempts to get airborne. In fact she is tasting every plant, trying to detect the mustard oils of Crucifers on which she lays eggs.

The female's potential range of foodplants is considerable. She will use almost any species of cress, although in Britain most eggs are found on water cress (*Nasturtium officinale*), lady's smock (*Cardamine pratensis*), garlic mustard (*Alliaria petiolata*), and hedge mustard (*Sysimbrium officinale*). These are common plants in woods and unfertilized grasslands but, like many butterflies, she is extremely selective about the sort of Crucifer that she chooses. Large, mature growths are invariably rejected in favour of seedlings or small, one-year-old, rosette-shaped plants, particularly those growing in moist recesses.

The pale, spindle-shaped eggs are very simple to find once one knows this butterfly's favourite spots. They are perhaps easiest to see in boggy grassland, but those in woods are by no means impossible to locate. Here, I generally search towards the bottom of ditches, in recently disturbed rides, or within the body of a wood, concentrating on quite shady, humid areas. The eggs may be on remarkably small plants. Although they are laid singly, I have frequently found three or four together on the undersurface of a water cress or lady's smock seedling, which consisted of no more than the four initial leaves, sprouting in old hoof-prints in a boggy meadow and along the crumbling banks of ditches and streams.

The eggs hatch after a week or two, and the caterpillar feeds only on the tender leaves, growing rapidly to pupate after about four weeks. It looks very like a Small White at this stage, except that there is no yellow line running down either side of the body, merely a circle of yellow around each of the spiracles. This is easily seen with the naked eye, and is shown in the enlarged segments of the two species, *(see opposite, and p.47).* Their chrysalises are harder to distinguish. Both exist in two main colour forms, regardless of the season. Those of the Green-veined White are presumably the better camouflaged, for I have yet to find either form in the wild.

# GREEN-VEINED WHITE · *Pieris napi*

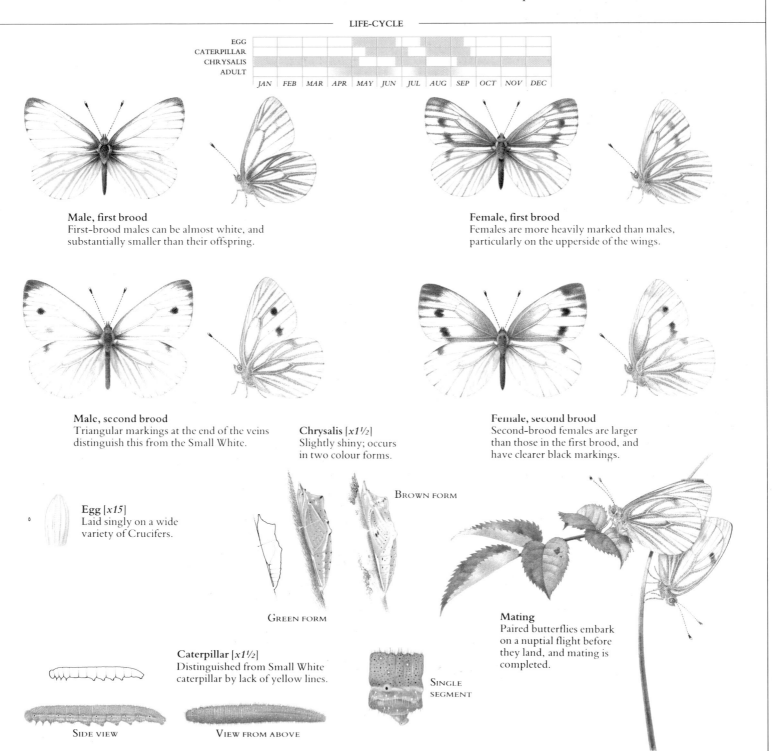

LIFE-CYCLE

| | JAN | FEB | MAR | APR | MAY | JUN | JUL | AUG | SEP | OCT | NOV | DEC |
|---|---|---|---|---|---|---|---|---|---|---|---|---|
| EGG | | | | | | | | | | | | |
| CATERPILLAR | | | | | | | | | | | | |
| CHRYSALIS | | | | | | | | | | | | |
| ADULT | | | | | | | | | | | | |

**Male, first brood**
First-brood males can be almost white, and
substantially smaller than their offspring.

**Female, first brood**
Females are more heavily marked than males,
particularly on the upperside of the wings.

**Male, second brood**
Triangular markings at the end of the veins
distinguish this from the Small White.

**Chrysalis [x1½]**
Slightly shiny; occurs
in two colour forms.

**Female, second brood**
Second-brood females are larger
than those in the first brood, and
have clearer black markings.

**Egg [x15]**
Laid singly on a wide
variety of Crucifers.

BROWN FORM

GREEN FORM

**Mating**
Paired butterflies embark
on a nuptial flight before
they land, and mating is
completed.

**Caterpillar [x1½]**
Distinguished from Small White
caterpillar by lack of yellow lines.

SINGLE
SEGMENT

SIDE VIEW

VIEW FROM ABOVE

# ORANGE TIP

*Anthocharis cardamines*

THE ORANGE TIP is the prettiest of the springtime butterflies, and is fortunately still a common species. The male is especially conspicuous, not simply because of his orange wingtips, but also because he is a patroller *par excellence,* and spends much of the day wandering through the countryside, searching every shrub and tussock for a mate. The female is more elusive. She hides among bushes for many hours each day, and has grey, rather than orange, tips to her wings. But she is equally attractive in her own way, and has the same exquisite undersides as the male. Not for nothing was this butterfly once called the "Lady of the Woods" or "Wood Lady", an admirable and superior description to its prosaic current common name.

**Distribution** *A common nomad breeding throughout the lowlands of England, Wales, and Ireland. Much more localized, but expanding, in Scotland.*

### COLOUR AND CAMOUFLAGE

Male Orange Tips are living examples of both warning coloration and camouflage. When flying, they are conspicuous and hence quickly spotted by predatory birds. However, they are also highly distasteful, because their bodies contain large amounts of bitter mustard oils, accumulated from their foodplants during the caterpillar stage. It pays for the males to advertise this fact, and the bright tips of the upper forewings act as a warning sign every time they fly. Once a bird has tasted an Orange Tip, it is reluctant to repeat the experience.

The resting butterfly sits still with its wings closed, and is less likely to be noticed. Only the under hindwings are visible, and now camouflage takes over as the most important form of defence. The exposed wing surfaces are delicately mossed with green, or rather with the illusion of green, for the lovely, lichen-like mottling is created from an intricate mixture of black and yellow scales. They offer near-perfect camouflage, especially when the butterfly rests on flowers of cow parsley (*Anthriscus sylvestris*) or garlic mustard (*Alliaria petiolata*), the latter being one of its principal foodplants. This is the only protection for females, which fly so seldom that orange wingtips are unnecessary.

The Orange Tip hibernates as a chrysalis, and the first males occasionally emerge in March following a warm spell, although late April is more usual. The main flight is from mid-May to early June. In exceptionally early seasons, there may be a small emergence of second-brood adults, which fly, and seem out of place, in high summer.

### A SPRING COURTSHIP

The natural history of this species is well known, thanks mainly to the recent work of Stephen Courtney. The adults in most regions live in loose, open populations, with both males and females wandering in no particular direction through the countryside, merely following hedgerows and wood edges as they search for mates or foodplants. This takes them into a wide variety of habitats in the south, including almost every garden. But they seldom stay long unless flowering Crucifers are present. Although honesty (*Lunaria rediviva*) and rocket (*Sysimbrium* spp.) will detain them in a garden, I prefer to grow lady's smock (*Cardamine pratensis*), both for its lovely, pale flowers and because the eggs that are laid on it are much more likely to survive.

Orange Tips behave differently further north, where they are much more localized and live in more or less compact colonies. In one that was studied in Durham, between 175 and 300 males emerged each year, probably accompanied by equal numbers of females. These spent their entire lives patrolling back and forth along a short stretch of riverbank. This appears to be a typical size for a northern colony. Low densities are also normal throughout most of the south, although there are many pockets where vast numbers can be seen.

For as long as the sun shines, the male Orange Tip flutters along hedges, shrubs, and bushes in search of a mate. His initial approach is not discriminating, and he investigates any white object, including Green-veined Whites, which emerge in abundance on most Orange Tip sites. However, they are soon

# ORANGE TIP · *Anthocharis cardamines*

## LIFE-CYCLE

| | JAN | FEB | MAR | APR | MAY | JUN | JUL | AUG | SEP | OCT | NOV | DEC |
|---|---|---|---|---|---|---|---|---|---|---|---|---|
| EGG | | | | | | | | | | | | |
| CATERPILLAR | | | | | | | | | | | | |
| CHRYSALIS | | | | | | | | | | | | |
| ADULT | | | | | | | | | | | | |

**Male**
The distinctive male emerges about a week before the female; underside of hindwings mossed with green.

**Female**
Similar to other Whites but undersides of hindwings mossed with green.

**Egg [x15]**
Greenish-white when first laid, gradually becoming orange.

**Caterpillar on seed-pod**
Mature caterpillar feeds on the seed-pods of Crucifers.

**Resting adult**
At rest, forewings are concealed by the camouflaged hindwings.

BROWN FORM    GREEN FORM

**Chrysalis [x1½]**
Two colour forms occur but the brown form is by far the most common.

**Egg-laying**
Eggs are laid singly under flower-buds.

**Caterpillar [x1½]**
Caterpillars may be cannibalistic if they meet on the same foodplant.

rejected, for they lack the female Orange Tip's scent. Almost nothing will stop a male once he has recognized a female of his own species. He forces his way through the densest foliage, whereupon mating occurs if she is a virgin.

The female eventually emerges to feed and lay eggs. She has a swift, no-nonsense approach compared to the investigative flutterings of most butterflies. Flying mainly along hedgebanks and the margins of fields, rides, and glades, she brushes against or alights on the taller plants, quickly taking off again if they prove not to be flowering Crucifers. Suitable foodplants are recognized first by sight from the air, and then chemically, through sensitive cells on her feet. A single egg is laid on the underside of a flowerbud before she quickly departs to find another plant.

The pale, spindle-shaped egg is easy to find if you examine the undersides of Crucifer flower-clusters in June. It becomes even more conspicuous a day or two later when it turns pink and then deep orange. The best plants to examine are isolated, unshaded flowering Crucifers that are growing within 1 m. (3 ft.) or so of a hedgerow, bank, or wood edge. Prominent plants are the butterfly's particular favourites, for only on large Crucifers is there sufficient food to support even one butterfly. The vast majority of British eggs are laid on lady's smock on heavy soils, and on garlic mustard on dry sites.

When young, the Orange Tip's caterpillars are cannibalistic, and so soon thin themselves out if more than one egg is laid on the same flower. However, such cannibalism is a rare event because females can smell eggs that have already been laid, and will reject any plant that bears an egg.

## THE CATERPILLAR'S DEVELOPMENT
The eggs hatch after a week to a fortnight, and the small caterpillar burrows into the flower, which by now is well expanded. It feeds on the developing seed, and soon sits as a black, long-haired maggot exposed on the seed-pods. It is said that these hairs are really glands, and that they produce tiny droplets of sweet liquid to attract ants, which attend and protect the caterpillars as they do many Blues (see p. 99). If true, this must be very rare in England, for I have examined hundreds of young caterpillars in the wild, and have yet to find one being attended by ants, or to hear of anyone else who has.

The growing Orange Tip caterpillar soon feeds only on the seed-pod of its plant, becoming beautifully camouflaged as it grows. It lies along the top of the pod, eating inwards from the tip.

Eggs and caterpillars contend with a host of natural enemies, despite the elaborate camouflage of the later stages. The chief dangers early on in life come from invertebrate predators that climb the foodplants at night, and from the cannibalism of other caterpillars. Once larger, birds are the main hazard and on some sites, over a third of the survivors then succumb to *Phryxe vulgaris*, a parasitic fly (see p.123).

The caterpillars that escape leave their foodplants to pupate. No one knows exactly where pupation occurs, but most, almost certainly, are in bushes and tall vegetation where the virgin females sit in spring. The chrysalis is exceptionally beautiful and, like those of most other Whites, exists in two colour forms.

## REGAINING GROUND
Despite its many natural enemies, the number of Orange Tips seen in any year depends mainly on the weather during the previous year, when the eggs were laid and, in the longer term, on the availability of suitable foodplants. Management can have a major effect. It is common to find that a meadow full of lady's smock and eggs has been grazed or mown long before the caterpillars have left to pupate. Similarly, the policy of spraying many road verges in June – to increase the visibility along roads – must have destroyed countless thousands of caterpillars in the past, although this practice has diminished in recent years.

Such losses probably do no more than depress Orange Tip numbers in any region, preventing it from reaching the abundance often seen in abandoned meadows and woodland glades. Far more serious has been the widespread agricultural improvement of meadowland, which has eliminated lady's smock from the vast majority of damp meadows in the British lowlands.

Despite this loss of foodplants, the Orange Tip is still remarkably common throughout southern England, Wales, and Ireland, and is still found in almost every wood and sheltered lane, and along a great many hedgerows and ditches. It becomes distinctly scarcer further north where, as already related, it lives in more self-contained populations. Nevertheless, large concentrations occur throughout the lowlands of Scotland, and both here and in northern England the Orange Tip has been steadily expanding in range for at least 40 years. To a large extent, this is a case of the butterfly regaining the ground it lost after the early nineteenth century, which is nothing compared to the massive loss of habitat further south. Nevertheless, it is an extremely welcome change, and in some places Orange Tips have spread and are breeding far beyond any historically known range.

# GREEN HAIRSTREAK

## *Callophrys rubi*

No BRITISH butterfly has a wider range of foodplants than this Hairstreak, and few European species can match a distribution that extends from the chilly coast of Lapland to arid Mediterranean *maquis*. Yet the butterfly is seldom common: in Britain, it abounds only on lowland English heathland and in warm western valleys from Cornwall to Inverness. It survives elsewhere in a handful of localities in most counties, and while not yet rare, it is a localized species that is declining everywhere.

Green Hairstreaks emerge once a year. After a warm spring, the adults first appear in late April, reaching a peak from mid-May to mid-June, although stragglers survive well into July. The butterflies usually live in small, self-contained colonies. A typical colony produces no more than 5 to 10 males each at the peak of the flight period, representing a probable emergence of between 30 and 50 butterflies over the whole season. However, the species can be much more abundant. For example, I have watched Green Hairstreaks teem by the dozen in Cornwall, hopping and jinking a few centimetres above lesser gorse *(Ulex minor)*, their vivacity contrasting with the sleepy atmosphere produced by the warm still air, heavy with the almond scent of furze blooms and the drone of bees. This kind of sighting is not unique, and the species is reported to be abundant, too, on some moors in western Scotland.

### PERCHING POSTS

The Green Hairstreak is a charming butterfly to watch. Males are highly territorial, and sit for long periods spaced around the edges of their breeding sites, each perched on a prominent shrub. They always sit with closed wings, and adjust their body temperature either by leaning sideways to catch the sun or by positioning themselves head-on to avoid it, in the same way as the Grayling *(see p.181)*. Males usually perch 1 to 2 m. (3 to 6 ft.) up, and can be hard to spot among the fresh green leaves. To find them, search particularly along the lower edges of a

**Distribution** *A widely distributed species that is rare through most of its range; many counties now have just a handful of surviving colonies.*

breeding site, tapping any prominent shrub that is in full sunshine. It is surprising how often a male will flip out from under your nose. Stand back and wait when this occurs, for after a few angry circuits he will return to his vigil, often alighting on the original leaf.

I once marked every male in a small Devonshire colony, and was surprised to find how constant these perching posts were over the season, yet how often different individuals swapped between them. Each would occupy his perch for perhaps an hour before launching into the air to investigate a passing insect. If his quarry was another male, a ferocious battle would ensue, with the rivals spiralling and looping around each other in tight circles until one was eventually vanquished. Females were pursued with greater persistence, during which time another male often stole the occupant's former perch. This game of musical chairs carried on all over the site, with males constantly changing places as perches became vacant on different shrubs.

### A UNIQUE COLORATION

The male Green Hairstreak is not only easy to photograph and watch while perching, but is also remarkably tame. It is simple, in cool weather, to persuade one to crawl on your fingers, where he will happily probe for salts should your hand be slightly sweaty. He can be examined in detail if you orientate his head towards you and blow gently as you lift him, which makes him tighten his grip. Notice the black oval eye, ringed by gleaming bands of white and black, and the exceptionally hairy fringes and mouthparts, or palps, that gave this creature its family name of *Callophrys,* which is Greek for "beautiful eyebrow". The wings are lovely too: they have a velvety look when fresh, a tail that is reduced to a mere stump, and a hairline that ranges from a continuous white streak, through the typical series of dashes, to being absent altogether on a few specimens. The colour is their most unusual feature, for this is the only

British butterfly to have wings that are truly green. The Orange Tip (*see p.53*) and Bath White (*see p.205*) both have a pretty, olive mottling on their undersides, but theirs is an illusion created by an intricate mixture of black and yellow scales, rather than by green itself.

## EGGS AND CATERPILLARS

The female Green Hairstreak is more elusive, but can be found slowly fluttering around shrubs and ground plants, frequently alighting to crawl and probe fresh leaves or buds to determine whether these are suitable for egg-laying. She uses a wide range of plants. The main British hosts are bilberry (*Vaccinium myrtillus*) on acid moors, gorse (*Ulex* spp.) on heaths and neutral soils, and rock-rose (*Helianthemum chamaecistus*) on chalk and limestone downs. Other foodplants include broom (*Cytisus scoparius*), bird's-foot trefoil (*Lotus corniculatus*), various vetches (*Vicia* spp.), dyer's greenweed (*Genista tinctoria*), the flowers of buckthorn (*Rhamnus* spp.) and dogwood (*Cornus sanguinea*), and bramble (*Rubus fruticosus*). The last is especially used in woods, and was probably a more important food in the past when British woodlands were open, sunny, and more suitable for breeding. Indeed, bramble was the only foodplant known to early entomologists, which is why the butterfly has the specific name of *rubi*, suggesting that it uses no other.

Despite the wide range of foodplants, females are fussy over their choice of plants for egg-laying. No thorough study has been made, but I, like many others, have noted that they lay among the tenderest young tissues, which probably contain the most nitrogen, an element essential for the caterpillar's growth. The female has an unusually flat ovipositor, which enables her to inject eggs into the tightest crevices of plants, such as deep between the soft growing points of gorse leaves. The egg itself is thin-shelled and flexible, and is moulded by the space into which it is squeezed. This is in marked contrast to the robust shells of the hibernating eggs of our four other Hairstreaks, and thinner than the waxy, white eggs of most other Lycaenids. This characteristic accounts for the green, shiny look of Green Hairstreak eggs.

Green Hairstreak eggs hatch after a week or two, and the small caterpillar burrows into the nutritious, soft plant tissue. It lives more openly as it grows older, but even then is extremely difficult to find, due to the excellent camouflage of its green and yellow body. On gorse, one trick is to search for a tip that is grey and withered, in which case the caterpillar stands out. However, most of the wild caterpillars I have seen are those that I have watched from the egg stage. They are unexciting creatures that live hunched over the growing-tip of their foodplants, with their heads buried deep in its tissues.

By August the caterpillar is fully grown. After this stage it deserts the foodplant to search for a pupation site, where it remains as a chrysalis until the following spring. The only one I have found in the wild was deep inside an ant nest. This is probably where all Green Hairstreaks hibernate, because tests have shown that the chrysalis is highly attractive to ants. Not only do the ants lick the secretions that ooze over the hairy, brown cuticle, but they also appear to be attracted, or at least appeased, by the cluckings and churring made by the chrysalis's sound organ. Most Lycaenid butterflies seem to communicate in this way with ants, but the Green Hairstreak is remarkable for the loudness of its stridulations, which are clearly audible to the human ear as a series of squeaks. Indeed, it was in this species that the extraordinary phenomenon was first noted, over 200 years ago.

## A LOCALIZED DISTRIBUTION

Colonies of Green Hairstreak are found in a wide range of habitats, including sunny woods, wet moors, and dry chalk downland. The two features common to most sites are that they are warm and sheltered, and that shrubs are always present. No one has yet explained why this is such a local butterfly in most of its range, although its need for an abundance of succulent foodplants and high densities of ants may be part of the story.

At present, the largest British colonies are found in the west, from the huge populations that sometimes develop on bilberries in Scotland, to those of the Welsh, Devon, and Cornish coasts, where European and dwarf gorse are the main foodplants. In the west of Britain, Green Hairstreaks can still be expected among dunes and in any warm, sheltered valleys that contain its foodplants, as well as on most lowland heathland throughout the country where gorse is common.

There may indeed have been local increases on some neglected heaths in recent years, for example in the Suffolk Sanderlings. These, however, are dwarfed by the losses that have occurred through habitat destruction elsewhere and from the general tidying up of the countryside. It is usual, also, to find a small population on any southern chalk or limestone down where rock-rose is common, provided the site contains reasonable areas of scrub.

Abandoned railway cuttings are another important habitat in counties that lack downs, heaths, or moors, as also were woods at one time. Today, woodland colonies are few and far between, almost certainly because modern woods tend to be too cool and shady for this sun-loving insect. Despite these losses, this remains the most widely distributed of the five British Hairstreaks, and easily the commonest of the group in Ireland, Scotland, and northern England.

# GREEN HAIRSTREAK · *Callophrys rubi*

### LIFE-CYCLE

| | JAN | FEB | MAR | APR | MAY | JUN | JUL | AUG | SEP | OCT | NOV | DEC |
|---|---|---|---|---|---|---|---|---|---|---|---|---|
| EGG | | | | | ▓ | ▓ | | | | | | |
| CATERPILLAR | | | | | ▓ | ▓ | ▓ | ▓ | | | | |
| CHRYSALIS | ▓ | ▓ | ▓ | ▓ | ▓ | | | ▓ | ▓ | ▓ | ▓ | ▓ |
| ADULT | | | | ▓ | ▓ | ▓ | | | | | | |

**Male upperside**
Each forewing has a light scent patch (sex-brand).

**Male underside**
This is the only British butterfly with green wings.

**Female upperside**
The forewings lack the sex-brand seen in the male.

**Female underside**
Markings are indistinguishable from those of the male.

**Male**
*Punctata* form, with white streak on forewings.

**Female**
*Caecus* form, lacking white streaks.

**Perching adult**
Male on gorse flower, ready to dart out at any passing insect.

**Egg** [*x22*]
Thin-shelled; laid in crevices in a wide variety of foodplants.

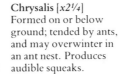

**Chrysalis** [*x2¼*]
Formed on or below ground; tended by ants, and may overwinter in an ant nest. Produces audible squeaks.

**Caterpillar** [*x2¼*]
Feeds on a variety of foodplants, depending on habitat.

**Caterpillar on gorse** [*x1½*]
Perfect camouflage protects the caterpillar while it feeds.

# BROWN HAIRSTREAK

## *Thecla betulae*

THIS IS THE largest, brightest, and perhaps most attractive of our five native Hairstreaks. Unfortunately, few people ever see the adult in the wild, for although the butterfly is scarce rather than rare, it spends almost its entire adult life perched out of sight on a tree-top. The golden-coloured females are somewhat easier to spot, because they briefly descend in August and September to lay eggs on twigs of blackthorn *(Prunus spinosa)* and its relatives, along hedgerows, wood edges, and around sheltered patches of scrub.

I had the pleasure of studying the ecology of this butterfly in all the stages of its life-cycle during a six-year period in the 1970s. My main site – a hotch-potch of clearings, wood edges, and overgrown hedges on the Wealden clays of west Surrey – contained one of the largest known colonies in Britain. Nevertheless, only about 40 adults emerged in the worst year, and no more than 300 survived in the best, when they laid just over 4,000 eggs. By comparison, there were at least a million Purple Hairstreak eggs in some years, laid on the oaks growing in the same area.

Brown Hairstreak eggs are laid at low densities over wide areas of countryside, although it is not unusual to find two, three, or even four eggs on a particularly suitable young twig. The colony I studied was supported by nearly 6,000 blackthorn bushes growing along 42 km. (26 miles) of hedges and wood edges, compressed into an overall area of about 30 ha. (75 acres). This, however, was an unusually compact example. Most Brown Hairstreaks breed over considerably larger areas encompassing hundreds of hectares. Yet, even on large sites, the same areas are used for breeding year after year, with very few eggs laid beyond the traditional boundaries.

## THE ROLE OF "MASTER TREES"

This widely dispersed distribution presents the Brown Hairstreak with some difficulties when it comes to finding a mate, for no more than one or two adult butterflies may emerge per

**Distribution** *Very local in wooded regions in the south. Common only in the Burren, southwest Wales, north Devon, and the west Weald.*

kilometre of hedgerow during the three- to four-week emergence period. Like the Purple Emperor *(see pp.115-118)*, the species solves the problem by using "master trees" – particular tree-tops where all the males perch and to which virgin females fly as soon as they emerge. Very few master trees have been discovered in Britain. All known examples are ashes growing near the lowest point of the basin of countryside that contains a colony. All, too, are large, bushy trees that tower high above the canopy of the adjoining woodland.

In the site I studied, the same ash tree was used year after year, and I never saw males anywhere else. Using binoculars, it was possible to watch the butterflies fidgeting and wandering over the leaves in sheltered pockets on the canopy, basking in the sunshine or drinking the sticky honeydew that coats so many ashes in August. Sometimes they took to the air, spiralling in rapid loops before returning to the leafy platform.

Adult males appear to spend their entire lives perched on the master tree, except in occasional years when they descend to feed on flowers. They are extremely tame when feeding and can be approached closely and photographed. But these descents are rare and unpredictable, and probably occur only when honeydew is scarce on the master tree.

## TREE-TOP COURTSHIP

The courtship and mating of the Brown Hairstreak has been observed only once, so elusive are the butterflies on their high tree-top canopies. No one knows quite how long the females remain on the master tree, but my own observations suggest it may be for the six to 10 days that it takes for their eggs to mature. They then disperse over the extensive breeding areas. There is evidence that only a limited number of females remains within the fixed areas of the colony, and that once 15 or so have gathered on the master tree, the surplus emigrates far beyond the colony boundaries. This limits individual colonies to a fixed size – one considerably below that which could be supported by the surrounding blackthorn bushes. Quite why this should be is, as yet, unknown. It may be an instinct that has survived from primeval times, when the Brown Hairstreak lived in a very different landscape of mixed woodland and clearings, and had to colonize the periodic gaps that arose when decrepit trees were blown over in the ancient Wildwood. Nowadays, however, there are few unoccupied breeding sites, and it seems likely that most females that desert their colonies perish in our modern agricultural landscape.

Females that remain in the colony fly only on the warmest days, and are seldom seen before 10 a.m. or later than 4 p.m. They spend long periods basking in weak sunlight, with their wings opened wide, allowing the dusky upper surfaces to absorb the maximum warmth. As the sun gets warmer, less and less of the wings are exposed until, in the hottest weather, they are kept tightly closed. The shiny undersides and white hairs on the lower half of the body then reflect rather than absorb the light, and prevent the butterfly from overheating.

It is unusual for a Brown Hairstreak to fly in air temperatures lower than about 20°C (68°F). The females then descend in rapid, jinking flights, hugging the wood edges or hedgerows and seldom crossing bare ground. Their golden colour is particularly noticeable in flight, so much so that they were once thought to be a different species from the duller males, and were known as Golden Hairstreaks.

## EGG-LAYING

Unlike the males, female Brown Hairstreaks regularly feed on late-summer flowers such as fleabane (*Pulicaria dysenterica*), bramble *(Rubus fruticosus)*, and thistles. Each female feeds in distinct bouts, punctuated by long periods of egg-laying, when she flies along woodland edges and hedgerows, periodically alighting on a projecting leaf. She then taps the upper surface with her front legs, tasting it through the chemical receptors near their tips. If the plant is a blackthorn, or another species of *Prunus,* she next begins a curious, crab-like descent down the twig, edging sideways and backwards into the bush while probing every nook and cranny with the curved tip of her plump, rounded abdomen.

This slow, methodical examination may take several minutes, but a suitable spot is usually found, and she squeezes out a single, bun-shaped egg. This is always laid on bark, on young growth usually at the base of a spine, or where one-year-old wood branches from a two-year-old stem. In Britain, the vast majority of eggs are laid on blackthorn, although I know a few sites where bullace *(Prunus insititia),* supplements it. The eggs are generally no more than 1 m. (3 ft.) above the ground.

The Brown Hairstreak has one generation a year, and is one of our last butterflies to take to the air. Adults emerge in late July and August, but egg-laying females are seldom seen before mid-August, and reach a peak of activity in early September. There is little time for the egg to develop, so it enters hibernation when the embryo is a mere ribbon of white tissue suspended in the rich fluids within the shell. Our three other woodland Hairstreaks, by contrast, hibernate as fully formed little caterpillars within the egg.

## EARLY DEVELOPMENT

The eggs remain on their twigs for eight months before hatching in late April and early May. They are gleaming white, with a beautiful raised sculpture over the surface, rather like intricate icing on a cake. Despite being widely spread, the eggs are easy to find from November to April, when the dark blackthorn twigs are bare. It is, in fact, far easier to see the egg than any other stage of this elusive butterfly: I have often found a hundred or more in a day on a good site. To locate them, look particularly on the lowest projecting growth that is both exposed to the sun yet sheltered from the wind. Small suckers, just a year or two old, projecting from the body of a shrub also tend to be selected.

Between half and three-quarters of the eggs hatch on undisturbed sites, with an unidentified disease accounting for most deaths. Predatory insects also kill small numbers, although, unlike other Hairstreaks, they are only rarely attacked by parasitic *Trichogramma* wasps. There are, however, very few undisturbed Brown Hairstreak sites in Britain, and the majority of eggs in most colonies are destroyed by hedge-trimming. A severe trim can remove every egg from a hedge, but on average about one-fifth survive on cut hedges. Uncut woodland edges form vital sanctuaries for the survival of the species.

In spring, the tiny caterpillar takes up to a day to nibble a neat, round hole in the top of its shell before squeezing out, leaving the empty case so firmly attached to the bark that this can be found up to a year later. The caterpillar immediately crawls into an unfurling leaf-bud, but emerges about a fortnight later, after the first moult, to live the rest of its life dangling upside down on a silk pad spun on the undersurface of a leaf. It sheds its skin twice more, looking the same but growing larger each time. Wedge-shaped in profile, with yellow stripes on a pale green background, it is extraordinarily well camouflaged beneath the leaf. Despite this, up to four-fifths of caterpillars are found and killed by predators. Harvestmen, spiders, and insects are the main culprits during the first month, and the moment they grow too large for these enemies, they are instead picked off by willow warblers, tits, and other insectivorous birds.

Locating the caterpillars is not an easy task, although it is by no means impossible if you patiently turn the leaves of a bush known to have contained eggs. A surer method is to beat the bushes sharply with a stick, and to sort through the variety of caterpillars that tumbles onto a sheet held beneath. It is a method that I avoid, though, for the branches are left twisted, broken and brown later on in the year, when the adults are around, reducing the pleasure when one returns to watch them.

## ANTS AND PREDATORS

The slug-like caterpillars remain motionless on their pads all day, but slowly wander over the bushes at dusk, browsing on the tenderest leaf-tips. Each usually returns to the same pad after its meal, although a new one may be spun nearby every week or so. Then, between 40 and 60 days after hatching, the caterpillar becomes a mottled purple colour and crawls to the ground to find a pupation site. It is known to be highly attractive to ants at this stage, although I have yet to see a wild caterpillar being tended by them.

Ants certainly tend the chrysalis, which calls them with chirruping noises, as some Blues do. I have seen few wild chrysalises, but, through following many caterpillars that were placed in natural positions, I am convinced that the majority pupate in cracks in the ground, in tussocks, or within the curl of a dry, dead leaf. Some were soon found by ants and buried in a loose cell of dry earth, and tended incessantly for the four weeks before emergence. It may be that, in the wild, all chrysalises are tended by ants, or even that they enter the nests, as does the Purple Hairstreak (*see p.64*).

Despite the presence of a retinue of ants, this is a dangerous stage in the butterfly's life-cycle. Small mammals, in particular, find the speckly brown chrysalis irresistible, and very large numbers are eaten. Up to four-fifths of the whole colony was killed during the pupation period on my Wealden site. The main culprits appear to be mice and shrews. In captivity, both show an extraordinary ability to sniff out chrysalises. Once one is unearthed, a shrew pounces on it in a frenzy of excitement and squealing, tearing and scattering the case into tiny fragments, while gobbling up the sticky contents. A mouse is more sedate. It sits up on its hindquarters, holding the chrysalis in both hands, as a squirrel might a nut. It then neatly nibbles the chrysalis until not even the hard cuticle remains, and then washes its paws and face before scurrying off to root up another one.

Both shrews and mice could find and eat up to one chrysalis a minute in my captive pens. Large beetles, by comparison, managed about one chrysalis a week. In this case the shell is slit right around the edge, as if cut by an old-fashioned tin opener, and the jagged halves are prised apart to enable the beetle to feed

on the rich contents. Only rarely have I found this damage in the wild, and it appears that ground beetles pose very little danger to Brown Hairstreak chrysalises in comparison to small mammals, which cause great damage.

## A HEDGEROW HABITAT

Brown Hairstreaks lay enough eggs to withstand these heavy losses, provided their habitat remains intact. A colony needs several kilometres of bushy hedgerows or woodland edges, and at least a third of these must remain untrimmed in any one year. Suitable breeding sites occurred more frequently in the past, when hedges were cut by hand. The trim was neither uniform nor as deep as it is today, while the practice of layering ensured that every hedge was left uncut for roughly two years out of ten. Most modern hedges are annually trimmed down to uniform rectangles, often more in the name of neatness than from a necessity to keep them stockproof.

The widespread grubbing up of hedgerows has also contributed to the disappearance of this butterfly from East Anglia and many flat regions of Britain. Nevertheless, it is not declining as rapidly as many species, and remains common in a few regions, although much overlooked.

There are three areas where this Hairstreak is so widespread that one can hope to find eggs on any suitable-looking stretch of blackthorn. One is on the heavily wooded clays of the western Weald, stretching from Horsham to Haslemere. The second is in the sheltered, low-lying valleys sandwiched between Exmoor and Dartmoor, from as far west as Torrington and extending eastwards in a band across Somerset, around the southern borders of Sedgemoor as far as the limestone base of the Polden Hills. The third is in similar countryside in the southwest quarter of Wales. There are several other scattered colonies in addition to these – one in the Blackmoor Vale of Dorset, perhaps three in Hampshire, others in Bernwood Forest near Oxford, and also in sheltered valleys in Gloucestershire. There are also one or two colonies in Worcestershire and Lincolnshire, but the butterfly has disappeared from the vast majority of eastern and northern sites, including the whole of East Anglia and the Lake District.

There are no authentic records of the Brown Hairstreak from Scotland, and for many years there was fierce controversy about its occurrence in Ireland. Fortunately, recent surveys have confirmed that this most elusive of butterflies maintains a very healthy stronghold among the shrubs and scrub growing over a wide area of the Burren. There is every reason to hope, therefore, that this lovely Hairstreak will be rediscovered in its other reputed localities, in the southern counties of Cork, Waterford, Wexford, and Kerry.

# BROWN HAIRSTREAK · *Thecla betulae*

## LIFE-CYCLE

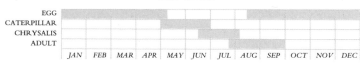

| | JAN | FEB | MAR | APR | MAY | JUN | JUL | AUG | SEP | OCT | NOV | DEC |
|---|---|---|---|---|---|---|---|---|---|---|---|---|
| EGG | | | | | | | | | | | | |
| CATERPILLAR | | | | | | | | | | | | |
| CHRYSALIS | | | | | | | | | | | | |
| ADULT | | | | | | | | | | | | |

**Male**
Wing-tails orange, but otherwise predominantly dark. Underside is marked with white stripes.

**Female**
Larger than male, with an orange-gold band on each forewing. The white stripes on underside are more pronounced.

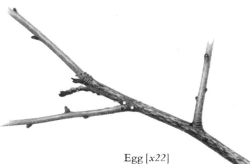

**Male**
Rare aberrant form *unistrigata* with reduced stripes.

**Female**
Rare aberrant form *uncilinea* with broken stripes.

**Egg [x22]**
Laid singly on blackthorn twigs, near the junction of one- and two-year-old growth.

**Caterpillar [x2¼]**
After first moult, caterpillar lives beneath leaves of foodplant.

**Chrysalis [x2¼]**
Formed on the ground, where it is tended by ants.

**Basking adult**
Females spend much of their lives basking in the sun, flying only on warm days.

# PURPLE HAIRSTREAK

## *Quercusia quercus*

THIS IS THE commonest Hairstreak in England and Wales, but colonies are often overlooked because the adults spend most of their lives in tree-tops. Individuals occasionally descend to flowers, but these butterflies tend to be faded and tattered, and approaching the ends of their lives.

The Purple Hairstreak is easy to identify when seen at close quarters. It is the only British Hairstreak to have an eye-spot next to the short tail, and the only one with blue or purple markings on the upperwings. The uppersides are frequently displayed, for the adults bask with their wings open, unlike their relatives, the Green, Black, and White-letter Hairstreaks, which always sit with folded wings.

***Distribution*** *The commonest British Hairstreak, much overlooked. Probably present in every southern oakwood, but scarce in the north and in Ireland.*

### TREE-TOP COLONIES

Like most Lycaenids, Purple Hairstreaks live in self-contained colonies, and are rarely seen far from the oaks on which they breed. A single isolated tree can support a colony, but most populations are confined to woods. Numbers fluctuate enormously from one year to the next. I once counted the hibernating eggs for seven years running on the same boughs of 14 oaks on a site in Surrey. There were only 26 eggs on these branches between 1973 and 1974, but three years later the number had increased to almost 1,500. These were on only a minute proportion of the oak boughs on the site, and the whole wood must have contained well over a million eggs that year, producing about 100,000 adults. Such population explosions have always been a feature of Purple Hairstreak colonies and tend to occur after warm springs and summers. Numbers were particularly high, for example, in the early 1980s.

This butterfly has one generation a year and hibernates as a fully formed, unhatched caterpillar inside the egg. The first adults emerge in early July, reaching a peak towards the end of the month, then flying throughout August and often lasting into September. On emergence, they fly immediately to a tree-top, but little is known of its subsequent behaviour. Some entomologists believe that the two sexes aggregate for mating on particular "master trees" *(see p.116)* but there is little evidence of this. The aggregations I have seen involved butterflies that had gathered to feed on tree-tops that were exceptionally sticky with aphid honeydew. Ash trees are particularly popular.

Purple Hairstreaks seldom fly, least of all in dull weather. Most of their lives are spent perched in sheltered, sunny nooks on the canopy, where they rest, bask, or slowly walk in circles, dabbing at the leaves for honeydew. It is possible to walk beneath a tree bearing several hundred Purple Hairstreaks without being aware of their presence. I search for the butterflies by tapping the lower boughs of oaks. It is surprising how often an adult is dislodged, and occasionally scores fly up together in a shimmering cloud of purple and silver.

The adults are more active on sunny days. Males launch themselves after any passing female, or engage in prolonged aerial battles with rivals, spinning and diving at high speed above the tree-tops. From below, they look like a handful of silver coins that has been tossed into the sunlight. Most sightings are of females later in the season. These have a more drunken flight, as they weave around oak boughs searching for places to lay eggs.

### EGG AND CATERPILLAR

The eggs are laid on branches that are in full sunshine and, for preference, partly sheltered from the wind. They are laid at all heights over the canopy and most are found on the southern edges of trees. Each is about the size of a pinhead, but is reasonably conspicuous after the oak leaves have fallen, looking like a small, pearl-grey bun stuck on the base of a plump flower-bud, or on the rough parts of adjoining twigs. Although laid singly, two or three may be found together in good years. Hatching occurs in April, just as the oak flowerbuds are beginning to break. The tiny caterpillar bores into the heart of a

# PURPLE HAIRSTREAK · *Quercusia quercus*

## LIFE-CYCLE

| | JAN | FEB | MAR | APR | MAY | JUN | JUL | AUG | SEP | OCT | NOV | DEC |
|---|---|---|---|---|---|---|---|---|---|---|---|---|
| EGG | | | | | | | | | | | | |
| CATERPILLAR | | | | | | | | | | | | |
| CHRYSALIS | | | | | | | | | | | | |
| ADULT | | | | | | | | | | | | |

**Male**
Male's purple sheen appears almost black from certain angles. Both sexes have an eye-spot next to the wing-tail.

**Female**
Reduced purple area is visible from all angles. Underwings are very similar to those of male.

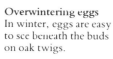

**Overwintering eggs**
In winter, eggs are easy to see beneath the buds on oak twigs.

**Variation**
Very rarely aberrations occur like this specimen with obscured markings.

**Egg [x22]**
Laid in ones and twos on all species of oak found in Britain.

**Chrysalis [x2¼]**
Formed on or below ground, sometimes in ant nests.

**Caterpillar [x2¼]**
Colour and shape camouflages the developing caterpillar on oak buds.

**Basking adult**
Adults feed and bask, with their wings open, on the tree canopy.

bud, and feeds out of sight on the tender tissues. The first skin is shed around 10 days later, and at about that time the caterpillar emerges to spin a silk web around the base of its expanding bud, which traps the brown scale-leaves when they peel off their buds, making a cocoon.

The mottled, woodlouse-shaped caterpillar is perfectly camouflaged in its cocoon, emerging only under the safety of darkness to browse on fresh oak leaves. This affords it considerable protection: about half the caterpillars hatching from 104 eggs I once studied in a Surrey wood survived on oak trees, whereas four-fifths of the colony died during the three- to four-week period between leaving their trees and emerging as adults.

## THE ROLE OF ANTS

There has always been some uncertainty about where the Purple Hairstreak forms its chrysalis. Some people say that it does so under moss on branches, but I have never found them there, nor know of any first-hand evidence that this is so. Previous collectors certainly found them while sieving soil for moth chrysalises on the ground beneath oaks. Having failed to find any myself, I recently began a systematic search of every crack, tussock, and patch of soft earth beneath an oak that had held a large number of caterpillars. Working outwards from the trunk, I found nothing in the first five metres, until I reached the outer edge of the oak boughs, where the grass grew in sparse clumps. I then pulled open a tussock that contained a large nest of the red ant *Myrmica scabrinodis*. As the crusty earth walls subsided and the ants poured out, I was amazed to find two Purple Hairstreak chrysalises in the heart of the brood chamber. Further searching soon uncovered chrysalises in four more nests, including those of the ant *Myrmica ruginodis,* but none of the 76 other antless tussocks that I examined contained anything.

This discovery does not prove that every Purple Hairstreak forms its chrysalis inside an ant nest, but it is likely that this is the case. Both caterpillar and chrysalis attract ants, and the latter is also able to "sing". It would be intriguing to know whether the fully grown caterpillar finds its own way into the nest, or is dragged there by the ants. The last explanation is a distinct possibility, for red ants carry home any sweet object that they can drag, and the caterpillar, with its swollen lobes that are easy to grip, is just light enough for determined ants to carry.

If, as is likely, the Purple Hairstreak depends on ants for its survival during the vulnerable chrysalis stage, this might explain why certain woods consistently support far larger colonies

ATTRACTING ANTS
*The chrysalises of most Lycaenid butterflies are protected by ants. They attract ants with secretions from microscopic pores, and by squeaking like adult ants.*
  *Chrysalis "songs" are produced by the toughened edges of two abdominal segments. These bear a set of teeth and grooves, which squeak when they are rubbed together.*

ENLARGEMENT

GROOVES    TEETH

than others. The ideal site for this butterfly is probably a wood that contains oaks of mixed ages, so that the canopy undulates, providing a large surface area of warm, sheltered boughs, and sunny clearings beneath which ant nests exist in large numbers. Old-fashioned coppices that also contained standard timber trees probably fulfilled all these conditions. However, the butterfly has survived remarkably well in modern woods. Even in conifer plantations, it is common practice to leave a scattering of oaks as nurse trees, or to have a fringe around the edge for cosmetic reasons. These can support remarkably high densities of Purple Hairstreaks, and even isolated hedgerow, park, or garden trees can support a small colony, at least in the south.

Thus, despite some losses as a result of the mass planting of conifers in so many woods, the Purple Hairstreak is comparatively unscathed, and still exists throughout its traditional range. It is especially common in southern England and lowland Wales, occurring in almost every wood that contains a reasonable scattering of oaks, and even being found in many places where oaks are scarce. Colonies are few and far between further north, but are probably much overlooked. The Scottish entomologist, George Thomson, considers that colonies can be found in almost all suitable habitats north of the border. But the butterfly appears to be genuinely scarce in Ireland, where it is largely confined to hillside oakwoods between Wicklow and Derry, and around the southern coast.

# WHITE-LETTER HAIRSTREAK
## *Strymonidia w-album*

THIS VIVACIOUS little Hairstreak is usually seen as a silver speck, tumbling in the July sunshine and circling around a tree-top. Its flight period overlaps with both the Black and the Purple Hairstreak, and it can be mistaken for either relative on the wing. All three species fly in the same erratic way, and all have a sheen to their undersides that glints, at certain angles, in the sun. The Purple Hairstreak *(see p.63)* looks very different when settled, but White-letter and Black Hairstreaks are similar. In addition to the distinguishing features described on p.69, the White-letter Hairstreak actually has the blacker wings of the two. Indeed, it was known as the "Dark Hairstreak" to early collectors.

In practice, the White-letter Hairstreak's dusky uppersides are never seen in the wild, for the butterfly always settles with its wings closed, regulating its body temperature in the same way as the Grayling, by standing at different angles to the sun *(see p.182)*. The markings on the undersides are fairly constant. Individuals may vary in the boldness of the white hairline and in the length of the tail, but major aberrations, such as the famous specimen we illustrate, are extremely rare.

## A DIET OF HONEYDEW

Adult White-letter Hairstreaks emerge during the first week of July in a typical year, and are on the wing for at least a month. Each colony breeds on either a small clump of elms *(Ulmus* spp.*)* or a single tree. Most are found on the sunny edge of a wood, but there are many others that are supported by an isolated grove or a single hedgerow tree.

Solitary adults have occasionally been reported from a variety of unusual habitats in recent years, perhaps because their breeding elms had succumbed to Dutch elm disease. But, as a rule, this is a highly sedentary species: hedgerow colonies remain strictly around each breeding tree, and even in woods, the adults seldom fly further than one or two tree-tops away, often settling on a neighbouring oak or ash that is sticky with aphid

*Distribution Widespread but extremely local species that has declined greatly due to Dutch elm disease. Elusive and often overlooked where it does occur.*

honeydew – their nourishing principal food. A typical colony contains a few dozen adults, although in occasional years the butterfly is more abundant. Even then it is usually elusive. There are a few sites where the adults regularly descend to feed on privet *(Ligustrum vulgare),* creeping thistle *(Cirsium arvense),* and other summertime flowers, and this occurs widely in certain years. But this is rather a rare event, caused, I suspect, when honeydew is in thin supply on the tree-tops. The whole colony generally remains hidden on the canopy.

It is easy to underestimate the numbers present in a White-letter Hairstreak colony. I remember once sitting for more than an hour beneath an oak in Monks Wood in Cambridgeshire, watching through binoculars as the adults spun up above the canopy to alight on the leaves. I guessed that there were perhaps 20 or 30 butterflies altogether, and then climbed an adjoining tree for a closer look. Here I had a good view over about half of the oak's canopy, and I was astonished to see at least 70 White-letter Hairstreaks, hidden high above the ground. Some slowly rotated their hindwings as they perched in the sunshine, while others walked over the leaves, trailing their proboscis between their legs. From time to time one would encounter a patch of honeydew, causing it to twitch and spiral around while it dabbed at the sticky syrup.

## EGG-LAYING

Pairing probably also occurs on the canopy, although I know of no one who has seen this take place. The egg-laying female is more conspicuous. She flutters around her breeding elm before alighting to crawl crab-like along the twigs, probing every nook with a plump, bent abdomen before laying a single egg on a rough patch of bark.

The egg is shaped like a miniature flying saucer, and is one of the most attractive of all British butterflies. Many are killed by parasitic *Trichogramma* wasps in their first three weeks of life, but they appear to be immune from mid-August onwards. By this time, each contains a perfectly formed little caterpillar, which remains in the egg until the following spring.

White-letter Hairstreak eggs are laid at all heights on elm trees, and are easy to spot on low boughs once the leaves have fallen. They are, indeed, somewhat easier to find than the adult butterfly. Most eggs are laid beneath flowerbuds, in forks, and particularly on the wrinkled girdle scar at the junction of the current and previous year's growth, usually on a sunny sheltered twig. Common elm (Ulmus procera), smooth-leaved elm (U. carpinifolia), and any of the hybrids may support a colony, but the favourite foodplant is wych elm (U. glabra).

## CATERPILLAR AND CHRYSALIS

The eggs hatch just as the elm flowerbuds are swelling, usually in mid- to late March. The tiny caterpillar lies first on the dark sepals, burrowing its head into the opening bud to feed on the soft tissues within. It gradually changes colour as it grows, in much the same way as the Black Hairstreak (see p.71), although in this case, the camouflage bears a remarkable resemblance to an expanding elm bud. By the second moult, the caterpillar has developed a pretty lilac saddle, and moves from bud to bud scooping out the contents but leaving the outer scales intact. If the tree is more advanced, it hides and feeds among the flowers.

As it grows older, the caterpillar feeds increasingly on leaf-buds, and finally on the fully expanded leaves. At this stage it rests on a silk pad spun beneath the leaf, which it closely resembles. Despite this camouflage, fully grown caterpillars are quite easy to make out as dark silhouettes if you stand beneath an elm in early June, looking upwards at any branch that supports fruit.

The chrysalis is also formed beneath an elm leaf or, less often, at a fork on a twig. Brown, speckled, and hairy, it looks exactly like a elm bud, yet is again fairly easy to find. Like most Lycaenid chrysalises (see p.64), it possesses a sound organ and sings a curious rasping song. I know of no one who has found the chrysalis being attended by ants, but this is probably because, among British species, only the wood ant (Formica rufa) climbs trees, and few White-letter Hairstreak colonies occur in the places where these abound.

## THE EFFECT OF ELM DISEASE

The White-letter Hairstreak has traditionally been regarded as a local species in England and Wales, but there is no doubt that a great many colonies were overlooked in the past. At one time, it occurred in all counties south of Yorkshire, and was especially common throughout the Midlands and in the Welsh Borders. Colonies also occurred in many parts of lowland Wales and the West Country but, for some unexplained reason, have always been much scarcer in these regions.

The situation has changed dramatically in the past 20 years. Dutch elm disease has caused a devastating loss of elm trees, and a large number of White-letter Hairstreak colonies have disappeared as a result. It is particularly unfortunate that this butterfly has such a preference for mature, flowering elms, for it is exactly these specimens that are most vulnerable to the disease. Young trees, suckers, and elm hedges may also be infected, but it is only when they attain flowering size that they generally succumb and die. The Hairstreak colonies do not always perish: there are several examples of them persisting on the young suckers that regenerate around dead stumps. But such cases of survival seem to be unusual; certainly, most of the colonies that I knew in the early 1970s have disappeared.

On the credit side, the preferred foodplant of the White-letter Hairstreak – wych elm – has been less severely affected by disease than the other species of elm, especially in the north of the butterfly's range. Moreover, it has recently become clear that this Hairstreak has always bred on a much higher proportion of elm trees than had previously been supposed. Thus it is worth searching any flowering elm for this butterfly within its range, including isolated trees in regions of intensive agriculture.

Despite the elm disease epidemic, the White-letter Hairstreak still survives, and its remaining strongholds are, as ever, in central England, from Yorkshire in the north down to Hampshire in the south, and extending as far west as Cheshire, Staffordshire, Herefordshire, and Worcestershire. It is still present, and probably much overlooked, in East Anglia, southeast England, Wales, and the West Country. There is also a possibility that the occasional Scottish colony survives, although there has been no definite record for at least a century. It does not, however, occur in Ireland.

# WHITE-LETTER HAIRSTREAK · *Strymonidia w-album*

## LIFE-CYCLE

| | JAN | FEB | MAR | APR | MAY | JUN | JUL | AUG | SEP | OCT | NOV | DEC |
|---|---|---|---|---|---|---|---|---|---|---|---|---|
| EGG | | | | | | | | | | | | |
| CATERPILLAR | | | | | | | | | | | | |
| CHRYSALIS | | | | | | | | | | | | |
| ADULT | | | | | | | | | | | | |

**Male**
Pale spot (sex-brand) distinguishes the male from the female.

**Female**
Ground-colour of female's wings is slightly paler than the male's.

 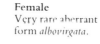

**Male**
Aberrant form with reduced white stripe on underside.

**Female**
Very rare aberrant form *albovirgata*.

**Egg [x22]**
Laid singly; overwinters on twig of elm.

VIEW FROM ABOVE    SIDE VIEW

**Chrysalis [x2¼]**
Pupation usually occurs beneath the leaves of the foodplant. The chrysalis is anchored to the plant by a silk girdle.

**Feeding male**
Adult feeding at flowers of creeping thistle. Nectar is used only occasionally as a supplement to the usual diet of aphid honeydew.

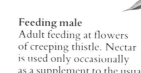

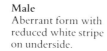 

**Caterpillar [x2¼]**
Camouflage conceals the caterpillar among elm buds, and later among expanded leaves.

# BLACK HAIRSTREAK

*Strymonidia pruni*

THIS LITTLE BUTTERFLY has an attractive caterpillar and chrysalis, but as an adult it is undeniably plain. Nonetheless, naturalists come from far afield to see it. This is partly due to its rarity, and partly because the butterfly is delightful to watch, whether spinning high above the canopy of an ash, tumbling in the June sunshine over immense banks of blackthorn, or settled on a leaf, tap-dancing and fidgeting as it drinks the honeydew.

### DISCOVERY AND DECEPTION

The native Black Hairstreak is restricted to one basin of low-lying clays that stretches from Peterborough to Oxford. It was one of our last butterflies to be discovered, with the southern colonies not being found until 1918. As so often happens, it took a schoolboy, W. F. Burrows, to locate these, in Bernwood Forest's Hell Coppice. No one believed him at first – least of all Oxford's professional entomologists – but an expedition was eventually mounted and Burrows's find was officially verified. Other rarities were soon discovered in the same wood, and "see you in Hell" quickly became a catchword among the University's butterfly collectors.

There was controversy, too, surrounding the first British discovery. This was in 1828, when an entomological dealer, a Mr. Seaman, visited Monks Wood, Cambridgeshire, and caught some small dark Lycaenids. These were exhibited in the belief that they were White-letter Hairstreaks *(see p.67)*. However, the great Victorian entomologist, Edward Newman, spotted the mistake, whereupon Seaman changed the name of the locality to "Yorkshire" to give himself a monopoly over this valuable new species.

Seaman's selfishness was ineffective, for Professor Babbington of Cambridge also took specimens in Monks Wood in 1829, and by 1837 the curate of Polebrook – the Rev. William Bree – discovered it in his parish at Barnwell Wold in Northamptonshire. Bree was a hospitable man, and Barnwell soon thronged with leading Victorian collectors.

**Distribution** *A rarity confined to small patches of blackthorn in about 40 west Midlands woods; also introduced in one area of the Surrey Weald.*

Barnwell Wold contained an extraordinary range of rarities, most in large numbers; the Purple Emperor, Chequered Skipper, Wood White, Duke of Burgundy, and six Fritillaries were there, together with all five Hairstreaks and Barnwell's greatest prize – the only substantial colony of Large Blues known at the time. Sadly, these rarities have long since disappeared, leaving the Black Hairstreak as the sole relic of this classic collecting ground.

### A HONEYDEW DIET

The Black Hairstreak is an elusive butterfly with a comparatively short flight period. Adults can generally be seen during the last 10 days of June, and for the first week of July, but this varies by several days depending on the warmth of the spring. They are not easy to find even at the peak of the emergence, since most colonies are confined to very small parts of a wood – perhaps 100 m. of sheltered edge, or one particular glade. They seldom move far, and scarcely fly at all on some days, preferring to sit out of sight, on a tree-top. Field maple *(Acer campestre)* and ash *(Fraxinus excelsior)* are their favourite resting sites, probably because the leaves are often coated with sweet aphid honeydew.

Although most colonies contain just a few dozen adults, large numbers of Black Hairstreaks gather together on good sites, leaning with closed wings, sideways to the sun. They then tap the leaves with their forelegs to detect honeydew, or slowly crawl from leaf to leaf with their tongues trailing between their legs, lazily drinking these sticky secretions.

### BEHAVIOUR AND IDENTIFICATION

At other times, there is greater activity, with adults spiralling through the air at high speed in a characteristic jerky flight. The jerkiness is exaggerated by the fact that the underwings reflect the sun, creating a silvery flash on every upbeat. This makes the flying adult extraordinarily difficult to distinguish from a White-letter Hairstreak, or even a Purple Hairstreak. Both of these commonly occur on Black Hairstreak sites, and overlap with the last Black Hairstreak adults in July. The White-letter and Black Hairstreaks also look similar at rest: unlike the Purple Hairstreak, neither opens its wings to bask, so only the undersides are visible.

Despite its name, the Black Hairstreak is more golden than the dusky White-letter Hairstreak. It has a line of black spots along the inner edge of the orange band on its hindwings, whereas the White-letter Hairstreak has a line. This is a far safer distinguishing feature than the white hairline halfway in from the edge opposite the tails, which can look like a sideways-on W in both species.

When it does descend to ground level, the Black Hairstreak compensates for its normal inaccessibility by being extremely tame. Adults will often bask for long periods and can be closely approached: in cooler weather, I have often had them crawling over my fingers. They are also oblivious to any distraction when feeding. Although honeydew is undoubtedly their main food, they also descend to the flowers of privet (*Ligustrum vulgare*) and dog-rose (*Rosa canina*). Both shrubs are common among the blackthorns (*Prunus spinosa*) on most Black Hairstreak sites, and their scents, pouring forth on a warm summer's day, are more evocative of this little butterfly than any picture.

### ELUSIVE EGGS

The female Black Hairstreak is mated almost immediately on emergence, sometimes before her wings are fully dry There is then a gap of a few days before egg-laying begins. Up to 30 eggs can be laid in a day, each placed singly on a *Prunus* twig. Blackthorn is by far the commonest foodplant in Britain, but entire colonies have been supported by its relative, the wild plum (*Prunus domestica*).

The eggs remain on their twigs for nearly nine months before hatching in spring. They are surprisingly difficult to spot, even in winter when the twigs are bare. To find two or three in an hour is very good going, whereas one might find a hundred Brown Hairstreak eggs for the same amount of searching. Most are laid on twigs that are from one to four years old. To find the eggs, search sheltered, sunny *Prunus* bushes of all ages and at all heights, for, contrary to popular belief, the eggs are not confined to the twigs at the tops of ancient bushes.

The Black Hairstreak egg varies in colour from pale yellow to rich brown, and by spring many have a green coating of algae that makes them even harder to spot. The first three weeks of life are particularly dangerous, many eggs being killed by minute parasitic wasps. By August, each egg contains a perfectly formed caterpillar, which is immune to further attack. Roughly two-thirds of the eggs survive. They hatch from

mid-March to late April, while the *Prunus* is still in tight bud. The caterpillar slowly nibbles a neat hole in the top of the egg-shell, often taking two days before it can squeeze out, leaving the empty shell so firmly fixed to its twig that it can be found, still cemented in position, up to a year later. The caterpillar immediately crawls onto a plump flowerbud, which it pierces with sharp jaws. However, rather than entering the bud to feed, it can reach the soft tissues in the furthest corners by means of a very long and thin extensible neck, leaving the remainder of its body resting outside on the brown scale-leaves.

The chestnut-coloured caterpillar is superbly camouflaged at this stage, and the resemblance becomes even more remarkable as the *Prunus* buds break and expand. The little caterpillar first develops a white "saddle" that matches the breaking bud on which it lies. As the leaves expand, it moves to the base of a clump, its appearance gradually changing to match its background. By late May, it sits exposed in sunshine among a fresh clump of leaves, eating the tender tips by day, but almost indistinguishable from them due to its fleshy green body and the purple tips on its serrated back, exactly like the edge of a young *Prunus* leaf. Several stages of this changing pattern, which occurs continuously rather than at moults, are illustrated on p.71.

The chrysalis, too, is a masterpiece of disguise. It resembles a bird-dropping and is attached quite openly to the top of a leaf or, more often, to a twig. With practice it is quite easy to find, for the camouflage is by no means perfect, but search at the beginning of the chrysalis stage, in early June, for by the time the adults emerge, up to four-fifths may have died. Willow warblers seem to be the chief predators.

### RELICS OF AN ANCIENT LANDSCAPE

Black Hairstreak numbers fluctuate considerably from one year to the next. Larger numbers emerge after a warm May and June, probably because the vulnerable caterpillars and chrysalises develop quickly in warm weather, leaving little time for them to be eaten by birds. There are also big differences between the average sizes of colonies on different sites. The largest are found where massive banks of blackthorn grow in exceptionally sheltered, yet sunny, situations. Typical examples are the south-facing edge of a glade, scrub of mixed ages growing on the sunny side of a wood, and where a tall, unkempt hedgerow runs parallel to a bushy woodland edge. Smaller colonies breed in slightly more exposed or shaded situations, such as in nooks along woodland edges or in the gaps beneath the canopy in a mature, open woodland.

Sunny banks of sheltered blackthorn are not particularly rare in the British landscape, so it is curious that just 80 colonies of Black Hairstreak have been found since 1828. All have been in the east Midlands forest belt, a string of ancient woodlands, relics of the once-continuous forest that extended from Rockingham to Narborough in the north, via the Huntingdon Fen edges, southwards through Yardley Chase, Salcey, Whittlewood, Waddon Chase, Grendon Underwood, and finally to Bernwood and Wytham near Oxford. At one time or another, it has occurred in more than half of the larger woods in this region.

The clue to this restricted distribution lies in the history of these ancient forests rather than in any intrinsic suitability they possess for Black Hairstreaks. True, the blackthorns are magnificent in this region, growing tall before blowing over when they become too massive for the shallow suckering root systems, but many Black Hairstreaks feed on small young plants. It is the extraordinary reluctance of the adults to fly far that explains why they became restricted to this part of England.

Only in these Royal game forests has there been an unbroken history of forest management that is sympathetic to the Black Hairstreak. Such management includes very gradual scrub clearance, with coppice cycles lasting 20 to 40 years before being cut again, and the encouragement of blackthorn regrowth because of the excellent cover it provides for game. Almost everywhere else in Britain it was commonplace to have much shorter coppice cycles, with any particular stand of shrubs being harvested up to 20 times in a century. This very sedentary butterfly could not colonize new shrubs quickly enough to keep pace with short coppice cycles, leaving the east Midlands as the only possible place for its survival.

The traditional management of east Midlands woods ended around the turn of the century, being replaced by more intensive forestry in some areas and by abandonment in others. This led to the extinction of a good many Black Hairstreak colonies and only about 30 survive today, in several cases thanks to enlightened conservation measures. Fortunately this is quite an easy butterfly to save, for it needs little space and only occasional management to maintain its breeding sites. Indeed, the Black Hairstreak has fared much better than most butterflies in the past 50 years.

## THE SURREY COLONIES

More encouraging still has been the recent spread of this butterfly outside its historical range. There had long been rumours of a Surrey colony, but these were dispelled when the original source was traced as a misidentified White-letter Hairstreak. However, as coppicing was abandoned in the Weald, the abundant blackthorn of the western clays often grew into massive, sheltered banks, apparently ideal for this little butterfly.

Their suitability was put to the test in 1952, when A. E. Collier, a master at Oundle School, moved south to Cranleigh.

Oundle is in the heart of Black Hairstreak country, and Collier took a few caterpillars with him. These produced about a dozen adults, which were released in a suitable-looking wood near Cranleigh, and promptly forgotten. Two years later, while walking in this wood, Collier had the delight of seeing a few Black Hairstreaks 100 m. or so from the original release point. These prospered for several years, but then the whole wood was converted into a cornfield.

No more Black Hairstreaks were seen for 15 years. Then, in 1975, while watching Purple Emperors in a glade about 1½ km. (1 mile) away, I was amazed to notice Black Hairstreaks jinking in abundance over the banks of thorn. Evidently a small group of colonists had reached another wood in the neighbourhood before reaching this site, and they were slowly spreading. In the next five years about five separate colonies developed in this area, which soon held more Black Hairstreaks than any other known wood in Britain. Unfortunately, much of this area has been cleared, but the Surrey Hairstreaks are keeping one jump ahead of the developers. In the 1980s they reached a scrubby, overgrown railway line, abandoned 20 years before.

## INTRODUCTIONS IN THE EAST MIDLANDS

It is particularly encouraging to find a rarity like the Black Hairstreak thriving in the Home Counties, but it does show how very slowly this little insect spreads. Presented with a vast area of predominantly suitable habitat, it has moved no more than an average of 100 m. a year. This suggests that there may well be other places in Britain where Black Hairstreaks can thrive, if only they could get there.

It seems likely that more and more introductions will be made as it is realized that this charming butterfly is locked in the east Midlands merely as a relic of a long-defunct form of woodland management. Indeed, there is good evidence that many colonies within its traditional range also originate from introductions. The great entomologist Lord Rothschild paid H. A. Leeds to catch "large numbers" of Black Hairstreaks between 1900 and 1917, for release in east Midlands woods. These were "doing well some years later", though, alas, no record remains of the exact woods that were used.

Even the famous colony at Monks Wood is itself an introduction. Early this century, Monks Wood stock was used to replenish a nearby wood at Warboys that had lost its colony. However, Monks Wood itself was largely felled during the First World War, and all the Black Hairstreak's breeding sites were cleared. When the butterfly had not been seen for five years, adults were caught in the Warboys colony, and released in Monks Wood. Here, nearly three-quarters of a century later, they can still be seen in excellent numbers.

# BLACK HAIRSTREAK · *Strymonidia pruni*

## LIFE-CYCLE

| | JAN | FEB | MAR | APR | MAY | JUN | JUL | AUG | SEP | OCT | NOV | DEC |
|---|---|---|---|---|---|---|---|---|---|---|---|---|
| EGG | | | | | | | | | | | | |
| CATERPILLAR | | | | | | | | | | | | |
| CHRYSALIS | | | | | | | | | | | | |
| ADULT | | | | | | | | | | | | |

**Male upperside**
Forewings have inconspicuous scent scale patches (sex-brands).

**Male underside**
Black spots distinguish both sexes from the White-letter Hairstreak.

**Female upperside**
Orange markings are more extensive than those of the male.

**Female underside**
Patterning similar to male's, but tails on hindwings longer.

**Egg** [x22]
Laid nine months before hatching; often becomes mottled with algae.

**Young caterpillar** [x2¼]
On hatching, the caterpillar feeds on flowerbuds.

**Mating**
The female mates soon after emergence, often on blackthorn twigs.

**Developing caterpillar** [x2¼]
As the buds burst, the caterpillar's camouflage changes.

**Mature caterpillar** [x2¼]
As the leaves expand, the caterpillar's colour changes to match its background. When fully grown, it is almost wholly green.

SIDE VIEW

VIEW FROM ABOVE

**Chrysalis** [x2¼]
Camouflaged as a bird-dropping; attached to a twig or leaf.

# LARGE COPPER

*Lycaena dispar*

NEARLY A century and a half has passed since our native Large Coppers disappeared. Yet the creature continues to fascinate, partly through the specimens in museums, and partly because a Dutch subspecies of the butterfly can still be seen flying at Woodwalton Fen, where a fragment of ancient habitat has been preserved among the agricultural prairie-lands of north Cambridgeshire.

This colony is delightful to watch, but there is also some sadness involved. For the Large Copper belongs to a landscape and a culture that had virtually vanished from England by the middle of the nineteenth century. It once bred in small clearings in the fenlands, in places where "the Bog Myrtle used to grow in profusion". Although abundant on a few sites, colonies seem always to have been extremely local in distribution. The first was found on Dozen's Bank in Lincolnshire, by the Secretary of the Spalding Gentlemen's Society. He named his discovery the "Orange Argus of Elloe", and painted an exquisite watercolour of a male in 1749. The painting, however, remained unknown for more than two centuries, and it was not until 1795 that the entomological world became aware of British Large Coppers, which had been found on a "moorish piece of land" in Huntingdonshire.

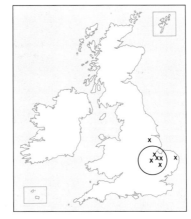

***Distribution** A fenland species extinct by the mid-nineteenth century. Colony of the Dutch race currently maintained at Woodwalton Fen.*

### THE BRITISH SUBSPECIES

The discovery of this handsome butterfly caused enormous excitement among the collecting fraternity. It was soon noted that British specimens were more beautiful and considerably larger than any known from the Continent, and were rightly considered to be of a distinct subspecies, named *L. d. dispar*.

The next 30 years saw the heyday of the Large Copper so far as English naturalists were concerned. Colonies were found in the Norfolk Broads, in Cambridgeshire, and possibly Suffolk but, most of all, in the old county of Huntingdonshire, in about 2,000 ha. (5,000 acres) of unbroken fenland surrounding Ugg and Whittlesea Meres. Although wild and inhospitable, this was nevertheless a worked landscape of peat and reed cuttings, with sheep and cattle grazing on the fen clearings in summer. The ancient communities maintained a patchwork of fen meadows, marshes, reedbeds, and waterways in which the great water dock (*Rumex hydrolapathum*) – the caterpillar's foodplant – was widespread and common. The butterfly itself was found "in spaces covered with sedge and coarse grass".

### A DISAPPEARING HABITAT

But already the fenlands were changing. The Earl of Bedford began the process when, in 1634, he employed Cornelius Vermuyden to introduce Dutch methods of drainage. By the nineteenth century, the fenlands of Lincolnshire and Norfolk had all but disappeared. Huntingdonshire and Cambridgeshire withstood the onslaught longer, and it was not until 1851 that Whittlesea Mere was drained and the last great obstacle to efficient agriculture was removed. Today the landscape is utterly transformed, and consists of seemingly endless expanses of flat, ploughed peatlands, crisscrossed by neat, parallel drains and virtually bereft of wildlife. It is a loss that we nowadays deplore, but that was viewed very differently at the time. Even the Rev. F. O. Morris, author of the most beautiful of all Victorian books on butterflies, took the change with Christian fortitude:

"Science, with one of her many triumphs, has here truly achieved a mighty and a valuable victory, and the land that was once productive of fever and of ague, now scarce yields to any in broad England in the weight of its golden harvest... The entomologist is the only person who has cause to lament the change, and he, loyal and patriotic subject as he is, must not repine at even the disappearance of the Large Copper Butterfly, in the face of such vast and magnificent advantages. Still he may be pardoned for casting 'one longing lingering look behind,' and I cannot but with some regret recall... the time when almost any number of this dazzling fly was easily procurable."

## DECLINE AND EXTINCTION

In fact, the extinction of the Large Copper slightly preceded the drainage of Whittlesea, with the last five specimens being caught at Holme Fen in 1847 or 1848, and a final colony lasting a further three or four years at Bottisham in Cambridgeshire. These losses were probably caused by the decline in traditional fenland management, which had been giving way to more intensive farming for many years: at least one colony disappeared when the reeds were burned back prior to agricultural improvement. Butterfly dealers were another hazard, and may have tipped the balance on a few sites. Certainly, vast numbers of specimens were taken. One collector gave this account in the early 1840s:

"It soon got known among the fen folk that [Large Coppers] were worth two shillings each in London, and two men came from Cambridge and secured a large number, which they took to London in boxes, and sold at sixpence each. I went down three years after, and got some of the larvae. They appeared to be very local, and most numerous where their food plant – the water-dock – was most abundant. The larvae were collected by all persons, young and old. I bought two dozen off an old woman for ninepence, from which I bred some fine specimens and sold them at one shilling each."

Many were later to write with regret that they had not secured more, so valuable did the old English specimens become once the butterfly was extinct. J. W. Tutt wryly charted their appreciation, culminating in the sale of 14 specimens for £71 15s. in 1900, and predicted that "these prices are as nothing to what may be expected in the not very distant future, when 'coppers' may produce figures approaching the prices for Great Auk's eggs". Perhaps because of their value; many specimens have survived in immaculate condition, and can be seen in museums around the country  The zoological department at Cambridge has a particularly fine series.

## CONTINENTAL LARGE COPPERS

Dutch colonies of Large Copper were discovered in Friesland early this century, in recently abandoned peat cuttings. They belong to a subspecies called L. d. batavus, but as can be seen from the illustration on p.75, are similar in size and markings to the old English form. They clearly had a common ancestry in northwest Europe before being divided, perhaps 6,000 years ago, when the continental land-link was broken by the rise in sea level.

Both are very different from the third subspecies, L. d. rutilus, which is found in marshlands throughout central and eastern Europe. This feeds on a wider variety of plants, has two rather than one generations of adults a year, and is significantly smaller, especially in the second brood. It also has duller underwings, but is a beautiful insect nonetheless, and is still locally common where European wetlands survive.

## COLONIES AND COURTSHIP

The natural history of Dutch Large Coppers has been thoroughly studied by Fritz Bink in the Netherlands and by Eric Duffey in England. It appears to have the same requirements as the old English subspecies, living in small, self-contained populations that range from a few dozen adults to several hundred. The butterflies emerge in early July, reach a peak in the second half of the month, and often survive well into August. They are very dependent on sunshine, jinking across fens at high speed while the sun is out and hiding in the reedbeds in gloomy weather. The males are as pugnacious as those of other Coppers, although they do not establish such obvious territories. Instead they sit on flowers or reeds, and dart up to intercept any insect that flies by. If this proves to be a virgin female, the pair soon lands on the reeds. Courtship is then a brief, fluttering affair, with the male first flapping his wings over the hen before the two butterflies couple.

The females mate shortly after emergence, but another three to five days pass before the first eggs are laid on the broad, glossy leaves of great water dock. They are extremely fussy in their choice of plants. They almost invariably avoid the large, leafy specimens growing on the edges of dykes, and the few eggs that are laid on these seldom survive the winter. Instead, they hunt for medium-sized plants growing in open marshland that is regenerating after a disturbance, particularly favouring specimens along the edges of taller vegetation.

It has been suggested that the females choose warm, sheltered plants for egg-laying, and that waterside specimens are simply too cold. There may be some truth in this, for the butterfly occurs at the extreme of its northern range in Britain and the Netherlands, and small-scale clearings among the reeds would undoubtedly be several degrees warmer than those on the edges of dykes. But they may also be seeking exceptionally nutritious plants. Bink showed that growth was hastened, and that larger butterflies produced, when the caterpillars fed on young, vigorous leaves that were rich in nitrogen.

Whatever the explanation for this fussiness, the egg is easy to find once one knows the sort of plants that are chosen. Indeed, with other students, I used to help Eric Duffey count every one of the thousands laid each year at Woodwalton Fen in the 1970s. Although laid singly, small clusters of two, three, or four eggs were often found together, usually beside the prominent leaf-ribs. They have a curious, robust sculpturing that is highly attractive when seen through a hand-lens.

## FROM EGG TO CHRYSALIS

The eggs hatch in mid-August, leaving conspicuous empty shells on the dock leaves. The little caterpillar starts feeding on the undersurface of its leaf, excavating shallow grooves like those produced by the Small Copper *(see p.77)*, and which are equally easy to find. The caterpillar then hibernates after one or two skin moults, still small and hidden on a silk pad spun on a twisted, dead leaf. These take some searching for, but are not impossible to find when water levels are low. Many, however, are submerged, and the caterpillar can survive for at least three months underwater in its hibernating stage. It is much more vulnerable when older, and isolated colonies are believed to have been lost through exceptional flooding in May.

The caterpillars re-emerge in spring, eating holes in the dock leaves but avoiding the midribs. This leaves a distinctive lattice looking not unlike a Swiss cheese plant. If these leaves are examined carefully in May, the fat, slug-like caterpillar can be found on the underside, usually resting on the midrib. It is sometimes attended by ants, for although it lacks a distinct honey-gland *(see p.99)*, there are secretory pores all over the body. These, unfortunately, do not save many caterpillars from being killed in their later stages, mainly by birds or, in some years, by parasitic ichneumon wasps and tachinid flies. Enough usually survive, however, to form plump, rounded chrysalises on the grass-stems and reeds near the docks.

## WOODWALTON FEN

The clue to the Large Copper's decline, both in England and the Netherlands, lies in the very fussy egg-laying requirements of the females. Whatever the primeval habitat of this species may have been, it has long depended on man to make piecemeal but regular clearings or cuttings in the fens. This, alas, ceased almost entirely in Britain, even in those fragments that were not claimed for agriculture. Woodwalton Fen is a prime example. Peat-cutting continued through the nineteenth century, and the fen in 1896 was still "full of flowers". Ten years later, the practice had ceased, and by 1910, when the Hon. N. C. Rothschild bought the land as a reserve, "the marsh meadowland was dominated by a thick growth of reed". This saved it from drainage and ploughing, but by 1926 much of the fen had become a birch and sallow carr woodland. This was partly due to 30 years with little interference, and partly because the water level fell as a result of increasingly intensive agriculture on the surrounding land.

At this stage Rothschild lent a hand, and about 9 ha. (22 acres) were cleared and planted with water docks, which had long been eliminated by carr. This was the famous "Copper Field", into which 25 male and 13 female Dutch Large Coppers were released in 1927. These were an immediate success, and in 1928 it was estimated that over a thousand adults emerged. The colony continued to prosper, but the management of the site was difficult, especially during the Second World War. From the earliest days the butterfly was "helped" by caging caterpillars to protect them from their enemies, and sometimes, too, its numbers were topped up with captive-bred specimens. This in many ways is a shame, but almost every naturalist is prepared to forgive this artificiality for the joy of watching the adults in July. The colony has died altogether once or twice, but the future offers some hope in that the water-table of the fen has now been raised, and large areas have been cleared and are partially flooded.

## OTHER INTRODUCTIONS

This was not the first re-introduction of Large Coppers, nor the most successful. As early as 1913, before the Dutch subspecies had been discovered, E. B. Purefoy cleared and planted a small bog at Greenshields, Tipperary, to which *L. d. rutilus* caterpillars and adults were introduced. The colony prospered for 43 years, without any caging or enrichments, until the bog became overgrown. It was cleared again in 1942, when Dutch adults were introduced. This colony survived without interference until the bog again became overgrown, in 1955.

Several other places have seen introductions. The most successful of these was at Wicken Fen near Cambridge, where Dutch Large Coppers flourished for about 10 years, disappearing only when the wettest part was ploughed to plant potatoes in the war. No other attempt has met with long-term success, although in a number of cases the butterfly initially thrived. The puzzle of the Large Copper's exact requirements has not quite been solved, but clearly conservationists are nearly there. The prospect is an exciting one, for there are few lovelier sights than Large Coppers darting by the dozen among the reeds.

# LARGE COPPER · *Lycaena dispar*

## LIFE-CYCLE

| | JAN | FEB | MAR | APR | MAY | JUN | JUL | AUG | SEP | OCT | NOV | DEC |
|---|---|---|---|---|---|---|---|---|---|---|---|---|
| EGG | | | | | | | | ▩ | | | | |
| CATERPILLAR | ▩ | ▩ | ▩ | ▩ | ▩ | ▩ | | | ▩ | ▩ | ▩ | ▩ |
| CHRYSALIS | | | | | | ▩ | ▩ | | | | | |
| ADULT | | | | | | | ▩ | ▩ | | | | |

**Male**
Subspecies *L. d. batavus*, introduced from Holland; undersides of both sexes slightly less bold than extinct English subspecies.

**Female**
Subspecies *L. d. batavus;* larger than male, with heavily marked uppersides but similar undersides.

**Male**
English subspecies
*L. d. dispar*, now extinct.

**Male**
Subspecies *L. d. rutilus*,
central and eastern Europe.

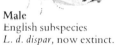

**Egg** [*x22*]
Laid singly, although several may be found on one leaf.

SIDE VIEW

VIEW FROM ABOVE

**Chrysalis** [*x1½*]
Formed on the stem of great water dock.

**Basking adult**
Subspecies *L. d. batavus* male basking on a leaf of the caterpillar foodplant, great water dock.

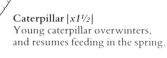

**Caterpillar** [*x1½*]
Young caterpillar overwinters, and resumes feeding in the spring.

# SMALL COPPER

## *Lycaena phlaeas*

THIS EXQUISITE insect is one of the liveliest and brightest of lowland butterflies in the British Isles. It is above all a creature of dry, dusty places, yet the occasional adult can be seen almost anywhere apart from the intensive arable prairies of East Anglia, and even here it has not been entirely eliminated.

The adult is unmistakable, and almost too familiar to many people to merit a detailed description. However, it is worth noting that this is a somewhat variable species, given to aberrations throughout its range, and existing as distinct colour forms in some places. In the north of Scotland, there is more gold and less black on the upperwings than further south, and in Ireland the underwings are distinctly greyer. By far the commonest and most attractive variety has a series of blue spots along the bottom edge of each hindwing; this is *caeruleo-punctata,* a form that is particularly common in northern Scotland, where up to half the adults in a colony may sport this livery. It is also common enough in the south – I saw several blue-spotted specimens in my garden during the warm summer of 1989.

Much rarer is an albino form, called *alba*. Here the normal copper markings are replaced by white, making a curiously attractive insect in the wild. The inheritance of this unusual characteristic appears to be controlled by a single gene. Being recessive, this probably finds expression in small, inbred colonies founded by single females bearing the gene. One of the small colonies near my home in Dorset produces a fair proportion of albino adults each year.

The Small Copper is variable, too, in the time of appearance. A first brood is generally seen in May, but can be a good month later in the north of Scotland. This, typically, is followed by a second emergence in July or August, and often by a third in September and October following a warm summer. There is even some evidence that it squeezes in a fourth brood in exceptionally hot years, but further research is needed before we can be sure of this. By and large, the butterflies in the second

**Distribution** *Common in rough grassland throughout lowland England, Wales, and Ireland; restricted to warm, sheltered sites in Scotland.*

emergence are more numerous than the first, but even so, colonies tend to be small. One comparatively large example in Cambridgeshire, which was measured by Jack Dempster, contained no more than 400 adults in high summer. Most colonies are much smaller than this, and the butterfly is usually seen in ones and twos.

Small Coppers generally live in close-knit colonies, often supported by small areas of land such as a well-drained bank, a road verge, or a patch of urban wasteland. Some individuals, however, are prone to wander, and are frequent visitors to country gardens where they both sup at flowers and establish territories, which they vigorously defend. One is even recorded to have reached the *Royal Sovereign* light vessel, over 12 km. (7 miles) off the Sussex coast.

## AN ENERGETIC ADULT

The adult, were it human, would be judged hyperactive, so fidgety are the movements and so rapid the flight. It cannot sit still even when feeding, but rotates its body on the flowerhead while constantly probing for fresh nectar. Night sees a halt to this frantic activity, when the butterfly roosts head-down on tall grass-stems. I have occasionally found Small Coppers roosting in aggregations, gathered on grass-stems like Blues *(see p.93)*, but this seems to be unusual, and more often than not a solitary sleeper is found.

Each male establishes a small territory in a warm, exposed position on a flowerhead or on the ground, often favouring discarded rubbish such as silver paper or a matchbox. It is sometimes said that he marks this territory with scent, but although an attractive theory, I have yet to read of any first-hand evidence. In fact, the male appears to have little need of a chemical deterrent, for he is a pugnacious scrapper that waits on his perching pad with wings ajar ready to hurl himself upwards at any passing insect. He usually returns after a brief skirmish, once again taking up his post. However, if the intruder is a female, she is pursued with zeal.

# SMALL COPPER · *Lycaena phlaeas*

## LIFE-CYCLE

|  | JAN | FEB | MAR | APR | MAY | JUN | JUL | AUG | SEP | OCT | NOV | DEC |
|---|---|---|---|---|---|---|---|---|---|---|---|---|
| EGG | | | | | | | | | | | | |
| CATERPILLAR | | | | | | | | | | | | |
| CHRYSALIS | | | | | | | | | | | | |
| ADULT | | | | | | | | | | | | |

**Male**
The male is smaller than the female, and has more pointed forewings.

**Female**
Egg-laying females flutter slowly over vegetation and are easily identified.

**Egg** [x22]
Laid singly; several eggs may be found on the same leaf.

**Colour variant**
Blue-spotted aberrant form *caeruleopunctata*.

**Colour variant**
Rare aberrant albino form *alba*.

**Perching male**
The alert male chases away any butterfly or other insect that enters his territory.

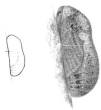

**Chrysalis** [x2¼]
Adults emerge about 3-4 weeks after formation of chrysalis.

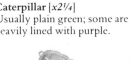

**Caterpillar** [x2¼]
Usually plain green; some are heavily lined with purple.

**Feeding damage**
Young caterpillars eat grooves in the leaves of sorrels. These are easily spotted, as are the eggs, which are usually laid near the midrib.

The Small Copper's courtship is so swift that it is hard for the eye to follow, although the Danish entomologist, H. J. Henrikson, gives a good reconstruction: there is first a rapid zig-zag flight, a metre or two (3 to 6 ft.) above ground level, with the two insects flying in close formation. They then crash-land and rest before resuming the aerial courtship. Finally the female, followed by the male, descends into the ground vegetation, where mating occurs.

## EGGS AND THEIR DEVELOPMENT

The female is more circumspect when egg-laying, and flutters slowly above ground level, often settling to crawl over and tap the vegetation with her antennae in an attempt to find suitable plants. Like most butterflies, she is exceedingly choosy. The eggs are more or less restricted to the common sorrel (*Rumex acetosa*) and to sheep's sorrel (*R. acetosella*), but only certain forms of these plants are chosen. Springtime butterflies will lay in quite tall but sparse vegetation. Typically, they choose sorrels that are 10 to 30 cm. (4 to 12 in.) high, and crawl down to deposit their curious, golfball-like eggs under tender leaves or, very often, on the joint between leaf-stalk and blade. Later broods almost invariably choose small, sprouting sorrels that are growing in warm, exposed positions, often selecting plants with no more than two or three little leaves.

I suspect that this seasonal distinction is not as curious as it seems. Like other Lycaenids, the females probably favour young sorrel growth because this contains a high concentration of nitrogen and other nutrients. In summer, the same conditions would be found only on smaller regenerating growths. This may also explain the occasional record of eggs being laid on broad-leaved docks, occurring when none of the sorrels has fresh leaves, but when some of the docks do.

Whatever the explanation, there is no doubt that fresh, small sorrels can be peppered with Small Copper eggs after a good summer. F. W. Frohawk describes finding an extreme example on 17 October 1933, with "over 300 eggs and many young larvae upon very small plants of Sorrel growing on a dry bank in a space of 15 or 20 yards".

This is, indeed, one of the easier butterfly eggs to find, and it is well worth collecting one or two. The sculpture of the eggshell is fascinating when seen through a lens, and the caterpillar is easy to rear and attractive – a fleshy, green grub, occasionally adorned with pink stripes, whose sluggish gait gives no hint of the vivacity of the adult.

Small Copper eggs hatch after one to two weeks, and the little caterpillar eats a small groove on the underside of its sorrel leaf, leaving the upperside intact. It fits snugly in this channel, which it elongates for a day or two before starting another. Soon the whole leaf looks as if it has been vandalized from beneath with a miniature chisel, and these silvery grooves are one of the easiest ways of detecting the butterfly.

Caterpillars eat larger portions as they grow older, again perforating the sorrel leaves in a characteristic way, although the creature beneath can be hard to find. Finally, after about a month, an attractive, dumpy chrysalis is formed. I know of no one who has found this in the wild, but I suspect, from examining its structure in captivity, that it may sometimes form an association with ants. The caterpillar can certainly attract them, although I have yet to see ant attendance in the wild.

## SMALL COPPER COLONIES

Colonies of the Small Copper can be found throughout most of the British Isles, and are absent only from the high ground of northern England and Scotland, from the extreme northwest of Scotland, and from the Orkneys, Shetlands, Outer Hebrides, and remoter isles. The butterfly is particularly common in the south, although many colonies have been eliminated from the most intensively farmed areas. This is a butterfly to look out for especially on warm, well-drained soils, for example on heaths (where sheep's sorrel is the main food), on chalk and limestone downs (where common sorrel is eaten), and above all, in rough patches of wasteland, on warm banks, embankments, dunes, and old quarries. Road verges also often support appreciable numbers, as do dry wood edges and the sides of ditches.

The Small Copper is not numerous every year, but its numbers can swell markedly during warm summers, unless there is a drought, in which case the sorrels shrivel and become unsuitable for breeding. Fortunately this is a sufficiently mobile butterfly to overcome any temporary setback, and it remains a delightful member of our fauna, easily spotted by amateur naturalists almost everywhere.

# SMALL OR LITTLE BLUE
## *Cupido minimus*

THIS DAINTY little butterfly has a wider distribution than any Blue, other than the Common *(see p.93)*, with colonies as far apart as John o'Groats in northeast Scotland, and Kerry in southwest Ireland. But, despite being widely scattered, it is rare in almost every region it inhabits. Even in its strongholds of Gloucestershire, Salisbury Plain, and south Dorset, it is no more than locally common.

Why the Small Blue should be so much scarcer than its foodplant, flowering kidney vetch *(Anthyllis vulneraria)*, is unknown, but a need for unusually sheltered conditions may be one answer. Colonies are seldom found on open downs or exposed cliffs. Instead, most of the butterflies breed in sunny nooks, where the soil is thin and crumbly and the plant cover sparse and warm. Dune slacks, old quarries, and steep embankments are all favourite habitats, and when visiting these places in late June, it is worth searching kidney vetch flowers for the tiny, blue eggs.

*Distribution Widely distributed, with occasional small colonies throughout most of its range. Common only in the Cotswolds and Portland.*

### BRITAIN'S SMALLEST BUTTERFLY
The natural history of this – the smallest of all British butterflies – has been thoroughly studied in recent years by Ashley Morton. Adult Small Blues are highly colonial, and are often confined to no more than 200 square metres (2,000 square ft.) of land, supported by perhaps two dozen kidney vetch plants. Typical colonies contain under 30 adults each, and breed in the same isolated patch for generation after generation. This is not to say that larger colonies do not occur – I have seen Small Blues teeming by the hundred in the Cotswolds and on the Isle of Portland, and sites with over a thousand individuals each are known to exist – but these are few and far between, and the vast majority contain only a few dozen butterflies.

A typical emergence begins in mid-May, with peak numbers flying about three weeks later. A few linger on into July, and almost overlap with a small second generation that emerges in ones or twos throughout high summer on most southern sites.

### BEHAVIOUR AND IDENTIFICATION
As a beginner, it is easy to overlook this butterfly, but its colonies are quite easy to locate once its distinctive behaviour becomes familiar. Males gather in a sheltered nook, usually a sunny depression at the base of a slope, where there is a scattering of shrubs or tussocky grass. There they perch for most of the day, 30 to 120 cm. (1 to 4 ft.) above the ground, with neighbours between 1 and 2 m. (about 3 and 6 ft.) apart. Their smoky black wings are held half-open towards the sun, so that the silvery blue dusting of scales is clearly visible.

Virgin females fly to these perching sites and are rapidly courted by the males, which spin upwards to investigate any small butterfly passing overhead. But there is no elaborate courtship, and once mated, the female leaves the perch areas strictly alone, concentrating instead on patches of kidney vetch, where she feeds, rests, basks, and lays eggs in its yellow florets.

Adult Small Blues feed almost exclusively on bird's-foot trefoil *(Lotus corniculatus)*, horseshoe vetch *(Hippocrepis comosa)*, or kidney vetch, creating a charming sight against the yellow blooms. Males also have a penchant for wet, salty patches, and in the Alps and the Cevennes I have seen them by the hundred, jostling together along the stony borders of streams and probing the moist soil with their tongues. This seldom happens on British sites, where males gather instead to feast on the unsavoury substitute of dog dirt.

The butterflies also congregate in loose groups to roost, with each perched head-down on tall vegetation. Curiously enough, these roosting sites are in distinct spots that are visited every evening, and may be some distance from the feeding and egg-laying sites, or from the males' perches.

Both sexes look weak and fluttery in flight, and much bluer than would be expected from seeing the colour of the settled butterfly. With practice, this is an easy species to distinguish on the wing, although beginners often confuse it with the more silvery looking Brown Argus *(see p.89)*. When the butterflies are at rest there should be no confusion: the little, round wings have distinctive undersides of clear silver-blue, peppered with black dots, and no trace of the orange found on most Blues. The Small Blue is, indeed, rather like a miniature Holly Blue *(see p.103)* from below, and the largest examples almost reach Holly Blue size, occasionally causing a puzzle.

## EGG AND CATERPILLAR

The female Small Blue spends much of her life fluttering around kidney vetch flowers, probing the yellow florets for a suitable egg-laying spot. She concentrates on prominent plants growing in warm, sheltered depressions, and inserts a single egg between the tightest florets of a young flowerhead that is still largely in bud. She then rubs her abdomen all over the buds, probably to deposit a scent that will deter other females from laying there. As with the chemicals from Whites, its effect wears off after a day or two, and it is not uncommon to find three or four eggs on the same flowerhead of an especially prominent vetch.

The eggs hatch after one to three weeks, and the young caterpillar burrows deep inside a floret to feed on the developing anthers and seed. It is cannibalistic at this stage, and if two or more caterpillars enter the same floret, a battle to the death ensues. As they grow older, the grey-pink caterpillars become easy to find once more, for they live openly on the flower clusters. Each lies head-down while it bites a series of holes into the base of flowers in order to feed on the seed. This damage is noticeable long after the caterpillars have left to pupate; their droppings also remain as a tell-tale sign.

After the third moult, when Small Blue caterpillars enter the final stage of their growth, they possess all of the ant-attracting organs described on p.99, except for the paired tentacles. They can also produce rasping "songs" every bit as loud and persistent as those of the Adonis Blue. In captivity, the caterpillars are highly attractive to ants, but are seldom attended by them in Britain, probably because few of our native species climb the 20 cm. (9 in.) or so to reach kidney vetch flowerheads. In central Europe I have examined scores of these vetches, and never once found a Small Blue caterpillar without ants present.

By late July the caterpillars are fully fed, and desert their flowerheads, which by now are beginning to disintegrate and shed seed. Each caterpillar settles on the ground, reputedly in a crevice, under soil and especially under moss, where it remains dormant for nine months. Then, in late April or early May, it seeks a pupation site, again under vegetation on the ground. It may well be earthed up by ants at this stage, for the chrysalis also attracts them. It is even possible that some chrysalises are protected by ants over winter.

## A SHRINKING HABITAT

The most productive places to seek this charming little Blue are nooks with kidney vetch flowers, not necessarily in profusion, but in a sunbaked, sheltered terrain of rough and broken ground, ensuring an annual supply of fresh seedlings. Typical sites include warm limestone pavement and abandoned lime- and chalkpits. Here the vetch can take root deep in fissures between rocks that are too inhospitable to support the coarse grasses that often swamp it on deeper soils.

Small Blue colonies also occur on unstable ground, where bare patches of fresh earth are constantly being exposed. Examples include steep, thin-soiled banks and calcareous sand dunes, composed of fragmented seashells. Railway lines and road verges are also excellent places: I know of four isolated colonies on the cuttings of dual carriageways in southern England, where the butterflies hop from flower to flower right up to the kerb, oblivious to the constant stream of passing traffic.

There are a few places where the butterfly breeds on open downland. Chief among these are almost every unfertilized, steep valley in the Cotswolds. Other open sites include the south-facing slopes of the Mendips, and Salisbury Plain, where Small Blues teem in several areas, including the Army ranges at Porton and the nature reserve at Martin Down.

Outside the Cotswolds and Salisbury Plain, the Small Blue occurs in scattered pockets throughout the central southern English counties, and is frequently encountered where kidney vetch grows in south Dorset and the Isle of Wight. A very few colonies exist along the North Downs, South Downs, and in the Chilterns, as they do along the coast of south Wales. North of this the butterfly is now extremely scarce, and has disappeared from the vast majority of former sites. There are, nevertheless, about 13 small populations that breed on warm undercliffs along the northeast coastline of Scotland, four inland Scottish sites, and another on the Galloway coast.

## A MISSED OPPORTUNITY

Although it is likely that additional colonies of the Small Blue have been overlooked in the British Isles, there is no doubt that this is a scarce species that has declined very severely in recent years. It is unfortunate, therefore, that few new road cuttings through the southern chalklands and limestone are tailored towards supporting this butterfly. For it is not only simple to create a new breeding habitat in many places, it is often cheaper than the normal practice of producing smooth, graded slopes that are then coated with a rich layer of topsoil. This results in a uniform, dense sward that may be ideal for several common species of butterfly, but which is unsuitable for those, like the Small Blue, that have less robust foodplants.

# SMALL OR LITTLE BLUE · *Cupido minimus*

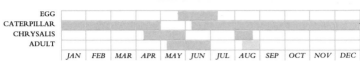

| | JAN | FEB | MAR | APR | MAY | JUN | JUL | AUG | SEP | OCT | NOV | DEC |
|---|---|---|---|---|---|---|---|---|---|---|---|---|
| EGG | | | | | | | | | | | | |
| CATERPILLAR | | | | | | | | | | | | |
| CHRYSALIS | | | | | | | | | | | | |
| ADULT | | | | | | | | | | | | |

**Male upperside**
The forewings have a scattering of blue scales at their bases.

**Male underside**
Neither sex has any orange on the undersides.

**Female upperside**
The forewings lack any trace of blue.

**Female underside**
The undersides of both sexes are similar.

**Large adult**
The biggest Small Blues can have wingspans of 25 mm. (1 in.)

**Small adult**
The wingspan in some adults can be as little as 16 mm. (0.6 in.)

**Perching male**
Males spend much of the day perching on vegetation, with their wings half-open.

**Egg** [x22]
Laid deep within the flowers of kidney vetch.

**Chrysalis** [x2¼]
Formed in April or May, under vegetation.

**Feeding adult**
Males sometimes probe moist ground for mineral salts.

**Caterpillar** [x2¼]
When fully grown, the caterpillar hibernates until the following spring.

**Caterpillars on kidney vetch** [x1½]
The caterpillars are easy to find among the seedheads.

# SILVER-STUDDED BLUE

*Plebejus argus*

THE SILVER-STUDDED BLUE is one of two characteristic butterflies of English lowland heath, and has come to be a symbol of this diminishing habitat. Unfortunately, the butterfly has declined enormously during the present century, and is now virtually absent from four-fifths of its former range. The stronghold, as ever, remains the Hampshire Basin, a sandy exposure of Tertiary deposits which encompasses all the heathland of the New Forest. Here, at least, the Silver-studded Blue can be seen by the thousand, fluttering and shimmering above furze and heathers through the hottest days of high summer.

Colonies are not confined to heathland, however. In Cornwall, Silver-studded Blues breed on several coastal dunes, and the species was once locally common on northern mosses, principally in the old county of Westmorland. More surprisingly, a few scattered colonies also once bred on the chalk downs of Kent, Surrey, Hampshire, and Dorset. This was the so-called *cretaceus* race, characterized by its slightly larger size and paler blue males.

These colonies, alas, have disappeared, with one possible exception rumoured to survive in Kent. But there are two spectacular areas of limestone where the butterfly has been known since Victorian days, and where it is still comparatively abundant. One is the Isle of Portland, which supports about 30 colonies, some extremely large, in the rocky, flower-strewn terrain of abandoned quarries. The other is the beautiful limestone stacks of Great Ormes Head, on the northern coast of Wales. Here my brother Chris Thomas found 10 colonies in 1983, of which a quarter contained 30,000 adults or more.

## THE NORTH WALES COLONIES

The Silver-studded Blues on Great Ormes Head are remarkable in a number of ways. As adults, they are unusually small, and the females have a noticeably bluish tinge. Furthermore, they emerge at a slightly different time – about two to three

**Distribution** *A declining species now rare outside southern English heathlands. Still abundant on many Dorset and New Forest heaths.*

weeks earlier – than all other populations, typically appearing in mid-June. These differences are sufficiently marked for this often to be considered a distinct subspecies, *P. a. caernensis*.

In comparison to other colonies, these diminutive Silver-studded Blues have survived very well. For while the butterfly has disappeared from almost all heaths north of Berkshire, *caernensis* populations have actually increased, partly through human help. In 1942, A. J. Marchant released 90 adults into the Dulas Valley, a region of rough limestone grassland some 13 km. (8 miles) east of Great Ormes Head. They have been a remarkable success, slowly spreading to 16 sites in the next 40 years, and supporting a combined total of perhaps 90,000 adults in the early 1980s.

## REGIONAL FORMS

Among Silver-studded Blues colour variations abound. The illustration on p.85 shows both the *cretaceus* and *caernensis* forms of this butterfly, along with an example from the extinct colonies of Westmorland, where the females were even bluer than those in north Wales, and were considered to belong to yet another subspecies, *P. a. masseyi*. It can be seen that these differences are really rather slight, and that the only consistent geographical variation (apart from the early emergence at Great Orme) is that females have bluer wings the further one travels north.

The idea that these represent true subspecies, each adapted to a different habitat, was quashed by Chris Thomas. He has shown that *caernensis* and *argus* populations use identical types of breeding site within the grassy limestone and heaths that they respectively inhabit, and that each will readily lay eggs in the alternative habitat if transferred.

To make identification more difficult, there are also many minor colour forms – and sometimes aberrations – within any one population. For beginners, females can be particularly perplexing. Here, the silvery-blue centres to the black spots along the outer edge of each underwing are a sure means of identification. However, they are not always present, and are extremely small on other individuals.

Males can be distinguished from the Common Blues that often fly among them by the thick, black borders to their wings, and darker, leaden-blue colour, which gave rise to the butterfly's early English name of "Lead Argus". Unlike Common, Adonis, and Chalkhill Blues, neither sex has a black spot more than halfway into the body on the underside of the forewing. Our two Brown Arguses also lack this spot, but have different patterns on their hindwings, with the two spots at the top arranged in the shape of a colon (:) rather than sideways on (··). Initially these differences may seem small and confusing, but with experience, it soon becomes second nature to notice them.

## SEDENTARY COLONIES

Like most Blues, this species lives in tight, close-knit colonies, which the adults are extraordinarily reluctant to leave. Although both sexes fly readily on sunny days, this is a slow, fluttering affair, seldom more than a few centimetres above the ground with frequent turns when an obstacle is encountered.

The life of the adult butterfly is brief. Chris Thomas, Mike Read, and Neil Ravenscroft independently marked adults in several populations in Wales, Devon, and Suffolk during the mid-1980s, and found that the average lifespan of both sexes was just four or five days. Very few moved more than 20 m. (60 ft.) over that period, and flights of over 50 m. (160 ft.) were exceptional. Thus neighbouring breeding areas separated by a hundred metres or so of gorse are to all intents and purposes isolated, and their populations wax and wane independently of each other. Longer flights do occur, but they are extremely rare. In ten summers working on the chalk downs of Swanage, I have only twice seen a Silver-studded Blue that had presumably strayed from the last populations on the Dorset heaths, just 1 km. (½ mile) to the north.

These feeble powers of dispersal make this butterfly singularly ill-suited for survival in the modern world, for breeding areas are becoming increasingly isolated, and, on heathland at least, are seldom suitable for more than a few years in any one patch. Thus, in north Wales, the Silver-studded Blue was quite unable to colonize the Dulas Valley naturally from the large populations close by to the west. However, once there, it did manage to spread to 15 other spots, moving at the snail's pace of about 1 km. (½ mile) a decade.

## LIFE IN A COLONY

Where it does occur, the Silver-studded Blue can be extremely numerous. Populations containing tens of thousands of adults have been measured in Wales, Suffolk, and Devon, and it is clear that many in Dorset, Hampshire, and Surrey are equally large. These make a wonderful show first thing in the morning, for the butterflies gather in communal roosts, often on tussocks of purple moor grass (Molinia caerulea), where several hundred may be found stretching their wings in the first sunshine of the day. Most colonies, however, contain between a hundred and a thousand adults, and some just a few dozen individuals. The last can be supported by as little as a 0.1 ha. (¼ acre) of ideal breeding habitat, although most large populations breed in considerably bigger areas.

The Silver-studded Blue has one adult generation a year. Apart from at Great Ormes Head, the adults typically emerge from late June onwards, reach a peak in mid-July, and last well into August. They are highly active, although less apt to visit flowers than many species. Males make short patrolling flights, fluttering between the sparse patchwork of dwarf bushes that characterizes most breeding areas, in a continuous search for females that have just emerged from their chrysalises. Courtship is then brief, consisting of little more than a short, buzzing flight by the pair as they weave between the low vegetation, before the female drops to the ground to mate.

The female is choosy when egg-laying. She makes short, fluttery flights over the vegetation before dropping to lay a single white egg, usually on a stalk or tough piece of vegetation. At Great Ormes Head and the Isle of Portland, the eggs are inserted just under the edges of mats of rock-rose (Helianthemum chamaecistus), bird's-foot trefoil (Lotus corniculatus), or wild thyme (Thymus serpyllum), where these spread onto bare limestone boulders. They remain there all winter, and are remarkably easy to find. On heaths, the egg-laying females concentrate on sparse patches where young heather or gorse sprouts through the sand in the first years after a clearance. This preference for fresh clearings is especially obvious in the north, reflecting the butterfly's need to lay in places where the ground is several degrees warmer than the bulk of the vegetation.

## ASSOCIATION WITH ANTS

It has recently become clear that this species has a closer relationship with ants than any other butterflies, other than the Large Blue (see pp.105-108). There is still much that is unknown, but it appears that the young stages are inseparable from a single species of black ant, Lasius niger, although the closely related L.alienus may possibly also be used. From Scandinavia it is reported that the Silver-studded Blue seeks areas where ants are plentiful, and from Spain, there is clear evidence that the female can detect this species of ant, and deliberately lays near its nests.

This may well explain the specialized behaviour of the Silver-studded Blue in the British Isles, for females certainly lay in the very places where this ant is most abundant. It may also explain the curious observation of "literally hundreds" of eggs found on the undersides of bracken fronds in Suffolk. Not only does bracken create a warm microclimate in its canopy, but the fronds also possess nectaries whose sole function is to attract ants.

The egg hibernates with a perfectly formed caterpillar inside, which hatches towards the end of March. The caterpillars feed on a range of plants, particularly bird's-foot trefoil and rock-rose on limestone sites, and on gorses *(Ulex* spp.*)*, ling *(Calluna vulgaris),* and other heathers *(Erica* spp.*)* on heaths. But in every case, they concentrate on the tenderest young shoots, which sprout from the plant in the pockets of warm soil where the eggs were laid.

It has been reported that ants carry the caterpillars about – they certainly tend them with all the assiduousness shown towards the Adonis Blue *(see p.99).* But the relationship here seems closer, and captive caterpillars often become mouldy and die if reared without ants, so copious are their sticky secretions. The chrysalis, too, is almost always formed in the brood chambers of an ant nest. John Pontin, an expert on ants, tells me he found Silver-studded Blue pupae lined up in rows along the passages and brood chambers of *Lasius niger* nests in the New Forest. The same has been reported from Spain, where over 20 chrysalises were found in a single nest. How they got there – whether they were dragged or crawled – is as yet unknown.

Chris Thomas has also noticed another extraordinary aspect of this relationship which has not, so far as I know, been reported from any other butterfly. On emergence, the adult's furry body is wet with droplets of liquid. These are highly attractive to ants, which form an accompanying posse as the butterfly crawls to the surface to blow up its wings. Up to four ants may remain standing on the body until the process of inflation is complete.

EMERGING UNDER ESCORT
*After emerging from its chrysalis, a butterfly must inflate its wings before it can fly. This is a dangerous point in the life-cycle, because the flightless butterfly is exceptionally vulnerable to predators. The ants that surround a Silver-studded Blue after it emerges may help to protect it from attack.*

## A SHRINKING HABITAT

The typical habitat of the Silver-studded Blue is somewhere unusually warm, most frequently on heathland, where there are both ants and a constant supply of fresh plant tips. Reasonable expanses of such areas are nothing like so common as they once were. The vast majority of lowland heaths have been destroyed altogether, at least outside the Hampshire Basin, and those that do survive are nowadays seldom farmed. At one time, burning or grazing in regular small patches produced an almost annual supply of fresh breeding sites on heathland, each adjoining the previous year's clearings. Today, disturbances are few and far between. Entire heaths are often abandoned for many years, only to be accidentally burned in summer fires. With its feeble powers of dispersal, this butterfly is simply incapable of spreading to new sites on the few occasions when regenerative vegetation is suitable for breeding.

This problem of isolation is much more serious at the north of the Silver-studded Blue's range, where very few colonies now survive. The butterfly is still strong, however, on Holy Isle off Anglesey, and, as already described, on limestone further east along the north Welsh coast. Witherslack and all the northern mosses lost their populations sometime before the last war, and the same is almost certainly true of the few Scottish populations. The situation in the Midlands it is little short of a disaster, with one small colony remaining on a fragment of heath sandwiched between two trunk roads. A similar fate has befallen the Breckland colonies, although one or two others survive in Norfolk, as do five or six on the Suffolk Sanderlings. There are strong colonies, too, on some Cornish dunes, but the major populations occur on the southern English heaths. Even here, there have been considerable losses, with only a few colonies remaining in Berkshire, Ashdown Forest, and the lovely pebble heaths of east Devon.

The story is a considerably happier one on the west Surrey heaths, while in Dorset and the New Forest the Silver-studded Blue can be expected on almost every piece of heathland that looks suitable. Perhaps because of the warmer springs in this region, colonies are less restricted to gently south-sloping hills or to areas where there has been a clearing in the previous five years. Although more or less absent from the mature, dry heaths, they are frequently encountered on the so-called humid heath – as opposed to the really boggy areas – where the soil is somewhat peaty and where the butterflies hover around the clustered bells of cross-leaved heath *(Erica tetralix).*

# SILVER-STUDDED BLUE · *Plebejus argus*

## LIFE-CYCLE

| | JAN | FEB | MAR | APR | MAY | JUN | JUL | AUG | SEP | OCT | NOV | DEC |
|---|---|---|---|---|---|---|---|---|---|---|---|---|
| EGG | | | | | | | | | | | | |
| CATERPILLAR | | | | | | | | | | | | |
| CHRYSALIS | | | | | | | | | | | | |
| ADULT | | | | | | | | | | | | |

**Male**
Typical coloration of the most common form of the species, found on heaths and dunes.

**Male upperside**
*Cretaceus* form, found only on chalk and limestone habitats.

**Female**
Common form of the female usually has no blue on the wings, unlike the rarer forms.

**Male**
*Masseyi* form, from Westmorland, now extinct.

**Female**
*Masseyi* form, showing exceptionally blue wings.

**Male, *caernensis* form**
The smallest form, found in north Wales

**Female, *caernensis* form**
Females of this form are noticeably bluish

**Male underside**
*Cretaceus* form; slightly larger than the common form.

**Egg** [*x22*]
Laid on a variety of plants, depending on habitat.

**Chrysalis** [*x2¼*]
Formed underground, within the chambers of an ant nest.

**Resting adult**
Adult resting on gorse, the caterpillar foodplant on heaths.

**Tentacles**
Tentacles at the rear of the caterpillar are erected to stimulate the ants into "milking" the honey-gland.

**Caterpillar** [*x2¼*]
The caterpillar is tended by ants as it feeds on young shoots.

**Feeding adult**
On heaths, bell heather is a frequent source of nectar.

# NORTHERN OR SCOTCH BROWN ARGUS

*Aricia artaxerxes*

THIS DUSKY little insect was probably one of the first cold-hardy butterflies to recolonize Britain when the last great Ice Age receded, roughly 12,000 years ago *(see p.172)*. Today it is restricted to scattered hillsides in Scotland and northern England, existing as two distinct British forms, as befits a creature that may have been isolated from continental populations for 10,000 generations or more.

### A QUESTION OF STATUS

The Northern Brown Argus closely resembles the Brown Argus in both behaviour and appearance. Indeed, for much of this century, they were considered mere subspecies. However, research has since shown that there are crucial differences and now they are universally accepted as separate species.

The one sure way of distinguishing between our two *Aricia* butterflies is in the number of broods each produces a year. The Brown Argus invariably has two, whereas the Northern Brown Argus has one. The latter can emerge in late May in southwest Scotland, although June is more usual, and it is usually a good month later on the east coast.

Scottish specimens nearly always possess a gleaming white mark in the centre of each forewing, and the spots on the under-wings are very faint, with most having no black pupil. In northern England, the butterflies are different in having distinctly spotted undersides, and seldom any white marks on the uppersides. They are known as the *salmacis* form, and look much more like the Northern Brown Arguses of the Continent.

Most British colonies of Northern Brown Argus are small. The two at Castle Eden Dene, in Co. Durham, appear to be typical – perhaps even on the large side – yet between them contained no more than 75 to 100 adults when measured on the peak days of emergence between 1970 and 1972. The butterflies appear, also, to be rather more sedentary than the Brown Argus. At Castle Eden Dene, no mixing of adults has been detected between the colonies located adjacent to each other on

*Distribution A very local species on northern limestone and alkaline soils; probably much overlooked in the northern half of Scotland.*

either side of River Dene, where the butterflies still breed in exactly the same spots that their predecessors used 150 years ago.

The egg is laid mainly on rock-rose *(Helianthemum chamaecistus)* but unlike that of the Brown Argus, is placed on the upper surface, where it gleams in the sunshine and is extremely easy to find. The caterpillar hibernates when fairly small, and resumes feeding the following spring. It is tended by ants, on the Continent at least, and possesses the full array of ant-attracting and appeasing organs. The chrysalis also has an association with ants, and sings to them in the same way as the Brown Argus.

### ENGLISH AND SCOTTISH COLONIES

This is a butterfly of warm northern hillsides. It is chiefly found on alkaline ground, especially limestone, where large, bushy rock-roses grow in abundance. I have found the eggs on steep, grassy slopes in the Peak District, but other colonies breed in more rugged terrain – in abandoned quarries, coastal valleys, limestone pavement, and sheltered cliffs. Some sites are at considerable altitude, up to 460 m. (1,500 ft.).

The Northern Brown Argus is a charming butterfly to watch, and its sites, too, are often beautiful. The most southerly of the English colonies are in the Derbyshire Peak District, with other centres in the Yorkshire Wolds, the Vale of Pickering, Upper Wharfedale, Cumbria, and the mouth of the Dene in Co. Durham. These are all of the *salmacis* form, as were many other northern English populations which disappeared long ago.

Many more colonies are known in Scotland, where the butterfly is probably often overlooked. It is still distinctly local, but good concentrations exist around the southwest coast, and there are major colonies throughout north and northeast Perthshire. The species also flies in scattered colonies further north. Northern Brown Arguses were once plentiful in the border counties of southern Scotland, but most of these colonies disappeared in the nineteenth century.

# NORTHERN OR SCOTCH BROWN ARGUS · *Aricia artaxerxes*

## LIFE-CYCLE

| | JAN | FEB | MAR | APR | MAY | JUN | JUL | AUG | SEP | OCT | NOV | DEC |
|---|---|---|---|---|---|---|---|---|---|---|---|---|
| EGG | | | | | | | ▨ | ▨ | | | | |
| CATERPILLAR | ▨ | ▨ | ▨ | ▨ | ▨ | ▨ | | | ▨ | ▨ | ▨ | ▨ |
| CHRYSALIS | | | | | ▨ | ▨ | | | | | | |
| ADULT | | | | | | ▨ | ▨ | ▨ | | | | |

**Male upperside**
Scottish specimen, with distinct white forewing marks.

**Male underside**
Spots much fainter than those of the similar Brown Argus.

**Female upperside**
Forewings have white marks and orange margins.

**Female underside**
Underside spots poorly developed, as in male.

**Egg on rock-rose**
Egg is conspicuously positioned on the upper surface of a leaf.

**Male**
*Salmacis* form, from northern England, lacks white forewing marks.

**Female**
*Salmacis* form, both sexes have clearer spotting on undersides.

**Egg [x22]**
Hatches within about a week of being laid.

SIDE VIEW

VIEW FROM ABOVE

**Chrysalis [x2¼]**
Tended by ants; less pink than chrysalis of the Brown Argus.

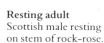

**Feeding adult**
Male *salmacis* form feeding on flower of bird's-foot trefoil.

**Caterpillar [x2¼]**
Initially feeds on underside of leaves; enters hibernation when small.

SINGLE SEGMENT

**Resting adult**
Scottish male resting on stem of rock-rose.

# BROWN ARGUS

*Aricia agestis*

A<small>T FIRST SIGHT</small>, the Brown Argus seems rather a dull little butterfly, with both sexes superficially resembling the brown form of the female Common Blue *(see p.93)*. It does, nonetheless, have a charm of it own, resulting from its lively behaviour, an unexpected shimmer of silver when it flies, and the rich chocolate and orange colours on the upperwings of fresh specimens. It is not a particularly common species, but lives in small, localized colonies on unfertilized southern downland, in several coastal dune systems, and in a scattering of other localities such as southern heaths and woods.

The Brown Argus was largely neglected by early entomologists, and features in few books of any antiquity. When it does appear it is under a variety of names, including the "Edg'd Brown Argus" and the "Brown Blue". Identifying the butterfly is often tricky. In flight, it can be mistaken only for the Small Blue *(see p.81),* due to the silvery reflection as the sun catches the underwings. However, identifying the perched butterfly is more difficult. One feature to look out for is the lack of blue on the upperwings. Also, in contrast to Common, Adonis, and Chalkhill Blues, there is no spot nearer to the body than halfway in on the undersurface of the forewing. The pair of black spots near the top outer edge of the lower hindwing forms a figure of eight or colon (:) instead of being sideways on (··) as in other Blues.

There is some variation in the markings of individual butterflies. In males, the orange spots on the uppersides can be reduced to mere pin-pricks, whereas these merge to form an orange band on some females. In one particularly attractive variety, called *subtus-radiatus,* the spots on the underwings are distorted and form long streaks.

## COLONIES AND MOVEMENT

Little was known until recently about the natural history of this butterfly, apart from the identity of its main foodplants, the fact that its caterpillars are often tended by ants, and that its

***Distribution*** *Generally scarce; found mainly on chalk and limestone downs, cliffs, and dunes. Commonest on chalk in Dorset and the Isle of Wight*

populations fluctuate in size. These fluctuations are unusual in that they seldom occur in synchrony on nearby sites. Thus it is common to find that the butterfly is having one of its best years on one down, while numbers have inexplicably dropped on others.

Insight was recently shed on this and other mysteries by the researches of Nigel Bourn, based at the research station at Furzebrook in Dorset. The Brown Argus has two adult broods a year, the first from mid-May to late June, the second from July to September. Both are protracted, so much so that although the average lifespan of an individual adult is roughly four days, it is usual for the earliest males of the second brood to be flying before the last tattered females of the first have died. Most colonies are small, containing just a few dozen adults, and even in good years the best sites support no more than five to seven hundred individuals.

Bourn also discovered that although the adults live in self-contained areas, there is much more interchange between adjoining sites than is the case, for example, with Adonis or Silver-studded Blues. These latter species travel, on average, about 10 to 20 m. (30 to 60 ft.) from their birthplaces, but Brown Argus adults move ten times further.

## COURTSHIP AND EGG-LAYING

At night, adult Brown Arguses roost in the lower parts of their site, clustered in groups head-down on grass-stems, often in the company of Common and other Blues. At daybreak they bask communally for a few minutes, with wings stretched wide to absorb the warmth of the sun. The rest of the day is spent in solitary pursuits. Males either perch on the ground with open wings or patrol the lower parts of their site, while any virgin female advertises herself by sitting astride a grasshead. A male soon alights alongside, and both then embark on a short and sinuous nuptial flight, meandering just above ground level before settling on a grass clump to mate.

# BROWN ARGUS · *Aricia agestis*

## LIFE-CYCLE

| | JAN | FEB | MAR | APR | MAY | JUN | JUL | AUG | SEP | OCT | NOV | DEC |
|---|---|---|---|---|---|---|---|---|---|---|---|---|
| EGG | | | | | | | | | | | | |
| CATERPILLAR | | | | | | | | | | | | |
| CHRYSALIS | | | | | | | | | | | | |
| ADULT | | | | | | | | | | | | |

**Male upperside**
In flight, both sexes appear silvery by reflecting sunlight.

**Male underside**
No spot on forewings is nearer than halfway in to the body.

**Female upperside**
Orange markings are bolder than those of the male.

**Female underside**
Orange spotting on undersides can vary considerably.

**Feeding**
Young caterpillar produces distinctive transparent patches on rock-rose leaves.

**Perching adult**
Male resting on the flowerhead of ragwort.

**Egg** [*x22*]
Laid singly on the underside of the foodplant's leaves.

SIDE VIEW

**Chrysalis** [*x2¼*]
Formed on the ground beneath the foodplant, probably in association with ants.

VIEW FROM ABOVE

**Colour variant**
Rare aberrant form *subtus-radiata*, with elongated black spots.

**Mature caterpillar** [*x2¼*]
Fully grown caterpillar is usually attended by ants, making it easy to locate on its foodplant.

VIEW FROM ABOVE

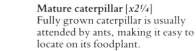

SIDE VIEW

SINGLE SEGMENT

**Basking adult**
Female on the flowerhead of wild basil.

It takes another day or two before the female's egg-load ripens, whereupon she embarks on low, fluttery flights, frequently alighting to search for caterpillar foodplants, twitching and tapping the vegetation with her feet. Rock-rose *(Helianthemum chamaecistus)* is the sole food used on most sites, but storksbill *(Erodium cicutarium)*, dovesfoot cranesbill *(Geranium molle)*, and probably other cranesbills can be used.

An egg-laying female becomes agitated when she encounters a foodplant, but tests each carefully before deigning to lay. Most plants she rejects outright, and instead concentrates her eggs on a minority of plants that have exceptionally thick, fleshy leaves and also unusually high concentrations of nitrogen. Sheltered, sunny depressions and plants with some bare chalk rubble around them are also particularly to her liking. Few rock-roses meet these specifications, but those that do range from large mat-like plants to virtual seedlings.

A survey of downs that support Brown Argus colonies has revealed that the condition of these plants, rather than their number, is of paramount importance to the butterfly. By and large, the species does well during a warm summer, but those colonies that breed on steep, thin-soiled downs, where water can be in short supply, find that their foodplants become unsuitable for eggs and caterpillars during periods of drought. On sites with deeper soils, the rock-roses remain lush and healthy, with the result that their Brown Arguses flourish.

The Brown Argus's egg is a pale, blue-green disc, and is nearly always laid on the undersurface of a leaf. It hatches after a week or two, and the small caterpillar begins to feed on the soft, rich interior of the leaf, eating a neat circle of tissue, then larger patches beneath the leaf. The upper leaf-layer is left intact, which creates shiny patches that are easy to spot in the wild.

## RELATIONSHIPS WITH ANTS

The Brown Argus caterpillar is the same shape as those of its close relatives, but can be distinguished by the deeper green ground-colour and the pink stripes, which blend beautifully with rock-rose shoots, and also with the pink-veined leaves of storksbills. Although it feeds openly by day, the fully grown caterpillar would be extremely hard to spot were it not for its attendant ants. If you scan likely rock-roses until you notice an excited group of ants, often there will be a caterpillar beneath them. It helps to know, however, that at the slightest disturbance, the ants will desert the caterpillar, which rolls off its leaf, and is then almost impossible to find.

In its final stage, the caterpillar possesses all the organs described on p.99. It whips its entourage into a frenzy of excitement by frequently everting the paired tentacles, especially when it walks, and by pumping visible droplets of honeydew out of a large and active honey-gland. In addition, microscopic secretions are exuded like sweat over the rest of the body, and doubtless we shall find that this caterpillar, too, sings to its ants.

## CHANGES IN THE LANDSCAPE

Nearly all Brown Argus sites are warm, south-facing chalk and limestone downs, but as already indicated, the butterfly has a much more restricted distribution than its foodplant. Rock-rose itself has sadly declined, for although it has the ability to dominate low turf, the plant is easily eliminated by ploughing or the application of fertilizer. Once lost, it may take decades or possibly centuries to return.

Although no precise records exist, there is little doubt that the Brown Argus has suffered enormously due to loss of its foodplant. Between 1811 and 1970, agricultural improvement and conversion to arable use destroyed 80 to 90 per cent of semi-natural downland in its stronghold, the county of Dorset. It may, indeed, have suffered more than other rarities like the Adonis Blue, because the gentler slopes and flatter land have fared worst. It is exactly this ground, with its more nutritious soils, that encourages the lush growths of rock-rose needed by this species. About one third of Dorset's Brown Argus colonies have disappeared since World War II. Some have been the victims of intensive agriculture, others have been casualties of reduced grazing from the mid-1950s to the early 1980s, which led to many low-growing rock-roses being shaded out.

## THE BROWN ARGUS TODAY

The Brown Argus remains, however, a locally common butterfly in Dorset, where there are still perhaps two or three hundred colonies, largely confined to the steep southern escarpments of downs. There is also a good scattering of populations in similar situations in Wiltshire, Sussex, Surrey, Kent, and the Isle of Wight, as well as in the Cotswolds and the Chilterns. It has become rare towards the north of its British range, for example in Warwickshire, Northamptonshire, and Cambridgeshire, although the beautiful limestone cliffs of Anglesey and north Wales still support strong colonies.

Most other populations are on cliffs or calcareous sand, for example along the coasts of north Cornwall, south Wales, and Norfolk, and in the surviving fragments of Breckland. Not every colony is supported by rock-rose, and the butterfly's ability to make use of some species of storksbill and cranesbill is responsible for a thin scattering of colonies elsewhere in southern England, and on soils other than chalk. It is possible, therefore, to encounter this delightful insect in woodland glades and rides on clays, and even on acid heaths. Such populations are, however, invariably small and very rare.

# COMMON BLUE

*Polyommatus icarus*

As its name implies, this is by far the commonest and most widely distributed Lycaenid butterfly found in the British Isles, and is the only Blue present on most small islands. Any warm patch of waste ground is likely to hold a few individuals, but its main habitats are ancient downland, rough pasture, dunes, sunny banks, and heaths, where it is regularly seen.

The brilliant lilac male will be familiar to all naturalists, and is a regular visitor to country gardens, where it sups on flat-headed flowers and establishes small territories, battling with hoverflies and other innocent passers-by. The female is less conspicuous: except when egg-laying or feeding, she remains out of sight, perched among the vegetation until the eggs in her abdomen mature. She also has duller markings, at least in the south.

***Distribution** A common species on rough grassland, absent only from intensive farmland, mountain tops, and the northern Shetlands*

## REGIONAL VARIATIONS

Females differ greatly in the amount of blue and brown colour present on their wings, both within colonies and between regions. In some the ground-colour is uniformly brown, although most have a dusting of blue scales towards the base of their wings. "Brown" females predominate in many southern colonies, but they may often be mixed with others that have variable amounts of blue on their wings, making it difficult to define the butterfly's characteristics.

The preponderance of blue markings increases the further one travels west and north, culminating in a magnificent form called *mariscolore,* which is regarded as a distinct subspecies by some entomologists. It lives in Ireland and northwest Scotland, including several Scottish isles, and is one of the most beautiful of all British butterflies. Not only are the wings a clear deep blue, but the orange spots are also enlarged almost into a band, and it is distinctly larger than southern specimens. So striking is its appearance that English entomologists sometimes mistake it for more spectacular species such as the Large Blue or Adonis Blue; the literature on butterflies is bedevilled with such mistakes.

## ATYPICAL FORMS

The Common Blue produces atypical forms or aberrations, although less frequently than Adonis or Chalkhill Blues. For example, the spots on the undersides may vary in size and shape, and the colour of the male's upperwings is occasionally paler, as in the example we illustrate on p.93, which is the *pallida* form of the butterfly.

For all this variation, there are a few constant features that distinguish both males and females from related species. The outer fringes of the wings are clear white and not crossed with dark lines or chequering as in Adonis and Chalkhill Blues. On the underside of the forewing, there is a spot about a quarter of the way out from the body which is absent from the Silver-studded Blue and our two Brown Arguses. Finally, there are orange marks around the edge of the hindwings, which is not the case with Holly, Small, and Large Blues. Thus the Common Blue is relatively easily identified.

## LIFE-CYCLES AND COLONIES

The number of broods and emergence dates of this butterfly vary considerably in different parts of the British Isles. In the south there are always at least two emergences, the first from mid-May to mid-June, the second lasting from late July into September. F. W. Frohawk, who reared many Common Blues in Kent, maintained that the second brood was no more than a partial one, because many of its caterpillars enter hibernation in June rather than develop to form adults. On the other hand, the species sometimes fits in a third generation in October after an especially warm summer.

Further north there is time for just one generation a year, which emerges on different dates according to the local climate: the warmer the climate, the earlier the emergence. George Thomson gives an authoritative account in *The Butterflies of Scotland.* Briefly, Common Blues may be flying in late May in southwest Scotland, although a prolonged emergence from June to late August is more usual. But in the northeast, for example on Speyside, they are seldom seen before the second week of July and are really August butterflies. Further south, in Yorkshire, the butterfly may switch between one and two broods a year according to the warmth of the season.

Common Blues live in reasonably discrete colonies, though they wander more than most close relatives. Thus the occasional stray has been picked up on lightships, and new patches of habitat tend to be colonized quite quickly. But it is not a true nomad like the Holly Blue, and most individuals fly, pair, and lay within the breeding grounds from which they emerged.

## TERRITORIES AND ROOSTS

Although this is easily the commonest British Blue, surprisingly little is known of its behaviour. Much of the information comes from Deryk Frazer and Roger Dennis, working in the county of Kent. Male Common Blues are distinctly territorial, and either perch or patrol in search of females, frequently skirmishing with rivals and other butterflies such as the Small Copper, which is equally combative. Typical flights are short and rapid in both sexes, as Common Blues flit from one flowerhead to the next.

When settled, the wings are opened fully only in weak light, so as to absorb maximum warmth from the sun. This occurs mainly first thing in the morning and in late afternoon, which are the best times to examine and photograph the Common Blue. Adults are easily approached then, and there is the added bonus that many may congregate on clumps of tall grass, settling on the tops to catch the last rays of the afternoon sun, and waking in the morning from their communal roosts. These roosts tend to occur on banks or in sheltered hollows, where both sexes rest head-down, two or three per grasshead, often accompanied by other Blues.

The lovely females come into their own when laying eggs. They make short, fluttery flights just above ground level, frequently alighting to crawl over low-growing herbs, twitching and drumming their feet to test the quality of different growths. Each female dips her antennae when she finds potential egg-laying sites, and rubs the leaves with the tip of a half-curved abdomen. Eventually, when a suitable plant is found, the abdomen is bent double before it recoils like a buffer, leaving a tiny pale green egg on the leaflet.

## COMMON BLUE FOODPLANTS

I have watched females lay many times and have found more than a thousand of their eggs. They use a fairly wide range of leguminous plants, but the commonest by far is bird's-foot trefoil *(Lotus corniculatus)*. Other well-used foodplants, which can apparently support an entire colony of this butterfly, are greater bird's-foot and lesser trefoils *(Lotus uliginosus* and *Trifolium dubium)*, black medick *(Medicago lupulina)*, and various rest-harrows *(Ononis* spp.*)*.

More important, probably, than the species of plant is the luxuriance of its growth. Eggs are invariably laid on the soft growing tissue of the youngest leaflets, while tough fully grown plants are ignored. This can lead to different plants being used in the two generations, as Roger Dennis recorded in Cheshire, where the first brood laid principally on lesser trefoil, but the second brood switched to bird's-foot trefoil in August when the lesser trefoil was largely withered.

Common Blue eggs turn white as they dry, and are easy to find. Most are laid on the midribs towards the base of tender leaflets, especially on the upper surfaces of small plants that are sprouting back into leaf after a disturbance, or growing beside a track or on a warm, sheltered bank. This is a simple species to rear, making an interesting exercise, although the caterpillar is plainer than those of other Blues. It emerges from the egg after a week or two, and starts feeding on the undersurface of its leaflet, excavating mouthfuls of soft mesophyll. As with most Blues, the upper epidermis is left intact, creating silvery blotches on the leaves that are also easy to find. Whole leaves are eaten by the older caterpillar and, unless it enters hibernation, growth is complete after six weeks.

## A CASUAL RELATIONSHIP WITH ANTS

The caterpillar is green and furry in its final stage, and beautifully camouflaged on the foodplant. It feeds by daylight, easing itself sluggishly over leaves and barking a tuneless song, too soft for human ears, which appears to be created by the rhythmic protrusion of its shiny black head, that pops in and out as it walks. The song, almost certainly, is to attract ants. But although this caterpillar also possesses the other ant-organs described on p.99, its powers of attraction are weak. Only 19 of the 25 undisturbed caterpillars that I watched for long periods in the wild were being tended, and then usually by just a single worker ant rather than the clusters that smother Adonis and Chalkhill Blue caterpillars when they emerge to feed.

Only once have I seen ants showing real enthusiasm for a Common Blue caterpillar. This was in Devon, where both the red ant *(Myrmica sabuleti)* and the great wood ant *(Formica rufa)* were common. I watched the caterpillar several times during the day, and it was always being milked by one or other of these species. Twice they fought for it: the first time a red ant was in possession, and easily saw off a feeble challenge from the more excitable wood ant. Later the opposite occurred: by now a wood ant was in control and there were frequent skirmishes as a red ant, in its typically persistent way, scurried back and forth

# COMMON BLUE · *Polyommatus icarus*

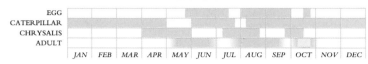

| | JAN | FEB | MAR | APR | MAY | JUN | JUL | AUG | SEP | OCT | NOV | DEC |
|---|---|---|---|---|---|---|---|---|---|---|---|---|
| EGG | | | | | | | | | | | | |
| CATERPILLAR | | | | | | | | | | | | |
| CHRYSALIS | | | | | | | | | | | | |
| ADULT | | | | | | | | | | | | |

**Male upperside**
Brilliant lilac-blue; outer fringes of wings clear white.

**Male underside**
Both sexes have a spot on the forewing near the body.

**"Brown" female upperside**
Predominantly brown, with varying blue near wing-bases.

**Female underside**
Both sexes have orange marks on edges of the hindwings.

**Female**
*Marsicolore* form, found in Ireland and northwest Scotland.

**Male**
Rare aberrant form *pallida*, with pale upperwings.

**"Blue" female upperside**
An extreme example, with brown restricted to the wing edges.

**Egg [x22]**
Laid singly, often on bird's-foot trefoil.

**Chrysalis [x2¼]**
Formed on the ground; probably tended by ants.

**Caterpillar [x2¼]**
Feeds during the day on tender leaves.

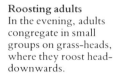

**Roosting adults**
In the evening, adults congregate in small groups on grass-heads, where they roost head-downwards.

**Feeding adult**
Common blues feed at flat-headed flowers, such as hawksbeard.

under the foodplant, sneaking up from beneath the caterpillar to take quick licks of its body. The wood ant was perched squarely on the back of the caterpillar (which continued to munch trefoil, oblivious to the battle) and at each attack reared back and up on its hindlegs, spraying formic acid at the red ant. It is tempting to think that the ant in possession held some territorial advantage over the intruder, but more observations are needed to be sure.

The chrysalis, also, attracts ants, through secretions which ooze out of microscopic pores and an ability to crackle into song. It drones on in long bursts of noise, less staccato than those of the caterpillar but equally tuneless, like a clicking ratchet or a football rattle. It seems probable that chrysalises are tended in the wild, and I once found one beneath a slate, inside a red ant nest. The chrysalis lasts roughly a fortnight before the adult butterfly emerges.

### THE DANGERS OF DROUGHT

Colonies of Common Blue exist in a wide variety of places where the foodplants are common. Each typically consists of a few tens or hundreds of adults, in contrast to the many thousands of Adonis, Chalkhill, and Silver-studded Blues that are found on their best sites. Common Blue numbers also fluctuate greatly from one year to the next. By and large, when there is a warm, wet spring in the south, there is high breeding success in the summer brood, and this in turn leads to large numbers the following year. But the population can crash as a result of a hot, dry summer, probably because there are few lush vetch leaflets for egg-laying.

A population crash certainly took place after the great drought of 1976, as the Butterfly Monitoring Scheme data at Monks Wood clearly demonstrates. I spent most of that summer in Devon, and remember one south-facing slope where almost all the foodplants had shrivelled by the time second-brood females were flying. These unfortunate mothers had to search for the few green wisps of trefoil that were growing in deeper soils and shaded by gorse. Even these were parched and miserable, but became peppered with eggs. I suspect that the

majority later died, for Common Blues were virtually absent from the area the following year, and took two to three seasons to recover to their normal numbers.

### COMMON BLUE HABITATS

In most years, this is a widespread and common butterfly, so much so that it is simpler to list the areas where it does not occur. It is absent, for example, from all land higher than about 550 m. (1,800 ft.) in Scotland and Wales, and although colonies are known from the warm southern sand dunes of the Shetlands, it is probably missing from the rest of those islands. Elsewhere, it may be found wherever its foodplants are abundant, even on islets that are less than 0.5 ha. (1 acre) in area. The largest colonies inhabit warm chalk and limestone downs, with those breeding on cliffs, undercliffs, and dunes a close second. Numbers tend to be lower elsewhere, but the butterfly is nonetheless common on banks, cuttings and roadsides, on lowland heaths with moderately rich soil, and on patches of wasteland. These sites are fairly well drained, but colonies will also be found on much heavier soils – in unfertilized pasture, marshy areas, and along ditches, where whole colonies appear to be supported by greater bird's-foot trefoil.

Although primarily a butterfly of open grassland, the Common Blue is frequently encountered in the glades and sunny rides of woods, or breeding on leguminous plants along the edges of woods. This, indeed, is almost the only habitat in which the butterfly survives in parts of Cambridgeshire and East Anglia, where intensive agriculture has eliminated much grassland and woodland, and where its foodplants are not now present in the open countryside. For despite being one of the commonest butterflies in Britain, there is no doubt that countless populations have been lost from lowlands due to the efficiency of modern agriculture and the general tidying up of the countryside. There was, moreover, a time when trefoils were actually sown in pasture to sweeten the hay and enrich the soil with nitrogen, which is a far more sensible way of fertilizing leys and hay crops than adding synthetic nitrates.

# CHALKHILL BLUE

## *Lysandra coridon*

A S ITS NAME IMPLIES, this beautiful butterfly is highly characteristic of the southern chalk and limestone downs to which it is confined. It is not particularly common, but inhabits most of the unfertilized southern grasslands where its foodplant, horseshoe vetch *(Hippocrepis comosa)*, still grows.

No one is likely to mistake the milky blue of the males, although when flying in full sunshine they can look surprisingly like Marbled Whites *(see p.179)*, so pale are the wings. The chocolate-brown females are a different matter and give rise to much confusion. However, there is a distinct chequering to the white fringes along the wing edges, which distinguishes this species from all except the closely related Adonis Blue *(see p.101)*. These two females can be extremely difficult to separate: the only way to be certain of either is to examine the spots around the margins of the uppersides: these are edged with white in this species but are edged with blue on the female Adonis blue – a distinguishing feature.

***Distribution** An inhabitant of unfertilized southern English chalk and limestone downs. A local species, abundant in some places.*

### CURIOSITIES AND COLLECTORS

Although most Chalkhill Blue colonies consist of only the typical adults, a great many also contain aberrations. In this species, however, we have included some of the many aberrations, to demonstrate the bizarre variety that can exist. Although the forms with strangely spotted undersides are intriguing, by far the commonest varieties are the blue *tithonus* and *semi-syngrapha* forms of the female. Curiously enough, it is unusual to find both varieties within the same population.

The most famous population was at Royston golf course, near Cambridge, where *semi-syngrapha* and other forms were common for several years before the last war. The scramble to net them led to accusation and counter-accusation between rival collectors. One man, to everyone's disgust, simply sat in the car while his chauffeur caught dozens for inspection. Another bred these forms and released them near Princes Risborough, but this ended in failure. In time, even the varieties at Royston disappeared.

### CHALKHILL BLUE COLONIES

Chalkhill Blues live in discrete, isolated colonies, whence males occasionally wander, to be found far from the nearest breeding site. There is one generation a year, with the first adults usually seen in mid-July, reaching a peak a month later and often lasting well into September. Numbers vary considerably between sites and in different years. Two colonies of no more than medium size contained around 10,000 and 18,000 adults when measured, both breeding in under 2 ha. (5 acres) of land. Many colonies are much smaller, however, and here only a few individuals will be seen. On the other hand, the largest examples probably contain hundreds of thousands of adults in their best years. Such outbreaks are unusual, and I have seen them only twice in Britain – at Fontmell Down in Dorset in the 1970s, and on the slopes of Old Winchester Hill in Hampshire in the 1980s.

Adults behave similarly to the Adonis Blue, gathering to roost by night on tussocks of tall grass near the base of a hillside. Often there are two or three per grass-stem, with perhaps a score in the same small clump. They make a lovely sight when the sun first reaches them in the morning, for all bask together for a few minutes, communally opening their wings to absorb the maximum warmth.

### FLIGHT AND EGG-LAYING

The main occupation of males is to flutter a few centimetres above the sward in an incessant search for mates. Females, by contrast, seldom fly, except to feed or lay eggs. Chalkhill Blues visit a wide variety of flowers, but on most sites scabiouses *(Knautia, Scabiosa,* and *Succisa* spp.), knapweeds, and hardheads *(Centaurea* spp.) are common and frequently used. Males also gather to drink water; on the Continent, I have often seen hundreds grouped on pebbles near alpine streams. When laying eggs, the female Chalkhill Blue flutters and crawls over the turf searching for horseshoe vetch. Eggs are laid singly, usually on stalks and tough woody parts as well as on neighbouring vegetation. The female of this species is much less fussy than that of the Adonis Blue, which chooses only the shortest vetch plants available. Chalkhill Blues will use these – I have often found eggs of both species on the same plant – but they use more overgrown vetches as well. Yet they do not seem completely unselective, and lush, nitrogen-rich plants appear to be favoured, as they are by the Brown Argus. Females certainly prefer large vigorous vetch clumps, and there is some reason to believe that the butterfly is commonest on sites where grazing has just been relaxed, releasing the close-cropped stumps to produce a luxuriance of delicate leaflets.

As befits an egg that will endure the winter, the shell is robust and heavily sculptured; even without a hand-lens, it is easily distinguished from that of the more delicate Adonis Blue. Chalkhill Blue eggs are simple to find on good sites; I often encounter them while working on Adonis Blues, finding several hundred in a good season. A search is best made in late summer, for an increasing number fall off during the autumn to complete their hibernation on the ground, where they are almost indistinguishable from the tiny chippings of lime or chalk.

### FEEDING BY NIGHT

The Chalkhill Blue caterpillar is fully formed by late summer, but remains within the shell until late April. At first, it behaves very like the similar-looking Adonis Blue *(see p.101)*. Apart from the difference in timing and size (Adonis Blue caterpillars are almost fully grown when Chalkhill Blue eggs hatch, and there is little overlap in the second generation), Chalkhill Blue caterpillars can be distinguished by their slightly paler bodies and their decidedly paler bristles. They are also nocturnal, emerging at dusk to browse on the vetch leaves.

Despite their nocturnal habits, the caterpillars are as attractive to ants as are those of the Adonis Blue, and possess similar secretory organs. No doubt they also make sounds, but this has yet to be proved. I have never seen a Chalkhill Blue caterpillar browsing at dusk that was not attended by ants. In some cases these include the yellow ant *Lasius flavus,* a subterranean species that will often follow the caterpillars above ground after dark.

### A SINGING CHRYSALIS

The chrysalis is harder to find, but well worth searching for in June, when it may be concealed inside earthen cells moulded by ants beneath vetches, or in the brood-chambers of ant nests. It is also adapted to attract ants. Although lacking the caterpillar's honey-gland, it possesses secretory pores which exude a film of amino acids (the chemical building blocks of proteins), a particularly desirable food source to an ant colony at this time of year.

More remarkable still is the sound organ, which is formed by two toughened segments of the thorax. It is folded in a deep V that penetrates far into the body in this species, where it is attached by a powerful muscle to the opposite wall. As can be seen in the illustration on p.64, one side of the V contains a series of tiny teeth, and the other a file. The muscle contracts to rub the two together, and so create sounds.

The sound produced by the chrysalis clearly stimulates and agitates the ants that surround it. This is particularly evident when an emerging adult struggles to free itself from the pupal case, bringing together a posse of protective ants.

### STATUS AND DISTRIBUTION

Unfortunately, this beautiful and fascinating butterfly has become scarce this century, as many flat sites have been ploughed and fertilized, and most steep downland abandoned as grazing land. However, it has experienced nothing like the decline of the Adonis Blue, and has generally survived on its traditional sites so long as the horseshoe vetch itself has persisted. Typical sites today include the southern slopes of open downland, ancient monuments, ramparts and banks on the chalk, and old abandoned quarries.

A few Chalkhill Blue colonies once bred as far north as Lincolnshire, where one survived as recently as 25 years ago. Today, its northwestern limit is marked by a handful of colonies in the Cotswolds, while in the east, it survives on fragments of unspoiled chalk grassland near Cambridge. It becomes more common, although still local, on herb-rich downs in the Chilterns, and is present on most sites south of this where horseshoe vetch survives in reasonable abundance. Thus there are strings of colonies along both the South and North Downs, and many isolated populations breed on the chalk hills of Hampshire. It is frequent, too, on many untouched areas of Salisbury Plain, especially in the dry valleys around the edges, but colonies are surprisingly localized in the Poldens and Mendip Hills to the west. Its strongholds now are the Isle of Wight, Wiltshire, and the escarpments of Dorset, where it is still to be expected in any unfertilized valley that harbours horseshoe vetch. This includes the limestone coast and the Isle of Portland, where magnificent populations survive. Many of these are protected, lying either within nature reserves or on the vast coastal properties of the National Trust.

# CHALKHILL BLUE · *Lysandra coridon*

LIFE-CYCLE

| | JAN | FEB | MAR | APR | MAY | JUN | JUL | AUG | SEP | OCT | NOV | DEC |
|---|---|---|---|---|---|---|---|---|---|---|---|---|
| EGG | | | | | | | | | | | | |
| CATERPILLAR | | | | | | | | | | | | |
| CHRYSALIS | | | | | | | | | | | | |
| ADULT | | | | | | | | | | | | |

**Male**
Milky blue upperwings are unlike those of any other Blue, and look very pale in full sunlight.

**Female**
Very similar to female Adonis Blue, although slightly larger; spots around the base of the upperwings are edged with white.

**Colour variant**
Female of the *tithonus* form, with blue wings.

**Colour variant**
*Caeca* form, from Watson Collection, British Museum.

**Colour variant**
*Antiextrema* form, from Watson Collection, British Museum.

**Colour variant**
*Flavascens* form, from Watson Collection, British Museum.

**Egg** [x22]
Laid on or near the foodplant; hibernates and hatches in spring.

**Chrysalis** [x2¼]
Formed underground inside an ant nest, or in a cell moulded by ants beneath the foodplant.

**Feeding adult**
Chalkhill Blues visit kidney vetch and many other flowers.

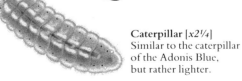

**Caterpillar** [x2¼]
Similar to the caterpillar of the Adonis Blue, but rather lighter.

**Resting adult**
Female resting in dull weather on flower-bud of hardhead.

# ADONIS BLUE

## *Lysandra bellargus*

THE ADONIS, along with the Chalkhill Blue, is the quintessential butterfly of southern English chalklands. Although increasingly rare and localized, it can still be seen by the hundred on warm downs stretching from Dorset to Kent, where the brilliant blue butterflies hover over a turf yellow with horseshoe vetch (*Hippocrepis comosa*). This spring flight is followed by a second emergence in late summer, providing a magnificent finale to the season when the Browns, Skippers, and Chalkhill Blues are either extremely tattered, or have disappeared.

### COLOUR VARIATION

The sheer brilliance of the male's wings has long attracted attention, and collections exist containing drawer upon drawer of this one species. It is all the more collectable due to the fact that the wing markings vary considerably in some colonies. The male's blue, for example, is almost violet in some cases and turquoise in others. This is much more apparent in the wild, where the strength of sunlight and the extent to which scales have been lost also affects appearances: there are always a few individuals which, in flight, are almost impossible to distinguish from the Common Blue (*see p.93*). At rest, the latter is more violet, while the Adonis Blue has fine black lines that cross the outer white fringes and just enter the body of the wing.

These chequered fringes are also a good way of distinguishing the female, although note that the Chalkhill Blue (*see p.97*) is very similar. She is a lovely chocolate brown on most sites, much given to variation on some. The commonest aberration, which I see by the hundred in the Isle of Purbeck, is called *semiceronus*. In this, the ground colour is wholly or partly blue, resembling a male with orange spots around the base. Other varieties have underwing spots that are distorted or reduced.

Adonis Blues live in close-knit colonies, with little or no movement between those on adjoining downs. I have marked thousands of adults over the years, and found that they fly very freely over herb-rich, open downland, but almost always turn

***Distribution*** *A rarity confined to unfertilized, well-grazed, south-facing downs in southern England, principally in Dorset and the Isle of Wight.*

back when they encounter a barrier or a ploughed field. Thus I have yet to detect any mixing whatsoever between four neighbouring colonies I have studied, even though each is separated by just 50 to 100 m. (roughly 150 to 300 ft.) of chest-high scrub. Of course the odd individual must occasionally migrate, but this is clearly a rare event. It has greatly hampered the recovery of this species when its habitat was recreated on certain downs in the 1980s. New colonies were largely restricted to sites that were a stone's throw away from surviving ones.

### COURTSHIP AND EGG-LAYING

Male Adonis Blues are much the more conspicuous sex because, in addition to their vivid markings, they spend long periods hovering just above the turf, slowly flying up and down the hillside in a perpetual search for virgin mates. Females are pounced upon almost immediately they emerge, and are often swamped by males before their wings are dry. This accounts for the many individuals seen with slightly crumpled wings.

After pairing, the female spends long periods resting on the ground. Typical Adonis Blue sites contain a short, broken turf with numerous little pits and depressions that catch the sun, and it is in these that she especially lingers, waiting for her egg-load to ripen. When it has, she flutters slowly over the turf, dropping frequently to crawl over the caterpillar's foodplant, horseshoe vetch. However, she is highly selective in her choice of plants. She usually rejects large clumps in favour of small, short sprigs growing in turf that is just one or two centimetres tall, especially when situated in a warm depression or hollow, such as an old hoof-print on a steep, south-facing slope. Warm boundary banks are also much favoured. Indeed, it is remarkable how many Adonis Blue colonies are entirely restricted to ancient fortifications. Spectacular examples include the battlements of Maiden Castle and Hod Hill in Dorset, and the fascinating Bockerly Dyke, which snakes its way between the boundaries of Dorset, Hampshire, and Wiltshire, supporting high densities of butterflies on a ribbon of turf no wider than a metre or two in some places.

The white, pin-head-sized eggs are found mainly on the underside of terminal leaflets, and are easy to spot if you gently lift the branches with a pencil. Although laid singly, there may be 30 to 40 on the best plants in a good year. They hatch after a week or two, and the tiny caterpillars start nibbling at the undersurfaces of the leaves. They are microscopically small, translucent, and extremely hard to see at first, but their presence is obvious from the feeding damage which appears as numerous little pale circles on the leaflets, each with the opaque upper cuticle left intact. Later, entire leaves, shoots, and fruits are devoured. The caterpillars feed throughout the day, and are camouflaged from after their first moult onwards. They would be very difficult to find were it not for the fact that they are attractive to ants, and are often surrounded by large clusters. This is not an unusual feature among Blue butterflies, although the relationship in this species is particularly strong.

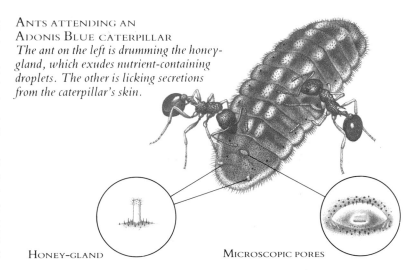

ANTS ATTENDING AN
ADONIS BLUE CATERPILLAR
*The ant on the left is drumming the honey-gland, which exudes nutrient-containing droplets. The other is licking secretions from the caterpillar's skin.*

HONEY-GLAND                 MICROSCOPIC PORES

## ORGANS TO ATTRACT ANTS

I have had the pleasure of watching over a thousand wild Adonis Blue caterpillars being tended by ants. The relationship begins after the first moult, and continues almost incessantly until the butterfly has emerged from the chrysalis. The caterpillar possesses three distinct organs that attract ants. The most obvious is the honey-gland. This consists of a slit across the seventh segment back from the head, which forms the opening to a complicated gland housed deep in the body. Fleshy, slightly raised lips surround this slit, which, on high magnification, can be seen to contain bizarre clusters of knobs and plates (mechanoreceptors), looking rather like medieval clubs.

The caterpillar also possesses microscopic pores, and an extraordinary pair of tentacles situated either side of the honey-gland, one segment back. These are normally kept hidden within the body, but are periodically unfurled like the expanding horns of a snail. At the tip of each is a circle of hairs that finally spring open, looking very like a chimney sweep's brush. Their exact function is still in doubt. They are extended by the caterpillar particularly when it crawls from one leaf to another, or when the ants have wandered off. They may contain a chemical that activates the ants, which become highly agitated when these are extruded.

Another extraordinary feature of the caterpillar was discovered in 1989 by Phil De Vries of the University of Texas. He had already found that the caterpillars of certain Riodinids (relatives of our Duke of Burgundy) produce strange songs by rubbing two ribbed tentacles behind the head against striations on the head capsule. These arouse and possibly pacify ants, which themselves make all sorts of noises, for example to spread the alarm when faced with danger. No such organ has been found on a Blue's caterpillar, but De Vries knew that a few American Blues sang. It was therefore with considerable excitement that we tested the Adonis Blue. We found that not only did the caterpillar sing, but that the tune was loud compared with other species, although below our feeble threshold for hearing. It has an eerie loveliness: a sort of rasping, barking noise that is especially apparent when the caterpillar crawls, reinforced by regular high-pitched squeaks that overscore the tune.

## PROTECTION BY ANTS

Any species of ant may attend Adonis Blue caterpillars, but on English chalk it is usually the red ant *Myrmica sabuleti* or the black ant *Lasius alienus,* which are the only really common species in the places where this butterfly breeds. The ants are obsessive in their attention, and the caterpillar receives considerable protection not only from other carnivorous ants, but also from parasitic wasps. The armed guard extends around the clock, for ants follow the caterpillar down to the soil surface when the day's feeding is complete, often burying it for the night in a pile of loose earth, which they often work into a firm crusty cell around it. These cells sometimes contain up to eight Adonis Blue caterpillars together, with perhaps a dozen ants doing sentry duty around them. Cells are also constructed around moulting caterpillars, a process that may take two or three days.

The chrysalis also has every bit as intimate a relationship with ants, relying on a combination of song and amino acids

## GROUND TEMPERATURES UNDER HORSESHOE VETCH

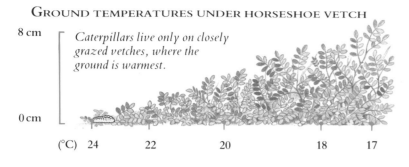

*Caterpillars live only on closely grazed vetches, where the ground is warmest.*

8 cm

0 cm

(°C)  24    22    20    18  17

secretions, in the same way as the Purple Hairstreak *(see p.64)*. Adonis Blue chrysalises are not easy to locate. Some undoubtedly enter crevices and cracks in the ground, where they are quickly buried and then tended by ants. I have found an equal number, however, inside ant nests, resting among the brood in the warm uppermost chambers. Whether they are attracted or carried to these, or merely enter the nests because these have soft soil, I have no idea. In any case the chrysalis receives constant attention until it emerges three weeks later. With a burst of crackling song, it breaks open the pupal case amid a sea of agitated ants, before crawling to the surface to spread its wings.

It is unlikely that an Adonis Blue colony could survive were it not for the protection of ants. This is true of other Blues, but is perhaps one reason why this particular species is very fussy in its breeding requirements. Adonis Blue caterpillars must be tended from the earliest days of March until the end of October. The Chalkhill Blue, by contrast, requires ants only from mid-May to August.

For ant colonies to be active so early and so late in the year demands an abnormally warm environment, and the caterpillar itself may need warmth. Whatever the precise reason, Adonis Blue colonies are restricted to the hottest localities in England – south-facing southern hillsides – and then only to sites where the soil is thin and the turf so closely grazed that the sun can bake the ground.

### A HISTORY OF DECLINE

Adonis Blue populations have declined dramatically during the present century, but have always been scarce. This was, indeed, one of the last British butterflies to be discovered, and for many years was known either as the "Clifden Blue" or "Deptford Blue", after two of its earliest localities. The main populations have probably always been in Dorset and the Isle of Wight,

where the chalk is warmest. These remain its stronghold today, having suffered much less than elsewhere when unfertilized downland was abandoned and when most sites became overgrown with the disappearance of rabbits in the 1950s. This led to a spate of extinctions almost immediately, as swards become too tall for breeding. Colonies that were documented in Kent declined from a few thousand adults to extinction in just two years after rabbits disappeared. This was a common occurrence throughout southern Britain, and by the 1970s only 2 per cent of former sites still supported the butterfly outside Dorset, even though horseshoe vetch remained abundant on most.

By the late 1970s, the Adonis Blue was at an all-time low in Britain. As a result of one survey, I estimated that about 75 colonies survived, of which half were in Dorset and most very small. It seemed likely that the species would be lost to Britain around the turn of the century if the decline continued unabated. This, happily, has not been the case. Many nature reserve managers are now managing their sites more effectively for this butterfly. These sites include much downland owned by the National Trust, such as the beautiful Hog's Back of the Purbeck Hills, and its extension between the Needles to Ventnor on the Isle of Wight, where there is a string of protected populations. In addition, the widespread return of rabbits, and an increase in grazing grants, has meant that many downs that had been ungrazed for 25 years returned to some sort of short turf in the 1980s. Several of these have been repopulated, either naturally or by deliberate introductions, and today there are perhaps as many as 150 colonies in the country.

### ADONIS BLUE COLONIES

Current Adonis Blue colonies just extend into the Chilterns, Oxfordshire, and Berkshire, and there is a series of large populations along the North Downs escarpment of Kent and Surrey. Several more breed in East Sussex, from the Seven Sisters to Lewes and Brighton, although most unfertilized downland in that county is unsuitable since it faces north. Few colonies have survived in Hampshire, but there are several in Wiltshire along the undulating edges of Salisbury Plain. By far the main concentrations remain in Dorset and the Isle of Wight, where one can still expect to see the butterfly on any stretch of escarpment that is steep, south-facing, unfertilized, and grazed. On the best sites – especially those scarred by cattle during winter – the populations can be huge, with tens of thousands emerging in the second generations of a good year. However, numbers fluctuate widely, regardless of site management, and plummet on poor sites following a series of cold summers.

# ADONIS BLUE · *Lysandra bellargus*

LIFE-CYCLE

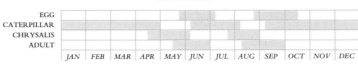

| | JAN | FEB | MAR | APR | MAY | JUN | JUL | AUG | SEP | OCT | NOV | DEC |
|---|---|---|---|---|---|---|---|---|---|---|---|---|
| EGG | | | | | | | | | | | | |
| CATERPILLAR | | | | | | | | | | | | |
| CHRYSALIS | | | | | | | | | | | | |
| ADULT | | | | | | | | | | | | |

**Male**
The brilliant colour of the male is brighter than that of any other Blue.

**Female**
Similar to the female Chalkhill Blue, but pale hindwing scales are blue, not white.

**Female colour variant**
Aberrant form *semiceronus*, common on some sites.

**Male colour variant**
A rare and extreme form caught at Ranmore, Surrey, in 1972.

**Feeding adult**
Second-brood adults often feed at the flowers of marjoram.

**Egg [x22]**
Laid singly on horseshoe vetch; many may be found on the same plant.

**Chrysalis [x2¼]**
Formed on or under the ground, in association with ant nests.

**Adult on horseshoe vetch**
Horseshoe vetch is used as a source of nectar by adults and a source of food by caterpillars.

**Caterpillar [x2¼]**
Made conspicuous by the constant presence of ants.

# HOLLY BLUE

*Celastrina argiolus*

THE HOLLY BLUE differs from its close relatives in being a butterfly of shrubs rather
than grassland, and in roaming the countryside
instead of living in tight-knit colonies. It is a
regular visitor to gardens, and can be found in the
heart of most cities in southern England. I shall
never forget my astonishment on being shown
the largest population I have ever seen, in the
grounds of the John Innes Institute – a small oasis
of walled gardens among the concrete and asphalt
of south London.

### THE GARDEN BLUE

This is a species that can confuse beginners,
who often glimpse a flash of blue as it flits over
a tree-top or wall. While it is reasonable to
assume that any blue butterfly seen flying high
among bushes could be a Holly Blue, this is not
an infallible guide. I have seen Common Blues
*(see p.93)* ascend to considerable heights, and even settle on tree-
tops to drink aphid honeydew.

Identification is easier when the butterfly is at rest. The silver,
black-spotted undersides, without the slightest trace of orange,
can be confused only with the those of the Small Blue *(see p.81)*,
which is scarce and very much smaller. Furthermore, while the
upperwings of the male Holly Blue are similar to those of a
Common Blue, its fringes are distinctly chequered around the
forewings, whereas those of the Common Blue are clear white.
The female Holly Blue has especially lovely uppersides that are
heavily tipped with black, particularly in the second emergence
in midsummer. These are distinctive in flight, giving an inky
blue impression very similar to a smallish Large Blue *(see
p.107)*. Indeed, the Holly Blue is responsible for more false
reports of Large Blues than any other butterfly.

There are usually two emergences of Holly Blues a year, the
first from mid-April to June, the second in late July and August.
There is reputed to be an occasional third brood in hot years, as
occurs further south on the Continent, while it is claimed that
there is just one midsummer emergence in the northwest of its

**Distribution** *Numbers fluctuate
greatly: in good years, seen in ones
and twos almost everywhere within
its range, but scarce at other times.*

range. However, I have yet to see this substantiated, and two generations seem to be the
norm in Scandinavia.

### FOOD AND FOODPLANTS

Adult Holly Blues behave rather like Hairstreaks,
resting among bushes at night and hopping in
the sunshine around the canopies of bushes.
They settle quite often on leaves, where they
fidget in the sunshine with wings firmly closed,
preferring to drink honeydew than nectar. Only
in weak sunshine do the wings open, and then
seldom more than 90 degrees, giving just a
glimpse of the beautifully marked uppersides.
They resemble Hairstreaks, too, in being
extremely tame, and can be closely approached
during their frequent descents to ground level.
Males, in particular, congregate to feed avidly
on the salts in patches of mud, especially during
midsummer droughts. I remember finding half-a-dozen drinking together on one muddy stream-bed in 1976. Like many
butterflies, they are also not averse to dung, benefiting from the
minerals that it contains.

Egg-laying females are often seen in gardens, fluttering
slowly around the contours of shrubs and pausing to hover over
any potential foodplant. Eggs are laid singly at the base of
flowerbuds and very young fruit of various shrubs, and less
often on fresh leaf-buds. In spring, by far the commonest host-
plant is holly *(Ilex aquifolium)*, whereas most midsummer eggs
are laid on the flowers of ivy *(Hedera helix)*. However, spindle
*(Euonymus europaeus)*, dogwood *(Cornus* spp.*)*, snowberry
*(Symphoricarpos* spp.*)*, and heathers are also used, and I know
whole colonies in the West Country where the sole food in both
generations is gorse *(Ulex* spp.*)* flowers.

### CAMOUFLAGED CATERPILLARS

Eggs are easy to find in good Holly Blue years, when favoured
bushes are peppered with scores of the tiny white discs. You
will notice that most are laid on somewhat prominent bushes

# HOLLY BLUE · *Celastrina argiolus*

LIFE-CYCLE

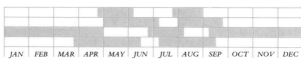

| | JAN | FEB | MAR | APR | MAY | JUN | JUL | AUG | SEP | OCT | NOV | DEC |
|---|---|---|---|---|---|---|---|---|---|---|---|---|
| EGG | | | | | | | | | | | | |
| CATERPILLAR | | | | | | | | | | | | |
| CHRYSALIS | | | | | | | | | | | | |
| ADULT | | | | | | | | | | | | |

**Male, first/second brood**
Males from the first (spring) and
second (summer) broods are similar.

**Female, second brood**
Second-brood females have broad
black margins to the upperwings.

**Female, first brood**
First-brood females have
less black on upperwings
than in second brood;
underside identical.

**Parasitic wasp**
The grubs of *Listrodomus
nycthemerus* kill large numbers
of developing caterpillars.

**Basking male**
Male basking on ivy, the
foodplant of the second
brood caterpillars.

**Egg** [*x22*]
Laid singly at the base
of flowerbuds, usually
of holly and ivy.

**Chrysalis** [*x2¼*]
Second-brood chrysalises
hibernate, producing adults
the following April.

**Caterpillar** [*x2¼*]
Camouflaged markings vary greatly,
but plain green is the most usual form.

**Caterpillar on ivy** [*x1½*]
Damage to the developing
flowerbuds makes the caterpillar
easy to find.

growing in warm sunny positions, especially beside a wall, or in a hedge or wood edge. If you have a garden in southern Britain, it is well worth growing one or more foodplants of this lovely Blue, for its delicate hues make a delightful contrast to the gaudier livery of Tortoiseshells, Peacocks, Red Admirals, and Whites, which are all that most people manage to attract. Cultivated and variegated varieties of holly and ivy are perfectly acceptable, so long as they are unshaded and produce fruit.

The egg hatches after about a fortnight, and the little caterpillar attaches itself to the side of the young fruit. It then bores a small hole in the skin, and eats the contents, with the head, which is mounted on the end of a long neck, scouring out the inner surfaces. It switches to fresh berries as it grows, leaving distinctive round holes on the withered fruit; these are very easy to find both on holly and ivy, as can be seen in the illustration. Larger ivy berries may also be completely devoured, but the cups remain as evidence, and there is often much bleeding of sap. In either situation this conspicuous damage should soon lead to the discovery of the caterpillar, marvellously camouflaged against the side of a fruit. Nearly all are a clear fleshy green, but others come with a variety of markings ranging from pretty pink to maroon stripes down the back and sides; we illustrate an extreme example.

## INTERACTIONS WITH ANTS

The fully grown caterpillar has a full array of ant-attracting organs *(see p.100),* although these are seldom used in Britain, probably because we have very few tree-climbing ants inhabiting the areas where Holly Blues breed. The caterpillars are, however, lavishly attended in captivity, and I have seen one being milked for its sugary secretions by the red ant *(Myrmica ruginodis)* on a low wall draped with ivy in Somerset.

The caterpillars could certainly do with some protection, for they are frequently attacked by a parasitic ichneumon wasp *Listrodomus nycthemerus,* which can be seen patiently cruising around holly and ivy blooms. It punctures the young caterpillars with a long stiletto of a sting, and injects eggs into their bodies. These develop inside the caterpillar as it grows, later emerging as adult wasps, one per Holly Blue chrysalis. This beautiful parasite has no other host than the Holly Blue, and it is reputed to be in some part responsible for the dramatic fluctuations of the butterfly, although no scientific study has been made of this up to the present day.

The mature caterpillar leaves its shrub to pupate, and acquires a purple mottling rather like the pre-pupal Brown Hairstreak. No one, to my knowledge, has ever found a Holly Blue chrysalis in the wild, but its speckled brown colour and strong ant-attracting capabilities make it likely that pupation occurs on or near the ground, where it is probably tended by ants. Captive ants certainly find the chrysalis highly attractive, due to its secretions and, probably, a powerful song *(see p.64).* Springtime chrysalises hatch after three to four weeks, but those from the midsummer brood hibernate.

## FLUCTUATING NUMBERS

Adult Holly Blues are considerable wanderers, once appearing in a district, increasing for a few years and then quickly declining. Permanent populations do exist, especially in its more wooded habitats, but even so there is probably much movement between neighbouring areas. Although notorious for erratic fluctuations, there is some pattern in that numbers tend to build up over a series of warm summers, and plummet immediately after a cool one.

The best places to see this butterfly are in sheltered, sunny gardens and woods. In good years the adults will be seen fluttering in ones and twos almost anywhere along the hedgerows of southern England and lowland Wales, with more localized concentrations further north, in the Lake District and the Isle of Man. It has been recorded from Scotland on just five occasions, and even in our most intensive agricultural regions, such as the East Anglian fenlands, although here it is restricted to overgrown churchyards and neighbouring gardens.

The Holly Blue is one of the few British butterflies that appears more or less to have held its own during the present century, although it was once considerably more widespread in northeast England. There is a little anecdotal evidence to suggest that it was scarcer in certain periods of the nineteenth century, and the earlier entomologists gave no indication that it was common. Indeed few mentioned it at all, and when they did they often created a new name, again suggesting that it was a local species. It was, for example, first known as "The Blue Speckt Butterfly", with the female called "The Blue Speckt Butterfly with Black Tips". "Azure Blue" and "Wood Blue" were alternative names in the nineteenth century, and it was only comparatively recently that the name Holly Blue gained acceptance, and was universally adopted.

# LARGE BLUE

## Maculinea arion

ABOUT EIGHTEEN THOUSAND SPECIES of butterfly are known from around the world, but none has a more curious lifestyle than the European Large Blues. These five species make a nonsense of the mutually beneficial relationship that normally exists between ants and Lycaenids butterflies. For whereas ants usually protect caterpillars while they browse upon their foodplants, and in return drink sweet secretions from the larval honey-gland *(see p.99)*, the caterpillars of Large Blues live like cuckoos inside ant nests, eating the ant grubs and often destroying the nest.

Sadly, this small group – the *Maculinea* – are among the rarest and most endangered insects in the world. We in Britain had only one species, and that became extinct here in 1979. The Large Blue was not particularly big: the wingspan of a typical adult only slightly exceeded that of a large male Chalkhill Blue, and miniature specimens the size of a Small Blue were apt to emerge on every site. But their markings were always lovely, although seldom constant. Male Large Blues generally had the finer black margins, and fewer and smaller upperside spots, but the heaviness of these marks varied considerably between individuals and, to a lesser extent, between sites.

**Distribution** *Colonies once mainly in the Cotswolds, and along the Devon and Cornish coasts. Extinct in 1979; reintroduced in Devon.*

### ESCAPE INTO THE AIR

I had the pleasure of working with these butterflies for 18 years, and of living among them for six summers on one site. I can therefore confirm, and in some instances add to, the remarkable observations made by Dr. T. A. Chapman, Capt. E. B. Purefoy, and F. W. Frohawk, who unravelled the main features of its lifestyle early this century.

The adult Large Blues emerge from the last week of June to mid-July; each, on average, lives five days. Before taking to the air, the adult must first escape from its ant nest. The chrysalis, like the caterpillar, lives underground, usually just below the soil surface in a warm earthen cell. It is attended by a dozen or more ants, which incessantly lick secretions off its body. The chrysalis also possesses a sound organ similar to that of the Purple Hairstreak *(see p.64),* which produces rasping bursts of song while the hatching adult splits open its pupal case and struggles to shake itself free.

Emergence occurs between 8.00 a.m. and 9.30 a.m., when the ants are rather sluggish, but the noise soon whips them into a frenzy of activity, and they accompany the butterfly as it crawls up the narrow passages to the outside world. Once above ground, they mill excitedly around, while the butterfly makes its way up a shrub and inflates its wings.

### SEARCHING FOR THYME

The butterfly rests for about 45 minutes while the expanded wings set hard. It then flies to the lowest part of its site. Typical British breeding grounds consist of steep, south-facing hillsides, and the males spend the rest of their lives near the bottom, patrolling back and forth in the morning sunshine. This activity diminishes around noon on hot days, and the males roost in the shade of a shrub or tussock. They reappear in late afternoon to drink nectar from wild thyme (*Thymus praecox*).

Virgin females also flutter down the slope and are soon intercepted by the males. There is a brief aerial courtship before the two butterflies land on a shrub or the ground, and pair for about an hour. They then part, he to feed then resume his patrol, she to hide until her eggs are ripe.

Some females lay eggs on the afternoon of their emergence, but the main bout occurs on the second day of life. Each flutters slowly up and down the breeding slope, hovering just above the short turf before alighting on wild thyme. After twitching and rotating on a flowerhead, the butterfly curves her plump abdomen almost double before plunging the tip into a tight young flowerbud. A single egg is injected into the inflorescence before the abdomen slowly recoils.

Many females are killed by spiders, dragonflies, or birds before laying a single egg, but those that survive can produce two or three hundred each. By the end of the season, an average of about 60 eggs will have been laid per female in the colony.

## CANNIBALISTIC CATERPILLARS

The eggs hatch after 5 to 10 days, and the minute caterpillar burrows into a thyme flower to feed on the pollen and seed. Although the eggs are laid singly, a large flowerhead growing on the edge of a thyme plant often receives four or five during the few days that it is in bud, and I have found over 100 eggs on a single plant. Most are destined to die, for the caterpillar is cannibalistic before its first moult and only one ever survives on each flowerhead. This is beneficial rather than harmful, for it thins out the caterpillars in places where the density is high, and reduces the chances that the ant nests will receive more caterpillars than they can support.

The caterpillars develop quickly on thyme but put on little growth. After two to three weeks, each weighs roughly a milligram (about 30 millionths of an ounce), yet has already completed all its skin changes and developed the organs needed for the next phase of its life. These include a minute honey-gland *(see p.99)* capable of secreting sweet droplets to attract ants.

## ADOPTION BY ANTS

I have watched several hundred Large Blue caterpillars being adopted by red ants, but the sight never loses its thrill. The tiny caterpillar completes its final skin moult at any time of day, but remains hidden in the thyme flower until 5 to 7 p.m. It then flicks off the flower and drops to the ground, where it hides beneath a leaf or in a crevice. By doing this, it greatly enhances the chances of being found by a red *Myrmica* ant, for these forage mainly in the early evening and search very close to the ground.

The caterpillar is soon discovered on a good site, and the ant taps its body, stimulating the honey-gland into producing a minute drop of liquid. This causes great excitement. After drumming the gland with its antennae for a few minutes, the ant rushes away to recruit about a dozen nest-mates. These crawl all over the little caterpillar, milking its gland and licking and prodding its body with their mandibles. But they eventually wander away, leaving the caterpillar with the original ant that discovered it. She is far more possessive; I have occasionally seen fights to the death when an ant from a different colony tried to milk the caterpillar as well.

Milking may last for up to four hours, but eventually the caterpillar rears up to signal its readiness for adoption. This causes a frenzied response from the ant, which is now tricked into believing that the caterpillar is one of its own grubs that has somehow escaped from the nest. For in the dark of the brood chamber, red ants recognize their young by a combination of

ANT IMITATION
*When ready for adoption, the caterpillar rears up on its prolegs, tucks its head, and inflates its first three segments like a balloon. It now closely resembles an ant grub.*

stimuli including size, hairiness, scent, and how firm the skin is to touch. The tiny Large Blue caterpillar already possesses the size and hairiness of an ant grub. It acquires its distinctive smell through being milked by the ant, for the odour of the nest is dissolved in volatile waxes that coat the body of every ant, and rubs off onto the caterpillar. The final stimulus is provided by the rearing and distortion of the caterpillar's body, which causes its normally flabby skin to be firm and taut, exactly like an ant grub. The ant immediately snatches the rearing caterpillar up in its jaws, and runs with it back to the nest. It carries the caterpillar underground and places it among the ant brood.

## A CUCKOO IN THE NEST

Once inside the nest, the caterpillar scrabbles among the ant brood, trying to puncture the skin of a grub. When this eventually bursts, the caterpillar slowly eats the fluid tissues. Between feeds, it rests on a small pad of silk spun on the wall of the brood chamber.

The caterpillar grows quickly in the nest, and soon turns into a bloated white maggot that dwarfs both the ants and their grubs. It crawls into the deep recess to hibernate, and resumes feeding near the surface in spring. By the time it pupates in late May, the caterpillar is about a hundred times heavier than at the time of adoption, and has consumed as many as 1,200 ant grubs. In fact, most caterpillars die long before this stage. The few that survive are those fortunate enough to have been adopted into a particularly large nest of one species of ant, *Myrmica sabuleti*.

Up to five different species of *Myrmica* live on some sites and all adopt the Large Blue caterpillars, and the Large Blue caterpillar mimics very accurately the identification chemicals and sounds produced by these insects. Interestingly, the other four species of Large Blue found on the Continent are equally specialized, but in each case a different *Myrmica* species is used.

Life in an ant nest is full of danger for the caterpillars, despite their disguise. Many are killed by worker ants which, acting

# LARGE BLUE · *Maculinea arion*

## LIFE-CYCLE

| | JAN | FEB | MAR | APR | MAY | JUN | JUL | AUG | SEP | OCT | NOV | DEC |
|---|---|---|---|---|---|---|---|---|---|---|---|---|
| EGG | | | | | | | | | | | | |
| CATERPILLAR | | | | | | | | | | | | |
| CHRYSALIS | | | | | | | | | | | | |
| ADULT | | | | | | | | | | | | |

**Male**
Smaller and generally less heavily spotted than the female, with finer black wing margins.

**Female**
Forewings heavily spotted with black – a characteristic unique among British Blues.

**Colour variant**
Aberrant *alconides* form, found most often in males.

**Colour variant**
Aberrant *imperialis* form, found most often in females.

**Feeding adult**
Adults feed on the nectar of wild thyme; caterpillars feed on its pollen and seeds.

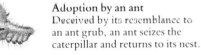

**Adoption by an ant**
Deceived by its resemblance to an ant grub, an ant seizes the caterpillar and returns to its nest.

**Egg [x22]**
Laid singly on the flowerbuds of wild thyme.

**Chrysalis [x2¼]**
Formed within an ant nest, where it produces sugary secretions.

**Feeding on grubs**
After being carried inside the ant nest, the caterpillar attacks and eats the grubs.

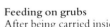

**Caterpillar [x2¼]**
At first, the young caterpillar feeds on wild thyme flowers. After adoption by ants, it feeds voraciously on their grubs.

**"Milking" a caterpillar**
An ant taps a caterpillar with its antennae, to stimulate production of secretions.

under the influence of their queen, kill large grubs that might develop to become her rivals. Starvation is also a threat, particularly in nests that contain two or more caterpillars.

## DECLINE AND DISAPPEARANCE

With such a specialized life-cycle, it is not surprising that the Large Blue has always been rare in Britain. It was discovered near Bath late in the eighteenth century, and about 90 colonies were found during the next 150 years. Most were in remote parts of southern England, at least a day's horse ride from the nearest railway station. This gave the butterfly a tremendous cachet among Victorian collectors, second only to that of the Large Copper.

The first British site where collectors could almost guarantee to secure specimens was at Barnwell Wold in Northamptonshire. This sustained heavy collecting for about 20 years, but in 1860 about 200 adults were taken at rest by one dealer in the course of a wet summer and the colony never recovered.

With the demise of the Barnwell colony, entomologists turned their attention to two other areas where it had recently been discovered: three small colonies in the limestone Polden Hills of Somerset and some large ones along the beautiful stretch of Devonshire coastline south of Salcombe – the Bolt Head to Bolt Tail cliffs, where enormous numbers were caught. The Rev. F. R. Elliot wrote of a friend who "in the summer of 1859 took as many as a hundred specimens in one day… which were later sold for half-a-crown apiece".

There were bitter debates about the wisdom of such collecting, and many appeals were made for some restraint. But this had little effect, and when the south Devon populations crashed in 1875, collectors turned to the Cotswold colonies that had been discovered 17 years earlier.

But as had occurred elsewhere, the Cotswold populations all but disappeared in the 1880s and remained in very low numbers until the twentieth century. They were, in fact, to recover and become locally common again in the 1920s and 1930s, but entered a terminal decline in the mid-1950s, becoming extinct 10 years later.

It was not until 1891 that the finest British colonies were discovered, along the Atlantic coast of Cornwall and Devon. This came as an enormous relief to Victorian entomologists who believed the butterfly to be on the verge of extinction elsewhere. They responded by arriving in droves, and contemporary reports claim that over 1,000 butterflies, "and probably double", were taken each year from 1895 to 1914 between Tintagel and Millook, with no apparent harm to the populations. Unfortunately, a considerable decline set in during the 1920s, at least in the traditional collecting grounds south of

Bude. Thereafter the butterfly was seen in insignificant numbers, disappearing finally from Crackington Haven in 1963.

There was still one stronghold, however, along the coast north of Bude, where the Large Blue bred in almost every valley up to Clovelly in the 1950s. It was exceptionally abundant on some sites, with individual valleys probably supporting up to 10,000 adult butterflies. However as in the Cotswolds, a sharp decline started in the mid-1950s, and within 18 years, the butterfly was extinct here too. This left one small colony on Dartmoor that disappeared in 1979.

## RABBITS, ANTS, AND BUTTERFLIES

Despite the large numbers taken by collectors, almost all these extinctions were caused by agricultural change. About half the old breeding sites were simply destroyed, mainly by ploughing and seeding. The remainder look superficially unchanged, and most still contain a sward of fine grasses dominated by mats of thyme. But these have altered too, in a subtle way. All were heavily grazed when they supported Large Blues, but farmers have abandoned these unproductive pastures for lusher, flatter land. As described on p.100, the effect was not serious until the 1950s, for huge populations of rabbits maintained a close-cropped turf. But once myxomatosis was introduced, the turf grew dense and tall.

Tall, shaded turf is as fatal to this butterfly – or rather to its ant host – as it is to the Adonis Blue (see p.101). The cooling of the soil that occurs when a short sward grows just a few centimetres taller results in the rapid disappearance of *Myrmica sabuleti*. Its nest sites are often taken over by other species of red ant, but these are unsuitable for the Large Blue, and the butterfly disappears as quickly as its host.

## THE FUTURE OF THE LARGE BLUE

Now that conservationists are aware of the specialized needs of this butterfly, they are attempting to recreate suitable conditions on a few former sites. By 1980, one owned by the National Trust seemed once again ready for the butterfly. This prompted a programme of re-establishment, in conjunction with David Simcox, the Nature Conservancy and World Wide Fund for Nature. After much searching in northern Europe, we located colonies in Sweden that appeared to be identical to the former British races. These were introduced as a trial in 1983, with immediate success. Indeed the butterfly increased for five years, before experiencing a slight fall in 1989, caused by a severe summer drought. At the time of writing, it is still uncertain whether we will be able to maintain this colony permanently, or succeed in our ambition of re-establishing the Large Blue on another five former sites, but the initial results are promising.

# DUKE OF BURGUNDY

## *Hamearis lucina*

Few British butterflies have experienced a more rapid and more worrying decline than the Duke of Burgundy. Although never particularly numerous, it once inhabited most large woods in the south, where it fed on half-shaded primroses that grew in regenerating clearings. Almost all these colonies have gone – victims of the decline in coppicing – leaving a rump of perhaps 250 populations in scrubby patches of downland. This has always been a poor alternative as a habitat, and most of these sites contain a mere handful of adults: all must be considered vulnerable.

### A LINK WITH THE TROPICS

It would be sad indeed were we to lose this little insect, for it is the only European representative of that wonderful tropical family, the Metalmarks, or Riodinidae, that finds its greatest diversity in Central America. Our Duke, to be sure, is one of the dullest and least interesting members of the group, with little of the subtle beauty of so many other adults. Nor, so far as is known, does it share any of the extraordinary adaptations that many Metalmarks have evolved to attract ants.

This is a charming butterfly, nonetheless, with much of the perky behaviour of a Hairstreak or Blue combined with the chequered wing pattern of a Fritillary. It was indeed known as the "Duke of Burgundy Fritillary" until recently, and the markings give rise to some confusion. The distinctive features that separate it from the Fritillaries are two clear-cut bands of white marks running parallel down the underwing, and spots around every wing edge.

### THE CONTEST FOR TERRITORIES

The Duke of Burgundy lives in small, close-knit colonies, typically consisting of a few dozen individuals, although there are two or three places where several hundred occur. Not all are alive on the same day, and you would do well, on a typical site, to see more than five or six adults on each visit. A typical

*Distribution A rapidly declining species, rare in most of its range; locally common only in the Cotswolds and on the edges of Salisbury Plain*

lifespan is five to seven days, with the first males emerging in late April after a warm spring, although May is more usual. Emergence then continues in ones and twos, building up to a peak towards the end of the month and dwindling away by mid-June.

The sexes behave rather differently. Males are much the more conspicuous sex, and can be located with ease, even on sites with low numbers, due to their distinctive territorial behaviour. Each selects a small bush or tussock and fiercely defends it against rivals through a series of spiralling dog-fights. Territories are generally in clearings towards the base of a hill, especially on the edges of sun-drenched shrubs that jut out into sheltered recesses. In woods, there is a strong preference to perch at the junction of two ridings, or in small sunny hollows near recent clearings. Each perch is used by a sequence of males throughout the season and, very often, from one year to the next. Here the male perches for long periods on a leaf, with wings half open, pointing backwards towards the sun, ever on the alert for any passing creature. A highly pugnacious butterfly, it soars up to engage any passing insect in prolonged, violent flights. But courtship itself is minimal, with none of the elegant behaviour patterns seen in the Browns and Vanessids.

### EGG-LAYING

Females are more elusive than males, and are generally seen only when laying eggs. This involves fluttering a few centimetres above the undergrowth in a series of jerky hops, punctuated by short glides. It is often said that neither sex visits flowers, but this is untrue: I have seen them several times on the blooms of hawthorn *(Crataegus monogyna),* and Matthew Oates, the country's expert on this butterfly, reports that buttercups *(Ranunculus spp.)* and other yellow flowers are also visited.

Duke of Burgundy eggs are laid on the undersurfaces of *Primula* leaves, with primrose *(Primula vulgaris)* used mainly in woodland, and cowslip (*P. veris*) in scrubby grassland. Extraordinary care is taken to choose a plant that is growing in a precise situation which, once one realizes this, makes the delightful glassy eggs very easy to find.

Both primrose and cowslip need warm, bare ground for their seedlings to germinate, and are often abundant in the year or two after a woodland is cleared, or on downland that is heavily trampled by cattle in winter – hence the name "cow-slip". However, they live a good many years, during which time it is common for them to become swamped by regenerating shrubs, or by tall, abandoned grassland. Eventually, they persist as anaemic non-flowering plants, whose large flabby leaves lie limply on the shaded ground, waiting for the next clearing to occur.

The female Duke of Burgundy invariably selects a *Primula* about halfway through this succession. In scrubby grassland, she chooses the widest and lushest green leaves of large flowering plants, preferring vigorous cowslips that are half-shaded by an encroaching shrub or tussock, yet not so swamped as to prevent the large vertical leaves from protruding above the sward. This is an unusual growth-form on most downs, where cowslips generally occur in more open patches of turf, and have a tight rosette of small, oval leaves that lie flat against the ground. However, the butterfly invariably avoids these, as it does heavily shaded plants with lank, limp leaves. Exactly the same is true of woodland primroses: almost all eggs are laid on the largest leaves of the flowering clumps.

When laying, the female Duke of Burgundy perches on the top of a leaf and reaches around below with her abdomen. The eggs are conspicuous glassy spheres, usually laid in groups of two to four, although up to 10 can be found together, and there may well be two egg-batches per plant. They are an attractive, opaque creamy-yellow when laid, developing a curious criss-cross pattern of lines shortly before hatching, caused by the long black hairs of the little caterpillar being visible through the transparent shell.

## FEEDING AND HIBERNATION

Duke of Burgundy eggs hatch after one to three weeks, and the tiny caterpillar crawls to the base of the stem. It rests in this position by day, emerging at night to rasp deep grooves in the fleshy *Primula* leaf. The damage it causes is quite distinctive, especially when the caterpillar grows older, for it eats large holes, leaving the veins intact until the leaf looks like a moth-eaten blanket. The final-stage caterpillar is a particularly voracious feeder, and can be found on warm July evenings after dusk if you search likely primroses and cowslips by torchlight. After six weeks of feeding, the fully grown caterpillar deserts its foodplant and forms a hairy, speckled chrysalis in dry nooks,

such as 30 to 60 cm. (1 to 2 ft.) up in the heart of a tussock of fine grass, among chalk scree, or even in the empty cases of beech nuts. Although it remains there throughout the winter, the chrysalis is extremely hard to find. It is, however, easily bred in captivity, which is well worth doing, for this is a delightful species in all its stages.

## SURVIVAL IN THE SOUTH

The Duke of Burgundy is, alas, a disappearing species that is now largely confined to central southern England. Although genuinely rare in most regions, typical small colonies are often overlooked, and it is worth searching any woodland clearing or downland coombe containing suitable *Primula* plants. On downland, the butterfly is best located by searching sheltered north-facing slopes, concentrating on the base of the hill, where the soil is slightly thicker and the cowslips less prone to summer drought. In woods, areas that have been cleared three to five years previously, and then left to grow, are the most promising.

The majority of colonies are confined to very small areas of their woods. Typical sites today are where a new plantation has been made on an ancient woodland site, while in the past the butterfly thrived on coppiced woods, coming into plots as they became slightly overgrown for Fritillaries, then moving on to another, a year or two later. Woodland colonies can be quite large for a brief period after an extensive plantation has been made. In Grovely Woods, near Salisbury, there were scores of this species in 1989, thriving a five-year-old plantation.

Such colonies are short-lived and unusual. Most are much smaller, concentrated mainly in woods and sheltered valleys in the Cotswolds and on Salisbury Plain. The Duke of Burgundy is still just common enough for one to expect to find a colony in a suitable-looking habitat in both these regions. It is much rarer elsewhere. A scattering of colonies exists along the South and North Downs of Kent, Sussex, and Surrey, and perhaps a dozen survive in Hampshire, including one very large population on the nature reserve at Knor Hill. There is a similar number of colonies in Dorset, mainly on the northeastern chalk, and three or four in Somerset. The only other real concentration is in the Chilterns, but these populations are also sadly diminished.

Other colonies survive in the larger woods around Oxford, and further north on the same clays in parts of Rockingham Forest, near Peterborough. These are perhaps the only populations left that are not on chalk or limestone. Apart from them, there is a small cluster of colonies in Cumbria, north of Morecambe Bay, and another on the North Yorkshire Wolds, where again it is represented on nature reserves. These offer the best hope for a butterfly that is already extinct in Scotland, Wales, East Anglia, and most of northern England.

# DUKE OF BURGUNDY · *Hamearis lucina*

## LIFE-CYCLE

| | JAN | FEB | MAR | APR | MAY | JUN | JUL | AUG | SEP | OCT | NOV | DEC |
|---|---|---|---|---|---|---|---|---|---|---|---|---|
| EGG | | | | | | ▓ | | | | | | |
| CATERPILLAR | | | | | | ▓ | ▓ | ▓ | | | | |
| CHRYSALIS | ▓ | ▓ | ▓ | ▓ | ▓ | | | ▓ | ▓ | ▓ | ▓ | ▓ |
| ADULT | | | | | ▓ | ▓ | | | | | | |

**Male upperside**
Both sexes have spots around all wing edges.

**Male underside**
The forelegs of the male are reduced and not used for walking.

**Female upperside**
Orange markings in the female are generally brighter than in the male.

**Female underside**
Both sexes have two bands of white marks on the underwings.

**Colour variant**
Markings may be more heavy on some individuals.

NEWLY LAID EGG

EGG PRIOR TO HATCHING

**Egg [x22]**
As the egg develops, the hairs of the young caterpillar may be seen through the shell.

**Egg-laying**
Small groups of eggs may be laid on the same leaf by different females.

**Chrysalis [x2¼]**
Formed in vegetation or on the ground; lasts for nine months.

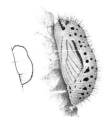

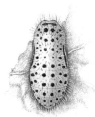

SIDE VIEW

VIEW FROM ABOVE

**Perching male**
Males spend much of their week-long lives defending territories against rivals.

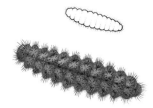

**Caterpillar [x2¼]**
Feeds nocturnally on the leaves of *Primula* spp., leaving distinctive damage.

# WHITE ADMIRAL

*Ladoga camilla*

THE WHITE ADMIRAL is a very special butterfly, beloved by naturalists from England to Japan. It has an elegance unmatched by other species, and strange but attractive young stages. It is, moreover, one of our few butterflies that is on the increase. Although still scarce enough to arouse excitement, it is not so rare that every locality is protected and known.

## COLOUR FORMS

No book can completely do justice to the White Admiral's dainty movements, or convey the character of a creature so ideally suited to gliding in and out of dappled shade among the branches of mature woodlands. The undersides are particularly beautiful and, seen close to, there is no other butterfly with which this can be confused. Hopeful beginners sometimes mistake high-flying adults for the Purple Emperor *(see p.117)*, but the White Admiral is considerably smaller, has a silhouette of rounded rather than pointed wings, and a graceful, flitting flight. It hugs the contours of the woodland canopy instead of rising higher and battling with the breezes above the tree-tops.

Adult White Admirals do not have constant markings: there are two named varieties which, although never common, are encountered in some years with reasonable frequency, and in certain woods more than in others. One of these is the *obliterae* form, in which the white markings are considerably reduced. The other is the scarcer *nigrina* variety in which the upperwings are universally black. Both types can be obtained by chilling captive chrysalises in a refrigerator, and it is possible that they are produced in the wild from caterpillars that pupate in low-lying frost pockets.

## LIFE IN THE CANOPY

There is just one brood of White Admirals a year, beginning in late June after a warm spring and usually reaching a peak in the second or third weeks of July, with tattered adults lasting well

***Distribution** Has spread to reoccupy many former sites in the past 50 years. Mainly seen in large woods, especially in Hampshire, Sussex, and Surrey.*

into August. It is essentially a woodland butterfly, and the adults are normally seen in ones and twos. This is not to say that it has small populations, rather that the adults are somewhat elusive, and spend much of their lives on the canopy, where they bask on oak leaves and drink aphid honeydew. Some, however, are attracted to ground level, where they cluster on the blossoms of bramble *(Rubus fruticosus)* in sunny rides, or sip at water or the dissolved salts in dung, from about 9.30 to 10.30 a.m.

Both sexes have a swift and elegant flight, consisting of minor whirrings of the wings punctuated by long, graceful glides. Their manoeuvrability is remarkable. Barrett, the famous entomologist, described this better than anyone nearly a century ago: "This special grace seems to arise from the habit of the insect of sweeping down over the trees to near the ground, then rising a little, gliding into every opening, taking the curves of the branches and high bushes with the perfection of ease, sweeping rapidly away, or soaring over the trees, to return in a few minutes to the same spot."

The males, especially, seem to soar in this way, launching themselves off large trees and other vantage points in sunny glades and rides. The females are more retiring and circumspect, especially when immature, and their matings seldom seen. These, I am told, occur out of sight in late afternoon high up on the woodland canopy.

## EGG-LAYING

Fat, fecund females descend to ground level, where they flutter slowly through shadier woodland, searching for spindly growths of honeysuckle *(Lonicera periclymenum)* on which to lay their eggs. They choose those straggly, trailing wisps that dangle in the half-light around a tree-trunk or beneath a bough, that clamber in the vegetation overhanging ditches, or weave through the shrubs bordering rides. Each female lays very quickly once she has found a suitable spot. She alights with a

# WHITE ADMIRAL · *Ladoga camilla*

LIFE-CYCLE

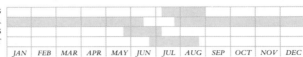

| | JAN | FEB | MAR | APR | MAY | JUN | JUL | AUG | SEP | OCT | NOV | DEC |
|---|---|---|---|---|---|---|---|---|---|---|---|---|
| EGG | | | | | | | | | | | | |
| CATERPILLAR | | | | | | | | | | | | |
| CHRYSALIS | | | | | | | | | | | | |
| ADULT | | | | | | | | | | | | |

**Male upperside**
Slightly smaller than female, with
forewings more pointed.

**Male underside**
Patterning of both sexes is similar
on upper- and underside.

**Female**
Females are most easily seen when they
descend to ground level to lay eggs.

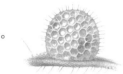

**Egg [x15]**
Hairy, with a shell
divided into cells; laid
singly on honeysuckle leaves.

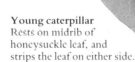

**Young caterpillar**
Rests on midrib of
honeysuckle leaf, and
strips the leaf on either side.

**Colour variant**
Aberrant form *obliterae,* in which
the white bands are obscured.

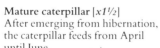

**Mature caterpillar [x1½]**
After emerging from hibernation,
the caterpillar feeds from April
until June.

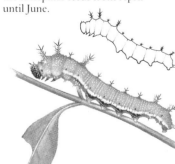

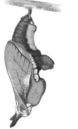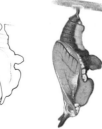

SIDE VIEW    VIEW FROM ABOVE

**Chrysalis [x1½]**
Suspended from a pad of orange
silk attached to a stem or leaf.

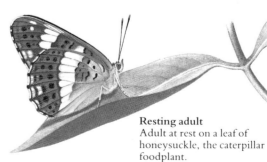

**Resting adult**
Adult at rest on a leaf of
honeysuckle, the caterpillar
foodplant.

flutter sideways onto the leaf, then arches her abdomen until it touches the opposite edge, and finally glues a single glassy green egg to its upper surface.

White Admiral eggs have a curious cellular shell with projecting hairs, and look rather like minute sea-urchins. They are fairly easy to find, and last one or two weeks before hatching. The young caterpillar is even simpler to spot, and is probably the easiest stage in which to find this butterfly. It feeds, sometimes as late as October, by nibbling the egg-leaf back at right-angles from the tip, but leaving the midrib intact and projecting. It rests for most of the day on the far tip of the midrib, a tiny, crusty brown object, hidden on a silk "faecal cushion" that is adorned with its droppings, with further knobs of excrement trapped in a skein of silk over its back. This unsavoury disguise is abandoned after a week or two, when the little caterpillar sits exposed on its midrib.

As autumn progresses, each caterpillar manufactures a shelter, called a hibernaculum, out of the honeysuckle leaf, and in this it spends the winter. It first fastens the stalk to the stem with silk, to prevent the leaf being shed, and then chews off the outer two-thirds of the leaf, before folding the remainder over the midrib.

The small caterpillar emerges to resume feeding in spring, resting at first on the base of rosettes of sprouting leaves, where its spiny brown body is well camouflaged against the leaf-scales. It turns green after the final moult, and is extraordinarily hard to spot as it rests, with head and tail end raised in a curve, on a tender honeysuckle leaf. The chrysalis is even more beautiful, and hangs suspended like a half-dead leaf, twisted and beginning to brown, and bedewed with beads of water or rain. It is not difficult to find, dangling beneath the honeysuckle on which it has recently fed. It hatches after two to three weeks.

## NUMBERS AND CLIMATE

Little was known about the ecology of this lovely butterfly, until Ernie Pollard studied the colony in Monks Wood, Cambridgeshire, in the 1970s. He found there was one key period in the life-cycle that determined whether numbers would be high or low in any year. This hinged mainly on the weather in June: large quantities of both chrysalises and larger caterpillars are devoured by birds, but in warm seasons these periods are short, so fewer are killed. Conversely, in cool summers they remain vulnerable for very much longer, and only a few survive.

Pollard's research, coupled with the known egg-laying preferences of the females, does much to explain the extraordinary fluctuations in this species over the centuries. When first recorded, it was quite widely distributed in southern England, extending as far north as Lincolnshire. It was, however, distinctly local in most counties – for example, only four colonies were known in Dorset in all the years up to 1913. It was plentiful enough in some large woods, notably the New Forest, but only in the major timber-growing areas is it likely that conditions were shady enough for breeding. The White Admiral does not thrive in freshly cut coppices, the condition of most woods in Victorian days and before.

## AN EXPANDING HABITAT

A sharp contraction of range occurred in the second half of the nineteenth century, perhaps partly due to the very cool summers in some of those decades, and by the early years of this century, its status was at an all-time low. But a very much happier state of affairs was soon to follow. During the present century, commercial coppicing virtually ceased, and a great many broadleaved woods and old coppices were neglected or left to grow mature timber crops. Although the sun-loving Fritillaries rapidly disappeared, the woods, in many places, provided ideal breeding grounds for this insect of partial shade. Moreover, the massive new conifer plantations of the past 50 years, although rightly deplored by all naturalists, nevertheless also provide good breeding conditions for White Admirals, albeit for a shortish period in their middle age, when the trees are beginning to close up, but before the woodland floor is cast into deep shade.

The White Admiral responded swiftly to capitalize on this increase in habitat, at least in certain parts of the country. By 1942, White Admirals had reached northwards to Lincolnshire, and had more or less reoccupied their former range. The spread in other directions has been more gradual. Although in Dorset colonies were reported to be steadily increasing in 1913 to 1923, by the 1950s, only 47 new sites had been located, with just one in its current stronghold, the Blackmoor Vale. By the late 1970s and early 1980s, however, we found the butterfly in about 100 distinct localities, and it still seems to be spreading westward.

This is not to say that the White Admiral has done nothing but expand in recent decades. Numbers have been very low in some years – notably those with cool summers – and it is probably already being shaded out of certain conifer plantations as these mature. Further losses from plantations are likely in the future, but happily the butterfly's fate seems secure in many southern broadleaved woods and coppices. It is certainly quite widespread today, to be found in almost every slightly shaded wood of any size from Dorset to Kent and as far north as Oxford, with many scattered but more localized colonies in Devon, Somerset, Gloucestershire, the southern Midlands, and East Anglia. This, altogether, represents a most heartening turnaround, and some slight recompense for the loss of most sun-loving butterflies from our English woodlands.

# PURPLE EMPEROR

*Apatura iris*

THERE ARE FEW greater thrills for any naturalist than to stand beneath an oakwood in high summer and watch male Purple Emperors soaring and wheeling above the canopy. They are large, pugnacious butterflies, that glide effortlessly through the air with short flicks of their wings, flashing every shade of purple in the sun. But spectacular though they may be, these are also scarce and elusive insects. Only seldom does the casual naturalist see one, even in its strongholds of south Wiltshire and the western Weald.

### THE "NOBLE FLY"

The combination of beauty, rarity, and elusiveness quickly elevated the Purple Emperor to become a great prize among early lepidopterists. Butterfly literature is littered with hyperbole about "this noble Fly" and "Royal Game". And understandably so, for no one forgets his or her first sighting of this creature, or can fail to be delighted by its young stages. Moses Harris, in the eighteenth century, was more restrained than most when he wrote of his "unspeakable pleasure" on having received three caterpillars from "an ingenious Aurelian", and when the then unknown chrysalises hatched out as Purple Emperors. Later, in Victorian times, the Rev. Morris, as usual, was less inhibited in his enthusiasm. This extract is from two pages of suitably purple prose that were devoted to the capture of his first three specimens:

"The 19th of July, 1852, must ever be the most memorable one... for on that day did I first see the Emperor on his throne – the monarch of the forest clothed in his imperial purple... One! two!! three!!! 'Allied Sovereigns'... I hope that Her Gracious Majesty *[Queen Victoria]* has no more profoundly loyal subject than myself, and I may therefore relate that, while plotting and planning 'an infernal machine' against His Imperial Majesty's liberty and life... in the shape of a fifty-foot net, and without any reference therefore to what is now going on in France, or any allusion to the career of Louis Napoleon, my toast that

*Distribution A scarce and elusive woodland species that is often overlooked. Mainly found in Hampshire and the western Weald.*

evening after dinner was (with as much sincerity as in the minds of the French), 'Vive l'Empereur'." There was no incongruity to the mind of a Victorian collector about his love of this butterfly on the one hand and his very strong desire to catch and kill it on the other. "You can't think how I put my whole soul into egg and butterfly collecting when I'm at it, and how I boil over with impotent rage at not being able to attain the object of my desires", wrote Frederick Courtney Selous when rain had prevented him from collecting Purple Emperors, some years before he found fame both as a big-game hunter and as the prototype of Alan Quatermaine. "I... raced across and took him easily. Strange to say, as soon as I had caught him, I felt a pang of sorrow I hadn't got *two*", wrote another Victorian on catching his first Emperor.

But most that was written concerned methods of catching this butterfly. Of particular interest were the respective merits of using a long-handled net to sweep males one by one off their favoured perching posts, or of capitalizing on their love of putrid flesh and excreta by luring them down. For it was soon discovered that, in some years at least, male Purple Emperors descended to gamekeeper's gibbets, and could "easily be captured while enjoying the luxurious juices of a dead cat, stoat or a rabbit, or of a seething mass of pig's dung". There was much discussion about the allure of different baits. It was generally held that fox and dog droppings were much superior to those of deer and horse, and a large number of male Emperors was caught in this way.

### HONEYDEW, SAP, AND SALTS

Butterfly collecting has now largely been replaced by watching and photography, but even in its heyday it is unlikely to have inflicted serious harm on this particular species. For it is impossible to catch more than a small proportion of a population, and the adult Purple Emperor is sufficiently mobile to spread back from one wood to the next. It is not, however, a migrant or a vagrant. Rather, a single colony usually breeds over a very large area of land, which encompasses several woods and copses.

Adult Purple Emperors emerge from the first week of July onwards and survive well into August. Although they hatch at extremely low densities, the sexes soon meet through flying to the highest point in the neighbourhood, where the males establish territories.

Mating occurs in the afternoon, leaving the morning and early evening free for other activities. Neither sex ever visits flowers, but instead drinks the aphid honeydew that coats many broadleaved trees in summer. Honeydew is no more than the partly digested sap of plants; both male and female Purple Emperors will also fly long distances to major bleeds, where sap weeps and congeals over damaged tree-trunks and branches.

Only the males descend to feed on other matter. This mainly occurs in the morning, especially between 10 and 11 a.m. Their love of dung and rotting flesh has been described, although they are by no means always attracted to these. I have more often found males drinking dew along rides or nearby roads, from which they probably obtain vital salts. Puddles are a particular attraction, especially during dry weather, causing them to probe deep into the mud with their strong, yellow probosces. This is a sight worth searching for in our better Emperor woods for, although you are unlikely to find more than one individual a morning, it usually drinks for several minutes before taking off, and is always extraordinarily tame.

## COLOURS BY REFRACTION

Mud-puddling males drink with closed wings if the sun is bright, displaying beautiful undersides with an eye-spot and pattern in the outer half that must look frighteningly like a predatory bird, such as a hobby, to any smaller bird hopping near it on a tree-top. But in weak light the wings are held open, exposing their purple sheen. This is usually shown over the whole wing in illustrations, but in the wild the wings often appear black, or have just a small portion gleaming purple. For it is only when light refracts through the scales at certain angles that this glorious colour appears. The exact tint varies with the intensity of light and with the angle of the wing to the sun. Males battling high above the canopy in strong sunshine emit a cascade of purple flashes that is unforgettable to anyone who has been in a suitable vantage point to see it.

Male Emperors take to the air from about 11 a.m. onwards. They first indulge in comparatively low-level soaring in and out of the upper branches of trees. Large distances are covered in the process, and they often move from one wood to the next, if possible flying along tall hedgerows and shelter belts. They

gradually ascend as they fly, and by noon begin to gather in the highest-lying woodland in the neighbourhood, often, but not always, on the summit of a hill. There they establish territories high up on prominent trees. One tree in particular is always occupied throughout the season and year after year. This is the so-called "master tree" or "master oak", which in reality can be of any species.

## MASTER TREES

There is a considerable mystique about master trees, much of it summarized in a fascinating book, *Notes and Views of the Purple Emperor,* by Heslop, Hyde, and Stockley. Many conflicting claims have been resolved in recent years thanks to the patient observations of Ken Willmott, on which much of this account is based. It was widely believed, for example, that no colony of Purple Emperors could survive the felling of its master tree. This is certainly not the case, but there may be a grain of truth in that the males possibly move to a different wood in the neighbourhood if there is no focal tree left to attract them.

Everyone who knows this butterfly well has their own favourite master tree, which is often a closely guarded secret. The earliest collectors soon learned that not only is the same tree used every year, but that particular branches or even leaf clumps are always occupied. These are usually on the edge near the top, where the males can perch with wings half open, facing outwards and slightly downwards, ready to launch themselves after females or intruders. Silver-washed Fritillaries are rapidly seen off, but the battles with rival males are remarkable. The combatants climb high into the sky, clashing their wings and flashing purple all the while.

Males also swoop down to investigate other shiny objects, and are well known for "attacking" car windscreens that gleam upwards in the sun. I was myself once the object of attack in a glade beneath a master oak in Surrey. I was wearing a white wind-cheater at the time, and a male immediately descended to fly in tight circles around my chest, encircling me four or five times before soaring back to his perch. It was a memorable experience, for the sun was shining quite brightly and the colours that accompanied every wing-beat were breathtaking when seen so close.

Each male occupies the same perch all afternoon, although he regularly abandons it to make brief circuits around the tree-top or wood. But if he disappears for too long from a key point, another male soon arrives to take his place. This, too, was known to early collectors. Barrett, for example, wrote a century ago of a "Mr. Tugwell *[who]* has taken half a dozen in succession from the same branch, and has known dozens to be secured from it in different years."

# PURPLE EMPEROR · *Apatura iris*

LIFE-CYCLE

| | JAN | FEB | MAR | APR | MAY | JUN | JUL | AUG | SEP | OCT | NOV | DEC |
|---|---|---|---|---|---|---|---|---|---|---|---|---|
| EGG | | | | | | | | | | | | |
| CATERPILLAR | | | | | | | | | | | | |
| CHRYSALIS | | | | | | | | | | | | |
| ADULT | | | | | | | | | | | | |

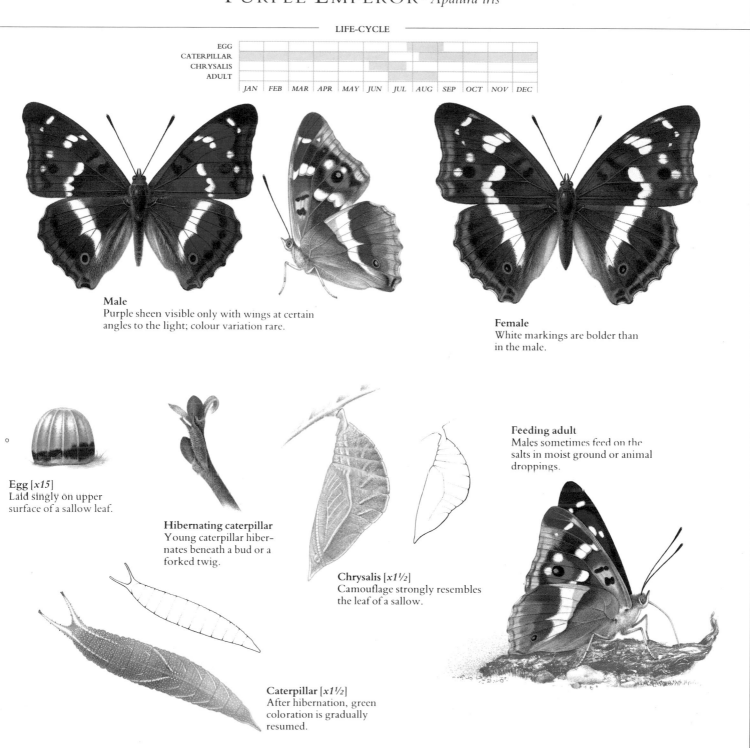

**Male**
Purple sheen visible only with wings at certain angles to the light; colour variation rare.

**Female**
White markings are bolder than in the male.

**Egg [*x15*]**
Laid singly on upper surface of a sallow leaf.

**Hibernating caterpillar**
Young caterpillar hibernates beneath a bud or a forked twig.

**Chrysalis [*x1½*]**
Camouflage strongly resembles the leaf of a sallow.

**Feeding adult**
Males sometimes feed on the salts in moist ground or animal droppings.

**Caterpillar [*x1½*]**
After hibernation, green coloration is gradually resumed.

117

The female Purple Emperor is much more elusive than the male. She lacks his purple colour and skulks among the tree-tops, seldom being seen even when egg-laying. On her first morning of adulthood, she also flies gradually towards the highest point in the neighbourhood, ending up at the master tree if she has not already been accosted *en route*. She receives immediate attention there, and, if receptive, leads the male to a suitable platform for mating, high above the canopy and often several hundred metres from the master tree.

### EGG-LAYING

After mating, the females disperse throughout the woods and copses of their breeding sites in search for sallows *(Salix* spp.*)* on which to lay. They are pestered by males when they fly over high ground, but elude these by drifting straight down to the ground. The male spirals around a female as she falls, but soon loses interest and regains his perch, leaving the female to resume her search. The eggs are laid mainly on the broad, shiny leaves of goat sallow *(Salix capraea),* although the narrower leaves of common sallow *(S. cinerea)* are also often used. Certain types of tree are much preferred. These are always in accessible situations in woods, such as on the edges of rides and glades, or in the undulating canopy of a fairly young plantation. The females also strongly prefer comparatively large sallows, and above all seek trees that are partly, but not entirely, shaded. Many that are chosen are on the north side of a clearing. Few sallows fit these criteria, and the females fly swiftly through the shaded branches hunting them out.

Once she has found a suitable sallow, a female "strikes" the tree (as old collectors used to say) by flying at it and disappearing deep inside. Perhaps a dozen eggs will then be laid, singly and well spaced on the upperside of shaded leaves, usually near the crown of the tree. The great majority are laid above eye-level. The long hours spent searching for the eggs are repaid when you eventually find one, for they are highly attractive, each resembling, as one Danish naturalist wrote, a rum pudding. Although the egg is green when first laid, it soon develops a purple band around the base, and hatches after about 10 days. The tiny caterpillar then crawls to the tip of its sallow leaf and sits facing inwards towards the stalk.

### EARLY DEVELOPMENT

Caterpillars adopt the same position on a leaf for the rest of their lives. They are extraordinarily well camouflaged after the first moult, when an attractive pair of horns appears. At first they nibble the edges of the leaf beside them, causing characteristic damage that is quite easy to recognize in late summer. By early November, they make their second skin change and soon turn a

A SHORTENED SHADOW
*The caterpillar rests with the front half of its body raised in the air. This reduces its silhouette from below, and increases the chances of escaping the notice of predators.*

muddy brown. It is at this time that they desert the leaf for the winter, to hibernate on a pad of silk spun over the crotch of a forked branch, where again they are extremely well camouflaged.

Caterpillars resume feeding in spring, first on expanding leaf-tips, but adopting the characteristic perch at the tip, which is shown above, once the leaves are large enough to support them. Then, early in June, each crawls some distance from its "seat leaf", and forms a beautifully camouflaged pale chrysalis beneath the undersurface of a leaf.

### EMPEROR WOODS TODAY

Scattered colonies of Purple Emperor once occurred in the more wooded districts of Wales, East Anglia, Cambridgeshire, south Lincolnshire, and Kent, but the species has declined in the present century, and is probably now extinct in all these counties. It still survives in a few woods in the West Country, and in Dorset, Northamptonshire, and Nottinghamshire. However, the stronghold is central southern England. The extensive breeding grounds here encompass virtually every wood and copse in the western Weald, including many on the Surrey sandstones and chalk, in addition to the famous populations on Wealden clay. The species is not, of course, uniformly abundant throughout this area, but nevertheless breeds almost everywhere where suitable sallows exist. This includes many conifer plantations for the first 20 years or so after planting.

The populations of the west Weald are matched by those of east Hampshire, where again the butterfly can be found in almost every large wood or heavily wooded district. This area extends to the New Forest, although numbers are extremely low there, as has always been the case. Far superior are the woods a little way to the north, around the southern and western borders of Salisbury. These currently support some of the highest densities of Purple Emperor in the country, and there are several spots where one can guarantee to see the males. Fortunately, one of the largest populations in this region breeds in a vast nature reserve, where the requirements of the Purple Emperor are a key feature of the management policy. Finally, there is at least one fine population northeast of Oxford, extending well into Buckinghamshire, which breeds in the combination of conifer plantations and deciduous woods that form the sadly transformed remnants of Bernwood Forest.

# PAINTED LADY

## *Cynthia cardui*

THE PAINTED LADY is one of the world's most successful butterflies. It breeds mainly in warm, arid habitats, has no hibernating stage in its life-cycle, and its caterpillar perishes at temperatures lower than about 5°C (41°F). As a result, there is probably no place in Europe where this species is permanently resident, and yet in most summers, it is one of the commonest butterflies over much of the Continent.

European Painted Ladies stem mainly from breeding grounds around the desert edges of North Africa and Arabia, where vast numbers emerge in most years. These teem northwards across the Continent, reaching some part of the British Isles every year, and the Orkneys roughly two or three times a decade. In exceptional summers they penetrate far above the Arctic Circle, over 3,000 km. (2,000 miles) north of the winter breeding grounds. Whether this occurs in one flight, or over several generations, is unknown.

Similar migrations occur in all other continents except South America, leading to the unattractive alternative name of the "Cosmopolitan Butterfly" in the U.S.A. Less appealing still is "Junkbug", a derisory name given it by American collectors, reflecting the extraordinary abundance of this butterfly in some years. It was estimated, for example, that one Californian swarm contained 3,000 million adults. European names have been more flattering. Apart from an abortive experiment with the "Thistle" in the eighteenth century, the butterfly has been known as the Painted Lady or "Papilio Bella Donna" in Britain since 1699, "Belladonna" historically in Scandinavia, and "La Belle Dame" in France.

As can be seen from the illustration on p.121, the Painted Lady is quite distinctive. Aberrations such as the ones we show are rather rare, although beginners might note that the normal butterfly varies considerably in size – probably due to malnourishment as a caterpillar – and in its background colour. When newly emerged, the butterfly's wings are suffused with a beautiful fresh salmon-pink, but they fade to a jaded orange-brown as

*Distribution A regular immigrant. Usually common throughout lowland England and Wales; found almost anywhere in its best years.*

the butterfly ages. This is due to the gradual oxidation of pigments, a reaction that is reversed if even the most decrepit individual is exposed to chlorine in the laboratory.

### DEPARTURE AND ARRIVAL

There is still much to be learned about the migrations of this insect. Few observations have been made of the beginnings of these great journeys. One of the best occurred in the desert beside the Dead Sea in 1869, when, according to C. B. Williams, a Mr. Skertchley "noticed that the whole mass of grass, through which they were riding on camels, was in a state of violent agitation although there was no wind. When he dismounted he discovered that the cause was the emergence from the chrysalis of myriads of Painted Lady butterflies, which dried their wings and about half an hour later flew off together eastwards towards the sea."

It will be noted that these butterflies swarmed before they had mated, and were all of exactly the same age. What triggers such migrations is not clear, although some insects are known to have a switch in their behaviour that produces an irresistible urge to swarm when they occur above a certain density. It is equally unclear why Painted Lady swarms stop flying to settle, mate, and breed in a particular district. Possibly this occurs when they have reached a certain maturity and also encounter suitable land for breeding.

European migrations of the Painted Lady vary enormously in their size and flight-paths. In many years, vast numbers are seen streaming north across the Mediterranean, flying by day or night, flitting their wings powerfully and then gliding, so that they can rest on the wing. There have been many descriptions of these flights. Some occur at low densities on fronts that may be 150 km. (100 miles) wide; others in compact swarms, no more than 3 to 4.5 m. (10 to 15 ft.) across, making a continuous procession that can take several hours to pass. Although individual Painted Ladies fly at least a metre apart, the greatest flights cast a shadow over the ground and contain hundreds of thousands, even millions, of adults. Each moves northwards in spring, but seems less able to compensate for the wind than is the case, say, with the Red Admiral. Thus they may arrive in different parts of Britain at any time in spring and summer, depending on their exact point of origin and the prevailing wind direction they encounter on the way.

### LANDFALL IN BRITAIN

British immigrations of Painted Ladies generally contain much smaller numbers than the great continental swarms. They arrive as early as January or February in some years, when regular sightings are made along the south coast. It is more usual, however, for the main swarms to arrive in late May or June, often followed by further immigrations later in the summer, which mingle with the offspring of the early arrivals. The best documented immigrations occurred in 1980, when westerly winds first carried them on an anticyclone from Spain or North Africa, depositing large numbers in the Western Isles and west Wales. This was followed by another large immigration in late July, this time arriving on easterly winds all along the east coast of England and Scotland. These were probably the offspring of earlier flights to central and eastern Europe.

Southern England usually receives most of these immigrants. Having arrived, the butterflies fan out through the country and can be seen in any flowery habitat, although by far the greatest concentrations occur in dry, open places such as heaths, dunes, and downland. Each male soon establishes some form of territory, choosing a warm patch of bare ground, sand, or rock on which to settle. In weak sunshine he basks with wings spread wide, pressed firm against the dusty ground, and flies up to investigate any passing object. Females are courted with a zest that marks most of the Painted Lady's behaviour.

### A TENTED CATERPILLAR

Both sexes feed frequently on flowers. The females then disperse throughout the countryside in search of thistles on which to lay eggs. They lay on a wide range of species, but nevertheless have distinct favourites. Martin Warren describes how he found over 200 caterpillars on musk thistle *(Carduus nutans)* on the south Dorset Downs in 1985, but only one on spear thistle *(Cirsium vulgare),* and none on creeping thistle *(C. arvense),* both of which were abundant on the same sites. Other authors, however, name both spear and marsh thistles as the butterfly's favourites.

The Painted Lady occasionally lays on a wide range of different plants, including mallows *(Malva* and *Althaea* spp.*),* artichoke *(Cynara scolymus),* and nettles *(Urtica* spp.*).* Thus this is one of the few butterflies that can breed in intensive farmland in Britain, as even the best-kept farms often have the occasional thistle patch.

The small green egg is quite easy to find. Although laid singly, there may be several eggs per plant, mainly on the uppersides of the thistle leaves. Each hatches after about a week and the small caterpillar crawls to the undersurface of its leaf. Here it spins a pad of silk and feeds on the lower cuticle, leaving a silvery patch of epidermis above, which is also fairly easy to spot. It becomes very much more conspicuous as it grows, for it constructs a tent out of one or more folded leaves, fastened firmly by silk, and lives within this, eating all but the sturdiest ribs and spines. Successive tents are spun as it grows older, leaving very obvious abandoned quarters consisting of skeletons of spines, silk, and desiccated droppings. Finally, after its last skin moult, the caterpillar lives openly on its thistle, before forming a very beautiful, burnished chrysalis. This exists in two main colour forms, and lives suspended in a larger tent of vegetation, rather like that of a Red Admiral.

### PATTERNS OF IMMIGRATION

The egg, caterpillar, and chrysalis together last less than a month in warm weather, so several generations can occur in Britain in a hot year. This, together with the erratic immigrations, means that it is impossible to predict where and when Painted Ladies will be seen. As a general rule, they are less common than the Red Admiral but more common than the Clouded Yellow, although this is by no means invariably the case. Peak numbers are usually seen in July to September, but occur considerably later in some seasons. It is unknown whether British adults ever return south in autumn, although there is some evidence of this on the Continent. What is certain, however, is that the vast majority of caterpillars and chrysalises perish once the weather deteriorates, and probably the entire British population either dies or emigrates every winter. Thus we depend wholly on immigrants to replenish the British stocks every spring.

Fortunately, there is no sign that these influxes have abated. On the contrary, the recent status of the Painted Lady appears slightly better than in 1766, when Moses Harris wrote that "These Flies are not very common... yet there are particular Seasons when they are very plentiful, which happens once in about ten or twelve Years".

# PAINTED LADY · *Cynthia cardui*

## LIFE-CYCLE

| | JAN | FEB | MAR | APR | MAY | JUN | JUL | AUG | SEP | OCT | NOV | DEC |
|---|---|---|---|---|---|---|---|---|---|---|---|---|
| EGG | | | | | | | | | | | | |
| CATERPILLAR | | | | | | | | | | | | |
| CHRYSALIS | | | | | | | | | | | | |
| ADULT | | | | | | | | | | | | |

**Male upperside**
Background coloration fades
to dull orange as butterfly ages.

**Male underside**
Sexes are similarly marked on
both upper- and underwings.

**Colour variant**
Rare *rogeri* form, an extreme
example of aberration.

**Feeding adult**
Adults feed on a wide
variety of flowers,
including scabiouses,
as they roam.

**Egg** [*x22*]
Laid singly on a range of
foodplants, including
thistles and nettles.

**Chrysalis** [*x1½*]
Suspended under vegetation;
two main colour forms.

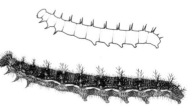

**Caterpillar** [*x1½*]
Solitary, living inside a
succession of tents made
of folded leaves.

**Parasitic wasp**
Small wasps, such
as this brachnonid
*Microgaster sub-
completus,* cause
the death of many
caterpillars.

# SMALL TORTOISESHELL

## *Aglais urticae*

THERE ARE FEW more common butterflies than the Small Tortoiseshell in the British Isles, and few that are held in greater affection. Except, that is, in Scotland, where it was once known as the "Devil's Butterfly" or, scarcely more flatteringly, as the "Witch's Butterfly". These unworthy names have long since disappeared, but some Scots continue in their singularity by calling it the "Red Admiral". The English, Welsh, and Irish names have been more constant: the "Tortoise-shell Fly" and "Nettle Tortoiseshell" are the only old variants that I have come across.

This is one of our loveliest butterflies, familiar to all who have gardens. The Small Tortoiseshell does vary slightly in size and appearance, depending on the temperature. Cool conditions result in unusually dusky individuals, very like the beautiful forms of Scandinavia; these are especially common in the north of Scotland after a cold summer. On the other hand, those emerging after hot summers tend to be brighter, with larger orange marks. These, and more bizarre forms, can easily be produced in captivity by rearing the chrysalises at different temperatures. Extremes are sometimes also found in the wild.

*Distribution A very common nomad that can be seen almost anywhere except on the highest mountain-tops and on the northernmost isles.*

### BROODS AND MIGRATIONS

Temperature and daylength also affect the number of adult emergences each year. There are usually two distinct broods in the south, one emerging in June and July, with their more numerous offspring appearing at any time from August to mid-October. The second brood goes into hibernation quite quickly, reappearing in the first warm days of spring to mate and breed, and often surviving well into May. However, after a cold, late spring, many first-brood (midsummer) adults also enter hibernation, saving their eggs for the following year. This tends to happen more frequently further north, and in Scotland there is usually just a single generation a year, emerging in July, hibernating and reappearing in March.

Adult Small Tortoiseshells do not live in distinct colonies but travel throughout the countryside, laying their eggs wherever suitable conditions are encountered. Typical adults move a kilometre or two a day, but some fly much further and even migrate across the English Channel. Migratory flights have been recorded in both directions; tired butterflies often rest on lighthouses up to 50 km. (30 miles) out to sea. F. W. Frohawk described one influx, coming from the southeast towards Swanage, Dorset, in August 1929. Although adults flew in singly, this went on for a week, and the eventual number of immigrants was considerable. Other large immigrations have been recorded, such as when hundreds of dead specimens were found off Flamborough Head in Yorkshire, but this is unusual. There is little doubt that the vast majority of our Small Tortoiseshells are resident, even on the remoter Scottish isles.

### FEEDING AND HIBERNATION

The behaviour of Small Tortoiseshells varies with the time of year. Those destined to hibernate are first preoccupied with feeding, which is why large numbers often gather in gardens from midsummer onwards, to gorge on nectar-rich buddleia (*Buddleia* spp.), valerian (*Centranthus* spp.), hebe (*Hebe* spp.), ice plant (*Sedum maximum*), and Michaelmas daisies (*Aster novae-belgii*). Much feeding also occurs on wild flowers, and adults gather in any habitat where these abound.

Having fed for several days, each adult looks for somewhere to hibernate. This is often in houses and outhouses, and many Small Tortoiseshells are thwarted by well-meaning but misguided householders who "rescue" them and release them outside. The exception is in modern, centrally heated houses, for the butterflies often awake when the heating comes on in the autumn, and waste vital fat reserves by fluttering around windows. Camouflaged underwings help to conceal the butterflies when they have entered hibernation.

# SMALL TORTOISEHELL · *Aglais urticae*

LIFE-CYCLE

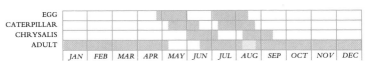

| | JAN | FEB | MAR | APR | MAY | JUN | JUL | AUG | SEP | OCT | NOV | DEC |
|---|---|---|---|---|---|---|---|---|---|---|---|---|
| EGG | | | | | | | | | | | | |
| CATERPILLAR | | | | | | | | | | | | |
| CHRYSALIS | | | | | | | | | | | | |
| ADULT | | | | | | | | | | | | |

**Female**
Aberrant *semi-ichnusoides* form produced by high temperatures during the pupal stage.

**Male**
The markings of both sexes are identical. Cool conditions produce duskier butterflies, which are seen particularly in northern Scotland.

**Male**
Aberrant *lutea* form.

GOLDEN FORM    BROWN FORM

**Parasitic fly [*x3*]**
The grub of the tachinid fly *Phryxe vulgaris* lives within the caterpillar, killing it before pupation.

**Egg [*x15*]**
Laid in large clusters; more than one female may lay eggs on the same leaf.

**Chrysalis [*x1½*]**
The colour varies from golden to brown, depending on the pupation site.

**Feeding adult**
Michaelmas daisy is a favourite nectar source in gardens in late summer.

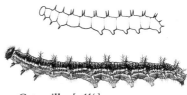

**Caterpillar [*x1½*]**
Bright colours warn that the body contains poisons. The amount of yellow and black is variable.

**Hibernating adult**
Camouflaged underwings conceal the butterfly during hibernation.

## COURTSHIP TERRITORIES

Adults awake in the first warm days of spring. Their behaviour is exactly the same as that of the summer-brood adults that go on to breed. At night, both sexes roost deep in nettle patches, where their dark underwings merge into the earthy background. Males become active around 10 a.m., and spend the next two hours flying through the countryside, with frequent pauses to feed and bask. This ceases around midday, after which they concentrate on mating. Each first establishes a territory, generally near a large nettle bed and almost always in a sheltered, sunny spot on the south-facing side of a hedge or wall. He then waits, basking on the ground, and soaring up to investigate every passing Small Tortoiseshell. Most turn out to be males, for there is considerable competition for perching places. Both spiral high into the air, then dive and ascend again, each striving to fly just behind and above his opponent. This is repeated until the intruding male flies off, leaving the victor to return to the exact spot he had left.

If, after 90 minutes, no female has flown past, the male abandons his post and sets up another territory, which he occupies until about 4 p.m. Any passing female is pursued at high speed, although it can take up to three hours before she succumbs. Mating finally occurs deep inside a nettle patch.

## THE SEARCH FOR EGG-SITES

Fertilized females spend the rest of their lives searching for egg-sites. As with most butterflies – and especially those that lay large egg-batches – great care is taken to choose the ideal plant. Common and annual stinging nettles (*Urtica dioica* and *U. urens*), are both used, but the Small Tortoiseshell has a strong preference for laying on young, tender plants that are growing in full sunshine on the edges of large nettle beds. There is generally no shortage of suitable sites in spring, but the summer emergence depends on a regrowth of young shoots, where patches were cut or grazed back earlier in the year.

Even in spring, the vast majority of nettles are rejected as unsuitable. This, sadly, includes almost all that are deliberately left or planted for the butterfly in gardens. These usually consist of small patches of nettle that are tolerated in a shady corner of the vegetable garden. But to be of any use to the butterfly, large clumps should be planted along the sunniest edges of garden beds, and some should be cut back in early June to produce tender regrowth in July.

Female Small Tortoiseshells congregate on suitable nettle beds, each laying 60 to 100 eggs at a time under the topmost leaf of an edge plant. They often choose leaves that have already been laid upon, and it is not unusual to find two females laying simultaneously on the same leaf. Vast clusters of up to a thousand eggs have been found, piled several deep and looking like green caviare. Once suitable nettles are known, it is quite easy to find these batches, but remember that the sting of young nettles is particularly fierce.

## SURVIVAL IN THE WILD

Small Tortoiseshell egg-batches hatch after 10 to 14 days, and the tiny caterpillars spin a dense web of silk over the growing leaf-tips. Large batches split into groups of about 200 each. They live communally within the web, emerging to bask and to eat. As each plant is defoliated, they spin new nests on adjoining nettles. Feeding damage is highly conspicuous, as are the nests of caterpillars themselves.

The caterpillars vary in colour from almost uniformly black to yellow with black spots, and are paler when young. Their bodies contain poisons, as well as spines in the later stages, and their colour serves as a warning of their toxicity. Most predators are alarmed by any animal with a black and yellow pattern, and the caterpillars' curious habit of jerking their heads in unison, when disturbed, perhaps acts as a further warning. These deterrents are enhanced by the presence of so many caterpillars together. However, they are by no means immune to attack by parasites: large numbers are often killed, either by ichneumon wasps or by tachinid flies.

The nests split up after the penultimate skin change, and each caterpillar lives alone for the remainder of its life. They are still easy to find as they bask on nettle leaves or devour the younger growth. The caterpillars disperse even further to pupate; chrysalises have been found 55 m. (60 yards) from the nearest nettles, generally suspended in a hedge or on a wall. They vary considerably in colour, ranging from lilac-pink washed with copper to dull brown, but all are beautiful. Unfortunately they are also highly vulnerable, and many are killed: birds are believed to be the main culprits.

Despite these enemies, the Small Tortoiseshell is thriving throughout the British Isles, and can be found in every type of habitat. There is no reason to believe that its numbers have declined in recent years. Even in East Anglia, where farmland is most heavily sprayed, their bodies have been found to contain insecticide residues, but only at one-hundredth of the danger level, and the butterfly remains common throughout the region.

The highest densities of Small Tortoiseshell occur on rich soils where nettles are abundant, but the butterfly is extremely well distributed and can be expected almost anywhere in the British Isles. It breeds on the smallest and remotest islands, and has been found at altitudes of 1,200 m. (4,000 ft.) on Scottish mountains, although the highest recorded breeding site was around 330 m. (1,100 ft.).

# LARGE TORTOISESHELL

*Nymphalis polychloros*

THIS SPLENDID Tortoiseshell mysteriously declined four decades ago, and is now our rarest indigenous butterfly. Indeed, I suspect that it is extinct as a British resident, and that most of the 120 or so sightings that have been made here since 1950 were either of specimens of the butterfly imported from the Continent or were misidentifications of other Vanessids. At best it is excessively rare – so much so that three times as many Camberwell Beauties and twice as many Monarchs have been seen in Britain during the past 40 years.

Such figures would have dismayed Victorian collectors, who regarded the Large Tortoiseshell as scarcely worth recording in wooded regions of the south. Edward Hulme, writing a century ago, is typically offhand: one "may sometimes come across a patch of spear-plume thistles in an open clearing in the wood, and here we shall probably find in plenty the Red Admiral, the Peacock and the Large Tortoiseshell." The really noteworthy Vanessid in those days was the Comma, a close relative of the Large Tortoiseshell whose increase this century *(see pp.134-136)* has been as remarkable as the latter's decline.

*Distribution An extreme rarity, once widely distributed in wooded regions of England and lowland Wales. Possibly now extinct as a resident.*

### COLONIES AND DISPERSAL

Like its close relatives, the Large Tortoiseshell is a mobile butterfly that flies through the countryside laying eggs wherever suitable conditions are encountered. There seem to have been more or less permanent colonies in the New Forest, Essex, and East Suffolk, but in general, it would appear in a particular district or wood, breed for a few years and perhaps become abundant, and then dwindle and disappear. This makes it hard to be certain that the species has entirely vanished as a resident, for there are no fixed sites where one can check on its occurrence.

The life of the Large Tortoiseshell most closely resembles that of the Peacock *(see pp.131-133),* with one generation of adults a year, emerging in July and August. Fresh adults are active in the morning and late afternoon, when they sup voraciously to build up reserves for a seven-month hibernation period. Like all Vanessids, they will visit garden flowers. They also share, with the Red Admiral and Camberwell Beauty, a passion for any sap bleeding from a wounded tree, and for the droplets of honeydew at the bases of leaves. At other times, they are hard to approach, and it takes a mere flit of their great tawny wings to send them soaring and gliding at high speed around the tree-tops. This elusiveness was well known to early collectors, who observed that "it requires nimbleness to take".

### COURTSHIP AND EGG-LAYING

Large Tortoiseshells hibernate a week or two after emergence, settling in dry piles of wood, garden sheds and, almost certainly, rotten holes in tree-trunks. They emerge the following spring to feed on the flowers of sallow *(Salix capraea),* and to bask on warm tree-trunks with wings held as wide apart as possible, reflexed backwards and pressing hard on the warm bark, as if to encircle the trunk. Females spend long periods in this pose, sitting head downwards, about 1 to 2 m. (3 to 6 ft.) up on trunks on the sunny side of a wood.

The Danish lepidopterist, H. J. Henriksen, gives a fine description of courtship. While the female basks on the trunk, the male at first hunts close to the ground, skimming above the surface with small flits of his wings. He glides between tree-trunks until he notices a female, whereupon he flutters up to within a few centimetres of her. She, however, flies off, with the male following perhaps 30 cm. (1 ft.) behind in a curiously sinuous flight. This can last several hours, but eventually mating occurs on a tree-trunk or under dead leaves on the forest floor.

Most Large Tortoiseshells mate in early April, and few survive the month. Having paired, females fly among the tree-tops searching for places to lay their large batches of eggs. In Britain, most are laid on the terminal twigs of elms *(Ulmus* spp.*),* particularly wych elm *(U. glabra),* sometimes along tall hedges or on suckering scrub, but more usually from 3 m. (10 ft.) up, and occasionally as high as the crown of a large tree. Sallows and willows are also often used as, more rarely, are poplars *(Populus* spp.*)* including aspen *(P. tremula),* birches *(Betula* spp.), wild cherry *(Prunus avium),* and pear *(Pyrus communis).* The eggs, which I have only seen in captivity, are most beautiful, being wrapped in a band of 100 to 200, completely encircling a young twig, and always on the sunny side of the tree.

## AN ARRAY OF DEFENCES

Large Tortoiseshell eggs hatch after two to three weeks, and the little caterpillars quickly spin a web of silk over the tender leaf-tips, which they chew in bouts of group-feeding. They remain together until fully grown, basking much of the time on their web. They are prickly even when small, and the full-grown caterpillar has a fearsome array of spines, each capable of piercing human skin. The large groups of caterpillars must be an unappetizing prospect for insect-eating birds, and they deter predators further by jerking their bodies in synchrony, making the whole web look like one twitching mass of spines, which is very disturbing to predators.

The webs of Large Tortoiseshells were once as easily found as the adults in many parts of southern England, and were one of the main ways that collectors obtained this species. It is ominous that there has not, to my knowledge, been a record of a nest of these caterpillars for nearly 40 years in Britain. This suggests that the few genuine records of adults emanate from escaped captive stock. It is still easy to collect webs in central Europe, and I know several people who have brought them back, and then tried to photograph the resultant adults in natural situations, only for these to escape. There have also been a number of deliberate releases.

Large Tortoiseshell caterpillars are generally fully grown by late June, when they leave their trees to form solitary chrysalises. These are situated on dead wood, such as on fences, wooden sheds, and probably among dry sticks. F. W. Frohawk describes how he watched the caterpillars drop off "the topmost branches of a lofty Elm", falling one after another to the ground, where they dispersed to search for pupation sites. I have again seen the chrysalis only in captivity: it is unspectacular, and must be hard to distinguish from a dead leaf in the wild.

## ABUNDANCE AND SCARCITY

On the Continent, as once in Britain, the Large Tortoiseshell is chiefly found in warm, sheltered, wooded districts, especially where elms, willows, poplars, or cherries are common. Although most frequent in woods, nests of caterpillars are also seen along avenues and tree-lined lanes, while adults can be found almost anywhere in years of abundance. The species has, however, always been subject to great fluctuations, which have yet to be satisfactorily explained. Long periods of absence or rarity are punctuated by shorter spells when the butterfly is locally common, and in occasional years, it builds up to an extraordinary abundance. This last happened in Britain in 1947-48.

In view of these fluctuations, and the almost migratory behaviour of the adults, it is difficult to tell just how widespread and common the Large Tortoiseshell once was. It has been recorded over the whole of southern Britain and the Midlands, and there are a few records extending up to Aberdeen, but none from Ireland. Although known to the earliest collectors, it was not thought particularly common, yet there were periods in the nineteenth century when it was comparatively abundant. Its strongholds were south Devon, the New Forest, Essex, east Suffolk, and Sussex, and here it could be extremely numerous in the outbreak years. Thus W.H. Harwood wrote in 1901 that caterpillars were "so excessively abundant in north Essex and on the southern side of the River Stour that I could have taken hundreds of broods had I required them".

There was then a period of about 40 years when the Large Tortoiseshell was distinctly scarce over most of southern England, although common enough still around Ipswich. Then, during the warm summers of the mid-1940s, there was one final build-up, and Large Tortoiseshells were again locally common, especially in southern East Anglia, Kent, Sussex, and the Isle of Wight. This revival lasted five years, before numbers suddenly dipped in 1949. The butterfly had virtually disappeared by the early years of the following decade.

Occasional genuine sightings are still made over wide areas of southern Britain, but there is no wood where one can expect, let alone guarantee, to see this butterfly. Most records are of solitary adults in a single year, although persistent sightings have been made over two or more years in north Wales, Buckinghamshire, Hampshire, West Sussex, and Wiltshire.

Although I strongly suspect that all genuine recent sightings have been of escaped or released continental stock, others believe that they are occasional immigrants from France. I remain to be convinced, because this is not a species that is picked up with other migrants coming ashore or flying around lightships. Furthermore, if this were an international migrant, one would have expected at least a few to have been recorded in Ireland during the periods of its greatest abundance.

One cannot be certain that it has disappeared however, nor that it will ever have a resurgence. However, this becomes less likely with every year that passes: there has never before been a period of low numbers anything like the current dearth.

# LARGE TORTOISESHELL · *Nymphalis polychloros*

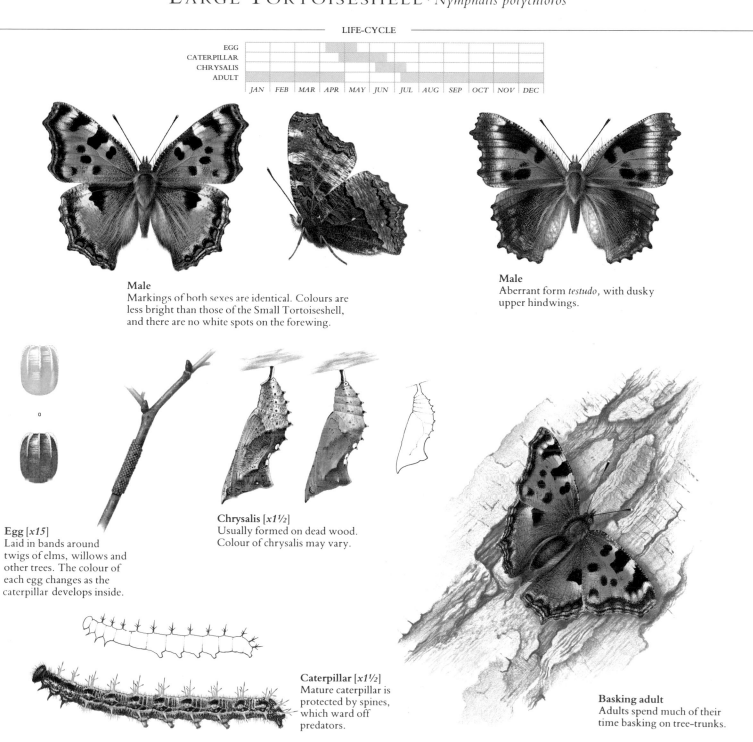

LIFE-CYCLE

| | JAN | FEB | MAR | APR | MAY | JUN | JUL | AUG | SEP | OCT | NOV | DEC |
|---|---|---|---|---|---|---|---|---|---|---|---|---|
| EGG | | | | | | | | | | | | |
| CATERPILLAR | | | | | | | | | | | | |
| CHRYSALIS | | | | | | | | | | | | |
| ADULT | | | | | | | | | | | | |

**Male**
Markings of both sexes are identical. Colours are less bright than those of the Small Tortoiseshell, and there are no white spots on the forewing.

**Male**
Aberrant form *testudo*, with dusky upper hindwings.

**Egg** [*x15*]
Laid in bands around twigs of elms, willows and other trees. The colour of each egg changes as the caterpillar develops inside.

**Chrysalis** [*x1½*]
Usually formed on dead wood. Colour of chrysalis may vary.

**Caterpillar** [*x1½*]
Mature caterpillar is protected by spines, which ward off predators.

**Basking adult**
Adults spend much of their time basking on tree-trunks.

127

# RED ADMIRAL

## *Vanessa atalanta*

THIS FAMILIAR INSECT is one of the largest and most magnificent butterflies in the countryside. It is not, however, a resident, and is killed in all but the mildest winters. Fortunately, large populations exist throughout central Europe, and migrants arrive in varying numbers each spring and summer to breed and spread. In good years, the Red Admiral reaches as far as the remotest Scottish isles and the highest mountain-tops. It is undoubtedly a powerful insect, with strong, expansive wings and a broad, robust thorax; however, it is still extraordinary to think that the black-and-scarlet butterfly seen gliding around the garden may already have flown halfway across the Continent.

### AN ANNUAL BUILD-UP

Little is known of the exact origins of British Red Admirals, even though the butterfly was the subject of some of the classic early studies of insect migration. It is generally believed to have two broods in Europe, and then to hibernate as an adult. This may well be true, but in Britain at least, there is little synchronization of broods such as occurs with the Small Tortoiseshell. Instead, there is a gradual build-up through the year, starting with rare sightings on warm February and March days, with real numbers being seen from May onwards, culminating in a peak during the autumn in late September and October.

Most early sightings are probably of individuals that successfully hibernate in Britain, although there are a few reports of very early immigrants as well. That this species can hibernate here has been demonstrated by several British naturalists, from F. W. Frohawk onwards. Unlike our other Nymphalid butterflies, the adults settle in exposed places, usually on tree-trunks or under branches, where the majority perish. Why so few survive is something of a mystery, for Red Admirals apparently overwinter in quite cold localities in central Europe, in contrast to the Painted Lady, which becomes restricted to frost-free regions in North Africa and the Mediterranean. In Spain, for

**Distribution** *A regular immigrant from southern Europe, common throughout the lowlands of England, Wales, and Ireland in most years.*

example, the Red Admiral is a resident species mainly in the Pyrenees, where winters are every bit as cold and as long as in Britain.

### ARRIVAL AND DEPARTURE

After hibernation, the adult Red Admiral has a strong urge to fly northwards. This lasts throughout May, June, and July, and brings varying numbers to Britain every year. Immigrants start laying almost immediately, but still spread northwards through the country, as do their offspring, and they are joined by fresh influxes from the Continent that last right through the summer. As a result, some adults reach Ireland and Scotland every year, and are often quite common there. It is usual to see a few individuals even in the Shetlands, while on the Continent they occasionally reach Lapland. From mid-August onwards, a change in behaviour takes place, and the Red Admirals start to return south. By mid-September, the traffic becomes more or less one-way. Nobody knows whether this is triggered by the diminishing length of the days, or whether it is simply an instinct of the final brood to emerge. Whatever the reason, the result is that large numbers sometimes gather along our southern coast in autumn. Some undoubtedly cross the Channel, but it is unclear how many make the attempt.

With so varied an origin, it is scarcely surprising that the number of Red Admirals fluctuates very markedly from one year to the next. In general, the species is commonest after a long, warm summer, and is sometimes very abundant indeed. I have never seen it more numerous than in 1989, when I could find 30 or 40 caterpillars within a few minutes in my garden throughout August and September, and see at least a dozen adults on my *Buddleia* every day. This, however, is nothing compared to the abundance that is occasionally reached. In October 1904, F. W. Frohawk saw up to 10 Red Admirals to the square yard, stretching over a mile of Sussex downland, all gorging on devil's-bit scabious (*Succisa pratensis*) to build up

# RED ADMIRAL · *Vanessa atalanta*

## LIFE-CYCLE

| | JAN | FEB | MAR | APR | MAY | JUN | JUL | AUG | SEP | OCT | NOV | DEC |
|---|---|---|---|---|---|---|---|---|---|---|---|---|
| EGG | | | | | | | | | | | | |
| CATERPILLAR | | | | | | | | | | | | |
| CHRYSALIS | | | | | | | | | | | | |
| ADULT | | | | | | | | | | | | |

**Male upperside**
Sexes are similarly marked on
both upper- and underwings.

**Male underside**
Brightly marked forewings contrast
with camouflaged hindwings.

**Colour variant**
Variation in the amount of red
and white occasionally occurs.

**Egg** [*x22*]
Laid singly on the
upper surface
of a leaf.

**Chrysalis** [*x1½*]
Normally formed within
the tent constructed by
the caterpillar.

**Feeding adult**
In late summer, adults are
attracted into gardens to
feed on flowers and
rotting fruit.

BLACK FORM

YELLOW FORM

**Caterpillar** [*x1½*]
Solitary, usually found
on nettles; lives within a
protective tent of leaves.

their resources before crossing the Channel, or settling down to hibernate. On the other hand, one might see one Red Admiral a week in a poor year in the south – still not exactly a rarity, but by no means a common insect either.

## ATTRACTING RED ADMIRALS INTO GARDENS

Not only are Red Admirals most numerous in early autumn, they are also much more conspicuous because they visit garden flowers to fuel up for the winter. As with all summer butterflies, *Buddleia* is a great favourite, and it is well worth pruning one hard in spring to ensure that there is a late flush of flowers to attract this magnificent butterfly. But the Red Admiral also has a partiality for sap and rotting fruit, finding windfall apples and split plums irresistible.

Your chances of attracting Red Admirals earlier in the year will be enhanced more by encouraging nettles (*Urtica* spp.) than by growing flowers. Although the Red Admiral appears to be far less fussy than its relatives, and will lay on semi-shaded shoots, the nettles must not be relegated to a gloomy corner if they are to be used for egg-laying. It is essential that the nettles are really vigorous, with plenty of fresh, green tips full of nutritious nitrogen. Many nettles are in this condition in May, but most Red Admiral eggs are laid in August, when nettles tend to be old, straggly and grey. It is therefore well worth cutting some patches in late June, to ensure a constant supply of fresh growth. This also encourages other Nymphalids.

## EGG, CATERPILLAR, AND CHRYSALIS

An egg-laying Red Admiral is quite easy to spot due to its rambling, fluttery flight, during which it fussily investigates every nook and cranny, giving the general impression of a broody hen. When a suitable nettle has been chosen, she quickly lays a small, green egg on the growing tip of the nettle, on the upper surface of the tender budding leaves. One egg is laid per tip, being placed in exposed places if the nettle is slightly shaded, or sheltered within a patch if the clump is large. Moses Harris, writing in 1766, had his own interpretation for the female's behaviour: "I have often perceived her, when about to lay an Egg, creep in among the Nettles; which I imagine is not only to place the Egg from the heat of the Sun, but likewise to see if those Nettles are frequented by Ants, these Creatures being very destructive to caterpillars".

Not every egg is laid on stinging nettles (*Urtica dioica*). Annual nettle, (*U. urens*) and its close relative, pellitory of the wall (*Parietaria diffusa*), are also used. But whatever the plant, the behaviour is the same. The egg hatches after about a week, and the tiny caterpillar spins a tent around itself by fastening a tender young leaf double with silk. Over the next four weeks it

A NETTLE-LEAF TENT
*In its final stage, the caterpillar fells a nettle top, spins the leaves together, and lives inside this tent, feasting on the tender crown.*

lives and feeds in a succession of nettle-leaf tents – or "Places of Security" as Moses Harris described them – each progressively larger and of a highly distinctive shape. Tents are extremely easy to find, and often several occur up a single stem, looking like plump packets of stuffed vine leaves. Be careful how you open these, for tents are made of the lushest growing leaves, and these invariably have the fiercest stings. Inside will be found the equally plump black-and-yellow caterpillar, with its body curled in the shape of a figure 6.

The caterpillar frequently abandons its single-leaved tent for the final bout of feeding, and constructs another that is equally conspicuous in its own way. It first selects a vigorous growing spike, which it fells by chewing two-thirds of the way through the stem, about 15 cm. (6 in.) below the tip. The upper section topples, but remains attached to the plant, and the caterpillar crawls into the downward-pointing terminal leaves, spinning them together in a cocoon. It may also form its chrysalis in this contraption if sufficient room exists. But more often it spins two or three large nettle leaves together, and pupates inside the shelter thereby created.

No British butterfly has a chrysalis that is easier to find in the wild than this species. Unfortunately, parasites also find them easy targets. In particular, beautiful black ichneumon wasps buzz around the nettles, injecting eggs via a long sting through the wall of the tent deep into soft, young chrysalises. It probably also stings caterpillars, but I have yet to witness this.

# PEACOCK

## Inachis io

This familiar insect has long been known as the Peacock, but the "Owl" would be more appropriate, as can be seen if you rotate the illustration on p.133 and view the adult upside down. Now the twin hindwings assume the image of a little or Tengmalm's owl, peering angrily from behind the forewings. The more one looks the more realistic this appears: the fur and scales between the eyes sweep back towards a dark, rounded profile that is topped by two small ear tufts. The butterfly's cigar-shaped body looks exactly like a beak.

This is, of course, no chance resemblance but another example of the remarkable mimicry and defensive markings that have evolved in butterflies. The underside offers a different image, but excellent camouflage nonetheless. By resembling bark, it makes the Peacock practically invisible when settled on a tree-trunk. This is the first line of defence. The second is to flash the wings open when an enemy comes near, simultaneously rubbing the forewings and hindwings together to produce a warning noise. This is easy to induce if you lunge at a resting Peacock, and the sound is startling enough to human ears. The shock to a mouse must be severe when, after sniffing to investigate an appetizing insect odour on the bark, a glaring owl suddenly looms above it, rustling and hissing dangerously.

We are fortunate that this fascinating butterfly is one of the commonest garden visitors in England, Wales, and Ireland, and appears to have held its own – perhaps even increased – in recent years. It has one brood a year, but the adults live for up to 11 months and can be seen on any sunny day, and occasionally even in winter. The emergence generally starts in late July and continues for another month or two. The adults then hibernate and reappear the following spring, when they mate and breed, mainly from March to early May. A few individuals linger on until late June, almost overlapping with the next generation.

The behaviour of this butterfly is now well known, thanks to excellent studies by Robin Baker. The Peacock is a nomad

**Distribution** *A common nomadic species found throughout the lowlands of England, Wales, and Ireland. Less common in Scotland.*

rather than a true migrant, for while it has a tendency to fly north in spring, and south in late summer, the furthest any individual had been shown to travel is about 95 km. (60 miles). Only seldom do they cross the sea.

### HIBERNATION

A Peacock's requirements alter according to the season. The freshly emerged adults of late summer have two priorities – to feed up for winter and to find a hibernation site. They begin in August, often visiting gardens, hedgerows and any flowery habitat, although the greatest concentrations occur in woods. At first they are quite mobile, but once an overwintering site has been found and autumn progresses, they tend to remain nearby. They will roost in their chosen site by night and feed every day until entering hibernation, usually in early September. By then, huge concentrations may build up, especially if it has been a good summer. I have counted up to 185 adults along a single woodland ride.

Peacocks choose dark crevices, sheds, or holes in trees in which to hibernate, but seldom enter houses, unlike their close relative, the Small Tortoiseshell. Large aggregations have occasionally been found in hollow trees and this could well be how most Peacocks hibernate. The Victorian lepidopterist Edward Newman found 40 together inside an oak, while A. B. Farn found "a large assemblage" and noted, as have others since, that the group produced a loud, hissing, snake-like sound when disturbed. This, like the flashing wings of non-hibernating adults, must be a considerable deterrent to enemies: most birds and mammals are afraid of snakes.

### THE DAILY ROUTINE

Adult Peacocks awake on the first warm days of spring to feed on a wide variety of wild flowers. The males sup mainly in the morning, but soon start wandering and travel, on average, about 500 m. (about ⅓ mile) a day. Their flights stop from about

11.30 a.m. onwards, when they begin to establish solitary territories on the ground. The process is complete by about 1 p.m. Typical territories are situated beneath the sunny edges of a wood or tall hedge, and are usually near a roost site; corners are especially favoured, for it is here above all that females are most likely to fly.

The male swoops up to investigate any dark object that flies over his territory. Even birds may be challenged, and Robin Baker found that the sexes could be distinguished by throwing a stick or lump of soil a metre or so above a Peacock. Females ignore the missile but males fly up to intercept.

Many intruders prove to be other males that are still searching for a territory. Most are seen off with ease, although the chase may continue for up to 200 m. (180 yards). Some, however, stay their ground, leading to spectacular dog-fights as each male tries to outmanoeuvre and fly above its opponent. This causes both to spiral upwards to a great height before plunging to the ground. The ascent may be repeated two or three times, but eventually one male achieves dominance and the other speeds off in search of another territory.

## COURTSHIP AND EGG-LAYING

Females that fly through male territories are pursued with a zeal and persistence that is scarcely deserved. Those that have already mated are particularly contrary and try to lose their suitors on and off during the afternoon, flying across country then suddenly folding their wings to drop from the sky into vegetation. Another escape strategy is to fly around the back of a tree and hide by settling on bark. Females may even lead an amorous male into another male's territory, escaping during the inevitable battle. A virgin is scarcely more solicitous, and it may be several hours before she finally succumbs.

Having mated, the next aim in any female's life is to lay eggs. Like most close relatives, the Peacock lays in massive batches, taking considerable care over where they are placed. Stinging nettle (Urtica dioica) is nearly always used, despite occasional reports of caterpillars being found on hop (Humulus lupulus). Egg-laying generally occurs around midday and is restricted to nettles that are in full sunshine at that time. Large, vigorous plants are usually chosen, especially those growing in sheltered situations such as in a woodland glade, along a wood edge or tall hedgerow.

Once she has selected a plant, the female hangs with closed wings beneath a tender young leaf, curves her abdomen onto the undersurface and slowly pumps out 300 to 500 sticky green eggs. They remain for one to two weeks, piled several layers deep. On hatching, the mass of caterpillars immediately spins a communal silk web over the nutritious growing tip of the stinging nettle. They live and feed within this web, until the leaf is a skeleton and the silk a grubby cobweb of shed skins and droppings. Fresh webs are spun periodically as the food supply is exhausted, but the caterpillars live and bask increasingly in the open the larger they grow.

## CATERPILLAR AND CHRYSALIS

Peacock caterpillars are easy to find at all stages of growth, and can be distinguished from those of the Small Tortoiseshell (see p.123) by their blacker white-specked bodies and by their much longer spines. They are presumably as conspicuous to birds and small mammals as they are to us, but evidently obtain sufficient protection from their awesome spines. These appear all the more formidable when the caterpillars are disturbed, for they jerk their heads and bodies in unison, making the spines sway in waves over the black mass. However none of this deters wasp parasites, which are responsible for the death of countless Peacock caterpillars of all ages.

The survivors are ready to pupate in successive batches from early June to mid-July. They invariably desert their stinging nettles at this stage and disperse to form solitary chrysalises: F. W. Frohawk gives an excellent account of how a band of fully grown caterpillars walked 3 m. (10 ft.) from their foodplant before climbing 4.5 m. (15 ft.) up an oak, still in one group, and then separated, each to pupate apart on the tree.

I have yet to find a wild Peacock chrysalis, but have reared them in captivity often enough. Their shape and colours are captivating, and there are two main types: one is blackish or grey, and this tends to be formed on dark tree-trunks or fences; the other is a much prettier yellow or golden shade, which gives good camouflage when suspended beneath leaves.

This species has less specialized requirements than many of the butterflies described in this book, and this may explain why it is still comparatively common in the British countryside. Open, sunny woodlands, rich in flowers, are its favoured sites, but the butterfly can be seen almost anywhere and on any soil. Numbers fluctuate considerably from one year to the next, and the Peacock is often more abundant after a cool wet summer, possibly because stinging nettles are lush and nutritious in such years. Unlike so many of the butterflies described, there is no indication that our Peacock populations have declined in recent decades. It remains a common species throughout the lowlands of England and Wales, and well distributed throughout Ireland, where it is believed to have increased in numbers.

Its status in Scotland is more confusing. From being widely distributed in the south in the nineteenth century, the Peacock declined and was often scarce until an expansion occurred in the 1930s. Today it is resident, and often common, in the west as far as north Argyll, but is largely absent elsewhere.

# PEACOCK · *Inachis io*

LIFE-CYCLE

| | JAN | FEB | MAR | APR | MAY | JUN | JUL | AUG | SEP | OCT | NOV | DEC |
|---|---|---|---|---|---|---|---|---|---|---|---|---|
| EGG | | | | | | | | | | | | |
| CATERPILLAR | | | | | | | | | | | | |
| CHRYSALIS | | | | | | | | | | | | |
| ADULT | | | | | | | | | | | | |

**Male**
Markings of both sexes are similar. Camouflaged undersides conceal the butterfly while it hibernates in crevices and holes in trees.

**"Blind" Peacock**
A rare aberration that lacks the blue pupils on the hindwings.

EGG [*x15*]

**Egg batch**
Large batches of eggs are laid on the undersides of nettle leaves, usually in sheltered situations.

**Chrysalis [*x1½*]**
Colour of chrysalis depends on the site chosen for pupation.

**Feeding adult**
In gardens, *Buddleia* flowers may attract many adults, which feed on their nectar.

**Caterpillar [*x1½*]**
The caterpillars are gregarious at first, but separate before pupation.

133

# COMMA

*Polygonia c-album*

THE COMMA is a familiar visitor to southern gardens, where it feasts alongside Peacocks, Red Admirals, and Small Tortoiseshells, building up reserves to last the winter. Although seldom as numerous as these relatives, this represents an astonishing change in fortunes compared to a century ago, when the Comma was on the verge of extinction and more or less confined to the Welsh Border Country. There were fewer than half-a-dozen records of the butterfly from about 1830 to 1929 in counties such as Suffolk, Surrey, Sussex, and Dorset, whereas today one expects to find it in almost every wood or scrubland.

### CAMOUFLAGE AND COLOUR FORMS

This is a particularly interesting and attractive species. The adult, with wings closed, offers one of the best examples of camouflage found among British butterflies. Its ragged outline, and the marbled pattern of grey, tan, and brown, with occasional green speckles, combine perfectly to resemble a dead oak leaf that has just begun to moulder. There even appears to be a crack in the centre where the "leaf" is breaking up – the white, comma-like mark that has given this species its name.

The normal male Comma is slightly darker than the female, but both sexes have a brighter golden form, called *hutchinsoni*, which is produced by the earliest caterpillars to develop in spring. These lovely Commas may constitute up to two-fifths of the midsummer emergence, but are not on the wing for long. They quickly pair, lay eggs, and die, in contrast to their darker siblings, which live for 10 months but do not breed until the following spring. The offspring of *hutchinsoni* Commas develop quickly to produce normal-looking adults in August and September; these feed for a few weeks before joining their uncles and aunts in hibernation.

Like other Tortoiseshells, Commas live in loose, open populations and wander through the countryside selecting places to feed, hibernate, and breed. They are not, however, true

*Distribution Common in woods and gardens throughout southern England and lowland Wales; range continues to expand in the north.*

migrants. There has never, to my knowledge, been a sighting at sea, nor any reliable record from Ireland, but adults undoubtedly roam widely at a local level. Thus the species managed to re-occupy southern England, early this century, within the space of just 25 years.

### SPRING AND SUMMER PEAKS

Adult Commas can be seen at almost any time from March to late October, but there are two main peaks – one in early April, the other from July to mid-September. The butterflies' requirements differ through the year, and this takes them into different types of habitat. For hibernation, they rely mainly on the dry parts of woods, settling low down on elevated tree-roots and other exposed surfaces, in places where drifts of dead leaves will later accumulate to complement their remarkable camouflage.

They awake quite early in March, and feed in the weak sunshine on the catkins of sallow (*Salix capraea*) and other spring flowers. Males, in particular, remain near the woods, feeding first thing in the morning and again in late afternoon, but otherwise spending most of the day looking for mates. Each establishes a separate territory in a sunny nook on the wood edge, beside a glade, or where two rides cross. He sits at this vantage point for long periods, poised a metre or two up on a prominent branch, leaning forwards with wings half-open. He intercepts any passer-by in a swift but economical flight, achieving high speed with no more than a rapid whirring of wings, punctuated by swooping glides. He soon overtakes and loops around the intruder. After a thorough investigation, he either returns to his perch or, if it is a female, gives chase.

### COURTSHIP AND EGG-LAYING

Pairing takes place high on a shrub or tree, and the female later wanders away to seek suitable places for her eggs. Many of these sites are too on woodland edges, but she will also investigate hedgerows, scrub, and especially hop-gardens. Hop

(*Humulus lupulus*) was undoubtedly the main foodplant in the past, when every village or farm had its own brew-house. The butterfly was once so plentiful in hop-gardens of southeast England that hop-pickers had their own name for the caterpillars, calling them "hop-cats", and knew the chrysalises as "silver-grubs". Hop remains a favoured foodplant, but is unavailable nowadays over large tracts of the countryside, forcing the vast majority of eggs to be laid on stinging nettle (*Urtica dioica*). Few eggs are also laid on currants (*Ribes* spp.) and elms (*Ulmus* spp.), but this is rare in my experience.

A female ready to lay flutters slowly around shrubs, periodically alighting to test leaves by tapping their surfaces with her legs, tasting each to see if it is suitable. The foodplant need not be in full sunshine – I have even found caterpillars deep in the shade of a north-facing wall – but most are laid in sunny sheltered nooks, on the tenderest sprouting leaves of hop or nettle. Although laid singly, the glassy, green egg is quite easy to find in good years; it is laid on the upper edge of the leaf, often on the extreme tip. Prominent stinging nettles beside a wood are preferred, and exposed plants growing in open fields are almost invariably avoided.

The *hutchinsoni* adults of midsummer behave in much the same way as the normal form in spring, and are therefore seen perching or egg-laying mainly around hedges and woods, where they are frequently mistaken for Fritillaries. However, the darker Commas that emerge in midsummer must prepare for hibernation, as do the offspring of *hutchinsoni* later on. Both broods spend long periods feasting at flowers, on rotten fruit, and oozing tree-trunks, bringing a succession of dark adults into the garden from mid-July to late autumn.

Comma eggs hatch after two to three weeks, and the little caterpillar immediately crawls under its leaf, where it spins a fine silk web and feeds on the tender tissue, making distinctive perforations. As it grows larger, the skin is shed four times, and the caterpillar increasingly comes to resemble a bird-dropping. At first it is small and crusty, a mere sparrow's dropping of black and white, sticking to the underside of a leaf. But the fully grown caterpillar is tan, with a gleaming splash of white, looking like a large deposit from a thrush lying curled in the open over a leaf. The chrysalis is strangely beautiful, resembling a withered leaf as it hangs on a thread beneath a hop or nettle.

## A HISTORY OF CAPTIVE BREEDING

Chrysalises can be found in the wild, but the caterpillar is easier to spot, and the egg is simplest of all. This is an easy species to rear, and of exceptional interest, on account of the changing camouflage from young to old caterpillar, followed by that of the chrysalis and adult. There is the added fascination, starting with springtime eggs, of producing both normal and *hutchinsoni* forms of the adults.

The trick of breeding golden Commas was first mastered by Emma Hutchinson, who also established that the species could be double-brooded. Mrs. Hutchinson's name was inseparable from that of the Comma in the late nineteenth century, and very properly lives on through its golden form. She lived near Leominster in Herefordshire, in the heart of Comma country at a time when the butterfly was exceedingly rare, and was famed for her generosity. Large numbers of Commas were collected from the hop-gardens there, or were bred artificially, enabling her to supply entomologists throughout the country.

F. W. Frohawk also bred *hutchinsoni* from a female sent by Mrs. Hutchinson in 1894. It says much for Frohawk's expertise that he kept this creature alive for 47 days, and obtained 275 eggs, which he reared on a variety of foodplants to produce 200 perfect adults. Forty-one were *hutchinsoni,* and with few exceptions came from the first adults to emerge, while virtually all that were of normal appearance derived from the later bouts of egg-laying. And there the story remained for nearly a century, giving rise to the myth that 20 per cent of springtime caterpillars produce *hutchinsoni* adults. In fact, there is a complex switching mechanism at work, which responds to the amount of daylight during the caterpillar's development.

## COLOUR FORMS AND DAYLENGTH

In Stockholm, the entomologist Soren Mylin has reared Commas both from Sweden and Oxford. She has discovered that English springtime caterpillars can switch their development, either into golden *hutchinsoni* adults that will breed the same summer, or into normal (dark) specimens that will hibernate. This is influenced by two main factors – the length of the day experienced by the caterpillars during their development, and whether the days become shorter or longer as they grow. When English caterpillars are given just 12 hours of light every day, all turn into dark, hibernating adults. But with 18 or 20 hours of light each day, 90 per cent turn into golden *hutchinsoni* Commas. The way the daylength changes during a caterpillar's life can tip the balance. In general, more *hutchinsoni* adult butterflies are produced if the days are growing longer and fewer if they are growing shorter.

This switching mechanism clearly allows the butterfly to take advantage of early springs and warm seasons. Warmer temperatures early in the year mean that the eggs are laid sooner, and hatch more quickly. By responding to daylength, caterpillars that have completed their development before the longest day can give rise to a second generation in the same summer. The caterpillar "knows" when it can comfortably fit in two generations a year, but also has an escape system, so that just one brood occurs in cool years, when conditions are unfavourable. In practice, a mixture of types is usually produced, with those caterpillars that pupate before the summer solstice (21 June) forming *hutchinsoni* adults and those (usually the majority) that are too late developing directly into dark, hibernating adults. Interestingly enough, Swedish Commas never form *hutchinsoni* in the wild, but can still do so if reared in artificial conditions that favour the golden form. They are, however, slightly less prone to do this than our British race.

## NINETEENTH-CENTURY DECLINE

As more is discovered about this lovely insect, the more fortunate it seems that it has recovered in Britain. There is perhaps no butterfly in the country that has experienced such dramatic fluctuations. To the earliest English naturalists it was not a particular rarity, and was the first of 36 butterflies illustrated by Moses Harris, who found it "very swift in Flight, and *[so]* timorous when settled that it is difficult to... lay the Net over it; they fly in Lanes, by Bank Sides, often settling in dry clayey Places, and against the Bodies of Trees".

The heyday of the Comma was perhaps the early nineteenth century, when it was widely distributed over England and Wales, and even reached Fife, Alloa, and Clackmannanshire. There then followed an extraordinary decline, beginning around 1818-20 in most southern counties. By 1830, it had more or less disappeared from a large stretch of southeast England, from Dorset to Kent and as far north as Lincolnshire. It also declined further north, where it had never been especially common. But, paradoxically, it either held on longer here or experienced a minor increase in the mid-nineteenth century. Thus Commas were seen in Derbyshire in 1855, and were present, and occasionally common, in Lancashire, east Yorkshire, and north Lincolnshire around that period, only to disappear again in the second half of the century.

Despite a few sightings in Kent and Epping Forest, the butterfly remained excessively rare and its demise was much lamented. "It is one of the receding species which we so greatly regret" wrote Barrett in 1893, and a Scottish entomologist wrote "it is very unpleasant to think that *P. c-album*, the butterfly of our youth, has left us for good and all".

## AN UNEXPECTED RECOVERY

The nadir of the Comma occurred between the turn of the century and about 1914. It is impossible to say whether it completely disappeared from all northern, central, and southeastern counties: although there were one or two isolated records per county, introductions and even frauds prevailed during this period. For example, one collector noted that "before 1881 hundreds of larvae and pupae were released in Surrey hoping to introduce the species, but without success".

What is certain is that the butterfly virtually disappeared, and could only be guaranteed in the Welsh Borders, especially Gloucestershire, Herefordshire, and Monmouth, and a few adjoining areas. Even here there were enormous fluctuations. In 1875, Mrs. Hutchinson wrote that "Pupae must have been very plentiful on the Hop plants cultivated here. I have had two hundred brought me, and thousands must have been thrown on the heap with the hop-bine, and burnt. Last year we had none".

Then, suddenly and inexplicably, came the recovery. This was first noticed in 1914, with single adults seen over most of the southern counties during the next 10 years, and regular sightings thereafter. In Sussex, for example, one was spotted at Eastbourne in 1915, and although none was seen in the early 1920s, it was "abundant" at Chichester in 1929, with "thousands" on the South Downs by 1935. Dorset had been colonized slightly earlier so that Commas were "everywhere" by 1929, but it was not until 1935-36 that Suffolk was fully re-occupied.

## THE TRIGGERS OF POPULATION CHANGE

Today the Comma is well established over the whole of lowland Wales and southern England, and still appears to be spreading northwards, although it has yet to penetrate further than Manchester in the west and Scarborough in the east. Quite why these fluctuations occurred is a mystery, although a few explanations have been advanced. There is no doubt, for example, that hop-gardens declined greatly during the nineteenth century, especially after 1870, and that the new techniques of bine-burning and washing with insecticides can only have exacerbated the situation during the 1880s. It is also true that stinging nettles have probably increased in the present century – particularly since the last war – as a result of nitrate use on farms. This, however, neither explains the sudden decline of this butterfly in the 1820s, nor its recovery early this century, before artificial fertilizers became common.

The weather has also been blamed for the Comma's fluctuations. This is unlikely to be the whole story, given the wide range of conditions under which the species lives on the Continent, although distinct physiological races probably help it to cope with such a variety of climates. It is, I suppose, possible that our Commas were ill-suited to the curious cold weather patterns of the nineteenth century, and that it took several generations for a better-suited race to evolve. But this is to speculate; for the present we can only be thankful that this beautiful ragged butterfly is again common in the British countryside, and hope that never again will it decline.

# COMMA · *Polygonia c-album*

## LIFE-CYCLE

| | JAN | FEB | MAR | APR | MAY | JUN | JUL | AUG | SEP | OCT | NOV | DEC |
|---|---|---|---|---|---|---|---|---|---|---|---|---|
| EGG | | | | | | | | | | | | |
| CATERPILLAR | | | | | | | | | | | | |
| CHRYSALIS | | | | | | | | | | | | |
| ADULT | | | | | | | | | | | | |

**Male**
Typical male. Camouflaged underwings conceal the butterfly during hibernation.

**Female**
The outline of the female's wings is less ragged than the male's, and the colour is lighter.

**Male**
*Hutchinsoni* form, produced by early spring caterpillars.

**Male**
Aberrant *suffusa* form, found in Oxfordshire, 1940.

**Egg** [*x15*]
Laid singly on the upperside of leaves of foodplant.

**Chrysalis** [*x1½*]
Formed low on vegetation, and camouflaged to resemble a withered leaf.

**Feeding adult**
*Hutchinsoni* adult on bramble, a nectar source in summer months.

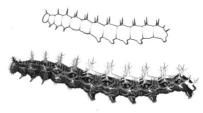

**Caterpillar** [*x1½*]
White splash on back mimics the coloration of a bird-dropping.

# SMALL PEARL-BORDERED FRITILLARY
## *Boloria selene*

THE CATERPILLAR of this species, and of the four Fritillaries that follow, feeds exclusively on the leaves of violets *(Viola* spp.*)*. All five butterflies were fairly common until the 1950s, then an extraordinary decline began which continues to this day. By far the heaviest losses have been in eastern England, where the Small Pearl-bordered Fritillary is now extinct or reduced to a few populations per county. It remains locally common in Wales, western England, and Scotland, where it can still be seen in abundance during June, gliding across woodland clearings, rough grassland, and moorland.

In many of the northern colonies, Small Pearl-bordered Fritillaries breed at low densities over extensive tracts of land, with larger numbers occurring in moist, sheltered pockets where the marsh violet *(Viola palustris)* grows. The adults can be extremely abundant in good years, and seem to be fairly mobile, with individuals flying from one concentration to another. In the south, their lifestyle is very different. Typical colonies consist of dozens rather than hundreds of adults, and many are restricted to small patches of isolated land. These adults are highly sedentary, and their slowness in colonizing new breeding sites can be remarkable.

**Distribution** *A declining species; colonies survive in woodland clearings throughout its range and on wild, sheltered grassland in the west.*

### EARLY DEVELOPMENT

Having mated, the females hide until their eggs are ripe. They then flutter slowly above the ground, sifting the air for the scent of violet leaves, and frequently alighting to tap the vegetation with their sensitive feet. All violets cause some excitement, but most are rejected for egg-laying. The main species chosen are marsh violet or common dog-violet *(Viola riviniana)*. Eggs are generally laid on medium-sized plants growing in open, sunny situations; this occurs when the ground vegetation is beginning to close over, about two to five years after a woodland clearing. In grassland, warm, sparse areas are chosen, especially patches recovering from a fire or from heavy trampling by cattle. The species also has a distinct preference for moist spots.

Once a suitable place has been found, the female scatters her eggs with little regard as to whether they land on violets or not. Some are neatly placed beneath their leaves as she scuttles crab-like over the vegetation, but many are dropped in flight. She hovers a few centimetres above the ground – usually over a moist depression – holding her abdomen still, pointed downwards as the white, cone-shaped eggs are squirted out.

The caterpillar hatches after about two weeks, and begins feeding on moist, sheltered violet leaves. After shedding its skin for the third time, it settles down to hibernate within a withered twist of vegetation. Feeding is resumed the following spring, but unlike most other Fritillaries, the caterpillar continues to be elusive. It hides in humid pockets beneath its foodplants, stretching upwards when hungry to nibble moon-shaped bites in the lobes.

### THE CHALLENGE OF A CHANGING HABITAT

There is no doubt that the Small Pearl-bordered Fritillary has been badly affected by the virtual cessation of coppicing in the present century. Central and eastern England have been worst affected. The butterfly has disappeared altogether from large areas of the Midlands and East Anglia; even on the western Wealden clays of Surrey and Sussex, it is reduced to a scattering of isolated colonies, mainly in young conifer plantations. The same is true of this species in Hampshire and Dorset.

The butterfly can still be seen on marshland, moorland, and moist grassland throughout the West Country, Wales, and the Lake District, and occurs in many woodland clearings in these regions too. It is also locally common in similar habitats over much of Scotland, occurring at altitudes of up to 800 m. (2,600 ft.) on Highland moors. Although present on several of the inner isles, the Small Pearl-bordered Fritillary apparently never recolonized the outer ones following the last Ice Age. It is absent, too, from Ireland.

# SMALL PEARL-BORDERED FRITILLARY · *Boloria selene*

**LIFE-CYCLE**

| | JAN | FEB | MAR | APR | MAY | JUN | JUL | AUG | SEP | OCT | NOV | DEC |
|---|---|---|---|---|---|---|---|---|---|---|---|---|
| EGG | | | | | | | | | | | | |
| CATERPILLAR | | | | | | | | | | | | |
| CHRYSALIS | | | | | | | | | | | | |
| ADULT | | | | | | | | | | | | |

**Male**
The underside has a more contrasting coloration than that of the similar Pearl-bordered Fritillary.

**Female**
The Scottish form *insularium*, shown here, is more brightly marked than butterflies further south.

**Colour variant**
Specimen caught in the New Forest in 1920.

**Basking male**
Males fly close to the ground, perching from time to time to bask in the sun.

**Egg [x22]**
Eggs are scattered near marsh violet or dog-violet.

**Chrysalis [x1½]**
Pupation takes place in vegetation near the violet.

**Caterpillar [x1½]**
Identifiable by two long, forward-facing spines.

**Resting adult**
*Insularium*-form adult resting on the leaf of a violet, the caterpillar foodplant.

# PEARL-BORDERED FRITILLARY

## *Boloria euphrosyne*

THIS IS THE earliest of the British Fritillaries to appear. It emerges in late April after an exceptionally warm spring, and was once known as the "April Fritillary". This, however, was before the Gregorian calendar was adopted and all dates were moved back by 11 days. Today it is usual to see the butterfly from about 7 May onwards.

The identification of medium-sized Fritillaries is apt to cause much confusion. This species can be distinguished from all but the Small Pearl-bordered Fritillary *(see p.139)* by the seven silver "pearls" along the borders of each lower underwing. The main difference between the two pearl-bordered species is on the lower hindwing: the Pearl-bordered Fritillary is more uniformly golden, and has two bright patches of silver on either side of a central pentagonal cell that houses a black dot. The Small Pearl-bordered Fritillary has a larger black spot in this position, surrounded by seven or eight patches of white or silver. It also has darker, brighter uppersides.

*Distribution A rapidly declining species, confined to dry, sheltered grassland in the west and to woodland clearings throughout its range.*

laid singly on or near violet leaves. As with related Fritillaries, any species of violet is used, although most English, Welsh, and Irish colonies are supported by the common dog-violet *(Viola riviniana),* whereas many in Scotland depend on the marsh violet *(V. palustris).*

When laying her eggs, the female Pearl-bordered Fritillary prefers young violets that sprout from warm, bare ground or which surface through a mat of dead vegetation, especially where there is an uneven tangle creating hot, dry hollows.

On heavy soils, and in northern Britain, egg-laying is often also confined to south-facing slopes, or even to the sunny sides of ditches and boundary banks where tiny strips of warm violets grow among the myriads of cooler plants found here and elsewhere in the wood. The egg hatches after about a fortnight. The caterpillar feeds intermittently from late June onwards, concentrating on the freshest leaves of established violets and, when available, grazing the dense flushes of seedlings growing in crumbly, warm soil. By September it has completed the fourth of five skin moults, and it then settles down to hibernate in a twisted, dead leaf. It usually reappears in early March, to embark on a month of serious feeding. Violet seedlings again are its preferred food, but almost as acceptable are the tender lobes of larger plants. Caterpillars are quite easy to find in early April, as they bask in the sun.

## COLONIES, COURTSHIP, AND BREEDING

This is a butterfly that lives in close-knit colonies. These vary enormously in size on different sites and from one year to the next. Many contain fewer than 20 adults, breeding in a minute portion of the woodland that they inhabit. But numbers can increase to thousands in the two to four years following a clearance, before falling just as rapidly as the breeding area becomes overgrown.

Each sex occurs in roughly equal numbers, but females are seen less often because they huddle in the vegetation or flutter slowly above the ground looking for egg-sites. Males, by contrast, are much in evidence. When not feeding on flowers, they spend most of every warm day gliding back and forth over the breeding area, scanning every crevice for a mate.

The female hides for a day or two after mating while her eggs ripen. She then embarks on short bouts of egg-laying. Eggs are

## THE ROLE OF COPPICING

Violets of a type that are suitable for this Fritillary grow mainly on dry soils or on banks in the first few years after a clearance. Most breeding sites are in woods or scrubland, although certain western colonies breed in rough grassland that is regularly burned back in winter, or has had the ground trampled by cattle and then left to recover. Some Scottish populations breed on warm, dry moorland, but here again the majority are in the shelter of woodland clearings.

# PEARL-BORDERED FRITILLARY · *Boloria euphrosyne*

## LIFE-CYCLE

| | JAN | FEB | MAR | APR | MAY | JUN | JUL | AUG | SEP | OCT | NOV | DEC |
|---|---|---|---|---|---|---|---|---|---|---|---|---|
| EGG | | | | | | | | | | | | |
| CATERPILLAR | | | | | | | | | | | | |
| CHRYSALIS | | | | | | | | | | | | |
| ADULT | | | | | | | | | | | | |

**Male upperside**
Markings are fairly uniform over the range in the British Isles.

**Male underside**
Seven silver "pearls" edge the hindwings of both sexes.

**Female upperside**
Larger than male, often with paler yellow marginal spots.

**Female underside**
Two bright patches of silver mark the inner hindwings of both sexes.

**Male**
Aberrant form *pallida* ranges from pale orange to white.

**Male**
Aberrant form *pittonii* has darker wing-bases.

**Egg** [*x15*]
Laid singly on or near dog or marsh violet.

**Chrysalis** [*x1½*]
Suspended in a nest of vegetation, just above the ground.

**Feeding adult**
Pearl-bordered Fritillaries often feed on bugle in spring.

**Caterpillar** [*x1½*]
Between feeds, the caterpillar often basks in the sunshine.

**Feeding adult**
Both yellow and purple flowers are visited by the adults. Here, a male feeds on a buttercup.

**PRINCIPLE BREEDING SITES OF VIOLET-FEEDING FRITILLARIES**

DARK GREEN AND SMALL PEARL-BORDERED FRITILLARIES
*Patchy grassland, where violets grow in clumps.*

PEARL-BORDERED AND HIGH BROWN FRITILLARIES
*Violets growing in warm ground, within a year or two of clearance.*

SMALL PEARL-BORDERED FRITILLARY
*Lush violets in woodland regrowth, a few years after clearance.*

FRITILLARIES ABSENT
*Mature coppice or shady woodland.*

SILVER-WASHED FRITILLARY
*Sunny woodland with an open canopy.*

In the past, ideal conditions were created annually in most British woods through the practice of coppicing. As all old collectors knew, the Pearl-bordered Fritillary bred "where the undergrowth has been cut down for two or three years and the ground is carpeted with wild flowers such as wild hyacinth, bugle, violet and primrose." This, however, is an ephemeral habitat, and this species is unable to thrive in the slightly older clearings so beloved by the Small Pearl-bordered Fritillary. It used, therefore, to move on to the next clearing after a year or two, leaving the older, slightly shaded violets to other Fritillaries. Only rarely does it breed in rides and glades.

## DECLINE FROM THE NORTH

The Pearl-bordered Fritillary was widespread and common in England, Wales, and Scotland up to the middle of the nineteenth century. It was almost ubiquitous in the woods of lowland Wales and southern England, except on the most waterlogged soils. A decline began towards the end of the century, coinciding with a period when many coppices were being abandoned. At first, this was serious only in northeast England and southeast Scotland, where suitable sites were probably always few and far between. Thus in 1934, F. W. Frohawk was still able to describe the butterfly as being "one of the commonest of our woodland butterflies in the spring and early summer months… [and] sure to be met with… in sunlit openings".

The situation today is very different. Modern woods may be suitable during the first years after a new planting, but are much too shady for breeding during the ensuing 50 to 70 years before the trees are felled. Even then, few isolated woods are colonized by this sedentary butterfly during the brief period that the habitat remains suitable again, if indeed any violets appear at all

after such a long period of shade. Among the Fritillaries, the Pearl-bordered is especially vulnerable to local extinctions due to its dependence on the very newest clearings. Small Pearl-bordered and Dark Green Fritillaries last several years longer, and sometimes also linger on in nearby sheltered grassland; the Silver-washed Fritillary breeds among trees, and often survives for many years in maturing broadleaved woods.

Because it was originally so common, the Pearl-bordered Fritillary has yet to become a national rarity. Nevertheless, it is probably now extinct in East Anglia, the east Midlands, and Lincolnshire, in addition to the areas from which it disappeared in the nineteenth century. It is, moreover, reduced to a handful of (mainly small) colonies in all southern counties east of Somerset, even in the New Forest and Dorset, where once it bred in extraordinary abundance. Most surviving colonies occur among the youngest trees in large conifer plantations. Nearly all face extinction in the near future.

The hopes for this species reside in the west. It is still not uncommon on dry, scrubby slopes in Devon, Cornwall, and west Somerset, in the Cotswolds, and in lowland Wales. It also survives in sufficient numbers in many of the woods of these regions for one still to expect, rather than hope, to see it in any fresh clearing. There are, in addition, groups of flourishing colonies in the Lake District, and in southwest and central Scotland, especially in coastal areas of Argyll, in Perthshire, and along the Spey Valley. It is rare, however, on the isles, with colonies known only on Rhum and Raasay. Finally, the Pearl-bordered Fritillary has a curious presence in Ireland. It is found only in the Burren, where it is comparatively common, breeding among the hazel scrub that grows sparsely on the warm limestone pavement of this beautiful region of Co. Clare.

# HIGH BROWN FRITILLARY

## *Argynnis adippe*

THIS HANDSOME FRITILLARY once bred in most large woods in Wales and southern England, and on a few rough and scrubby grasslands in the west. But an extraordinary decline afflicted the woodland colonies, beginning in the late 1950s and continuing to this day. As a result, this has become the most endangered butterfly in the country, and has virtually disappeared both as a woodland species, and from the eastern two-thirds of its old range. The decline continues, and colonies are lost every year.

At the time of writing, the High Brown Fritillary survives in scattered pockets on the Malvern Hills along the Welsh borderlands and in the West Country, and has one last stronghold among the beautiful limestone hills of the Lake District, at the extreme north of its traditional range.

***Distribution*** *One of our most rapidly declining species. Strong populations now occur only in the Malverns and southern Lake District.*

It would be tragic indeed if this butterfly were lost, for it is an impressive and beautiful insect, perhaps less fine than its close relatives – the Silver-washed and Dark Green Fritillaries – but magnificent nonetheless. I fear, however, that it has declined even more than the latest maps suggest, for many naturalists misidentify the Dark Green Fritillary for this species, on the assumption that any specimen seen flying in woodland is a High Brown Fritillary. This rough-and-ready guide held good 40 years ago, but today there must be a over a hundred sightings of Dark Green Fritillaries made in woods for every one of this species.

### SOME AIDS TO IDENTIFICATION

The importance of accurate identification makes it worth dwelling on the distinguishing features of these particular Fritillaries. By far the most obvious characteristic is on the underside, where the High Brown Fritillary has an extra row of small silver spots, each ringed by a reddish-brown halo, between the two bands of silver patches that extend down the outer edge halfway in on the hindwing. The Dark Green Fritillary has no markings in this gap, but usually has additional silver patches near the tip of the forewing, extending a short distance down the outer edge. In addition, as their names imply, the former species has brownish crescents around the outer silver patches on the hindwing, and the inner silver patches are often encircled by brown. The Dark Green Fritillary instead has green crescents, and the whole of the background to the inner two-thirds of the hindwing is tinged with the same beautiful olive-green. It should be noted, however, that this green tinge varies in intensity, and that the presence or absence of the little green spots is the only infallible guide.

These two Fritillaries are much harder to distinguish with their wings open. One trick is to look at the outer edge of the forewing, which is straight or slightly concave in the High Brown Fritillary, whereas it curves outwards on the Dark Green Fritillary. Basking males can also be distinguished by looking at the scent marks near the middle of the forewings. These are elevated, black, and shiny on the second and third vein up on the High Brown Fritillary, rather like a smaller version of the streaks on a male Silver-washed Fritillary. On the Dark Green Fritillary, they are flat, insignificant, and confined to the first two veins. It is unusual for the two species to be common in the same place.

### FINDING FOODPLANTS

In flight, the High Brown Fritillary is swift and powerful, and is hard to approach except when feeding on flowers, for then it becomes oblivious to everything around it. Both sexes soar high among the tree-tops, roosting on the uppermost branches in poor weather and at night. They float down when the sun shines, the males to search for virgin females, and the mated females to lay eggs. Male High Brown Fritillaries pound back and forth over the breeding areas, dipping rapidly to examine anything resembling a female.

Both sexes may wander some distance from their arid breeding sites, especially in dry summers when the flowers wither and die. I shall never forget seeing them in 1976, when the males gathered by the score in marshy meadows below the wooded fringes of Dartmoor. Here they jostled, four to a flowerhead, on marsh thistles (*Cirsium palustre*), gorging on the rich nectar. They were so abundant that I gave up bothering to photograph single specimens.

When laying her eggs, the female High Brown Fritillary flutters just above ground level, through warm, sunny areas that are sheltered by a sparse growth of bracken (*Peteridium aquilinum*) or shrubs. She responds to the scent of violets (*Viola spp.*), the caterpillars' foodplants, but seldom homes in on individual clumps. Instead, she lands nearby, and crawls around until she finds a sheltered spot with scattered plant cover.

The eggs are usually laid on twigs, dead leaves or even stones, and always near the ground, with three or four often around one patch. They are attractive, cone-shaped, and apricot-pink when laid, but soon turn a dull slate-grey as the little caterpillars develop inside.

Although fully formed after about three weeks, each caterpillar does not hatch until the following spring, when it bores out of the toughened shell before searching for violets. Having located a source of food, the young caterpillar feeds on the tender growing leaves, biting increasingly large lumps out of their lobes. It feeds throughout April and May, and can be found quite easily on the best sites, for it often basks openly in the sunshine, raising its body temperature to help digest its food. It is a most attractive creature that exists in two general colour forms when fully grown. The usual lighter form is shown opposite, but do not be surprised to find others that are dark brown, or even grey.

### THE IMPORTANCE OF COPPICING
In the past, High Brown Fritillaries bred in abundance in many of the larger coppiced woodlands of England and Wales, probably in comparable situations to the egg-laying sites among scrub and rough grassland today. I suspect they bred almost exclusively on short-lived sites, using established violet clumps that had survived in the shade of mature coppices, and which suddenly took on a new lease of life in the spring after a block was cut. After just one or two seasons, the site would become unsuitable, and only through a continuing cycle of coppicing (*see p.142*) could the butterfly prosper. This would certainly explain why the High Brown Fritillary has almost always been the first of the violet-feeders to disappear from a district following the abandonment of coppicing.

There can be no doubt that the decline in coppicing is responsible for this butterfly's disappearance, although it is surprising that the onset of the decline was so sudden. My belief is that rabbits may have played a part, for it is often forgotten that they once dominated the grazing on many woodland floors and were not just confined to heaths and grassland. At the very least, the loss of rabbit grazing when myxomatosis struck in the 1950s must have added to the shading effect.

### TODAY'S SURVIVORS
As late as the 1950s, the High Brown Fritillary still occurred widely in the woods of East Anglia and the southeast, and was even considered to be the commonest of the woodland Fritillaries in Sussex, being found "in local abundance in suitable spots throughout the county". Now it is a very great rarity, probably extinct in the entire eastern third of England, extinct too in Dorset and most Midland counties, and with no more than occasional reports from Hampshire and Wiltshire. It has also declined enormously in Devon and Somerset, but a few small populations survive, mainly in scrubby grassland on the edges of woods. It occupies similar habitats in the Welsh border country, having all but disappeared from the great forests, such as Wyre, in which it was recently abundant. Its stronghold there is now the southeastern slopes of the Malvern Hills, where it breeds in sheltered patches of rough grassland, in places where bracken casts a scattered but by no means dense shade. This is one of the few places where High Brown Fritillaries can be seen in any numbers, sweeping up the hillsides or fluttering around gaps in the bracken. It is heartening to know that the management of this area is specifically designed to encourage this and other Fritillaries.

### A LAKE DISTRICT SPECIALITY
The finest colonies by far are found on the southern hills of the Lake District, on the carboniferous limestone that surrounds Morecambe Bay. Matthew Oates, who has made the most comprehensive surveys in recent years, found the occasional adult in almost every suitable-looking place. That is not to say it is particularly common there, rather that it flies throughout this large area, breeding in small numbers wherever its habitat exists.

Among the many minor colonies are a few very large ones, breeding mainly among patchy scrub on the violets that flourish in the cracks between the natural limestone pavements in places such as Arneside Moss, Leighton Moss, and Gait Barrow. These three sites at least offer some hope for the future, for the first is owned by the National Trust and the other two are Nature Reserves. Indeed, from Gait Barrow comes the most encouraging news that, against all the trends elsewhere in Britain, the High Brown Fritillaries have shown a substantial increase. This is due to renewed management that involves exposing the violets so that they develop in the way that suits this species.

# HIGH BROWN FRITILLARY · *Argynnis adippe*

## LIFE-CYCLE

| | JAN | FEB | MAR | APR | MAY | JUN | JUL | AUG | SEP | OCT | NOV | DEC |
|---|---|---|---|---|---|---|---|---|---|---|---|---|
| EGG | | | | | | | | | | | | |
| CATERPILLAR | | | | | | | | | | | | |
| CHRYSALIS | | | | | | | | | | | | |
| ADULT | | | | | | | | | | | | |

**Male upperside**
Outer edge of the forewing is less rounded than the similar Dark Green Fritillary.

**Male underside**
Red-ringed spots on hindwings are a characteristic feature.

**Female**
Females are more heavily marked with black than males.

**Egg** [x15]
Egg turns grey as the caterpillar develops inside. Hatching is delayed until spring.

SIDE VIEW       VIEW FROM ABOVE

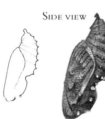

**Chrysalis** [x1½]
Formed in a loose web of silk. The leaf-like, brown coloration varies in hue.

**Feeding adult**
Flowers of bramble are a favourite nectar source.

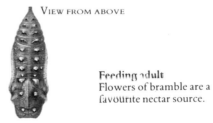

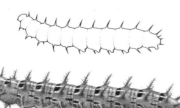

**Caterpillar** [x1½]
Light form; darker brown or grey specimens also occur.

# DARK GREEN FRITILLARY

*Argynnis aglaja*

THIS SPECTACULAR FRITILLARY inhabits dunes and wild grasslands from the Orkneys to the Channel Islands. Although seldom particularly numerous, it is not a species likely to be overlooked. So conspicuous is it that a single airborne male quickly catches the eye, particularly when it battles alone against the breeze or, in calmer weather, glides among the Browns, Blues, and Skippers that abound on most of its sites.

## FLIGHT AND CONCEALMENT

For all its powers of flight, the Dark Green Fritillary is not a particularly mobile species. The adults usually remain close to their sharply defined breeding grounds. These, in lowland England, are typically small in area, and each one is usually widely separated from the next. Other sites are more extensive, but even along the coast, there is little evidence that adults fly between them.

Male Dark Green Fritillaries spend most of every warm day on the wing, scanning the hillsides for hidden females. These sit in tussocks, and are probably located by scent. Mating quickly follows, low down in the grass. There is elegance as well as power in these patrolling flights: the wings whirr swiftly for a second or two, causing the butterfly to surge forward and then glide, before another burst of wingbeats becomes necessary. They seldom pause to rest, and the only realistic chance of seeing or photographing either sex is to wait beside purple flowers in the early morning or late afternoon.

Females remain hidden for the rest of the day, waiting for their burden of eggs to ripen. Each then embarks on a brief investigative flight, fluttering slowly above the grass and often alighting to tap vegetation as she sifts carefully through the scents rising from below. Her reaction to the scent of violets (*Viola* spp.) is spectacular. She spins around and makes brisk, jerky movements back and forth in their vicinity, squeezing herself deep into the tangled vegetation. Any violet will prompt her to lay, but clumps of robust, large-leaved species are most to

***Distribution*** *Widely distributed on downs, dunes, and rough grassland. Frequently seen along Irish and western coasts; very local elsewhere.*

her liking. Thus, in the north and on wet sites, marsh violet (*Viola palustris*) is preferred to most other species, as is hairy violet (*V. hirta*) on dry, calcareous soils.

Although catholic in her choice of violet species, the female is very choosy about where she lays. I suspect that the Dark Green Fritillary prefers lushness, coolness, or humidity around its violets, for it selects large clumps that protrude above a fairly dense sward, typically 8 to 15 cm. (3 to 6 in.) in height, or which grow sideways through a wall of dense grass into a sheltered, sunny spot. There is no holding a female once a suitable place is found. Her abdomen curves around, stabbing left and right, and a series of eggs is ejected in rapid succession.

The eggs hatch two to three weeks later, and the caterpillars immediately hibernate among the leaf-litter. They re-emerge in spring to take hurried bites out of large but tender violet leaves. They are nervous, rather wasteful feeders, especially when older, and they hide for long periods between scuttling from one plant to another to snatch a few bites from the lobe of a leaf.

## A SURVIVOR AMONG FRITILLARIES

This splendid butterfly is the commonest Fritillary over much of the British Isles, and the only species present in the far north and on many islands. Unfertilized, open habitats are its main abode, particularly where the turf is regularly disturbed and then left to grow tall again. Such conditions occur naturally on dunes and undercliffs along much of the coast, and have been created by farmers on rough, scrubby grazing and moorlands for centuries. Colonies also occur on unfertilized chalk and limestone downs, but only where grazing is light or erratic. A few colonies occur in woodland glades.

There is no doubt that countless inland colonies have been destroyed in the last 50 years, due to the elimination of the butterfly's foodplants. However, this remains the least threatened of Fritillaries, with the coast being its real stronghold.

# DARK GREEN FRITILLARY · *Argynnis aglaja*

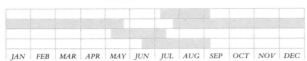

| | JAN | FEB | MAR | APR | MAY | JUN | JUL | AUG | SEP | OCT | NOV | DEC |
|---|---|---|---|---|---|---|---|---|---|---|---|---|
| EGG | | | | | | | | | | | | |
| CATERPILLAR | | | | | | | | | | | | |
| CHRYSALIS | | | | | | | | | | | | |
| ADULT | | | | | | | | | | | | |

**Male upperside**
Wings are more rounded
than those of the similar
High Brown Fritillary.

**Male underside**
Underwings are flushed
with green; those of the female
are similar.

**Female**
Ground-colour of the wings is
paler than in the male, especially
towards the margins.

**Egg** [*x15*]
Laid singly, close to any of
several species of violet.

**Chrysalis** [*x1½*]
Formed inside a loose cocoon
of silk and grass leaves.

**Female, Scottish subspecies**
The Scottish subspecies,
*A. a. scotica,* is more heavily
marked than southern specimens.

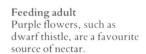

**Feeding adult**
Purple flowers, such as
dwarf thistle, are a favourite
source of nectar.

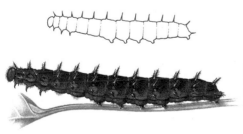

**Caterpillar** [*x1½*]
Feeds on the leaves of violets,
cutting out characteristic
moon-shaped patches.

# SILVER-WASHED FRITILLARY

## *Argynnis paphia*

ONLY ONE OF the 50 Fritillaries of Europe exceeds this butterfly in size, and none is more beautiful or more magnificent. It is, by some margin, the largest of the British species, with a male wingspan that is nearly 1 cm. (0.4 in.) wider than that of the Dark Green Fritillary *(see p.147)*. Fortunately, the Silver-washed Fritillary is less rare than most of its near relatives, although it too has shown worrying declines. At present, it remains common in most large woods, and many small ones, in Ireland, lowland Wales, and the West Country, and frequently flies and breeds along hedged lanes in these regions.

Silver-washed Fritillary colonies are strictly confined to woodland everywhere else in Britain. They were once found as far north as southern Scotland, but today are unknown beyond a line between the River Mersey and the Wash. South of this, the species is also extinct, or reduced to a scattering of small populations, in all the eastern counties of England. This, sadly, even includes the New Forest, once the most famous of all strongholds of this Fritillary. Its abundance there a century ago was legendary. According to reports documented by F. W. Frohawk, "it used to be in such profusion that it was common to see forty or more assembled on the blossoms of a large bramble bush".

***Distribution*** *Locally common in woods and scrubby lanes in south Wales, the West Country and Ireland; present in most large woods in the rest of its range.*

VALEZINA FEMALES

### COLOUR AND SCENT

Adult Silver-washed Fritillaries can be distinguished from other large Fritillaries by the beautiful markings on the underwings. These lack the large, clear-cut silver patches of High Brown and Dark Green Fritillaries *(see pp.145 and 147)*, but instead look rather as if they have been given a watercolour wash of delicate greens and silver streaks – hence both the current name, and its predecessor, the "Greater Silver-streakt Fritillary".

The upperside is equally distinctive in the male, due to four thick, black ridges along the veins of the forewing. These are scent glands, also known as androconial organs, that are formed from two types of modified scales on the wings. The behaviour of this Fritillary is comparatively well known, thanks to the classic research of Dietrich Magnus and others in Germany. It has one generation a year, with adults flying throughout July and August in Britain, and reaching peak numbers around 1 August. Most modern colonies contain no more than a few dozen adults in an average year, although populations of hundreds, or even thousands, fly on the best sites.

It is a considerably more mobile butterfly than the smaller Fritillaries. The adults glide at high speed above the tree-tops, flying from one end of their wood to the other in a matter of seconds, before descending into any sheltered opening in search of flowers, mates or places to lay eggs. In the West Country, they make frequent sorties along wooded lanes. However, little or no mixing has been detected between colonies in neighbouring woods in other parts of the country.

Adult numbers tend to be fairly stable in a particular wood from one year to the next, so long as no major felling occurs. But every so often, there is a spectacular increase. This generally takes place after there has been unusually warm weather in early summer. Few naturalists in southwest England will forget the staggering numbers that emerged in 1976, when Silver-washed Fritillaries could be seen even from a car, as they flew along every wooded lane in large parts of Devon, and when over 100 were visible at once in some woods.

SCENTED SCALES
*During courtship, the outer scales of the male's sex-brands burst open, showering scent scales over the female.*

MALE SEX BRAND

SCENT SCALES

OUTER SCALES

**AN AERIAL DANCE**
*The female (centre) flies in a straight line while the male repeatedly swoops under her, then up in front of her head.*

COURTSHIP CONCLUDED
*After their courtship flight, the female (right) lands on the ground. The male stands opposite with quivering wings, wafting scent scales over her. He then draws her antennae over the sex-brands on his upperwings, and the butterflies soon pair.*

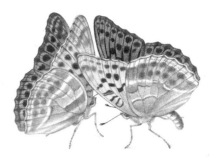

## AN AEROBATIC COURTSHIP

Adults of both sexes spend long periods on tree-tops drinking aphid honeydew, but they also frequently descend to flowers. The male matures after two to three days, and for the rest of his life is preoccupied with finding a mate. He seeks his females on the wing, flying along a zig-zag path, generally 1 to 2 m. (3 to 6 ft.) above ground level, and concentrating on rides, wood edges, and glades. The female is first recognized by her colour. He glides rapidly to investigate any golden object, but is especially attracted by movement. This was well known to the old continental collectors, who would make orange paper models and wave these on the end of fishing lines, netting the males that approached.

Even more irresistible to the male is the flickering pattern that is produced when a female flaps her wings. She, if willing, solicits him further by emitting a scent from the tip of her abdomen. This gives rise to a beautiful courtship flight, which can be seen throughout July in the glades and widest rides of all our larger western woods.

## EGG-LAYING

Female Silver-washed Fritillaries are comparatively inconspicuous until late July, when they begin egg-laying. They are then very much in evidence as they flutter slowly through their woods, weaving between the tree-trunks in search of suitable sites. They have very particular preferences, choosing much shadier places than any of the other Fritillaries whose caterpillars feed on violets. Thus they never lay in fresh clearings, although I have often seen females flutter around the edges of these, before crawling a short distance into the neighbouring older coppice growth to lay in the base of a dense stool. But most eggs are laid under trees, or rather on the trees themselves, for the pale, cone-shaped egg is usually deposited singly in chinks in the bark, nearly always on the mossy, north or west side of the trunk. Having found a suitable area, they then fly slowly above the ground, searching for the scent of violets. Any species attracts them, although the commonest in these situations is common dog-violet *(Viola riviniana)*. They hover over the clumps, sometimes brushing the violets with their wings before fluttering on to the nearest shaft of sunlight.

It is fascinating to watch the egg-laying female, as she crawls crab-like with closed wings up a tree-trunk, probing every crack with her plump curved abdomen, then pausing to press firmly into a chink for a second or two, before the tip slowly recoils. This is a sure sign that an egg has been laid. She often lays two or three more on the same trunk before moving on, usually to the next tree.

Although most eggs are laid between 1 and 2 m. (3 and 6 ft.) above ground level, I have frequently watched females through binoculars and seen them 6 m. (20 ft.) up, probing and laying along the mossy upper branches of ancient oaks. Indeed, any rough niche appears to be suitable. Eggs are sometimes laid on dead bracken, and I have even had some on my clothes on a few occasions. I simply stood still in an ideal spot, and the passing females alighted one by one on my trouser leg, probing the material as they crawled up. They would eventually reach a seam, invariably laying an egg in it. Five eggs were laid within a few centimetres on one afternoon, all so firmly affixed that it was impossible to detach them; alas, they perished in the wash.

## CATERPILLAR AND CHRYSALIS

The egg hatches after about a fortnight, but the little caterpillar does no more than eat the eggshell, before spinning a tiny pad of silk on which it hibernates, still on the tree-trunk. It descends to ground level the following spring, and immediately starts searching for violets on which to feed.

The caterpillar's feeding damage is easy to detect, for it leaves large, curved bites in the sides of the violet leaves. The caterpillar is much harder to spot. It spends most of the day basking in shafts of sunlight, often on dry, dead leaves up to

## TEMPERATURE REGULATION

**MAKING ADJUSTMENTS (1)**
*The butterfly keeps its body temperature near 32°C (90°F) by opening or closing its wings.*

**ABSORBING HEAT (2)**
*The upper surfaces of the wings are opened wide when the butterfly needs to absorb heat.*

**KEEPING COOL (3)**
*As it gets hotter, the butterfly raises its body above the ground, and begins to close its wings.*

**REFLECTING HEAT (4)**
*When it is too hot, the undersides are exposed in order to reflect the sun's heat.*

30 cm. (1 ft.) away from the violet clump. Although it lies quite openly, the spiny brown body and yellow stripes blend perfectly with the sunlit background.

By early June, the first caterpillars are fully grown, and wander in search of pupation sites. The few chrysalises found in the wild have generally been a few metres up in a tree or shrub, suspended beneath a leaf or twig, and looking very like a curled up dead leaf, with silvery patches.

### *VALEZINA* FEMALES

Entomologists eulogize over all stages of this Fritillary's life-cycle, but there is one form in particular that causes excitement. This is the lovely *valezina* type of female, in which the upperwings have a dusky, greenish sheen, and the underwings are distinctly pink. It looks strikingly different on the wing, and is quite common in some central southern populations. *Valezina* females were once thought to be more or less confined to the New Forest and neighbouring woods, but I have found them just as frequently in certain woods in the west Weald of Surrey, and I expect to see them every year in any population throughout north Dorset. Generally between 5 and 15 per cent of females are of the *valezina* type in the larger colonies within the species' main range. There is, however, an abrupt cut-off to the west, north, and east of the central south.

Just why *valezina* females are restricted to central southern England is a mystery, although the same patchy pattern occurs throughout the Continent. This form of the butterfly is controlled by a gene that finds expression only in the female. It is dominant over the normal form when Fritillaries of mixed parentage are bred in captivity, being produced in greater numbers, despite being rarer in the wild. This indicates that *valezina* females must be at some disadvantage in the field, which keeps their numbers down. They are, for one thing, considerably less attractive to males than normal females. They also behave rather differently, avoiding sunny clearings and rides and instead skulking in shady woodland. This is possibly because their dusky bodies are prone to overheating. They are certainly capable of flying in much cloudier weather.

### CHANGING FORTUNES

The increasing shade in many woodlands, created by the decline in coppicing and the planting of conifers, has caused the extinction of this fine Fritillary in large areas of its former range. Its need for fairly open woodland is strikingly demonstrated whenever trees are thinned, for the butterfly's numbers shoot up from a few individuals to many scores during the next few years. Although generally tolerant of much shadier conditions than the other Fritillaries that feed on violets, and often the last of the group to disappear, it cannot switch to breeding in rough, sheltered grassland. This means that it has disappeared from many shady woods in which the Small Pearl-bordered Fritillary lingers on in glades and along rides. Thus a great many populations of Silver-washed Fritillary have disappeared completely, both from mature conifer plantations, and from deciduous woods in which the canopy is more or less closed. This has been particularly severe on the heavy, flat soils of eastern England.

Today the Silver-washed Fritillary is probably extinct in the whole of East Anglia, Cambridgeshire, and Lincolnshire, and occurs in very few places in the Midlands and in Kent. It is still reasonably common in the heavily wooded areas of the western Weald, but its status in Hampshire is parlous – Victorian entomologists who once flocked to the county for the *valezina* form would be shocked by the decline, and by learning that the Purple Emperor now occurs in nearly 50 per cent more of the county's woods than this species.

Only slightly further west, the butterfly's fortunes improve dramatically. Colonies survive in most of the woods of Dorset and Wiltshire, and in considerably larger numbers in Avon, Gloucestershire, Devon, lowland Wales, and Ireland. Here it is so abundant in some years that it is hard to imagine that it could ever decline. Ominously, the same could have been said of the burgeoning New Forest populations, just 50 years ago.

# SILVER-WASHED FRITILLARY · *Argynnis paphia*

LIFE-CYCLE

| | JAN | FEB | MAR | APR | MAY | JUN | JUL | AUG | SEP | OCT | NOV | DEC |
|---|---|---|---|---|---|---|---|---|---|---|---|---|
| EGG | | | | | | | | | | | | |
| CATERPILLAR | | | | | | | | | | | | |
| CHRYSALIS | | | | | | | | | | | | |
| ADULT | | | | | | | | | | | | |

**Male upperside**
Four black ridges (sex-brands) lie on the veins of each forewing.

**Male underside**
Markings are "washed" rather than clear-cut.

**Female upperside**
Females have more extensive black markings.

**Egg [*x15*]**
Laid singly on tree-trunks, usually in bark crevices.

**Chrysalis [*x1½*]**
Camouflaged as a dead leaf. Adult emerges after 2-3 weeks.

**Female**
*Valezina* form, found principally from Dorset to the west Weald.

**Feeding adult**
Adult *valezina* form, feeding at the flowers of bramble.

**Caterpillar [*x1½*]**
Back is striped with characteristic yellow lines.

# MARSH FRITILLARY

*Euphydryas aurinia*

THIS LOVELY FRITILLARY is one of the most rapidly declining butterflies in Europe. It is primarily a wetland species, and the chief cause of its decline has been the relentless drainage of meadows for agriculture. This process has been going on for centuries, but the combination of modern farming methods and subsidies has resulted in a devastation that would have seemed inconceivable to Victorian entomologists. It is, indeed, barely a century since Marsh Fritillary caterpillars became so abundant in Co. Fermanagh that Irish villagers were forced to barricade their homes with peat bricks against the onslaught, and farmers raked up huge piles for burning. Questions were asked in the House of Commons about the problem.

Such outbreaks were a regular, but infrequent, occurrence throughout the nineteenth century. Another example occurred in Co. Clare, when the Rev. S. L. Brakey drove to see a reported "shower of worms", but instead found Marsh Fritillary caterpillars "so multitudinous in some fields that a black layer of insects seemed to roll in corrugations as the migrating hosts swarmed over one another in search of food".

### CHANGING PATTERNS

It would be wrong, however, to conclude that the Marsh Fritillary was ever common in the British Isles as a whole. Colonies were distinctly local, and, more often than not, numbers were low. A typical population was monitored by the distinguished geneticist E. B. Ford and his father in Cumberland from 1881 to 1935. They watched it through two periods when the butterfly was "excessively common", which were separated by 30 years when it was very rare indeed.

The Fords noticed that the adults varied enormously in size and wing pattern during the period when numbers were increasing, but that they then settled down to a uniform pattern. This however, was recognizably different from that of typical adults during the previous period of abundance. They concluded that

*Distribution A declining species on boggy, unfertilized grassland. Locally distributed in Ireland, and scarce or rare in the rest of its range.*

this species possessed great inherent variety in its genetic makeup, but that this was seldom expressed, because most variants were comparatively unsuited to the prevailing conditions. The majority of the variants survived only in the most favourable seasons, and it was in these years, too, that the colony expanded.

### EMERGENCE AND MATING

Marsh Fritillaries breed year after year in the same patch of grassland, which may be less than 0.5 ha. (1 acre), or over 20 ha. (50 acres) in size. They emerge once a year, starting in late May to early June, depending on locality, and warmth of spring. The males emerge first, and are by far the more conspicuous sex. By the time the females emerge, most males are quartering the ground in low, zig-zagging flights, searching for a freshly hatched mate.

A typical female emerges early in the morning, waits an hour or two for her wings to dry, then crawls out into the open to sit with wings held wide open. This soon attracts a male, who alights beside her. He walks around to the front and flutters his wings, which probably showers her with scent. Pairing quickly follows, and lasts for about two hours. The male then disengages, but not before he has sealed her genitals with a "chastity belt" of foam, which prevents any rival male from fertilizing her at a later stage.

The female spends the remainder of the day searching for a suitable plant of devil's-bit scabious (*Succisa pratensis*) for her eggs. Although just a few hours old, her swollen body may already contain 300 mature eggs – so many that flight is often impossible unless the weather is warm. She usually just crawls among the vegetation until she encounters a prominent, medium-sized plant, growing in a warm, sunny situation, with its leaves standing proud of the surrounding vegetation. She grasps the edge of a leaf between her legs, and curls her abdomen around to lay a batch of about 150 eggs, glued in neat rows to the undersurface. When this is complete, a second layer, and often a third, is cemented onto the first until, three hours later, the entire load has been laid. By then her body has become a slack and flabby bag, but she is now light enough to fly properly, and the last hours of the day are spent flitting between whatever flowers are available.

Many females are caught by predators on the day of emergence, but those that survive quickly develop more eggs, enabling some to lay a smaller batch on their second day, and possibly a third after that. These are often placed on plants that already contain eggs, and huge clusters can be found. Keith Porter, the entomologist on whose work much of this account is based, once found 1,500 eggs under a single leaf in Oxfordshire, probably originating from at least five females.

## TEMPERATURE REGULATION

The eggs hatch after about three weeks, and the tiny caterpillars immediately spin a dense and conspicuous silk web, which is perforated with tunnels that lead to the centre of the plant. The original scabious is usually devoured within a week, causing the caterpillars to crawl, *en masse,* to a nearby plant, where the whole process begins again. This continues until late August. The caterpillars then moult for a third time, change colour from brown to black, and spin a new and dense nest deep among the grass. They spend the winter inside this, huddled together in small groups, each suspended in a pocket of silk. The silk insulates the caterpillars in a warm blanket of trapped air, and on swampy sites the whole nest can remain submerged for several weeks without the caterpillars coming to harm.

The bristly little caterpillars reappear on the first warm days of spring to spin a fresh web over another communal scabious plant. The air is often cold at this time of year, and the caterpillars must raise their body temperature to around 35° to 37°C (95° to 98°F) if they are to digest their food. They achieve this by clustering together above the vegetation, to form a black mass that absorbs the warmth of the sun.

Nests of basking fourth-stage caterpillars are easily found in early spring, particularly on cool but sunny days. Caterpillars are also conspicuous in their fifth and sixth stages, even though they separate into small groups and eventually live singly. By now, they need to eat considerable quantities of scabious. The hungry caterpillars are surprisingly agile, and spread out over the entire site when numbers are high; it is not unusual for every scabious to be chewed down to an unrecognizable stump. If there is still insufficient food, the caterpillars wander far from their fields, and will tackle other plants, especially concentrating on honeysuckle *(Lonicera periclymenum),* in the surrounding hedgerows. But few survive once the devil's-bit scabious has been eaten, and starvation is a major cause of death.

## ATTACK BY PARASITES

Apart from hunger, the other main threats to Marsh Fritillary caterpillars are from ground beetles, spiders, bugs, and tiny parasitic wasps. Birds are seldom a problem, due to the protection afforded by the spiny bristles, and wasps are the greatest cause of death. Two species are involved, both of which live solely on Marsh Fritillary caterpillars. In southern England, Wales, and southern Ireland, they are mainly infected by the wasp *Apanteles bignelli,* whereas in the north, *A. melitaearum* is the major parasite. There is, however, a slight overlap; both parasites are found attacking colonies on Dartmoor.

The life history of these *Apanteles* wasps is an extraordinary example of how parasites can adapt to exploit their hosts. Each generation of caterpillars plays host to up to three generations of wasps, with individual caterpillars being attacked at any stage in their lives. Newly hatched caterpillars are afflicted in July, with the wasps injecting minute eggs into any caterpillar that has emerged from the safety of its nest. The eggs hatch into wasp grubs within the caterpillars' bodies. These first-generation grubs feed on the caterpillars' tissues, but do not cause their death until August, when the parasites are ready to depart to spin their own cocoons.

By the time that the wasps hatch from these cocoons, and are ready to infect the next batch of caterpillars, their prospective hosts are already spinning hibernation nests. So the second generation of *Apanteles* grubs spends the winter inside the medium-sized, fourth-stage caterpillars within their webs. Infected caterpillars are killed in spring, and adult wasps emerge from their cocoons a week or two later. This leaves time for these wasps to lay a third generation of eggs, which develop in the caterpillars as they enter their final stage.

The parasites in this third generation have a problem, for there are now no caterpillars available, and the wasps are unable to infect chrysalises, eggs, or adult butterflies. So they must wait for the next generation of caterpillars to hatch in July before they can continue their destructive breeding cycle. This apparent difficulty has been neatly solved in two ways. In the first place, the wasps appear to slow down the development of the affected caterpillars, so that they are still present when all the uninfected Marsh Fritillaries have pupated. Thus, the wasps do not themselves form cocoons until the adult butterflies of the next generation are emerging. At this point, the *Apanteles* spin especially dense cocoons encased in silk. Although the tiny adult wasps soon develop, they do not bite their way out for another four to six weeks, by which time a new generation of caterpillars is ready for infection.

These parasites inflict immense damage on a Marsh Fritillary colony: up to 70 wasps may emerge from a single caterpillar,

KEEPING WARM
*Marsh Fritillary caterpillars can become 20°C (36°F) warmer than their surroundings by basking on their web. Individual caterpillars commute down to the cool scabious leaves to feed, then return to the warm huddle to digest their meal.*

and in some years, three out of four caterpillars are killed. However, the parasite seldom gets out of hand, for it suffers a setback in certain years, when the infection rate drops to under 10 per cent of the Marsh Fritillary population. This apparently occurs when there is a cool but sunny spring. Marsh Fritillary caterpillars capitalize by basking and developing quickly, but the *Apanteles* cannot warm itself up inside its cocoon. The wasps therefore develop much more slowly, and many Marsh Fritillaries develop quickly enough to avoid being victims of the parasites in their last stage as caterpillars.

## A HISTORY OF DECLINE

It is impossible to say how many Marsh Fritillaries emerge on our best sites at the height of a population explosion, but it certainly runs into tens of thousands. However, typical British colonies seldom seem to contain more than 200 adults, and it is clear that many decline to a few dozen individuals in their worst years.

Whether large or small, there is no doubt that the number of colonies left in Britain is a minute fraction of the former total. On the Continent, the situation has become so serious that the Marsh Fritillary is one of the few European butterflies afforded special protection, including the preservation of all breeding sites. Sadly, at the time of writing the British government has opted out of this commitment, although the Irish government has agreed to it.

There are, perhaps, more Marsh Fritillary colonies in Ireland than in any other country north of the Mediterranean, but they are disappearing at an alarming rate. In addition to the straightforward destruction of sites, many unfertilized swamps are no longer grazed, which causes the devil's-bit scabious to become smothered by tall vegetation and unsuitable for butterfly breeding. Not that the Marsh Fritillary thrives under heavy grazing either: it is seldom, if ever, found in wet meadows where the sward is less than 15 to 25 cm. (6 to 10 in.) tall. Scotland also possesses fine populations, and there were some notable population explosions of Marsh Fritillary around Oban in the 1970s. The main Scottish centres are in the west, among damp, mossy moorland, and on acid raised and blanket bogs from Argyllshire to Inverness, and on the isles of Mull, Islay, Jura, Colonsay, Gunna, Rhum, Coll, and Tiree.

Scottish colonies are greatly outnumbered by the 200 or so populations that still survive in Wales and England. These are mainly in the west. In lowland England, agriculture has taken an especially heavy toll. The butterfly is now extinct in most of the eastern third of the country, including Sussex, which was once considered a stronghold. Further west there are scattered relic populations, and in Wales, the West Country, and Lake District, it is still worth looking on any marshy piece of land where devil's-bit scabious flowers in profusion.

## COLONIES ON CHALK AND LIMESTONE

Despite this background of declines, there is a small area of the country where the Marsh Fritillary has colonized a different type of habitat, and has actually increased over the past 50 years, although nothing like enough to offset declines on traditional sites. In the Cotswolds, Wiltshire, and Dorset, devil's-bit scabious also grows on unfertilized chalk and limestone downs. These were never colonized before the 1920s, probably because sheep and rabbits kept the sward too dry and short. However, as downland became overgrown, an increasing number of Marsh Fritillary colonies has been found on these hills, mainly on the warm but wet western slopes. Some of these new colonies are fairly large, and although Marsh Fritillaries may look out of place among the Adonis Blues and other chalkland species, it is a delight to see this endangered butterfly enjoying a modest recovery somewhere within its range.

# MARSH FRITILLARY · *Euphydryas aurinia*

LIFE-CYCLE

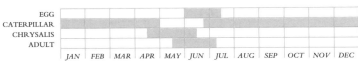

| | JAN | FEB | MAR | APR | MAY | JUN | JUL | AUG | SEP | OCT | NOV | DEC |
|---|---|---|---|---|---|---|---|---|---|---|---|---|
| EGG | | | | | | | | | | | | |
| CATERPILLAR | | | | | | | | | | | | |
| CHRYSALIS | | | | | | | | | | | | |
| ADULT | | | | | | | | | | | | |

**Male upperside**
Both sexes have a row of spots on the upper– and undersides.

**Male underside**
Neither sex has silver patches on the underside.

**Female upperside**
Females are often larger and slightly paler than males.

**Female underside**
Patterning is similar to that of the male.

**Female, Irish form**
The Irish form *hibernica* has a brighter and more contrasting coloration.

**Perching male**
Male on the leaf of the caterpillar foodplant, devil's-bit scabious.

**Egg [*x15*]**
Laid in large batches, sometimes three layers deep. The eggs gradually darken and hatch after about three weeks.

**Chrysalis [*x1½*]**
Suspended from a leaf or stem in low vegetation.

**Feeding adult**
Adult on the flowerhead of meadow thistle, a favourite nectar source.

**Caterpillar [*x1½*]**
Gregarious at first, dispersing and becoming solitary when fully grown.

# GLANVILLE FRITILLARY

## *Melitaea cinxia*

I HAVE HAD the pleasure of carrying out research on all eight British Fritillaries and, to my mind, the Glanville is both the loveliest and the most interesting. It is probably also the rarest, being confined nowadays to perhaps a dozen sites on the Isle of Wight, and to several more in the Channel Islands. Any of these sites is worth visiting in May. They are lovely in their own right, most being warm, sheltered undercliffs carpeted with wild flowers such as thrift *(Armeria maritima)* and bird's-foot trefoil *(Lotus corniculatus),* which form the butterfly's principal nectar sources. The Glanville Fritillary's delicate underwings are especially attractive seen against these pink and yellow blooms, and it is a fine butterfly in flight, whether gliding swiftly through still air or battling with whirring wingbeats against a sea breeze.

A typical emergence begins in mid-May, reaching a peak in early June, but declining quite rapidly so that few butterflies outlive the month. It is a variable emergence, however, much affected by the warmth of the season. Thus the first males may be seen as early as April during a warm spring, and in these years there is sometimes a small second brood in August if the weather holds.

**Distribution** *Confined to a few warm coastal cliffs and undercliffs on the Channel Islands and south coast of the Isle of Wight.*

### A DIET OF PLANTAINS

Adult Glanville Fritillaries live in fairly close-knit colonies, with most remaining in the chines or undercliffs where they emerged. There is, however, some interchange, and one frequently finds a group of caterpillars on plantains *(Plantago* spp.*)* along a cliff edge, resulting from an egg batch laid up to a kilometre from the nearest permanent centre. Strays are picked up all over the Isle of Wight, and they periodically form temporary colonies on the chalk downs and in northern parts of the island.

This butterfly is certainly the most agile of fliers. Males are especially active and conspicuous as they patrol back and forth above the seashore. Like all small Fritillaries, they constantly dip down to investigate any golden object, in the hope of finding a virgin female. The females themselves are less conspicuous, preferring to hide for long periods in dense tussocks. But for all their heavy burden of eggs, they are remarkably agile when they do fly, in sharp contrast to their close relative the Marsh Fritillary, which can just about lumber off the ground when egg-laden, and then only in hot weather.

Mating usually occurs around mid-day, and is a fairly conspicuous affair, for the female may continue to fly between flowers, dragging the male behind. She then starts searching for a site in which to lay her eggs. This takes a considerable time, for eggs are laid in batches of 50 to 100, and great care is taken in selecting a suitable spot. Most eggs are laid in sheltered nooks, where the ground is warm and well drained, and where abundant clumps of young ribwort plantains *(Plantago lanceolata)* grow vigorously in a short, sparse sward, with much bare soil around. The primrose-yellow eggs are deposited in layers on the underside of a young plantain leaf, where they hatch two to three weeks later, depending on the weather after laying.

### CONSPICUOUS CATERPILLARS

The Glanville Fritillary has the most conspicuous caterpillars of any British butterfly. They live gregariously from August until March, in dense webs of white silk, spun over the clumps of tender young plantains. The caterpillars spend much of the day basking on top of these webs, where their black, bristly bodies absorb warmth from the sun in the same way as the Marsh Fritillary *(see p.154).* However, they spend much longer basking than Marsh Fritillaries, and are also more conspicuous because they concentrate on small plantains.

As the caterpillars grow, they shed their skins several times, always within the safety of the nest. After the fourth moult, when the caterpillars are about 5 mm. (⅕ in.) long, they move to slightly taller vegetation where they spin much denser nests. These contain numerous little pockets of silk, suspended like

## GLANVILLE FRITILLARY · *Melitaea cinxia*

### LIFE-CYCLE

| | JAN | FEB | MAR | APR | MAY | JUN | JUL | AUG | SEP | OCT | NOV | DEC |
|---|---|---|---|---|---|---|---|---|---|---|---|---|
| EGG | | | | | | ▓ | ▓ | | | | | |
| CATERPILLAR | ▓ | ▓ | ▓ | | | ▓ | ▓ | ▓ | ▓ | ▓ | ▓ | ▓ |
| CHRYSALIS | | | | ▓ | ▓ | | | | | | | |
| ADULT | | | | | ▓ | ▓ | | | | | | |

**Male**
Males are slightly smaller than females, with angular wings.

**Female**
Females are often darker than males; the wings are more rounded.

**Male**
Aberrant form *wittei*, with less chequered markings; caught on the Isle of Wight, 1929.

**Feeding adult**
Bird's-foot trefoil is the main food source on many sites.

**Resting adult**
Adult on leaf of ribwort plantain, the caterpillar foodplant.

**Egg** [*x22*]
Shell has 16–20 vertical ridges, or keels.

SIDE VIEW    VIEW FROM ABOVE

**Chrysalis** [*x1½*]
Concealed deep inside dense vegetation.

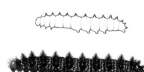

**Caterpillar** [*x1½*]
Mature caterpillar, shown here, feeds in the open on plantain leaves.

miniature hammocks within the nest, and here the caterpillars gather to hibernate in small groups. Hibernation nests are easy to find in September and early October, until the first gales of autumn blow surrounding grass clumps down over them.

## ESCAPE UNDERFOOT

The caterpillars remain dormant until March, when they swarm out on sunny days to spin a fresh web over the young, newly sprouting plantains. They can be extraordinarily abundant, concentrating on warm, open patches, such as footpaths, where it was feared that many were trampled by ramblers. They have, in fact, an escape mechanism, admirably described over 200 years ago by Moses Harris: "They are so remarkably timid that should you stir the Plant they are on, tho' never so little... they instantly roll themselves into the form of a Hedge-hog".

They also roll safely away into the vegetation, as I found when I tested their vulnerability by deliberately trampling on nests that contained a known number of caterpillars. These were recounted an hour or two later when the nests had regrouped, and even the heavy boots of my colleague, David Simcox, made little impact, killing an insignificant number of the caterpillars. Although a somewhat brutal exercise, the results were valuable, for otherwise certain key footpaths would have been diverted, and some lovely stretches of coastline closed to the public at a particularly beautiful time of year.

Glanville Fritillary caterpillars enter their final phase in April, and are extremely handsome when full-grown, with shining, russet-coloured heads and black, bristly bodies. At this stage the nests are abandoned, and the caterpillars swarm out over the plantains, greedily devouring the leaves. They still show a strong preference for young plants, but these are often exhausted, forcing the caterpillars to eat leathery old growths and, as a last resort, the strange lobed leaves of the buck's-horn plantain (*Plantago coronopus*). Even these are sometimes used up, and although the caterpillars can cover considerable areas quite quickly by running along paths and over short turf, many starve in certain years. Those that survive crawl into dense vegetation, and form solitary chrysalises, almost impossible to find.

## ON THE UNDERCLIFFS

Although the Glanville Fritillary is a common and widespread insect in warmer parts of central southern Europe, it is confined to exceptionally warm places in Britain, where there is also a regular supply of many thousands of young plantains. Such conditions occur along much of the southern coast of the Isle of Wight, although they may not persist for long in any one place. This spectacular coastline is famed for its many different geological formations: Glanville Fritillaries are found mainly on the well-drained sandstones, principally between Freshwater and Ventnor. They also breed on the south-facing slopes up several chines, but only in the first hundred metres or so in from the sea, where the ground is unstable and the vegetation sparse.

It is the instability of these cliffs and undercliffs that is responsible for the current prosperity of this rare butterfly. Some erosion occurs every winter, either as little slippages or major falls, and a flush of young plantains regenerates in the sandy exposures every spring. Many caterpillars are lost during the severest of landfalls, but plenty survive to repopulate the new patches. It is indeed far more serious if there has not been much slippage for more than a year or two. Then a tall, dense sward develops that is utterly unsuitable for egg-laying.

## EXTINCTION ON MAINLAND BRITAIN

The Glanville Fritillary has long disappeared from the British mainland, and although it is regularly reintroduced to suitable sites, none has survived for long, the most successful being a railway embankment in the New Forest, where the butterfly flourished for 17 years until the site itself was destroyed.

It is difficult to gauge just how widespread it once was, for there is disagreement over the authenticity of some early records. The last, and most famous, mainland colonies were on the southeast Kent coast between Folkestone and Sandwich, where the species mysteriously disappeared in the late 1850s.

Other mainland colonies apparently bred on rough ground beside woods. These, almost certainly, were irregularly tilled areas that were frequently disturbed and then abandoned, situated along warm, sheltered edges. There are few contemporary accounts, and the butterfly was always a rarity, although known from as far north as Lincolnshire in the 1690s. It was here indeed that this Fritillary was discovered, by Eleanor Glanville, after whom it was eventually named. Prior to this, the butterfly was first christened the "Lincolnshire Fritillary" and later downgraded to the "Dullidge Fritillary", after the more accessible populations around Tottenham and Dulwich; later still it acquired the apt but unexciting name of "Plantain Fritillary". Finally, some 40 years after Eleanor's death, the name was changed again, as described by Moses Harris in one of the most famous passages in early entomology:

"This Fly took its Name from the ingenious Lady Glanvil, whose Memory had like to have suffered for her Curiosity. Some Relations that was disappointed by her Will, attempted to let it aside by Acts of Lunacy, for they suggested that none but those who were deprived of their Senses, would go in Pursuit of Butterflies".

Fortunately, Eleanor Glanville's reputation survived this slur, and the will was established.

# HEATH FRITILLARY

## *Mellicta athalia*

THIS ATTRACTIVE, small Fritillary flies in a variety of warm habitats on the poorer soils of southern England. It breeds in patches where the vegetation has recently been cut, burned, or cleared, and has become extremely localized: colonies, nowadays, are found in a few sheltered valleys on Exmoor, in four abandoned hayfields in Devon and Cornwall, and in a handful of woods in Essex and Kent. Yet it is often abundant. Over 10,000 adults can emerge from a single colony, making a wonderful sight in June, with the males particularly in evidence, as they encircle small clearings, hunting for hidden females.

Rare as the Heath Fritillary is, its position today is a remarkable improvement on its status in the late 1970s, when many entomologists were predicting that it would soon follow the Large Blue to extinction. For although always a local species in Britain, the Heath Fritillary had been in continuous and severe decline for well over a hundred years. By 1980, it was found in just five woods in the West Country, and in the large woods at Blean, near Canterbury. The outlook, too, was depressing: two sites that had supported huge populations when they had been established as nature reserves had both lost their colonies, and management changes in the other areas made it unlikely that their Heath Fritillaries could survive.

*Distribution A great rarity found in sheltered Exmoor valleys, rough grassland near woods in Devon and Cornwall, and Kent.*

### BACK FROM THE BRINK

Following the loss of the Large Blue, rescuing the Heath Fritillary became a matter of urgency in butterfly conservation circles. Fortunately Martin Warren, at Furzebrook Research Station, was able to build up a detailed knowledge of the butterfly's requirements.

This emergency action produced a remarkable turnaround in the Heath Fritillary's fortunes. The butterfly once again teems on the old reserves, and several new ones have been established which now support flourishing colonies. Two successful introductions have also been made to carefully prepared former sites in Essex. In addition, there was an unexpected bonus in the early 1980s, when a number of large colonies was discovered on Exmoor. Several are on land owned by the National Trust, whose management plans now take account of the exacting needs of this creature. On the debit side, but underlining the need for active conservation, nearly every colony that has not received special management has, as predicted, become extinct in the last decade.

### SUN-LOVING INSECTS

It would have been tragic if this Fritillary had been lost, for it is an insect of charm and some beauty. It is on the wing in late May in the West Country, where it reaches a peak in the first third of June, and often survives well into July. Kentish colonies emerge a fortnight later, probably because spring temperatures are cooler there. Depending on the warmth of the season, most adults live for five to ten days, during which time they practically never stray from their breeding sites. Indeed, the very static nature of this butterfly is one of the major reasons why it has been unable to cope in the modern countryside.

Although female Heath Fritillaries spend most of their lives basking or hidden in the ground vegetation, the males are extremely conspicuous. They are sun-loving insects, seldom flying when the temperature drops below 18°C (64°F), and then only if the sun shines. But whenever conditions are suitable, they quickly take to the wing, and are airborne for nearly half the day. Theirs is a smooth, flitting flight, powered by little flicks of the wings, which are then stretched flat as they glide just above ground level traversing their clearings in search of mates. They often pause to feed on flat, open flowers.

### EARLY DEVELOPMENT

Females mate within a few hours of emergence, and wait several more days while their eggs ripen in the sun. Heavily laden, they then embark on ponderous flights, fluttering just above the ground vegetation before alighting to continue on foot. They pause to bask quite often in their wanderings, then burrow again in the undergrowth before settling to lay a batch of gleaming, pale green eggs. These are ejected at a rate of two a second, until a mass of perhaps 80 to 150 eggs has been laid, usually on the undersurface of a small bramble or dead leaf, close to a foodplant. Smaller batches are occasionally found, but these probably emanate from old females that have already made their first large drop.

The eggs soon turn an attractive lemon-yellow, hatching after two to three weeks. The young caterpillars eat the egg-shells and then move *en masse* to the nearby foodplant, where they spin a flimsy web. But soon they disperse into smaller bands, typically of 10 to 20 caterpillars apiece, and again spin fine webs as they roam from plant to plant. These are not at all difficult to find if you search on warm, sunny days in August.

After feeding for about a month, the spiny young caterpillars enter hibernation, sometimes in small groups but usually singly, fastened to a silk pad spun in the curl of a dry, dead leaf.

They reappear on the first warm days of March or April, to bask and feed whenever conditions permit. They are inactive when the air is colder than 12°C (54°F) and, like the gregarious caterpillars of the Marsh Fritillary *(see p.154)*, spend long periods basking in sunshine to raise their body temperatures high enough to digest food. By the time they are fully grown in May, the curious black-and-amber caterpillars can be found with ease on any site where the vegetation is sparse, basking on dead leaves in ones and twos, or lying openly in the sunshine on any of their foodplants.

## A WIDE-RANGING APPETITE

It is always curious when a rarity such as the Heath Fritillary turns out to have several foodplants, some of which are extremely common. The main food eaten by the caterpillars varies with the location. In woods, they generally eat cow-wheat *(Melampyrum pratense)*, a lovely plant of mainly light, acidic soils, which lives semi-parasitically on grasses. This is the only food of the eastern colonies, but on Exmoor, where cow-wheat is sparser, older caterpillars often switch to foxglove *(Digitalis purpurea)*, and, on occasions, eat a range of other species. Finally, in the abandoned hay meadows and other sites in Devon and Cornwall, ribwort plantain *(Plantago lanceolata)* and germander speedwell *(Veronica chamaedrys)* are the main food, although here again other plants may be tackled.

Given this lack of selectivity, a shortage of foodplants is clearly not responsible for the Heath Fritillary's decline. Instead, the critical factor – as with so many other rare butterflies – is that the plants must be growing in a relatively high temperature.

The Heath Fritillary breeds only in the warmth and shelter of recently formed woodland clearings, where its foodplants briefly flourish, but then become too overgrown for the caterpillars only three to ten years later. Its requirements are extraordinarily precise: in the densest coppices in Blean Wood, Heath Fritillaries will colonize an area in the first year after a clearing, increasing to perhaps 10,000 adults by the second year, only to be completely shaded out two years later. A similar sequence occurs on freshly burned heathland, and so, too, when a sparse hay meadow is abandoned, albeit on a slightly longer time scale.

## STAYING IN PLACE

The remarkable speed with which events can change for this species was recognized by the Victorian entomologists and collectors, who knew the Heath Fritillary as a butterfly that "followed the woodman".

It is a pity that more twentieth-century conservationists did not heed this saying for, when two nature reserves were obtained for the butterfly, neither was cleared on a regular basis and their vast Heath Fritillary colonies soon disappeared. But although habitat change has been identified as the cause of most disappearances, other factors are also involved.

Because adult Heath Fritillaries are so sedentary, they simply do not reach fresh clearings quickly enough unless these arise within 200 to 300 m. of an existing colony. Even in the woods at Blean, which are well populated by the butterfly, many isolated clearings are never colonized in the four years that they remain suitable.

It seems surprising, at first sight, that any butterfly should have evolved to become dependent on a habitat that lasts for just a few years in one spot, while at the same time lacking the mobility to discover new clearances as and when these arise. The same problem is seen in many other sedentary butterflies, including those Fritillaries that feed on violets, as well as the Silver-spotted Skipper and several Blues. I think there is a simple explanation, the key being that these species have been moulded by certain conditions that prevailed in the British countryside during the past 12,000 years, but have become badly unstuck in the present century, when radical changes have occurred in their habitats.

## THE EFFECT OF TEMPERATURE

To understand the paradoxical position of these butterflies, it is necessary to go back 13,000 years to the time when, at the height of the last Ice Age, all butterflies would have been eliminated from Britain. As the ice receded, our current species are believed to have reoccupied the country, spreading from southern Europe and beyond roughly 10,000 years ago. There

# HEATH FRITILLARY · *Mellicta athalia*

## LIFE-CYCLE

| | JAN | FEB | MAR | APR | MAY | JUN | JUL | AUG | SEP | OCT | NOV | DEC |
|---|---|---|---|---|---|---|---|---|---|---|---|---|
| EGG | | | | | | | | | | | | |
| CATERPILLAR | | | | | | | | | | | | |
| CHRYSALIS | | | | | | | | | | | | |
| ADULT | | | | | | | | | | | | |

**Male**
The amount of black on the upperside
varies between individual butterflies.

**Female**
The ground-colour of the female is
often lighter than that of the male.

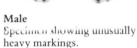

**Male**
Specimen showing unusually
heavy markings.

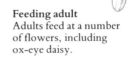

**Resting adult**
Male resting on the
flowerhead of a plantain.

**Egg [*x22*]**
Laid in batches of up
to 150, on or near the
leaves of a variety
of foodplants.

**Chrysalis [*x1½*]**
Formed inside a dead leaf,
usually near the ground.

**Feeding adult**
Adults feed at a number
of flowers, including
ox-eye daisy.

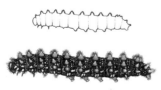

**Caterpillar [*x1½*]**
The caterpillars are
gregarious at first,
later dispersing.

161

followed a period of 5,000 or 6,000 years, when average summer temperatures were 2-3°C (3.5-5.5°F) warmer than today, rather similar, in fact, to those now occurring in central Europe.

Anyone who travels south to the Dordogne or Rhône Valley will be struck by the abundance of many species – and not just butterflies – that are rarities in southern Britain. A closer examination reveals that these breed in much more overgrown conditions under a warm climate: Adonis Blues, Large Blues, and Silver-spotted Skippers, for example, are found in knee-high limestone grassland in central France, and "woodland" species thrive not only in shadier woods, but also in hayfields and overgrown grasslands. Nor are these species confined to warm, south-facing slopes, as is often the case in England, but breed on all aspects and on flat ground. In other words, in regions where the climate is warmer, these heat-loving butter-flies can breed in most of the places where their foodplants occur, and are not restricted to a few exceptionally warm spots.

It is reasonable to suppose that the Heath Fritillary had similarly less exacting requirements when it reinvaded Britain after the Ice Age, because the climate was that much warmer. It may still have been fairly localized, for most of the country was under mature forest (the "Wildwood"), but at least it would not have depended solely on new clearings for its survival.

### MAN-MADE HABITATS
About 6,000 to 7,000 years ago, humans started to fell the Wildwood. It is likely that Heath Fritillaries immediately colonized these Stone-Age woodland clearings. Then, in about 2500 BC, the climate cooled by 4°C (7°F) or more. At this point, the artificial habitats created by man probably became vital to the survival of heat-loving butterflies. Thus Adonis Blues, Large Blues, and Silver-spotted Skippers may have become restricted to heavily grazed patches on the south-facing southern downs, where the grass was so short that the soil baked in the sun. Silver-studded Blues were probably confined to hot, freshly burned areas of heath, and in woodlands, several of our Fritillaries may have found warm refuges in the places that were regularly cleared through coppicing.

Following this change in the climate, it seems likely that not only did the Heath Fritillary become trapped in these man-made coppices (and on heaths that were burned back on a similar regular basis), but that it also became much more sedentary. For from now on, any individual that had a tendency to migrate beyond its wood would be likely to die without finding a new breeding site, whereas its less adventurous brothers and sisters were almost guaranteed to find fresh clearings in the adjacent piece of woodland. We know from records of the Swallowtail that butterflies can become less mobile when circumstances change in a way that puts migrants at a disadvantage. In that case, it took 30 years before structural modifications occurred to the Swallowtail's body. How probable, therefore, that British Heath Fritillary also became sedentary through being restricted to worked coppices for perhaps 5,000 generations.

### PERMANENT PROTECTION
It is hard to say just how widespread the Heath Fritillary became during the heyday of coppicing, for the practice was already in abeyance when the first comprehensive records of insects were compiled. It may always have been restricted to warm, light soils. But although clearly a local species in the eighteenth century, it was nonetheless common enough to be familiar to the first collectors. It was indeed described as early as 1699, and called the "May Fritillary" to distinguish it from the "April Fritillary" (the Pearl-bordered). Both names became inappro-priate after the calendar changed in 1751, and for much of the eighteenth and nineteenth centuries it was instead known as the "Pearl Border Likeness".

In retrospect, it seems likely that the gloomy predictions of this species' extinction would have been fulfilled, if the results of the research into its ecology had not been quickly put into practice. The Exmoor sites would perhaps have survived, but the others were on borrowed time by the early 1980s. The situation in the West Country was especially precarious, for the best sites had been planted with young conifers, and the colonies could not have lasted long. Fortunately the Prince of Wales intervened – for the sites were on Duchy of Cornwall land – and soon the conifers were grubbed out, and the rough, disturbed grassland restored. This prompt action has undoubtedly saved these populations, which are now thriving.

The situation in Kent is less satisfactory. Much of the Blean woodland is in private hands, and the butterfly may soon be eliminated from these areas. On the other hand, some parts are within nature reserves, and by making annual clearings close to existing Heath Fritillary colonies, and by broadening the rides to encourage greater movement, it has been possible to increase the butterfly's numbers. There is, moreover, the prospect of further introductions to reserves elsewhere, as has occurred with great success in Essex.

# SPECKLED WOOD

## *Pararge aegeria*

THE SPECKLED WOOD has coped more successfully than any other butterfly with the fundamental changes that have occurred in British woodlands. A lover of dappled shade, this attractive Brown has spread continuously since the 1930s through the abandoned coppices, mature deciduous woods, and conifer plantations of Wales, southern England, Ireland, and central Scotland. This represents a welcome return to many districts from which the butterfly had mysteriously disappeared in the second half of the nineteenth century, but it has also spread to some previously unrecorded regions. Much of this information has been gathered by Tim Shreeves of Oxford Polytechnic.

*Distribution Common in woods, scrub, and tall hedgerows throughout Ireland, lowland Wales and much of southern England.*

### OVERLAPPING GENERATIONS

Adult Speckled Woods can be seen at any time from late March until October. Their chocolate-and-cream markings are unmistakable, although these vary a little according to the season, and in different parts of their range. Females have slightly larger pale patches than the males, and both sexes tend to be darker later on in the year, when second- and third-brood adults emerge. We illustrate the seasonal variation of the main subspecies found in the British Isles, *P. a. tircis,* along with a subspecies called *P. a. insula* that is confined to the Isles of Scilly. In the latter, the pale patches are tinged with orange. The surviving Scottish populations belong to a third group called *P. a. oblita,* which has larger wings and more contrasting markings than the other subspecies. In addition, its undersurfaces often have a hint of purple around the outer edges.

Speckled Woods are on the wing for seven months of the year, even though individual adults seldom live longer than a week. The species has the unique ability among British butterflies to overwinter either as a caterpillar or as a chrysalis. Hibernating chrysalises produce the first adults of spring, but these overlap with others that spend the winter as caterpillars. This results in two peaks of emergence, the first in mid-May and the second in early June.

The offspring of both sets of adults then develop at variable rates, producing a second brood of butterflies that is strung out over a very long period indeed. The earliest born and quickest developers produce adults that overlap with the last stragglers from the first brood, but several weeks pass before the second brood reaches its peak, usually in late August or early September. Speckled Woods are at their most abundant in these months, even though it is believed that certain springtime caterpillars do not turn into adults that year, but instead enter a period of quiescence – or aestivation – before resuming growth in early autumn and then forming chrysalises that hatch the following spring.

There is usually a final emergence of fresh adults in autumn. These are the offspring of the second brood, with which they also overlap. This third brood is seldom very numerous, because by late summer most caterpillars develop slowly and overwinter, or form hibernating chrysalises. The main trigger that induces certain caterpillars to develop straight through to adulthood and others to hibernate is a combination of the length of daylight and the air temperature. As a rule, caterpillars that experience 12 or more hours of light a day go on to form adults in the same year, whereas those that receive less light either form hibernation chrysalises, or spend winter as caterpillars. There is, however, considerable variation in the response of different individuals to light and temperature. Different races and subspecies of the butterfly also vary in this respect.

### PERCHING AND PATROLLING

Speckled Woods live in self-contained colonies, although the females wander rather more than most "sedentary" butterflies. A large woodland colony contains several hundred adults in late summer, with the two sexes in roughly equal numbers. The males, however, are much more apparent. This is because females hide on tree-tops or in bushes for much of the day, emerging only to mate, feed, or lay eggs.

Both sexes roost at night and during cool weather, clinging to the undersurfaces of leaves, high up on tall shrubs, or in the tree canopy. They crawl around to catch the morning sun, basking with their wings held wide open and pressed flat against the top of a leaf, but closing them during the heat of the day. By this means, they regulate their body temperature to around 32°-35°C (90°-95°F). They also feed on tree-tops, drinking the sweet honeydew that coats many leaves in summer. But the butterflies are often forced to descend to flowers in autumn and spring, when honeydew is scarce.

When warm and well fed, the males float down to the ground where they either perch in sunlit spots for the rest of the day or patrol back and forth through their breeding area. They are looking for females in both cases. Certain individuals – especially those possessing four spots on the upperside of each hindwing – are more inclined to perch, whereas males with three spots (like those in our illustration) have a tendency to patrol.

When perching, the males usually settle about 1 m. (3 ft.) above the ground, on a stem of bramble *(Rubus fruticosus)* or on a frond of bracken *(Pteridium aquilinum)*. Each occupies a sunlit spot, where a gap in the canopy allows the sun to cast a pool of light on to the woodland floor. Small patches are occupied by a single male, which fiercely protects his territory against intruders. Large ones may have two or more males in residence. Every passing insect is investigated. When this proves to be another male, he is fiercely attacked in an aerial skirmish in which both insects spiral around each other, bumping and clashing their wings as they ascend towards the canopy. After a minute or two, the intruder flies away, allowing the original occupant to descend to resume his vigil.

Virgin females are also attracted to these patches of sunlight. But they, when challenged, generally drop to the ground, where a courtship dance follows that is similar to that of the Grayling *(see p.182)*. The female then leads the excited male to a tree-top, where mating occurs. Patrolling males indulge in the same intricate courtship, but find their mates on the wing.

### EGGS IN SUN AND SHADE

Most females mate just once, usually within a few hours of emergence. They then rest while their eggs ripen, before venturing forth on slow, fluttery flights. Eggs are laid singly on a wide variety of grasses, including wood false brome *(Brachypodium sylvaticum)*, cock's-foot *(Dactylis glomerata)*, and Yorkshire fog *(Holcus lanatus)*. Despite this lack of specificity, females are quite selective about the kind of plant that they choose. Small, isolated plants receive the most eggs, particularly those growing in sheltered situations where the air temperature reaches 24°-30°C (75°-86°F). This restricts egg-laying to the sunny edges of woods, rides, and hedges in spring and autumn, whereas during the heat of the summer, most eggs are laid in fairly shady places within the body of a wood or scrub.

The little caterpillar stays on the grassblade near its egg, resting on the undersurface and taking small bites from the edge inwards on and off during both day and night. The attractive, stumpy chrysalis is formed suspended beneath a grassblade or on nearby vegetation, usually within 20 cm. (8 in.) of the ground. Those that do not hibernate hatch after about 10 days.

### A DECLINE REVERSED

Despite its need for fairly warm conditions in spring and autumn, the Speckled Wood can tolerate shadier woods than any other British butterfly. In summer, it breeds under canopies that exclude between 40 per cent and 90 per cent of the light, and finds ideal conditions in a great many modern woods. In Scotland and much of England and Wales, colonies are more or less restricted to woodland, but in the south and in Ireland, they also occur along many wooded lanes, hedgerows, and patches of scrub, including that along most of the southern coastline. The butterfly also frequently breeds, albeit at fairly low densities, in country gardens.

There is no doubt that the gradual spread of the Speckled Wood has been assisted by the decline in coppicing. However, this does not explain all the changes in its status. The earliest accounts of the "Enfield Eye" or "Wood Argus", as it was once called, indicate that although it was seldom considered to be common, it nevertheless was very widely distributed throughout the British Isles, with the main subspecies, *P. a. tircis,* extending through northern England and southern Scotland.

The decline began from the 1860s onwards. This was very gradual, with local extinctions being continuously reported over the next 60 years. By then, the butterfly had disappeared entirely from most parts of its former range, and was more or less restricted to lowland Wales, southwest England, Wiltshire, and the heavier, wetter soils of Dorset and West Sussex. The old Irish records are too poor to be able say whether it declined there as well.

The recovery was also very gradual. It was first noticed in counties such as Dorset, that contained residual populations, as early as the 1920s. Since then the butterfly has spread to reoccupy much of its old range, and is now a common species found in almost every wood in most regions shown on the map *(see p.163)*. The expansion is occurring still. For example, the butterfly reappeared in Suffolk in the 1960s, after an absence of 70 years, entering via the newly afforested areas of the Breck. It has yet to colonize several of the wooded parts of East Anglia, but there is a chance of this in the next 20 years.

# SPECKLED WOOD · *Pararge aegeria*

## LIFE-CYCLE

| | JAN | FEB | MAR | APR | MAY | JUN | JUL | AUG | SEP | OCT | NOV | DEC |
|---|---|---|---|---|---|---|---|---|---|---|---|---|
| EGG | | | | | | | | | | | | |
| CATERPILLAR | | | | | | | | | | | | |
| CHRYSALIS | | | | | | | | | | | | |
| ADULT | | | | | | | | | | | | |

**Male, first brood**
Main subspecies, *P. a. tircis;* a first-brood adult with larger yellow spots than those that follow.

**Female, first brood**
Main subspecies, *P. a. tircis,* with large yellow spots typical of the first brood.

**Basking adult**
Males with three spots on each hindwing often behave differently to those with four spots.

**Male, second brood**
Subspecies *P. a. insula,* found on the Isles of Scilly, has more orange markings.

**Chrysalis** [x2¼]
The Speckled Wood can overwinter as a caterpillar or a chrysalis.

**Egg** [x15]
Laid singly on the underside of a grass-blade; size very variable.

**Caterpillar** [x2¼]
Caterpillars of all sizes can be found from spring until late autumn.

**Caterpillar on grassblade**
Camouflaged caterpillars feed on a wide variety of grasses.

SINGLE SEGMENT

# WALL

## *Lasiommata megera*

IN MOST YEARS, the Wall is quite common and widely distributed in wild grassland throughout the lowlands of England, Wales, and Ireland, but numbers plummet every now and then, leaving it restricted to scattered centres where its favourite habitat abounds. These are extensive areas of dry, unfertilized grassland, with a rugged, broken terrain, and an abundance of bare patches where this heat-seeking butterfly can toast in the sun.

By and large, the Wall is an easy species to identify. Flying adults are sometimes mistaken for Commas or Fritillaries, but at rest the bright eye-spots immediately indicate its membership of the Brown family of butterflies rather than the Nymphalids. It is, nevertheless, highly distinctive. No other Brown has such gleaming golden upperwings, or such an intricate pattern of zig-zag stripes on the undersides.

There are two full generations of Walls a year, the first appearing in May and early June, with their offspring flying throughout August and often well into September. In warm years in the south, the second emergence occurs slightly earlier, in July, and on these occasions there may be a third brood in early autumn. Numbers are usually about three times higher in the second brood than in the first, but even then most colonies are small compared with those of other Browns. The largest contain no more than a few hundred butterflies in their best years, and it seems likely that most colonies are reduced to a few dozen adults by springtime.

### FLIGHT AND TEMPERATURE

Generally, Walls live in self-contained colonies, but some individuals wander, enabling the species to spread quite quickly to ground lost after one of its periodic retractions. There are at least two records of adults reaching the Outer Dowsing light vessel, 50 km. (30 miles) off the Norfolk coast, and it is not unusual to find Walls visiting garden flowers, although most are more sedentary. Males typically live for just three days.

*Distribution Common in dry grassland throughout most of lowland England and Wales; more coastal in Ireland and at the north of its range.*

The adult butterflies spend much of the daytime basking in warm patches of bare ground, with their wings held two-thirds open and angled towards the sun. In this way they can raise their body temperature to about 8-10°C (14.5-18°F) higher than their surroundings. When their bodies reach 25-30°C, they are warm enough to fly. Many of the local movements made by the butterfly on different days can be explained by the need to keep their body temperature up. For example, on warm, windless days, males will be seen flying for long periods, particularly around hilltops. However, they cool down quite quickly during flight in windy weather, so exposed places are then avoided altogether, and they frequently have to alight to warm up on a patch of earth. On the other hand, the temperature can get dangerously high on hot summer days, and then the Wall retreats into the shade.

### A BOISTEROUS COURTSHIP

As with most butterflies, male Walls tend to emerge a few days before the females, although there is a considerable overlap. They gather at dusk in the sunniest parts of a site before settling, upside-down, to roost beneath fences, hedgerow leaves or under the lower boughs of trees. Most of the male's life is spent in a search for females, punctuated by short bouts of feeding on whatever flowers are available. Females are encountered in one of two ways: either by flying back and forth along sunny edges, such as paths, roadsides, hedges, banks, or even fence lines, or by perching at regular intervals on the ground along these same edges. Many people will have disturbed a Wall when walking along a path, and have noticed that it always settles on the bare ground a few metres ahead, only to be flushed up again and again. This is the perching male, waiting, while sunning himself, for a virgin female to fly down the track.

Patrolling males glide fast and low, generally 30 cm. (1 ft.) above ground level, travelling 30 m. (100 ft.) or so before backtracking along the same edge. On other occasions they zig-zag

# WALL · *Lasiommata megera*

## LIFE-CYCLE

| | JAN | FEB | MAR | APR | MAY | JUN | JUL | AUG | SEP | OCT | NOV | DEC |
|---|---|---|---|---|---|---|---|---|---|---|---|---|
| EGG | | | | | | | | | | | | |
| CATERPILLAR | | | | | | | | | | | | |
| CHRYSALIS | | | | | | | | | | | | |
| ADULT | | | | | | | | | | | | |

**Male**
The oblique line of scent scales (sex-brand) on the forewing is typical of the male.

**Female**
Females are larger and brighter than males, and lack the sex-brand.

**Female**
Rare aberrant *anticrassipincta* form, with larger and more distinct eye-spots.

**Basking adult**
Walls are often seen basking on bare, sunbaked ground, with their wings angled towards the sun.

**Resting adult**
Dull-coloured hindwings camouflage the butterfly when at rest on the ground.

**Egg [x15]**
Laid singly or in clusters on roots or leaves of grasses.

**Chrysalis [x2¼]**
Colour varies from bright green to almost black.

**Male**
Markings in the rare aberrant form *bradanfelda* are creamy yellow, rather than orange.

**SINGLE SEGMENT**

**Caterpillar [x2¼]**
Patterned with white warts and stripes, as seen in enlarged segment.

in drunken circles, continually scanning the earth and stopping to investigate likely objects. They skirmish with any flying insect that they encounter. If this proves to be a rival male, the two butterflies soar high into the sky in a spiralling dog-fight before diving towards the ground and separating, about 10 seconds later. Females are pursued with much greater persistence, and may even be courted in flight.

I have never seen the courtship of this butterfly, but am told that it is a brief, rumbustious affair. When pursued, the female soon alights on bare ground and starts fluttering her wings. The male crash-lands behind her, and works his way to the front, beating his wings so violently that the female may be wafted off the ground in a cloud of dust and scales. Then, facing his hen, he hammers her head with his two antennae before buffeting and bombarding her with flapping wings in a series of head-butts. This is all very different from the elegant courtship of the Grayling *(see p.182),* but the effect is the same: the male envelops his female with flying scent scales, and she in turn is mesmerized by their heavy, chocolate-like odour. They then quickly pair and disappear from sight into the surrounding vegetation.

Roughly one female in 10 will mate for a second or even a third time in later life, but most fertilize all their eggs from the one pairing. Much of the female's day is taken up by resting and basking, but when sufficiently warm, she embarks on a short, fluttering flight in search of egg-sites.

## EGGS AND CATERPILLARS

Walls lay in very dry spots and exclusively select grass that has an exposed vertical edge. In practice, this occurs in three distinct situations. One is where the ground has broken away beneath the tuft to form a miniature cliff; hoofprints, rabbit holes, and places where the soil has slipped along banks, sheepwalks, and path edges, are all typical examples. The spherical white eggs are often laid solely along the upper edges of pathways on downs that otherwise have a smooth and uniform sward, making them remarkably easy to find.

The other two places chosen for egg-laying are the sides of large, isolated tussocks of wild grasses, such as cock's-foot *(Dactylis glomerata)* and the beautiful wavy hair-grass *(Deschampsia flexuosa),* and where bents such as common bent *(Agrostis tenuis),* and black bent *(A. gigantea),* or the downy blades of Yorkshire fog *(Holcus lanatus),* form a wall of tall grass-stems beneath fences and under the edges of shrubs.

Wall eggs hatch after about 10 days, the caterpillar nibbling a slice across the top of the shell until it lifts off like a hinge. It then eats the whole shell before embarking on a tender blade of grass. Tor *(Brachypodium pinnatum)* and wood false brome

*(B. sylvaticum)* are favourites, in addition to those mentioned. The caterpillars from the summer brood of adults overwinter when half-grown, awaking on and off to feed on warm days. In contrast, those that hatch in spring take little more than a month to become fully grown. Although plain, the caterpillar is nonetheless rather attractive, having a slightly furry, blue-green body with minute white warts and faint white stripes along the sides.

The chrysalis too is attractive, but beautifully camouflaged and hard to spot as it hangs suspended for about two weeks on a grass-stem. Its colour varies somewhat. Most chrysalises are bright grass-green, but some are pale and a few almost black; we illustrate a typical example.

## PERIODIC DECLINE AND ITS CAUSES

Small Wall colonies can be found on almost any patch of open, unfertilized grassland that lies within the butterfly's range. Due to the fussiness over egg-laying, the Wall is particularly frequent on dry, sparse soils, such as grassy heathland, chalk, and limestone downs, but is common only in a bumpy terrain of sheltered hummocks and hollows, or where the ground has been broken or disturbed by cattle or man. Abandoned railway lines, quarries, derelict land, and undercliffs also support fine colonies. However, the butterfly is by no means restricted to light soils, and may be found breeding in small numbers on the dry edges of tussocks even on the heaviest of clays. But it is almost never seen where the sward is uniform and unbroken, nor under even the lightest woodland shade.

Since the last war, the Wall must have declined enormously, on a local scale, due to the extreme use of synthetic fertilizers on lowland grasslands; however, it remains widespread and sometimes common over large areas of the country wherever suitable habitat survives. In Wales and Ireland it is absent only from the mountain ranges, while in England it is missing from the Pennines and other northern hills. The northern limit extends just into Scotland, with scattered colonies in what was Dumfries, Kircudbright, Ayrshire, and Wigtownshire. These northern specimens are particularly beautiful and dusky, and were once considered to be a separate subspecies. We illustrate an extreme example. They were much more widely distributed in early Victorian times, reaching as far north as Aberdeen and Glasgow.

The Wall disappeared from vast areas during a series of exceptionally cold, wet summers in the early 1860s. Some ground was regained in the 1970s and early 1980s, but there were dramatic nationwide declines in the mid-1980s, again coinciding with four wet summers. In 1988, there was a considerable recovery in the best sites of southern England, but it is too early to say whether the recent declines have resulted in any long-term reduction in range, as occurred in the last century.

# SCOTCH ARGUS
## *Erebia aethiops*

THIS HANDSOME, dusky Satyrid was first discovered in the eighteenth century on the Isle of Bute, and has been recorded from many hundreds of localities since that time. As the name implies, virtually all of these are in Scotland, where it can still be seen flying in thousands over wet, sheltered, tussocky grassland in the August sunshine. It is also common in mountainous areas on the Continent, but is curiously absent from the rest of Britain, where it is probably now confined to just two colonies in the Lake District.

The adults live in well-defined colonies and seldom fly far from their traditional breeding sites. They are often the commonest butterflies where they do occur; Roger Dennis estimated that one Lakeland colony contained thousands, if not tens of thousands, of adults, and it is clear that many Scottish populations are as large. However, the single flight period is short, even on good sites. The first males emerge in the last days of July and only a few faded females last into September.

*Distribution Reduced to two large colonies in the Lake District, but widespread and locally abundant in sheltered grassland in Scotland.*

## A NEED FOR SUNSHINE

For a butterfly that inhabits some of the wettest regions of the British Isles, this species is extraordinarily dependent on sunshine. Adults occasionally fly in warm, overcast weather, but usually float to the ground the moment a cloud appears, vanishing deep into the tussocks. They are then surprisingly hard to spot, due to a close resemblance to dead leaves. But they emerge in numbers the moment the sun reappears, stretching their black wings to absorb as much heat as possible before launching themselves on jerky, rolling flights.

Males fly more often than females, and are especially active on bright windless days, when they weave tirelessly around the tussocks, each searching for females. They will investigate any brown object, including withered leaves caught among the grass. This, however, is not their only method of finding mates; at other times, they simply perch on grass clumps, resting just below the flowerheads, ready to chase every female that flies past.

## EGG-LAYING

Once mated, the female Scotch Argus feeds frequently on hawkweeds (*Hieracium* spp.), bramble (*Rubus fruticosus*), and heathers (*Erica* spp.), but spends most of her life resting or basking in open areas, slightly apart from the males. Only in the hottest weather does she embark on ponderous egg-laying flights, fluttering from one clump of purple moor grass (*Molinia caerulea*) to another. This is the only known foodplant in Scotland, although the butterfly invariably chooses blue moor grass (*Sesleria caerulea*) in Cumbria.

The attractively speckled eggs are laid singly, deep among tussocks, on plants growing in open though sheltered areas. As with the eggs of all species of *Erebia,* they are large and barrel-shaped, but unlikely to be found in the wild due to the dense vegetation in which they occur. However they are easily obtained in captivity: a female will even lay in the dark in a cardboard box, unlike most other butterflies, which are infuriatingly fussy over their laying conditions.

This ability to lay eggs in the dark suggests that the female Scotch Argus might not be quite so dependent on sunshine as is popularly supposed, and may be able to crawl among vegetation to lay her eggs on overcast days. As one so often finds, there are enormous gaps in our knowledge of this butterfly's behaviour, leaving considerable scope for amateur entomologists to make new observations.

## CATERPILLARS AND CHRYSALISES

Scotch Argus eggs hatch after about a fortnight. Like the Marbled White, the tiny caterpillar eats a neat groove around the shell, until it can push open a lid and squeeze out. More of the shell is then eaten, before it switches to feeding on grassblades. This continues for about four weeks, then the caterpillar settles down to hibernate on a dead piece of vegetation deep in the tussock. It is still very small at this stage, having usually completed a single skin moult.

Feeding resumes in spring, and as it grows older, the caterpillar becomes increasingly nocturnal. Although I have not searched for it myself, I am told that the fully grown caterpillar can be found in late June, hiding deep in a tussock by day or out on the grass-tips at dusk.

Finding the caterpillars can require a degree of exertion. As long ago as 1895, a Mr. Haggart of Galashiels warned that "no artificial light can be used as the larvae immediately drop down among the grass… the method is by no means enviable, even to the most ardent entomologist, as in the uncertain light it necessitates crawling on one's hands and knees amongst the grass, and there is always the risk of grasping those little brown slugs in mistake, which resemble the larvae very much in shape and colour". The caterpillar is, however, distinct from that of any other Scottish butterfly except, perhaps, the Ringlet, which has brown rather than green stripes.

The chrysalis is formed in moss or under leaf litter, in a thin web of silk spun at the base of the grass clump. It lasts for two to three weeks, and can be found with difficulty in the wild, by searching at the best Scotch Argus sites.

### AFTER THE ICE AGE

An ability to live in cool climates means that the Scotch Argus was probably one of the first butterflies to recolonize Britain after the last Ice Age, 11,000 to 12,000 years ago. The improvement in the climate was followed by a temporary return to Arctic conditions a few hundred years later, which would again have eliminated all but the most cold-hardy of our current species. In the extreme south, the Scotch Argus should have been among the few to survive, and should therefore have been among the front-runners to regain ground when the present temperate climate returned. It is surprising, therefore, that it has never been recorded from Ireland, and that it is absent from a number of apparently suitable islands, such as Islay and Jura. The lack of any Welsh colony is also a puzzle, as is the cause of its decline in England. At present, two large colonies are known in the Lake District, breeding on ungrazed tussocky grassland that is dominated by blue moor grass and sheltered by scattered shrubs. There were once several colonies in northern England, for example at Castle Eden Dene near Durham, at Fawdon in Northumberland, and at Grassington in Yorkshire.

The large Scotch Argus colony at Grassington was famous because it supported a highly distinctive race. The males had almost no orange on their upperwings, while that on the females was little more than on a normal male. Numerous collecting trips were made to this site – one Victorian excursion by the Yorkshire Naturalists' Union tells of hundreds being secured by the members, and of hundreds more that could easily have been taken. It is doubtful, however, that collecting caused the loss of this unique colony, which became extinct in 1955.

### NORTH OF THE BORDER

Scottish colonies have been very much more stable, with serious losses reported only from the old county of Berwickshire. The Scotch Argus is common in numerous sunny places where its habitat occurs, from sea level to about 500 m. (1,600 ft.). It can be seen particularly in warm sheltered valleys, among open scrub, and in rough ground beside woodland edges. Smaller colonies can be found in broad woodland rides and in young plantations, but they soon disappear from shady woods. It is less common on open moorland, but sometimes found where there is a little shelter. There are also colonies among the rough grass and rushes on raised beaches along the west coast.

There is some variation in the wing colour and in the size of the eye-spots in every colony. Scottish populations differ somewhat in appearance from the main European races, and themselves exist in two slightly different forms. The distinguished Scottish entomologist, George Thomson, has plotted the distribution of these, which form the basis of our map.

# SCOTCH ARGUS · *Erebia aethiops*

LIFE-CYCLE

| | JAN | FEB | MAR | APR | MAY | JUN | JUL | AUG | SEP | OCT | NOV | DEC |
|---|---|---|---|---|---|---|---|---|---|---|---|---|
| EGG | | | | | | | | | | | | |
| CATERPILLAR | | | | | | | | | | | | |
| CHRYSALIS | | | | | | | | | | | | |
| ADULT | | | | | | | | | | | | |

**Male upperside**
Upperwings are almost black
when the butterfly emerges.

**Male underside**
Ground-colour of
underwings grey
and deep brown.

**Female upperside**
Upperwings are more brown
than those of the male.

**Female underside**
Ground-colour
mid-brown; hindwing
barred with green.

**Colour variant**
Aberrant *croesus* form,
with larger eye-spots.

**Resting adult**
Adults only fly when the
sun shines, otherwise
hiding in vegetation.

**Egg** [*x15*]
Speckled pattern
develops after five days;
caterpillar hatches after
two weeks.

**Chrysalis** [*x2¼*]
Formed at the base of grass
tussocks, in moss or leaf litter.

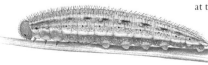

**Caterpillar** [*x2¼*]
Young caterpillar hibernates
at the base of grass tussocks.

**Basking female**
Females spend much of the
time basking, interrupted by
bouts of egg-laying.

# MOUNTAIN RINGLET

## *Erebia epiphron*

THIS SMALL and dusky butterfly is confined nowadays to a few bleak mountain-tops in the English Lake District, and to the Grampians and other mountainsides in Scotland. It is our only true alpine species, the sole relic of the first wave of cold-hardy butterflies that repopulated our lands when the last Great Ice Age receded, roughly 12,000 years ago. Although there was still another little Ice Age to come, the so-called "Lôch Lomond Readvance" of 9000-8200 BC, the ice flows and polar desert were then restricted to northern uplands, leaving a barren landscape of permafrost, tundra, and steppe across the south. Most butterflies were eliminated during this period, but there is every reason to believe that the Mountain Ringlet flourished throughout the chilly wastelands of latterday Surrey, Sussex, and Hampshire, and more or less continuously across the continental land link to central Europe.

The Loch Lomond Readvance ended about 10,000 years ago, giving way to a climate that was substantially warmer than our present one. From that time onwards, the European populations of Mountain Ringlets became separated into isolated groups, each restricted to zones of moist grassland at high altitude in the Pyrenees, the Vosges, the mountains of Harz, and to other centres in the Alps, Balkans, Appennines, and Dolomites.

***Distribution** Confined to high mountain grassland in the Lake District and Scotland; abundant where it does occur.*

### NINETEENTH-CENTURY DISCOVERY

Not surprisingly, our own Mountain Ringlets, having inbred for 10,000 generations, have evolved into a distinct subspecies from those now living in mainland Europe. Ours is called *E. e. mnemon,* and is smaller and duller than most of its continental counterparts. The distinction, however, is slight, for this is a highly variable butterfly with adults that differ in size, brightness, and in the number of spots within every colony. Nevertheless, there are even minor differences between the Scottish and English races, suggesting that these, too, have been isolated from one another for several thousands of years. Scottish specimens tend to have longer wings than those in England, with larger black spots.

Despite being our oldest surviving butterfly, the Mountain Ringlet was one of the last British species to be discovered, the first specimen being caught on 25 June 1809, on the slopes of Red Screes, above Ambleside in the Lake District. It took another 35 years before the first Scottish colony was found, at Rannoch in Tayside. But this is an easy species to overlook. Typical colonies are restricted to small parts of their mountains, and the flight period seldom lasts more than three weeks; one vast colony flew for just 12 days in the hot, dry summer of 1976. The exact date of emergence varies with the season and altitude, and may be two weeks early at low levels in north Scotland. However, in most colonies, the first males will be seen in late June after a warm spring, and from mid-July onwards in a cool year.

### LIFE AT HIGH ALTITUDE

Little is known about the natural history of this elusive butterfly, apart from a study by Keith Porter made at Scathwaite Fell in the Lake District. The main colony that was investigated bred on a barren, undulating plateau, 600 m. (2,000 ft.) high and surrounded by crags, rocky outcrops, and large expanses of scree. The butterflies were restricted to little more than 0.5 ha. (1 acre) of east-facing grassland, containing drier slopes of mat grass *(Nardus stricta)* surrounding springs, boggy hollows of *Sphagnum* moss, and stagnant, peaty pools.

In just 12 days, 650 Mountain Ringlets were marked on this small plateau, and the results confirmed that the butterflies live in strict colonies with little or no mixing between neighbouring hillsides. The numbers on the peak day – about 2,870 adults – corresponded to a total emergence of between 8,500 and 9,000 adults that year. This is typical of Mountain Ringlets: their sites may be few and far between, but where they do occur, the butterfly is often found in great abundance.

Adult Mountain Ringlets are greatly dependent on sunshine. They rest deep among the mat grass on cloudy days, with their

# MOUNTAIN RINGLET · *Erebia epiphron*

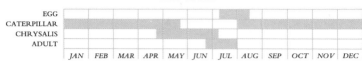

**LIFE-CYCLE**

| | JAN | FEB | MAR | APR | MAY | JUN | JUL | AUG | SEP | OCT | NOV | DEC |
|---|---|---|---|---|---|---|---|---|---|---|---|---|
| **EGG** | | | | | | | | | | | | |
| **CATERPILLAR** | | | | | | | | | | | | |
| **CHRYSALIS** | | | | | | | | | | | | |
| **ADULT** | | | | | | | | | | | | |

**Male, Scottish form**
The Scottish form is generally larger and
brighter than specimens found in England.

**Female, Scottish form**
Orange spots are brighter in the female,
and the wing ground-colour lighter.

**Male, Lake District form**
Males fly close to the ground,
searching for females.

**Female, Lake District form**
Females of both forms rarely
fly, and so are seen less often.

**Feeding adult**
On grassy hillsides, Mountain
Ringlets often use hawkweed as a
source of nectar.

**Egg [x15]**
Laid singly on the
leaves of mat grass.

**Chrysalis [x2¼]**
Formed in a loose
cocoon, deep within
a grass tussock.

**Resting adult**
Adults rest inconspicuously
with the forewings concealed
by the hindwings.

**Caterpillar [x2½]**
Sluggish caterpillar hibernates
when half-grown.

forewings tucked down so that only the well-camouflaged hindwings are exposed. They are extraordinarily easy to overlook until the sun shines. Then, hundreds suddenly emerge from the tussocks, all with their dark, velvety wings spread wide to absorb the maximum warmth. Females seldom fly, being weighed down by clusters of large, heavy eggs that distend their hairy black bodies almost to breaking point. On Scathwaite, at least 17 males were seen for every female, although the two sexes were probably present in even numbers.

On sunny days, male Mountain Ringlets patrol back and forth across their restricted breeding grounds, fluttering or gliding slowly around each tussock, and seldom rising more than 30 cm. (1 ft.) above the ground. They settle to investigate any brown object, including other males, dead moss, and the droppings and brown wool of the Herdwick sheep that half-heartedly graze these nutrient-poor uplands. Virgin females are courted and quickly mated, then left to mature on a warm clump of mat grass. They emerge only to lay eggs or feed. Tormentil *(Potentilla erecta)*, heath bedstraw *(Galium saxatile)*, and bilberry *(Vaccinium myrtillus)* are often all that is available, but if mineral flushes exist, there is often a carpet of wild thyme *(Thymus praecox)*, where the butterflies cluster to drink nectar.

The average lifespan of the adults has only once been measured, in the hot, dry summer of 1976. It was then a mere day and a half, but is likely to be three or four times longer under more normal conditions. Skylarks, whinchats, pied wagtails, and other birds are believed to be the main predators, and the Mountain Ringlet's distinctive behaviour on settling is a response to bird attack. On alighting, it sits for a few seconds with the wings wide open, so that any bird that had been attracted by its flight is more likely to peck the wings' eye-spots rather than the vulnerable body. It then closes its wings, keeping the forewings raised, again so that any following bird will strike a harmless area. Finally, the forewings are withdrawn between the hindwings, so that no further predators are likely to notice them. Pecked wings are visible on many adults.

## SURVIVING THE WINTER

Female Mountain Ringlets lay up to 70 eggs a day, given warm, sunny conditions. These are placed singly on the wiry, grey-green blades of mat grass, and are quite easy to find on good sites if you search the bases of tufts in late July and early August. They are surprisingly large for a butterfly of this size, and are creamy yellow at first, soon developing the rusty brown blotches that are found on so many Browns' eggs.

Each egg hatches after about three weeks. The caterpillar first eats the entire shell, then starts feeding on the tender tips of mat grass. By September, the half-grown caterpillar settles down to hibernate deep in the dense tussock, where it remains for six or seven months, gaining additional protection from the snow-drifts that invariably blanket the breeding sites. It can spend two years as a caterpillar if the spring is particularly late and the summer short, but most of them complete their growth in April and May, sluggishly crawling to the nutritious tips of mat grass between periods spent basking on the sides of tussocks.

Typical caterpillars pupate in late May or June, in a loose cocoon of silk and grassblades. The chrysalis is particularly attractive, and well worth searching for in the base of tussocks. Look early in the season, though, for it is believed that huge numbers are killed by the short-tailed voles that teem among the loose scree, found alongside most Mountain Ringlet sites.

## A CURIOUS DISTRIBUTION

There has been much controversy over whether Mountain Ringlets exist anywhere other than in Scotland and Cumbria. Mat grass is the dominant plant at high altitudes on most British mountains, yet it now seems certain that the butterfly is absent from the Pennines, Cheviots and, most curiously of all, from the massif of Snowdonia. Ireland poses a greater problem: three nineteenth-century records exist from Croagh Patrick, the eastern shores of Lough Gill in Co. Leitrim, and from Nephin Beg in Co. Mayo, although considerable doubt surrounds the last two records.

No such doubts surround the Cumbrian colonies, as abundant now as they ever were. Huge populations exist in suitable patches alongside streams and damp, swampy grassland down to 180 m. (600 ft.) above sea level, although most are between 460 and 760 m. (1,500 and 2,500 ft.) high; famous sites include Red Screes, Langdale Pikes, Stye Head Tarn, and Helvellyn.

The great majority of colonies are in Scotland, breeding on damp mountain pastures and, especially, on the sides of steep gullies. They are commonest between 450 and 730 m. (1,300 and 2,400 ft.) above sea level, but also occur down to 275 m. (900 ft.) and as high as 915 m. (3,000 ft.). The main concentrations are in the Grampians, on many mountains south of the Great Glen, from Glen Clova in the east to Ben Vane and Ben Nevis in the west. Further north, the Mountain Ringlet still breeds south of Newtonmore in Inverness-shire, and there is a single colony on Ben Lomond. There are also unconfirmed reports from as far north as Sutherland and, more dubiously, from the mountains of Galloway in the southwest. The latter have been quite well explored in recent years, and seem unlikely still to support a colony, if they ever did. However, the Scottish expert, George Thomson, considers the butterfly might yet be discovered in the remote mountains of the far northwest, or even on some of the Western Isles.

# GATEKEEPER

## *Pyronia tithonus*

THE GATEKEEPER is one of those curious butterflies which, like the Small Skipper, is considered to be either commonplace or extremely rare, depending on where one lives. Having lived entirely in the south, where it is common, I find it impossible to imagine high summer without seeing scores of Gatekeepers jinking along hedgerows and woodland rides before alighting to jostle for nectar on the flowers of bramble *(Rubus fruticosus),* ragwort *(Senecio jacobaea),* and fleabane *(Pulicaria dysenterica).* Yet it quite abruptly becomes scarce as one travels north, and is absent from the entire northern half of Britain and from all but the southern coast of Ireland.

The Gatekeeper's habitat – a combination of tall, wild grasses growing beneath sunny sheltered shrubs – is clearly abundant over much of the British countryside, but the butterfly can only make use of it south of a clear-cut limit. This, almost certainly, reflects its need for comparatively warm springs and summers. Many Gatekeeper colonies on the Continent experience much colder winters than in Britain, although the butterfly is absent from Denmark, northern Germany and all but the southern fringe of Poland.

This is perhaps the commonest of all our southern non-migratory butterflies, and was well known to the earliest British naturalists. Not surprisingly, it acquired a variety of names over the years. The "Hedge Brown", which to my mind is more appropriate but less attractive than Gatekeeper, is the only other name in common usage today, but the species was once also known as the "Hedge Eye", the "Small Meadow Brown" and, very confusingly, as the "Large Heath".

### EYE-SPOTS AND WING PATTERNS

The Gatekeeper is not a difficult butterfly to identify. The two sexes are rather different, with the male distinctly smaller and brighter, and possessing a dark, broad band of scent scales across the orange on each of the forewings. Beginners some-times confuse it with the larger but duller Meadow Brown *(see p.187).* One small but clear-cut distinction is that the tiny dots on the undersides of the hindwings are white on the Gatekeeper, whereas they are black on the Meadow Brown. In addition, Meadow Browns generally have just one white pupil in the large eye-spot on each forewing, whereas the Gatekeeper's eye-spot always contains two. This last feature is not an absolute rule, for one occasionally finds a Meadow Brown with two white pupils; this, however, mainly occurs in Scotland, far to the north of the Gatekeeper's range.

Unlike several of our Browns, the Gatekeeper shows little variation in wing pattern in different regions of the country, although it is not uncommon to find the occasional adult in any colony that has extra spots. Some heavily spotted varieties are very beautiful. We illustrate an example that is by no means an extreme case, and which is quite common in certain colonies in some years.

### GATEKEEPER COLONIES

The Gatekeeper's flight period is quite sharply defined, in contrast to that of the Meadow Brown, which emerges a good month earlier and which is still on the wing long after the last tattered Gatekeepers have vanished. This species first appears in the second half of July, quickly reaches a peak in the first week of August, and all but disappears by the end of the month, although there are a few colonies on the southern chalk that regularly last for two or three weeks longer.

Less is known about the natural history of this common little butterfly than of any other Brown. Like its close relatives, it undoubtedly lives in clearly defined colonies, with little or no migration between nearby sites. Thus adults are often seen in country gardens, but this results from colonies breeding in adjoining hedgebanks rather than from adults flying any distance to the flowers. It is very rare for Gatekeepers to appear in city gardens, even in counties where the species is abundant.

***Distribution*** *Local but very common along wood edges and hedgerows throughout lowland southern England and Wales. Mainly coastal in Ireland.*

Gatekeeper colonies vary enormously in size from a few dozen adults up to several thousand. This largely reflects the size of the breeding area, the smallest populations being confined to narrow strips along the bottoms of hedgerows, whereas the largest occur in open but scrubby woodland, where the terrain is crisscrossed by broad, sunny rides. Numbers also fluctuate within any colony from one year to the next, generally in synchrony from site to site. They tend to be particularly high in dry years, when summer temperatures are also warm.

Gatekeepers are almost always associated with shrubs. Their eggs are laid in the sheltered grasses below while the adults fly strictly around the bushes, except in woodland where they periodically ascend to the tree-tops to drink honeydew. However, they feed mostly on hedgerow and woodland flowers. Although they visit a wide variety, they are restricted to flat, open blossoms. This is because the Gatekeeper's proboscis is exceptionally short, and quite unable to penetrate the deep corollas of teasels *(Dipsacus fullonum)* and other tubular flowers, a feature shown on p.42.

### A GRADUAL DEVELOPMENT

Gatekeeper eggs are laid singly at the bases of shrubs. Some are deposited directly on leaf-blades, but most are attached to bark or simply ejected into the air, in the same way as the eggs of the Marbled White, Ringlet, and Meadow Brown. Unless an egg-laying female is followed, its pretty eggs are impossible to find, but are easily obtained in captivity by caging a freshly emerged female over a half-shaded clump of grass. They hatch after about three weeks, during which time the colour changes from pale yellow to white with rust-coloured patches, and then eventually to a rather dreary brown.

The tiny caterpillar first eats part or all of its eggshell, and then nibbles tender grassblades for the rest of its life. It is unknown whether it finds certain species more palatable, but there is reasonably good evidence that a wide range of fine and medium-bladed species are eaten, including couch *(Agropyron repens)*, various bents *(Agrostis* spp.*)*, fescues *(Festuca* spp.*)*, and meadow grasses *(Poa* spp.*)*. But in every case, the egg-laying females select tallish plants growing in sheltered, sunny spots. The caterpillar is sluggish and slow-growing, taking eight months between hatching and forming a chrysalis. It hibernates after making the first of four skin changes, choosing dried curled leaves deep in the body of a grass clump. Growth resumes in March or April, with the daytime spent head-down and hidden within the clump, then ascending to nibble the tender growing tips at dusk. This is not a particularly easy caterpillar to find, but it can be discovered on good sites by shining a torch on the taller grasses along the bottom of shrubs on warm evenings in May. Caterpillars vary somewhat in colour, but most are grey-brown with darker stripes, and all are slightly hairy. They are similar to those of the Ringlet, except that there is less pinkness to the pale stripes along their sides.

In a typical year, the grey, slug-like caterpillars complete their growth early in June, and settle down to form a much prettier chrysalis, suspended beneath a leaf-blade, again towards the base of a shrub. This is unlikely to be found in the wild, and hatches after three or four weeks.

### SOUTHERN ABUNDANCE

Gatekeeper colonies can be expected almost anywhere in the south where shrubs grow in warm, sheltered places and have tall wild grasses growing beneath them. A great many of the hedgerows of southern England and Wales support small numbers along their bases, and populations occur in almost every southern wood, breeding either along the outer edge or, where these exist, along shrubs bordering sunny, open rides. Enormous colonies breed also in many shrublands, including on heathland, sand dunes, and the scrubby undercliffs of many southern coastlines. Gatekeepers are, however, almost completely absent from the surroundings of some towns – for example few, if any, now survive in London's parklands.

The Gatekeeper is also common in suitable habitats throughout the lowlands of Wales, but is absent from all mountains. In England, it is probably the commonest summer butterfly in southwestern counties such as Devon and Dorset, but it becomes increasingly confined to woods in the Midlands. Colonies are absent from the southern Pennines, but extend north in sheltered coastal habitats on either side, petering out in Yorkshire to the east and in Cumbria to the west.

Old records exist for southern Scotland, but George Thomson, who has an unrivalled knowledge of Scottish butterflies, is inclined to doubt some of these. Although there has been some spread at the northern limits of its range in England, there seems little doubt that no genuine Scottish colonies exist today, despite interesting reports of a few individuals that bred for a year at least following releases or escapes in the southwest. Across the Irish Sea, colonies in Ireland are almost entirely confined to the south coast.

# GATEKEEPER · *Pyronia tithonus*

LIFE-CYCLE

| | JAN | FEB | MAR | APR | MAY | JUN | JUL | AUG | SEP | OCT | NOV | DEC |
|---|---|---|---|---|---|---|---|---|---|---|---|---|
| EGG | | | | | | | | | | | | |
| CATERPILLAR | | | | | | | | | | | | |
| CHRYSALIS | | | | | | | | | | | | |
| ADULT | | | | | | | | | | | | |

**Male**
Males have a broad band of dark scales (sex-brand) on each forewing, and a fuller orange colour.

**Female**
Females are larger and paler than males, and lack the sex-brand on the forewings.

**Eye-spot variant**
Aberrant *multiocellata* form, one of a range of eye-spot variants.

**Basking adult**
Adult male basking on the leaf of bindweed, with wings exposed to the sun.

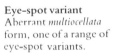

**Chrysalis** [*x2¼*]
Slung beneath a leaf at the base of a shrub.

**Egg** [*x22*]
Laid singly; gradually becomes mottled and then brown.

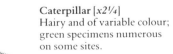

**Resting adult**
Male at rest on flower of traveller's joy.

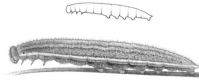

**Caterpillar** [*x2¼*]
Hairy and of variable colour; green specimens numerous on some sites.

# MARBLED WHITE

## *Melanargia galathea*

THIS IS ONE OF the loveliest insects to be seen in high summer on southern English downs. Despite its appearance, it belongs to the Browns – the family Satyridae – and the old English names of "Marmoress" or "Marmoris" (both ancient terms for marbling), "Our-Half Mourner", or "Marbled Argus" are all more appropriate than Marbled White and, to my mind, more attractive.

No other butterfly has such a striking black-and-white pattern. This is seen at its best in weak sunlight, first thing in the morning or in late afternoon, when the wings are held open to absorb the maximum warmth from the sun. Large groups bask like this on good sites, perched in clusters on tall scabious *(Knautia arvensis)* and knapweeds *(Centaurea* spp.*)*, generally in sheltered pockets towards the base of a hill. Too lethargic to move, basking adults can be approached very closely, and this is undoubtedly the time to watch, paint, or photograph them.

The flying season is short compared with other common Browns. The first adults appear in late June, reach a peak in mid-July and disappear before mid-August. They live in sharply delineated colonies, ranging in size from a handful of adults to several thousand on the finest sites.

So far as is known, the Marbled White has no elaborate courtship or social behaviour. Nor is the female at all fussy over egg-laying. She sits on a tall plant, pulsates her abdomen until an egg appears at the tip, then, with a little wriggle, flies off. The egg simply falls to the ground.

### CATERPILLAR FOODPLANTS

Marbled White eggs are quite large, unpatterned, and white, similar to those of the Speckled Wood and Wall, but less shiny. They hatch after about three weeks, with each caterpillar neatly nibbling a slit around the top until the lid is pushed open. It then squeezes out, eats the shell, and crawls into a small piece of dead vegetation, where it hibernates.

*Distribution Fairly common on dry, unfertilized grassland in southwest England, but scarce and local towards the north and east of its range.*

The first proper feed occurs in early spring. To begin with, the caterpillar sits along a grass-blade, nibbling at the leaf during the daytime. This behaviour changes as it grows larger, and after the third and final moult, the caterpillar becomes nocturnal, hiding head-downwards in the body of a grass clump by day and ascending to feed at night. Several species of grass may be eaten, including sheep's fescue *(Festuca ovina)*, tor *(Brachypodium pinnatum)*, cock's-foot *(Dactylis glomerata)*, and Timothy *(Phleum pratense)*. However, it has recently been discovered that red fescue *(Festuca rubra)* is invariably eaten at some stage, and appears to be essential if young caterpillars are to survive.

### A PUZZLING DISTRIBUTION

The Marbled White has a most curious distribution in Britain that has never been satisfactorily explained. It is a common butterfly over large areas of the southwest, especially along the coast. Here it occurs on all soils except the most acid, and on almost every unfertilized chalk or limestone hillside west of Surrey, from the Cotswolds southward. On warm, south-facing slopes, where the sward has been left to grow quite tall, it is particularly abundant, but it also breeds in very small areas and in a wide range of situations including woodland glades, sunny rides, and many of the wider road verges.

The Marbled White is very much scarcer elsewhere in southern Britain. Although locally common along a few stretches of the South Downs, it is absent from most of the North Downs apart from the eastern end in Kent. It is also a rarity in Wales, with most colonies centred on the Gower Peninsula. In central England, large colonies breed along many woodland rides in Oxfordshire and Buckinghamshire, but the Marbled White suddenly becomes extremely rare a little further north. However, there is an interesting group of colonies in the North Yorkshire Wolds, breeding mainly on south-facing slopes along dry river valleys, and on some roadside verges.

# MARBLED WHITE · *Melanargia galathea*

LIFE-CYCLE

| | JAN | FEB | MAR | APR | MAY | JUN | JUL | AUG | SEP | OCT | NOV | DEC |
|---|---|---|---|---|---|---|---|---|---|---|---|---|
| EGG | | | | | | | | | | | | |
| CATERPILLAR | | | | | | | | | | | | |
| CHRYSALIS | | | | | | | | | | | | |
| ADULT | | | | | | | | | | | | |

**Male**
Both sexes have similar upperwings; the male's
hind underwings have only a tinge of yellow.

**Female**
The hind underwings have a marked yellow
tinge, as does the leading edge of the forewing.

**Egg [x12]**
Eggs are dropped rather
than laid, near to the
foodplants.

**Chrysalis [x2¼]**
Formed at the surface of the
ground, under soil or moss.

**Caterpillar [x2¼]**
Covered in short hairs;
colour varies from yellow-
brown to light green.

**Basking adult**
Adults sit on prominent
flowers and grassheads early
and late in the day, warming
themselves in the sun.

**Resting adult**
The wings are kept tightly
closed during the heat of the
day, and when roosting.

**Male**
*Nigricans* form, a rare
aberration with much
heavier black markings
than usual.

# GRAYLING

## *Hipparchia semele*

THE GRAYLING, more than any of our butter-flies, is confined to dry, dusty places where the soil is poor and thin, the vegetation sparse, and the terrain so rutted or broken that the sun's rays bake the ground. Arid soils of all types may support a colony, yet this is a scarce insect in most counties, being common only on southern heaths, and on cliffs and dunes around the coast.

Like all Browns, the Grayling lives all year on its clearly defined breeding sites, although wandering adults are occasionally seen in gardens adjoining heaths, and even out to sea. Colonies vary enormously in size. In 1976, I spent one hot summer's day on Dartmoor, marking the adults to see how many lived in a typical colony. There were 55 alive on that day, equivalent to a total emergence of around 150 adults. That was on a 3-ha. (7-acre) hillside, but I have often found Graylings on much smaller sites, such as abandoned quarries, which must contain no more than 20 or 30 adults. On the other hand, some heathland and dune populations are vast, with tens, if not hundreds of thousands, of individuals.

This is one of the later butterflies to emerge. There is one generation a year, typically starting in early July, and reaching a peak towards the end of the month, with a few stragglers lasting into September. The timing is a little later in northeast Scotland, while on the limestone peninsula of Great Ormes Head in north Wales, there lives a curious dwarf race that regularly emerges much earlier, at the beginning of June.

***Distribution*** *Locally common on dry coastal grassland and dunes, and southern lowland heaths. Rare and declining elsewhere in its range.*

### RELUCTANT FEEDERS

The female Grayling is secretive except when laying eggs, so sightings tend to be of males. It is often said that the adult never feeds. This is untrue, but feeding is seldom a major activity, and mainly occurs first thing in the morning or late in the afternoon. Graylings visit a wide range of flowers, depending on the habitat; bell heather *(Erica cinerea)* is a particular favourite on heaths. And if there is any sap oozing from a tree-trunk, a salty

puddle, or a wooden stake sticky with resin, they find these irresistible at all times of day. Once they have fed, male Graylings disperse within their breeding sites to perch singly, usually on a bare patch of sand, rock or earth. Most of their sites are treeless, but where they can find elevation they do, resting a metre or so up on the sunny side of a tree-trunk, or boulder. I have often had them settle on my leg, especially when wearing jeans. They will even probe the material for sweat if the day is hot and sticky. They are extraordinarily tame when drinking, and can be gently stroked without taking fright.

### COURTSHIP AND MATING

Each male remains at his station for much of the day, awaiting the freshly emerged females that occasionally fly past. He then soars up and gives chase. In fact, the male Grayling will "buzz" any moving object, be it a butterfly, bird, person, or falling leaf. If it proves to be a female, she soon alights and the male lands behind her, before walking around so that the two are face to face. An unreceptive hen then flaps her wings with great vigour, to drive the male away. But if instead she stays still, he takes this as an invitation to begin the charming courtship that was first described in one of the classic studies of animal behaviour by the Dutch scientist, Nikolaas Tinbergen.

First of all, while still facing his hen, the male jerks his wings upwards and forwards in quick succession, so that the beautiful orange patch on the underside, with its two white-pupilled eye-spots, is clearly visible. Next, with the forewings and hindwings still held separate, he repeatedly flicks the forewings open and shut for perhaps a minute. This culminates with the quivering forewings being held wide open as he executes a deep bow to the facing female. Gently he folds his wings together, catching the female's two antennae and draw-ing them through his forewings as he straightens up. The tips of a butterfly's antennae are the main organs of smell, and these are dragged across the male's scent glands, which are conspicuous

THE GRAYLING'S COURTSHIP
*Towards the end of his elaborate courtship, the male (right) bows to the female with his wings apart. He catches her antennae and draws them over his scent glands.*

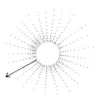

as a dark ridge across each forewing. Their scent is just detectable even to our feeble sense of smell, and has been variously described, for the Grayling, as having the faint aroma of sandalwood or an old cigar box. This is a powerful aphrodisiac to the female Grayling, and she responds immediately. Indeed, to all intents and purposes, the male has now seduced her, and he quickly withdraws his wings and walks around behind her to pair. Mating then takes place for 30 to 45 minutes, before they part to go their separate ways.

## TEMPERATURE REGULATION

Naturalists often wonder what a butterfly is doing when they see one perched or flying around. The male Grayling is preoccupied with his vigil for mates, while the female forays for egg-sites with equal persistence. But both sexes also spend much of their lives in regulating their body temperature. The bare terrain that typifies Grayling sites can bake in the sun of high summer, reaching temperatures of 40-45°C (about 105-115°F). On the other hand, these barren sites become very cool in overcast weather, and to be active a Grayling needs to keep its body temperature at around 32°C (90°F). They achieve this by exposing different areas of their wings and body to the sun, as illustrated opposite.

## EGG-LAYING

The female Grayling lays eggs in warm weather throughout the day. Each is placed singly on the caterpillar's foodplant or nearby, generally on a small tuft of young grass growing in a sheltered, sunny pocket of bare ground. Several of our native grasses are used, depending on the site. On chalk, lime, and shales, sheep's fescue *(Festuca ovina)* is a favourite, while many coastal and dune populations breed largely or wholly on marram grass *(Ammophila arenaria)*. My own searches have mainly been on acid shales and heaths, where I have found eggs almost entirely on the wiry, blue-green tufts of bristle bent *(Agrostis setacea)*. The egg is tricky, but by no means impossible, to find if you search small foodplants growing in suitable places. It is almost spherical and white, with a faint glow as if made of porcelain. It can be distinguished from the eggs of most Browns

REGULATING TEMPERATURE
*When it is too cold, the Grayling leans sideways on to the sun (above) to expose the maximum wing and body area to its heat. In hot weather (below), it stands head-on to the sun, on tiptoe.*

by its clean colour, lacking rust-like patches, and from those of the Wall and Marbled White by the distinct ribs that run from top to bottom.

The egg hatches after 10 to 20 days. The small, cream-coloured caterpillar feeds on the tender tips of the grass, and sheds its skin twice before settling down to hibernate deep in the tussock. It resumes feeding next spring, moulting twice more before attaining full growth in mid June. By now it is feeding exclusively at night, but is quite easy to pick out by torchlight if you scan the beam over the tips of grassblades. This must be done gently, however, for the caterpillar releases its grip and curls up into a ball at the merest rustling of the clump. It is then almost impossible to find, as it is by day, concealed in the depths of a tussock.

The caterpillar is beautifully camouflaged to match the grey, parched grasses among which it lives. Ringlet and Scotch Argus caterpillars may at first appear similar, but neither has such distinctive brown, yellow, and white stripes, nor so smooth a skin. The chrysalis is also well camouflaged for its background. It lives in a cell, lined with silk, below the soil surface.

## A PERFECT CAMOUFLAGE

It is the adult, though, that is the master of disguise. With its wings closed and the forewing tucked down so that both eye-spots are hidden, it is extraordinary how difficult this butterfly is to spot. Whether resting on sand, chalk rubble, or bark, the grey-brown and black marbling of the underwing blends imperceptibly into its barren background. But if startled, the forewing is immediately raised, exposing the bright eye-spot to frighten, or at least distract any enemy. Indeed, when watching this I often think how much more apt – and attractive – were the early English names for this butterfly before it became the "Tonbridge Grayling" and then simply the Grayling, like that unattractive fish. The "Rock-Eyed Underwing" or "Black-eyed Marble", as it was once known, are both more expressive of the character of this fine Satyrid.

This is our largest Brown, although it scarcely appears so when huddled, wings closed, on the ground. It seems considerably larger on the wing, due to a peculiar looping, gliding flight. This enables it to soar and swoop at high speed up and down rocks and cliff-faces, while its smaller relatives flap weakly below. It also appears very much paler when flying, for the straw-coloured bands of the upperwings are then exposed and offset the darker tones of the underside.

## DISTRIBUTION AND STATUS

Graylings vary slightly in appearance within any colony, and certain forms predominate in different parts of the British Isles. The main type, *anglorum,* is illustrated. This is found throughout England, Wales (except on Great Ormes Head), and southern Scotland. The finest colonies are on the southern heaths of Dorset, the New Forest, and Surrey, where it is the commonest Brown and is to be found everywhere that heath survives. It is also common in the more open, grassy areas, and in sunny rides among forestry plantations on these soils. It does particularly well where fine grasses are beginning to invade the sandy strips that are ploughed as fire-breaks.

Colonies were also common on steep, unfertilized chalk downs, in the days when rabbits kept the turf short, and scraped bare patches of soil. Almost all of these colonies have disappeared following the decimation of rabbits by myxomatosis, from the mid-1950s onwards. A very few scattered populations still survive on inland chalk or lime, and it is always worth searching for this butterfly in abandoned quarries.

The inland colonies on other soils have virtually disappeared during this century, except in Devon, Cornwall, and parts of Wales, where unfertilized rough grazing, on mica-schists and shales, such as those surrounding Dartmoor, sometimes support a colony. But the main British colonies, other than those on heathland, are to be found along the coast. Graylings may be present on any eroding cliff or undercliff, and are especially abundant among sand dunes; the adults fly throughout these areas, but it is only worth looking for the young stages on the driest summits, among the marram grass.

## REGIONAL VARIATION

There is a curious race of Grayling that lives solely on the southwest edge of the Great Ormes Head peninsula of north Wales. Its markings are much the same as other Graylings, but it is no larger than a Ringlet or a Speckled Wood. Another strange feature of this dwarf race is that it consistently emerges a few weeks earlier than Graylings elsewhere. It is thought that this race, called *thyone,* originated from Graylings that colonized this peninsula about 10,000 years ago, but which were then cut off from other populations for 3,000 years or so when, due to rising sea levels, these limestone stacks became islands.

A very beautiful form of Grayling is found in the northern half of Scotland. The markings show greater contrast than the southern type, with wider pale bands on the uppersides, and undersurfaces richly marbled with thick, jet-black lines on a paler white background. The contrast is greater still on Hebridean islands, where the broad pale bands are a bright yellow. These so-called *scota* Graylings are virtually confined to the coast, where they may be found in abundance.

The other named races of this variable butterfly live in Ireland. There are two types. The commonest, *hibernica,* is in many ways similar to the Scottish form, but can be distinguished by its warmer brown ground-colour; it, too, is restricted to the coast. There is, however, another type that occurs only on the limestone pavement of the Burren. Even in England, the Graylings that live on chalk and lime tend to be paler and more grey, but here the adults are so pallid that they have been given their own name of *clarensis.*

# GRAYLING · *Hipparchia semele*

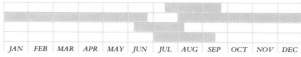

| | JAN | FEB | MAR | APR | MAY | JUN | JUL | AUG | SEP | OCT | NOV | DEC |
|---|---|---|---|---|---|---|---|---|---|---|---|---|
| EGG | | | | | | | | | | | | |
| CATERPILLAR | | | | | | | | | | | | |
| CHRYSALIS | | | | | | | | | | | | |
| ADULT | | | | | | | | | | | | |

**Male**
Dark markings (sex-brands) across the leading edge of the forewings produce a scent during courtship.

**Female**
Upperwings have broad yellow bands; both sexes always settle with their wings closed.

**Egg** [x22]
Strongly ribbed; laid singly on a small tuft of young grass.

**Chrysalis** [x1½]
Formed below ground in a silk-lined, earthen cell

**Burren form**
The pale-coloured *clarensis* race lives only in the Burren in Ireland. The female is larger than the male.

**Caterpillar** [x1½]
Mature caterpillar feeds by night, spending the day concealed in grassy tussocks.

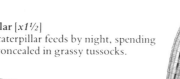

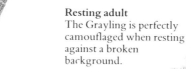

FEEDING CATERPILLAR

**Resting adult**
The Grayling is perfectly camouflaged when resting against a broken background.

# MEADOW BROWN

## *Maniola jurtina*

THIS LARGE but unspectacular Brown has declined greatly in recent years as a result of the agricultural improvement of most lowland grasslands. No longer is it remotely possible to write – as did C. G. Barrett a century ago – that there is "hardly a grassy field in the United Kingdom from which it is wholly absent". Yet this remains an abundant and widespread species. Colonies survive in almost every patch of wild grassland that is not very closely grazed, and the Meadow Brown probably still deserves its reputation of being the commonest butterfly in the British Isles.

Despite its abundance, this species is frequently confused with other Browns when on the wing, especially the Gatekeeper *(see p.177)* and the Ringlet *(see p.189)*. The Meadow Brown also varies somewhat in appearance in different parts of its range. The largest and most beautiful forms occur in the west and north – the race *iernes* in southwest Ireland and the Atlantic isles, *cassiteridium* in the Isles of Scilly, and *splendida* in the Orkneys, Hebrides, and mainland Scotland north of the Great Glen.

**Distribution** *Common in unfertilized grassland and woodland rides throughout lowland Britain; coastal in northern Scotland.*

### VARIATION AND NATURAL SELECTION

One apparently trivial way in which individual adults and whole colonies of Meadow Browns differ is in the position and number of the tiny black dots on the undersurface of each hindwing. Some individuals – particularly females – have no dots at all, whereas others have up to five dots per wing. Earlier this century, this variation was used by E. B. Ford and W. H. Dowdeswell of Oxford as the subject of some of the pioneering research on animal genetics. Working first in the Isles of Scilly, Ford and Dowdeswell found that Meadow Browns on the small, isolated islands were much more uniform in their pattern of dots than were those on the three large islands. They attributed this to the fact that the larger islands contained a greater variety of grassland habitats, and that certain forms of Meadow Brown survived better in some localities, while other patterns were favoured elsewhere. The end result, produced by natural selection, was a more diverse population on each large island, and one that was better able to exploit the full range of habitats. Hitherto, many scientists had believed that this sort of variation between isolated colonies was largely the result of chance, or was caused by the characteristics of the females that first colonized each site.

Ford and Dowdeswell also found differences in the presence and pattern of these same black dots on Meadow Browns in various parts of England. Colonies in the north tended to have fewer dots, whereas the Meadow Browns of west Devon and Cornwall were nearly as heavily spotted as those on the larger Scilly Isles. By and large, this regional variation occurs gradually as one moves from one part of the country to another, but there are many local pockets containing colonies with atypical adults.

### WING PATTERNS AND SURVIVAL

Geneticists argued for many years over the significance of these findings. Few originally thought that the presence or absence of the tiny dots could make much difference to the chances of a Meadow Brown surviving in the wild, yet, at the same time, many believed that very powerful forces must be favouring one pattern or another to produce such clear-cut differences. It came as something of a relief, therefore, when the entomologist Paul Brakefield found that this apparently trivial variation in dotting could be linked to real differences in the Meadow Brown's survival under different circumstances.

Brakefield discovered that the black dots were controlled by large groups of genes – called polygenes – and that some of these also controlled other characteristics of the butterfly. For example, certain genes have the dual effect of causing the caterpillar to reach maturity quickly, and also to develop into a large adult possessing a large number of dots, whereas Meadow Browns without these genes emerge late in the season, and tend

## ESCAPING ATTACK

**SURVIVAL IN THE OPEN (Below)**
*Sedentary females that live in patchy, open habitats are also inclined to be conspicuous. They, too, tend to have dots on their hindwings to deflect bird attacks.*

**SURVIVAL IN THE AIR (Above)**
*The dots on a Meadow Brown's hindwings may trick birds into pecking at the wings rather than at the vulnerable body. Meadow Browns that keep on the move – such as those living in poor habitats – have evolved heavily dotted hindwings.*

**SCARE TACTICS (Below)**
*Females without hindwing dots can also raise their forewings, exposing gleaming eye-spots, to frighten the predator away. These eye-spots tend to be larger than on more mobile Meadow Browns.*

**CONCEALMENT (Above)**
*Females that breed in grassland spend most of their lives out of sight in the uniform vegetation. They hide their forewings between the hindwings which generally have no dots, to betray them to birds.*

to be small and spotless. If either the early- or late-developing caterpillars in a colony suffer unusually heavy losses during spring, the colony will tend to switch from a preponderance of one pattern of spotting to another.

In addition, it is now clear that not only are these dots large enough to distract enemies in their own right, but that those butterflies that possess several dots on their hindwings also tend to have larger eye-spots on their forewings. The latter clearly attract the attention of predators, and any circumstance that favours the survival of Meadow Browns with large or small eye-spots inevitably also affects the number of hindwing dots in the colony. From this rationale, Paul Brakefield made an ingenious suggestion that accounts for the differences in the markings of male and female Meadow Browns, and for much of the local variation in their dot patterns.

### DISTRACTION AND CAMOUFLAGE

Male Meadow Browns are active creatures that spend much of the day searching for females, either by launching themselves from prominent perches on low vegetation or, more often, by weaving between grass clumps on erratic investigative flights. This makes them conspicuous to birds and mammals. It pays for the males to have a variety of dots near the outer edges of their wings, for these distract predators, deflecting their attacks towards this area and usually allowing the butterfly to escape with no more than a peck-mark.

Females, on the other hand, spend most of the day resting near the ground. They sit with their wings closed and over-lapping, so that only the undersurfaces of the hindwings are visible. The emphasis now is on camouflage. Survival is highest among individuals that do not attract any predators in the first place, and their camouflage is enhanced if there are no or few dots on the hindwing. Females also have a second line of

defence. If discovered, they quickly raise their forewings, exposing the gleaming eye-spot in a flash, in the hope of startling the predator into flight. To achieve this, females tend to have much larger eye-spots on their forewings than males, even though the hindwings contain fewer dots.

Brakefield also noticed that the nature of the habitat could account for some of the variation in dotting between individual males and females. Butterflies that have few or no dots are much better camouflaged on sites that contain uniform grassland, such as those that predominate in the north, whereas Meadow Browns with several dots merge better into mixed, scrubby backgrounds. In addition, butterflies that breed at low densities over large areas of mediocre habitat are forced to roam much more than those that emerge at high densities on ideal breeding sites. Thus, the Meadow Browns living in the former situation are more likely to be noticed – needing dots that deflect attack than those that live at high densities.

### HIGH-DENSITY LIVING

Meadow Browns may be crammed together in remarkable numbers on the best sites. The ideal habitat for this species consists of warm, open grassland, 0.5 m. (1½ ft.) or so in height, and containing an abundance of summer flowers and medium- or fine-leaved grasses. This situation exists on many lightly grazed downs, on undercliffs, in recently abandoned grassland, and in unfertilized hay meadows that are cut late in the season, after the adult butterflies have emerged. Up to 2,000 Meadow Browns can emerge in a single hectare on these sites.

Equally high densities can be found along the verges of some of the busiest roads in Dorset, while Meadow Browns are seen by the hundred in almost every sunny woodland ride in Britain in July. Very much smaller numbers occur in marginal habitats, such as tall, coarse grassland, or turf that is grazed fairly short.

A few dozen butterflies is also the normal complement on many small sites, such as the thin strips of grass that grow beneath almost every hedgerow.

## TAKING TO THE AIR

By and large, the Meadow Brown is a sedentary insect, which strays from its breeding sites only when these are disturbed or are of poor quality. The first males emerge in mid-June in a normal year, but some fly as early as May after an exceptionally warm spring. The date of peak numbers varies by up to four weeks from one year to the next, depending on June temperatures, but is usually reached in late July. There is then a gradual decline, with the butterfly disappearing on most sites by the end of August. However, the emergence is greatly prolonged on many warm southern chalk downs, especially those that are grazed fairly short. On these, adults continue to emerge throughout September, and it is by no means unusual to see fresh females in mid-October. Why this occurs is unknown.

Male and female Meadow Browns usually roost together in tall clumps of grass, then bask with their wings spread wide to absorb the early morning sunshine. When warmed, they are capable of flying in the dullest weather, and even in light rain. Both sexes feed avidly on a range of summer flowers.

## COURTSHIP AND EGG-LAYING

The males, as already described, spend much of the day hunting virgin females. Once found, there is a brief courtship during which the male envelops his partner in an unpleasant scent that has been variously described as resembling an old cigar box, musty hay, or dirty socks. Humans vary in their sensitivity to this; some find it exceedingly strong, whereas others can scarcely detect it. The female Meadow Brown, however, is entranced, and settles on a firm piece of vegetation, while the male grasps her with his claspers.

Female Meadow Browns generally mate on the first active day of their lives, and rarely need to pair a second time. Like the males, they live on average for about 5 to 12 days, lasting longer in cool, humid weather. The eggs ripen quite quickly, and are mostly laid between two and four days after the female mated. As with many butterflies, she first embarks on distinctive fluttering flights, flapping slowly just above the grass. She frequently alights in warm, sheltered patches of fine or short turf, and walks jerkily with wings closed in a sort of rocking movement, as she twitches her way excitedly through the grass tufts.

Moses Harris watched this over two centuries ago, and wrote that "the hens, when impregnated, cast forth their eggs but I cannot be certain whether they fix them to the blades of grass, or scatter them loose on the ground". In fact they do both: some are deposited with the utmost care, whereas others are simply squirted out, sometimes even in flight.

## EARLY DEVELOPMENT

It is not known exactly what prompts the female Meadow Brown to lay in particular patches of turf. Perhaps she selects a favourable scent within the field, or even chooses particular grasses. For although the caterpillar can feed on a wide range of grass species, it has distinct favourites. These are medium- or fine-leaved species, particularly meadow-grasses (*Poa* spp.), bents (*Agrostis* spp.), and rye-grasses (*Lolium* spp.). Very hairy or coarse grasses, such as purple moor grass (*Molinia caerulea*) are invariably avoided.

The young caterpillars feed by day in high summer and autumn, but are too small to be found with ease. They settle down for the winter in a grass clump, emerging during mild spells to nibble a few blades. They resume feeding in earnest in spring, and by March many have moulted for the second time and reached a size at which it is safer to feed by night.

Fully grown caterpillars are quite easy to find on the best sites, where there may be as many as 10 per square metre. They are also quite easy to identify, being hairier than the caterpillars of most Browns, and possessing "tails" that are distinctly white. They can be found by day deep in the base of favoured grasses, such as smooth meadow-grass (*Poa pratensis*), by looking for tussocks with blades that have clearly been eaten back. More will be seen after dusk if you scan the upper grassblades with a torch, especially on warm, damp evenings in May. However this must be done very gently, for the caterpillars are sensitive to the merest rustling and instantly drop to the ground, curled up in a ball.

Most caterpillars pupate by early June, and last two to four weeks before hatching. They are extremely variable in appearance, ranging from pale green with few dark markings, to almost white but heavily striated with broad, black bands.

## A BROAD DISTRIBUTION

Although many former colonies have disappeared due to the spraying and ploughing of ancient grassland, the Meadow Brown remains an extremely common lowland butterfly in almost all suitable habitats in the British Isles. It is easier to list the regions where it is scarce or absent. These include northern Scotland, where it is distinctly local throughout, the Orkneys, where it is confined to a few warm, south-facing slopes, and the Shetlands, where it has never been reliably recorded. Colonies are seldom found at altitudes above 200 m. (650 ft.) in the Highlands, Pennines, and Welsh hills, or above 300 m. (1,000 ft.) in the warmer atmosphere of Dartmoor.

# MEADOW BROWN · *Maniola jurtina*

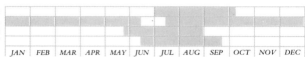

LIFE-CYCLE

| | JAN | FEB | MAR | APR | MAY | JUN | JUL | AUG | SEP | OCT | NOV | DEC |
|---|---|---|---|---|---|---|---|---|---|---|---|---|
| EGG | | | | | | | | | | | | |
| CATERPILLAR | | | | | | | | | | | | |
| CHRYSALIS | | | | | | | | | | | | |
| ADULT | | | | | | | | | | | | |

**Male upperside**
Typical males have virtually no orange on the upperwings.

**Male underside**
Black dots on the hindwings vary in number from none to five.

**Female upperside**
In both sexes, there is much variation in eye-spots and other markings.

**Female underside**
Eye-spot is exposed if the butterfly is threatened.

**Female, Irish form**
The Irish subspecies *M. j. iernes* is large and brightly marked.

**Female in late summer**
Towards the end of the summer, adults become faded and tattered.

**Feeding adult**
Creeping thistle is a favourite source of nectar in grassy places.

**Egg [*x22*]**
Laid singly, usually on grassblades, but sometimes in the air.

**Caterpillar [*x2¼*]**
Sluggish, hairy caterpillar feeds on a variety of grasses.

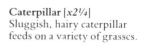

**Chrysalis [*x2¼*]**
Markings vary from highly striped to plain green.

# RINGLET

## Aphantopus hyperantus

THE RINGLET is an enchanting inhabitant of humid grassland over much of the British Isles. Flying mainly in July, it avoids the summer's heat by living in woods and cool, moist places where the air is damp and still. Earlier this century, F. W. Frohawk aptly described it as a "peaceful" butterfly, and there are few more refreshing sights than the dusky adults fluttering silently along rides, crossing glades, or bobbing among dense tussocks on a sticky summer's day.

This is a comparatively common butterfly, frequently overlooked due to a resemblance, in flight, to the male Meadow Brown *(see p.187)*. The Ringlet has much darker wings, that are bordered by a fine, white fringe that shines as it catches the sun. There should be no confusion when the butterflies settle: Ringlet uppersides are soft, velvety and uniformly dark, with none of the orange of a Meadow Brown, while the undersides are adorned with distinctive, gleaming eye-spots. It is these that gave this butterfly its name, two centuries ago, when the word "ringlet" was in common usage to describe any small circle, such as the fairy rings caused by fungus on a leaf. Other early names included the "Brown-eyed Butterfly", and the "Brown Seven Eyes".

***Distribution*** *Common and often overlooked in woodland rides and damp grassland in Ireland, lowland Wales, and southern lowland England.*

### EYE-SPOT VARIATIONS

The eye-spots may vary in size, shape, and number on different individuals. The most striking form, called *lanceolata,* has large and elongated spots, as can be seen opposite. It is a beautiful variety that is sometimes quite common in certain colonies, particularly in the south. It is also easily bred in captivity, as this characteristic is controlled by a single recessive gene that ensures that at least one in nine butterflies will turn out to be *lanceolata* if the offspring of one are paired with each other.

Other forms have few, small, or even no spots. We illustrate an extreme example called *arete,* but every intermediate can be found between this and the normal spotting. Another form, *caeca,* merely possesses the inner white dots. This, like the *arete*

Ringlet, becomes increasingly common as one travels north. The butterfly also tends to be smaller and greyer in Scotland, as it is in Scandinavia and at high altitudes further south.

### ALL-WEATHER FLIGHT

Ringlets are invariably found in self-contained colonies. These have been little studied, but standardized counts suggest that they range enormously in size from a few dozen individuals up to many thousands per colony on the best sites. Numbers also fluctuate considerably from one year to the next. In general, the butterfly benefits from a rainy summer but declines after a dry one. There was, for example, a severe reduction almost everywhere after the exceptional drought of 1976, and a rapid recovery during the cool, wet years that followed. This species is one of the most consistent of all butterflies in its time of emergence. The first males are seen on the last days of June, but the main flight occurs in July, peaking in the third week. There is then a rapid decline, with a few faded stragglers surviving beyond mid-August. They do, however, make the most of their short lives, and remain surprisingly active in gloomy weather when every other butterfly is grounded, even flying in light rain.

Male Ringlets spend much of their lives fluttering around grassheads and jinking between tussocks in a relentless search for mates. Both sexes also spend long periods at flowers, where they jostle for nectar among Meadow Browns and Gatekeepers on bramble *(Rubus fruticosus),* thistles *(Cirsium* and *Carduus* spp.),* or any other blooms that are available. They visit orchids on downland sites, which can cause problems because the sticky sacs of pollen adhere to their probosces, making it impossible to curl them away after feeding.

### AERIAL EGG-LAYING

Female Ringlets appear to be indiscriminate when it comes to egg-laying. They either sit high up on grassheads squirting

# RINGLET · *Aphantopus hyperantus*

## LIFE-CYCLE

| | JAN | FEB | MAR | APR | MAY | JUN | JUL | AUG | SEP | OCT | NOV | DEC |
|---|---|---|---|---|---|---|---|---|---|---|---|---|
| EGG | | | | | | | | | | | | |
| CATERPILLAR | | | | | | | | | | | | |
| CHRYSALIS | | | | | | | | | | | | |
| ADULT | | | | | | | | | | | | |

**Male**
Upperwings of fresh males are almost black;
their colour fades slightly with age.

**Female**
The ground-colour of females is slightly paler
than that of males. Wings of both sexes have
distinctive fringes.

*ab. arete*

*ab. lanceolata*

**Eye-spot variants**
Size and shape of the underside
eye-spots varies greatly.

**Orchid pollen**
Pollen sacs from orchids
may prevent the proboscis
being coiled up.

**Egg** [*x22*]
Dropped, rather than
laid, among grasses.

**Chrysalis** [*x2¼*]
Formed at the base
of grass tussocks.

**Adult feeding**
Wild privet is a frequent nectar
source on downland sites.

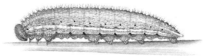

**Caterpillar** [*x2¼*]
Overwintering cater-
pillar feeds occasionally
on mild nights.

their eggs into the air or, less often, lay while hovering in a stuttering, stumbling flight. I suspect, however, that there is more to this than meets the eye, and that they are responding to the scent of certain grasses that wafts upwards on the cool and humid air.

I have watched Ringlets lay on many occasions, but have yet to find their eggs on the ground. They are, however, easy to obtain in captivity if a female is caged over a pot of moist grasses. Each egg is triangular in outline, with a wet, glossy sheen unlike that of any other Brown. It hatches after a fortnight and, if necessary, the little caterpillar can survive without food for a day or two while it searches for a suitable plant. The full range of grasses eaten in Britain is unknown, but all experts agree that the list is very short – often just one species being used on a particular site. Cock's-foot *(Dactylis glomerata)* and wood false brome *(Brachypodium sylvaticum)* are great favourites, but only where these coarse grasses grow as lush, uncropped tussocks.

The caterpillar lives about 10 months, hibernating while still quite small after the second of its four skin moults. It is impossible to find in the autumn, but can seen quite easily by searching tall grass clumps by torchlight on warm evenings in May. It is rather like the grey forms of the Marbled White and Gatekeeper caterpillars, but is hairier than the latter and lacks the former's distinctive pink tails. It pupates in mid-June, forming an attractively streaked chrysalis that rests at the bottom of its grass clump in a small cocoon of silk.

## WOODLAND AND HEDGEROW HABITATS

By far the best places to find this dusky Brown are the rides, edges, and glades of woods, where wild grasses have been left to grow into a dense strip or as isolated tussocks. In the southern half of Britain, most large or medium-sized woods contain a colony, so long as there are open, sunny spaces. But the species is by no means confined to woods, and can be encountered on any patch of rank, unfertilized grassland. Colonies are very much more common on heavy soils, and on the southern clays it is even a hedgerow species, being found along many ditches, hedge bottoms, and road verges. It is much less common on light soils, and although a few downland colonies exist, these tend to be on damp, north-facing slopes, or in coombes where the soil is deep.

Although common throughout Ireland, southern England, and lowland Wales, the Ringlet becomes much more localized as one travels north. It is nonetheless common, where found, over quite large areas of lowland Scotland, and inhabits several of the Western Isles. There is a curious absence of colonies in the Midlands and northern England, as well as around London, Glasgow, and Edinburgh. Local extinctions occurred in all these areas during the Industrial Revolution, and it has been suggested that this might be due to air pollution. I suspect it may equally well be associated with drainage and the disappearance of moist, abandoned grassland, for I have seen Ringlets in abundance in Poland, flying in some of the most polluted regions of Europe.

# SMALL HEATH

*Coenonympha pamphilus*

THE SMALL HEATH is one of the smallest and most successful of the 117 species of Browns found in Europe. Although seldom as numerous as, for example, the Meadow Brown or Scotch Argus, it nevertheless occurs over a wider geographical range and in a greater variety of habitats than any other member of its family. It also has an extremely long flight period in the south, where a complicated sequence of broods ensures that the tawny adults can be seen bobbing around wild grasses almost continuously from May to October.

Size and colour distinguish this common species from other brown butterflies. Among our small species, it is both lighter and more golden than the Dingy Skipper *(see p.29)* or the female Blues, but it has nothing like the brightness of the four golden Skippers. A drunken pattern of flight is also diagnostic, as it flops and bobs erratically just a few centimetres above the ground. Blues have a more purposeful flight, whereas Skippers characteristically dart back and forth at high speed.

Small Heaths vary in appearance, with unusually bright and dull adults often flying in the same colony. The size of the spots on both forewings and hindwings also differs. There is a tendency for adults to be duller and paler the further north and west one travels in Scotland, and the butterfly has been described as a separate subspecies, called *C. p. rhoumensis,* at the extreme of this range. This is also illustrated, although its status as a true subspecies is doubtful.

## PROTECTIVE EYE-SPOTS

Whatever the ground-colour, both sexes appear much brighter when flying, because the settled butterfly always sits with its wings closed. In dull weather, or when the butterfly has been sitting for some time, the forewings are tucked well down between the hindwings, so that only the grey hind undersurface is visible. However, like the Grayling *(see pp.180-183),* the Small Heath usually rests for a short while after landing with the

*Distribution Found in most patches of dry grassland throughout its British range, but seldom in large numbers. Absent from the Orkneys and Shetlands.*

forewings held aloft, which exposes a gleaming eye-spot set in a tawny triangle; this was no doubt responsible for one early English name – the "Golden Heath Eye".

The eye-spot is probably a ruse to trick insect-eating birds, that have noticed the butterfly land, into pecking at the wrong place. You will often find tattered Small Heaths with V-shaped cuts, made by a bird's beak, around the eye-spot. By deflecting the attack from head to wing, they at least live to tell the tale.

## COLONIES AND TERRITORIES

The Small Heath lives in self-contained colonies of limited size, with most adults flying and breeding in the same patch of grassland for their entire lives. Yet the odd individual of both sexes wanders more than is the case with most sedentary species, and isolated patches of fresh breeding habitat tend to be quickly colonized. Sometimes they make longer journeys. It is not unusual for the butterfly to be seen in gardens, and a few have been caught on lightships.

Next to nothing was known about the breeding behaviour of this butterfly until Per-Olaf Wickman recently studied it in Sweden; his findings tally so well with most casual observations in Britain that I have no doubt that our Small Heaths act in exactly the same way. Males live, on average, for about seven days and spend most of their lives searching for mates. Each tries to establish a territory by perching on the ground near a tree, a bush, or a hedge – all places where virgin females fly. Unfortunately, there are seldom enough perching points to go round, so rival males engage in prolonged aerial battles for possession. In general, the larger-winged individuals win, condemning smaller males to fly further afield, where they have little chance of mating. Wickman found that nearly 90 per cent of the pairings on his Swedish site were accomplished by the 60 per cent of males that managed to establish territories. This pattern broke down only on exceptionally hot days, when many territorial males deserted their perches in favour of flights.

Male territories seldom overlap with breeding areas, which are found in more open grassland. The virgin females emerging from these patches fly directly towards male territories, and then make themselves conspicuous by flying backwards and forwards a good metre (3 ft.) above the ground, soliciting the attention of any perching male. They, in fact, need little invitation, and will launch themselves after any insect passing by. Having attracted her mate, the female lands on the ground and the male advances with a combination of head butts and fluttering wings, almost certainly showering her with aphrodisiacs, as described for the Wall *(see p.168)*.

Females that have mated avoid male territories, and their rare flights are short, fluttery affairs, just above ground level. They search for open, wild grassland in which to lay eggs, landing where the sward is short or sparse. Each then wanders for a while, testing the vegetation before laying a single egg, usually on a blade of fine grass. In England a range of wild species is used, including meadow grasses *(Poa spp.)* and fescues *(Festuca spp.)*. Wickman found that four-fifths were laid on sheep's fescue *(F. ovina)* on his Swedish study site.

### HIDDEN IN GRASS

The egg of the Small Heath is large for the size of the butterfly, and is highly attractive. Young females lay particularly large eggs and eject them more rapidly than do the older females; they also lay green-shelled eggs, whereas after a hundred or so have been laid, the shells are yellow. No one knows the significance of this change, and both forms are well camouflaged against the grassblades on which they are laid.

Small Heath eggs last about a fortnight, during which time they turn pale and freckled, and then almost transparent just before hatching. The caterpillar lives low down in the sward, mainly in a small tuft of young grass. It emerges at night to nibble the nutritious tips, although I have also found final-stage caterpillars eating openly on dull days. They are by no means easy to spot, for the green-and-white striped body blends beautifully with the narrow leaf blades.

Southern Small Heaths have a complicated growth pattern that has not been thoroughly researched. Most caterpillars are quite large by the time they hibernate, although a few may be considerably smaller. They resume feeding in spring, and by late April the first of the pretty, striped chrysalises have been formed, dangling beneath grass-stems. These produce a first batch of adults in mid-May. Numbers build up to reach a peak a month later, then gradually fall during July, with the last stragglers overlapping with a second brood of adults in early August. The second peak is reached towards the end of that month. In warm years there may then be a third emergence in the autumn. But not every egg that is laid develops into an adult the same year: some offspring of the first brood hibernate instead, as do many or all from the second brood, and after a warm summer, three generations of caterpillars may be hibernating together. Hibernation probably explains why fewer Small Heaths emerge in the second brood than in the first in most years, with fewer still in the third brood, when this exists. This is especially the case after cool, wet summers: hot seasons tend to result in large emergences in August followed by small ones the following spring.

Northern Small Heaths belong to a different physiological race, and are less likely to produce second and third emergences, even when they are reared under artificially warm conditions. Thus there is usually just one emergence a year in Scotland. This varies in timing according to the weather in the season and the locality, but typically begins in the first week of June and lasts for three months until the end of summer.

### A UBIQUITOUS SPECIES

Colonies of Small Heath are found throughout the British Isles apart from the Orkneys and Shetlands. On mountainsides, they extend no higher than about 750 m. (2,500 ft.). Numbers fluctuate considerably from one year to the next, but are consistently large only on open, well-drained grasslands where wild, fine-leaved grasses dominate the sward. These habitats include dunes, heaths, and chalk or limestone downs that are grazed fairly short, but not nibbled down to the ground. Smaller numbers will be found almost everywhere else where wild grasses grow in open, sunny conditions, for example in unfertilized meadows, verges, wasteland, and woods. Nor is this butterfly restricted to dry soils. It is often seen in ones and twos on heavy clays and in marshes, although in these places breeding is probably restricted to local dry spots. Thus I have found many caterpillars in the glades of one swampy wood in the Surrey Weald, but only on the sides of ant hills, which protrude as islands above the surrounding waterlogged ground.

# SMALL HEATH · *Coenonympha pamphilus*

## LIFE-CYCLE

| | JAN | FEB | MAR | APR | MAY | JUN | JUL | AUG | SEP | OCT | NOV | DEC |
|---|---|---|---|---|---|---|---|---|---|---|---|---|
| EGG | | | | | | | | | | | | |
| CATERPILLAR | | | | | | | | | | | | |
| CHRYSALIS | | | | | | | | | | | | |
| ADULT | | | | | | | | | | | | |

**Male**
Generally smaller and brighter than the female; sexes otherwise similar.

**Female**
Ground-colour and size of spots is highly variable in both sexes.

**Male**
Subspecies *C. p. rhoumensis,* from Scotland; duller than forms found further south.

**Male**
Colour variants with brighter wings may occur alongside duller forms in the same colony

**Egg [x22]**
Large in proportion to butterfly; laid singly on grassblade.

**Chrysalis [x2¼]**
Suspended beneath grass stem; black streaking varies, and is sometimes absent.

**Mating**
Mating takes place within territories established and defended by the males.

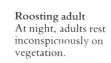

**Roosting adult**
At night, adults rest inconspicuously on vegetation.

**Caterpillar [x2¼]**
Camouflaged caterpillar lives low down in grass, feeding by night.

# LARGE HEATH

## *Coenonympha tullia*

THE LARGE HEATH occurs in a string of isolated colonies that stretch from central Wales to the Orkneys. It is one of our few truly wetland species, and flutters in high summer over countless small bogs throughout the north. It is also one of our most variable butterflies, so much so that it was once considered to be three distinct species, known as the "Scarce Heath", the "Marsh Ringlet", and the "Small Ringlet". These very roughly corresponded to the three forms of Large Heath recognized today – *scotica*, *polydama*, and *davus* – which are illustrated opposite. Other early names were the "Manchester Argus", commemorating the first known colony of this butterfly, long since destroyed by that conurbation, the "July Ringlet", and "Silver-Bordered Ringlet"; all more attractive names, to my mind, than the Large Heath, and less confusing, for it is not so long ago that another Satyrid butterfly, the Gatekeeper, was known by this name.

The variation in the markings of this butterfly was a great attraction for Victorian collectors. In this century, a number of scientists have studied this phenomenon, including Tim Melling of the University of Newcastle, on whose research much of this account is based.

**Distribution** *Very local species in peat bogs and wetlands, but often abundant where it does occur. Commonest in north Scotland.*

### BRIEF LIVES

Large Heath colonies can be found from sea level up to altitudes of about 760 m. (2,500 ft.). Typical habitats are lowland raised bogs, waterlogged peat mosses, upland blanket bogs, and damp, acid moorland – all flat, wet areas where the main caterpillar foodplant, hare's-tail *(Eriophorum vaginatum)*, grows in immense, shaggy tussocks. Most sites also contain an abundance of cross-leaved heath *(Erica tetralix)*, which is the favourite nectar source of the adults.

Adult Large Heaths emerge in mid-June on most lowland sites, but not until a month later at high altitudes. They usually reach a peak in mid-July, lingering on well into August, even though various studies indicate that individual adults live, on average, just three to four days. The main cause of death is thought to be attack by meadow pipits, which hop between the tussocks in search of prey. In one study, about a third of the Large Heaths examined had beak marks across their wings, but had escaped being eaten. Of more than a hundred meadow pipit droppings teased apart, practically all contained the remains of what may be presumed to be Large Heaths.

### THE BOGLAND BUTTERFLY

The Large Heath is a highly sedentary species, with little or no interchange between the butterflies of nearby bogs. Individual colonies may be very large, numbering up to 15,000 adults. Roughly equal numbers of both sexes emerge, but at first sight, males seem to predominate, due to the habit of females of hiding within the tussocks. The males sit with wings tightly closed, leaning sideways to the sun to warm up, for, like the Grayling *(see p.181)*, this is a species that never basks with its wings held flat.

The flight of both sexes is a slow, bobbing affair, that occurs in dull as well as sunny weather. Cold weather grounds the butterflies, as does high wind, but, even on a windy day, it is usually possible to flush a few by shuffling through the undergrowth. For, unlike most Browns, they tend to dart away through the air rather than drop into deep vegetation, when a potential enemy disturbs them.

### FROM EGG TO CATERPILLAR

The egg is laid on dead, brown leaves at the base of immense tussocks of hare's-tail or, on a few sites, of white-beaked sedge *(Rhynochospora alba)*. It is shiny yellow at first, but develops rust-coloured blotches after a week. After a further week it darkens, and the little caterpillar emerges. This starts feeding on the tender tips of its foodplants, and in late September, after two moults, it hibernates deep in the tussock. Here it can withstand long periods of immersion, and even being frozen solid.

# LARGE HEATH · *Coenonympha tullia*

## LIFE-CYCLE

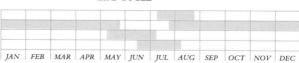

| | JAN | FEB | MAR | APR | MAY | JUN | JUL | AUG | SEP | OCT | NOV | DEC |
|---|---|---|---|---|---|---|---|---|---|---|---|---|
| EGG | | | | | | | | | | | | |
| CATERPILLAR | | | | | | | | | | | | |
| CHRYSALIS | | | | | | | | | | | | |
| ADULT | | | | | | | | | | | | |

**Male**
Dark *davus* form, found
in northwest England.

**Female**
*Davus* form; coloration slightly
lighter than the male's.

**Male**
*Scotica* form; the underside of this form
has few spots. Found in Scotland.

**Male**
*Polydama* form; an intermediate form found
in northern England, Wales, and Ireland.

**Female**
*Polydama* form.

**Female**
*Scotica* form; the palest of
all the variants.

**Egg** [*x22*]
Initially yellow, later
developing dark blotches.

**Chrysalis** [*x2¼*]
Suspended from a stem;
the boldness of the black
stripes varies.

**Feeding adult**
Adult clinging to the flowers
of cross-leaved heath, the
main nectar source.

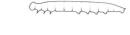

**Caterpillar** [*x2¼*]
Can withstand extreme cold;
may hibernate for two winters.

On northern sites, some of the caterpillars may spend a second winter in hibernation, taking two years to develop from egg to adult. More often, however, the caterpillars are fully grown in June, when they form their attractive, stumpy green chrysalises.

## LOCAL VARIATION

Colonies of Large Heath can be found locally throughout the bogs of Ireland, and in considerable numbers in the northern half of Scotland. They are present, too, on many islands, including the Outer Hebrides and Orkneys, but not, almost certainly, the Shetlands. The species is much more localized in the southern half of Scotland, although plentiful enough in parts of Northumberland and Cumbria. There was a time when it was also common and widespread on the Mosses around Manchester and Liverpool, but the vast majority of these have been drained and converted to farmland, or built upon. Finally, clusters of colonies are still found in the more mountainous areas of north and central Wales.

The great variation in the appearance of adult Large Heaths, both in different parts of their range, and also – except in the most northern colonies – within individual sites, has led to their classification into three forms. The largest, and most uniform, is *scotica*. Its wings are pale and grey, and are also virtually spotless, giving it an appearance rather like a very large Small Heath *(see p.193)*. It is the form found in all the isles and throughout northern Scotland, down to an abrupt boundary shown on the map on p.194. The *scotica* form is now known to constitute a separate subspecies.

Travelling south, the *polydama* form predominates. This is slightly smaller and darker than *scotica* and, above all, possesses appreciable eye-dots. It is found in Cumbria, Northumberland, and southern Scotland, as well as on one site in the Pennines, on the Lincolnshire and Yorkshire Moors, and on several sites in mid- and north Wales. It is also the predominant type in Ireland.

The third form, *davus,* is the most beautiful of all. It has richer, redder wings, and an array of large eye-spots, many with gleaming white pupils. It is the predominate type in lowland England and, for that reason, most of its colonies have been lost. Nevertheless, it is still to be found in good numbers along the coastal plain south of the Lake District, on the lowland Mosses of northwest England, in a small area of Shropshire, and at one site in lowland Lancashire.

It is fair to say, however, that these last two groupings are largely for convenience. There is much variation within both forms and, where they meet, one very much resembles the other. *Scotica* Large Heaths, on the other hand, certainly form a distinct and invariable group, and have probably been isolated from the southern populations for 10,000 generations or more.

## "HIDERS" AND "DEFLECTORS"

Quite why Large Heaths in various regions should have evolved such strikingly different markings is explained by the recent work of Tim Melling. He examined many colonies in the wild, and concluded that the reason was similar, but more clear cut, to that suggested for the Meadow Brown *(see p.185)*. It centres on which is the safest method of protection against bird attack – to be exceptionally well camouflaged while sitting with closed wings on the ground, or to develop wing eye-spots, which make the butterfly more conspicuous, but deflect any attack away from the vulnerable body.

Melling found a very close correlation between the number and size of spots on different Large Heaths and the hours of sunshine that their various sites typically received in June and July – the months when adults were on the wing. On warm, sunny, southern lowland bogs, and also on scrubby, sheltered ones, the adults tended to be much more active, and flew more frequently, than on cool sites. Their movements drew them to the attention of meadow pipits, which pecked particularly at the outer edge of the lower wings, if there were gleaming eye-spots there. This, Melling showed, gave the butterfly a good chance of escaping.

Over the years, less heavily spotted individuals tend to be caught by birds, while spotted ones tend to survive to do more of the breeding. Eventually, this leads to the development of a colony made up of *davus*-form Large Heaths. At the other extreme, on cool northern sites, it is seldom warm enough for the butterflies to take to the air, and instead, they spend long periods perched on the ground. For these butterflies, it is a far better strategy to escape the notice of birds in the first place. In these conditions, unspotted *scotica*-form individuals are more likely to survive. Finally, on intermediate sites, there is probably a balance between the advantages of being camouflaged and those of surviving bird attacks. This leads to the *polydama* form, which has intermediate markings on its wings.

This is, perhaps, an oversimplification of the system, but even so, it is typical of many of the subtle forces that affect the appearance and behaviour of insects. It certainly adds greatly to the fascination of watching this little butterfly, trying to weigh the balance as to whether each is a "hider" or a "deflector" in its battle for survival.

# INTRODUCTION TO RARE SPECIES
## VAGRANTS, RARE MIGRANTS, AND EXTINCT BUTTERFLIES

AT LEAST 50 SPECIES of butterfly have been recorded in the British Isles, over and above the 60 residents and regular visitors already described. These include two former natives, the Mazarine Blue and Black-veined White, which are extinct and have yet to be successfully reintroduced. They also encompass several migrants that occasionally fly here from overseas, but so seldom that even the most acute naturalist is unlikely to see more than four or five of them in a lifetime. Eight of these vagrants are described in the following pages, together with the Mazarine Blue and the Black-veined White.

This leaves about 40 recorded species that, on various grounds, are excluded from this concluding section. Many stem from genuine records, substantiated by photographs or specimens in museums, but are of exceptional rarity in the British Isles. Others include frauds, mistakes, and wishful thinking, for butterfly enthusiasts are no less susceptible than anglers to embroidering their tales.

There is genuine uncertainty about a number of strange species that feature in the earliest accounts of British butterflies. A few are simple mistakes due to the mixing of records or specimens. Other species may well have resided here once, to become extinct before being properly documented. These include three species of Copper – the Scarce, Purple-shot, and Purple-edged – as well as the so-called Arran Brown *(Erebia ligea)*. The case for believing the Coppers to have been British is not strong. However, many give the Arran Brown the benefit of the doubt.

There is no doubt that the reported sightings and capture of many species of butterfly are fraudulent. The origin of an individual butterfly can be extremely difficult to verify: I have had some experience myself over the Large Blue, when dead continental specimens have been claimed as English. Frauds are, in fact, much less common now than in previous centuries, when there were genuine new species to be discovered in remote regions, and when collectors were prepared to pay high prices for British rarities. There have, of course, also been many innocent introductions of foreign species to Britain, as well as many captive butterflies that have escaped. This has recently become common due to the proliferation of butterfly farms; it is not particularly unusual to see a gaudy South American species gliding around the gardens in the vicinity of a rearing house. Other species that have been caught in the British Isles once or twice probably owe their origin to being accidentally imported as chrysalises or caterpillars, sometimes literally in a bunch of bananas. Yet more are thought to be vagrants from other continents. One undoubted example, which crops up too rarely for a full account, is the American or Hunter's Painted Lady *(Cynthia virginiensis)*.

With the increase in international travel, it seems likely that more exotic species of butterfly will be transported to escape or be (illegally) released in the British Isles in future years. But it is remarkable how few species establish themselves here. One famous example that briefly succeeded is the European Map *(Araschnia levana)*, which was released in the Forest of Dean in about 1912, and bred for a few years. It is widely believed that it was exterminated by a collector who hated the idea of foreign butterflies in Britain. This, however, seems unlikely to be the entire reason for this butterfly's demise, it is more likely that its habitat was only marginally suitable.

There is today just one species of foreign butterfly, the Large Chequered Skipper *(Heteropterus morpho)*, that is known to have colonized part of the British Isles in recent centuries.

**AMERICAN PAINTED LADY**
*Since its discovery in Pembrokeshire in 1808, only about 19 genuine records have been made of this North American immigrant. It is, however, permanently established in Spain.*

**ARRAN BROWN**
*This handsome butterfly was reputedly discovered by Sir Patrick Walker on the Isle of Arran in 1803. The most recent specimen was caught by a schoolboy in 1969 on the western edge of Rannoch Moor.*

**LARGE CHEQUERED SKIPPER**
*This is believed to have been accidentally introduced to Jersey during the wartime occupation. Today, only a single colony survives on the island.*

# PALE *and* BERGER'S CLOUDED YELLOWS

## *Colias hyale* and *Colias alfacariensis*

THESE TWO Clouded Yellows are rare migrants to the British Isles and are extremely difficult to distinguish. Indeed, they were only recognized as separate species as recently as 1945, and there remains much confusion as to the true occurrence of each in Britain. To make matters worse, both also resemble the pale *helice* form of the female Clouded Yellow *(see p.39)* which, although scarce, has been considerably more common than either in the British Isles in recent years.

### IDENTIFYING ADULTS
On the Continent, some clue to the identify of these species may be gained from their location, as of the two, only Berger's Clouded Yellow reaches as far south as the Mediterranean countries. However, in Britain, as elsewhere, it is virtually impossible to distinguish between Pale, Berger's, and *helice* Clouded Yellows on the wing. All three species settle with their wings closed, which obscures the main distinguishing mark of the *helice* form of the Clouded Yellow – a broader black edge to the wings, especially the hindwings, that extends much further around the corner towards the body, along both the lower edge of the forewing and the upper edge of the hindwing.

Pale and Berger's Clouded Yellows are best distinguished by the shape of the leading edge of their forewings. This is curved in the former and straight in the latter, giving the Pale Clouded Yellow's wings an altogether more pointed look. In addition, male Berger's Clouded Yellows have a slightly warmer and more intense yellow ground-colour, the orange spot on the underside is brighter, and the dark markings are less distinct. However, all these characteristics vary within the two species. Although the shape of the forewing is a fairly good guide, for positive identification the butterflies must be killed and their detailed anatomy examined. Today, few naturalists have either the ability or inclination to do this, and so the identity of vagrants is often difficult to establish.

***Distribution** Berger's Clouded Yellow – the rarer of the two species – has not been recorded beyond the area shown above.*

### DISTINCTIVE CATERPILLARS
Another way around the problem of identification is to breed the two species in captivity, or, preferably, to watch egg-laying females in the wild. The Pale Clouded Yellow lays on lucerne *(Medicago sativa)* and probably other medicks and melilots *(Melilotus* spp.*)*, as well as, reputedly, on clovers *(Trifolium* spp.*)*, whereas Berger's Clouded Yellow restricts its eggs to horseshoe vetch *(Hippocrepis comosa)*. Both lay the typical long, bottle-shaped eggs of all Whites, and these turn orange or pink after a few days on the foodplant.

It is the caterpillar, however, that is really distinctive, and that confirms that these two very similar butterflies are in reality two separate species. As can be seen from our illustration, that of the Pale Clouded Yellow is similar to the Clouded Yellow's in being pale green with a fine, pale line down either side linking the spiracles, which are surrounded by rose-coloured circles. The Clouded Yellow caterpillar, which shares the same foodplants, is distinguishable by a short orange stripe either side of each breathing hole, with a black spot beneath each *(see p.39)*. The caterpillar of Berger's Clouded Yellow is totally different, and has the same basic colours of the Chalkhill and Adonis Blue caterpillars *(see p.97 and 101)*, which are also camouflaged to resemble horseshoe vetch. In this case, the cylindrical green caterpillar has bright yellow lines down its body and along both flanks, each punctuated by a pair of black blobs in every segment either side of each line. The chrysalises of all three Clouded Yellows are pale green, unlikely to be found, and almost impossible to distinguish.

The ecology and behaviour of these two butterflies is also rather different. Berger's Clouded Yellow is more likely to be seen on southern chalk downs, where horseshoe vetch is abundant, whereas the Pale Clouded Yellow generally settles in clover and lucerne fields. Of the two, the Pale Clouded Yellow is more docile, and spends much of the day hiding or feeding on lucerne, making strong zig-zag flights only in sunshine.

# PALE CLOUDED YELLOW
*Colias hyale*

# BERGER'S CLOUDED YELLOW
*Colias alfacariensis*

## LIFE-CYCLE

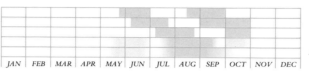

| | JAN | FEB | MAR | APR | MAY | JUN | JUL | AUG | SEP | OCT | NOV | DEC |
|---|---|---|---|---|---|---|---|---|---|---|---|---|
| EGG | | | | | | | | | | | | |
| CATERPILLAR | | | | | | | | | | | | |
| CHRYSALIS | | | | | | | | | | | | |
| ADULT | | | | | | | | | | | | |

ADULT

**Male**
Forewings slightly pointed; black edges to hindwings more extensive than those of Berger's Clouded Yellow.

**Male**
Forewings more rounded than those of Pale Clouded Yellow; brighter lemon-yellow coloration.

**Female**
Black dusting at base of wings is heavy in both sexes.

**Female**
Very similar to female Pale Clouded Yellow, but with paler and more rounded wings

**Chrysalis** [x1½]
Very similar to Clouded Yellow, but with a straighter head.

**Chrysalis** [x1½]
Well concealed among low vegetation; adult emerges after 1 to 2 weeks.

**Caterpillar** [x1½]
Hairier than Clouded Yellow caterpillar, and with a more granular appearance.

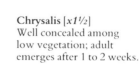

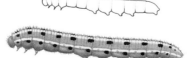

**Caterpillar** [x1½]
Camouflaged to resemble its sole foodplant, horseshoe vetch.

## PATTERNS OF IMMIGRATION

Both these species are irregular migrants, most frequently seen in Kent, Sussex, and the southeast. It is believed that most originate from central Europe, and having reached Britain they seldom wander far, even though they have a distinct urge to fly northwards in spring and south in autumn. Only a handful reach the Midlands, and both species are virtually unknown further north. Thus neither species has anything like the migratory powers of the Clouded Yellow, which arrives every year from southern Europe. These two, by contrast, are far more common in Holland than the Clouded Yellow. Unfortunately, although both hibernate as caterpillars and can survive quite cold winters, neither is able to withstand the dampness of the British Isles.

Both Pale and Berger's Clouded Yellows are generally seen in August or early September, with a few sightings in May and June, and some as late as October. It is likely that all early sightings are of immigrants, but that most seen from August onwards are their offspring. Both species are known to breed in Britain. Their occurrence has been highly irregular, and the records are confused due to misidentifications of *helice* Clouded Yellows and the uncertain identity of these two species. So far as one can tell, Berger's Clouded Yellow, which has a more southerly distribution in Europe, is considerably the rarer, and perhaps accounts for just one in ten sightings of these two species. Both tend to arrive in the same years, and were comparatively common on occasions in the years 1826 to 1950, when a total of 8,500 individuals were sighted – a seventh of the number of true Clouded Yellows seen in the same period. The ratio has been much lower in recent years, perhaps reflecting the intensification of agriculture and declining numbers, especially of Pale Clouded Yellows, in central Europe since the war.

## TWENTIETH-CENTURY RECORDS

Pale or Berger's Clouded Yellows were recorded in Britain as early as the eighteenth century. About a quarter of the 8,500 individuals seen up to 1950 were in one extraordinary year, 1900, when they were comparatively common throughout the south. There was then a lull until that celebrated decade for immigrants, the 1940s. Unlike the Clouded Yellow, which was common throughout the decade, these two species had just an exceptional five-year span from 1945 to 1949, when they were locally common in all but one year, and when a total of 1,979 specimens were reported. It is tempting to think that this had something to do with the disruption of agriculture in the latter stages of the war, which allowed Pale Clouded Yellows in particular to breed on the one- to two-year-old lucerne plants that they prefer. This, however, may be pure coincidence, for weather patterns too were unusual during this period.

There have been very few sightings of these butterflies since the 1940s, although I occasionally see both on the southern Dorset Downs. Pale Clouded Yellows, in particular, have declined in central Europe, but this does not necessarily mean that we will not enjoy another major immigration of these rarities. I well remember how this was said of the Clouded Yellow in the 1970s, only for all predictions to be confounded in 1983, when it temporarily became a common summer butterfly throughout southern England.

# BLACK-VEINED WHITE

## Aporia crataegi

THIS STRIKING and magnificent White will be familiar to any naturalist who visits the Continent in midsummer. Although on the wing as far north as Scandinavia, it is most common in central southern Europe, where sightings can more or less be guaranteed in any wild and wooded region. The adult is easy to spot, for its powerful, white or transparent wings, with their fine tracery of veins, are considerably wider than those of the Large White. It is impressive, too, in flight, as it soars effortlessly over a tree-top, or glides swiftly past with its wings held in a V.

In Britain, alas, the Black-veined White is now extinct. Although known to the earliest British entomologists, it was common only in a few regions, and then only for certain periods. Kent was the last great stronghold, and collectors can still be met who, as schoolchildren, peeled off the grey, cobwebbed hibernation nests, full of caterpillars, from apple and plum branches in orchards along the Stour. But the species mysteriously disappeared in the early 1920s, and all attempts at re-establishment have failed.

**Distribution** Extinct in the British Isles since the 1920s. The extent of its former range is shown here.

### SHEDDING SCALES

The Black-veined White is a moderately mobile butterfly, that would appear in a locality, breed in more or less isolated colonies for several years, and then die out again. There were also a few more permanent populations, but by and large these were extremely localized. In all areas, numbers would fluctuate enormously from one year to the next, and this is still the case on the Continent.

I have seen Black-veined Whites most often in the Dordogne and in eastern France, in the wooded foothills of the Alps, the Rhône Valley, and the beautiful Hautes Alpes. The butterfly is most easily found by looking especially along the scrubby edges of woods, in moist, damp valley bottoms, and in any flowering hay meadow nearby. Both sexes are avid feeders on flowers, and are easy to approach and photograph.

Black-veined Whites roost on tree-tops in wooded regions, although the old Kentish colonies would settle in cornfields, where they were found by the dozen in the best of years. In the morning there is a period of basking, before they begin to flutter and then soar in the growing warmth of the day. Pairing is also generally in the morning, and it is common to see them together, the female grasping the male tightly between her powerful wings. These rub backwards and forwards against her partner's, until many of the scales are missing, leaving a clear black network of wings against a translucent background. No one knows the point of this curious behaviour.

### EARLY DEVELOPMENT

British Black-veined Whites were generally seen in late June, reached a peak in early July and often survived into August. The eggs were laid in batches of 50 to 200, usually on the undersurface of a leaf. Blackthorn (*Prunus spinosa*) and hawthorn (*Crataegus monogyna*) were the two commonest foodplants, although apple, cherry, pear, and plum were all eaten in the orchards of Kent. This still happens in some fruit-growing regions of the Continent, where the Black-veined White is regarded as a pest in its periodic outbreak years.

The bright yellow eggs hatch after two to three weeks, and the mass of little caterpillars soon sets about the tenderest leaf-tips available, living in a group under a fine layer of silk. As they work down the stems they weave a more substantial web, which encompasses the entire group. According to F. W. Frohawk, who lived in Kent, the heart of Black-veined White country at the turn of the century, they would spend long periods hidden, with batches of one or two dozen caterpillars marching out of the nest in relays, to eat the same large leaf, sitting side by side in rows, before returning in a pack to digest this in the safety of the nest. In autumn, a much tougher, denser web is spun over the twigs making, as Frohawk noted, "a very secure and snug abode". The small caterpillars hibernate deep within, huddled together in small batches in pockets within the nest. They re-emerge and are at their most conspicuous in spring, as was well known to the very earliest British entomologists. Writing in 1766, Moses Harris described them "feeding very greedily on the Buds and young tender Leaves. Now is the best time to take them, they being easily seen on Account of their Size, as they lay on their Web altogether".

The caterpillars remain on their web until quite large, after which they usually split up into small groups. Each rests clasped along the twigs with the dense fringe of hairs pressed firmly against the bark, looking rather like the caterpillar of the Lackey moth. They are still quite easy to find at this stage and, as with many conspicuous and gregarious caterpillars, their hairs can provoke a small rash if touched. This is a form of protection against predators, and is reinforced by a foul smell that lingers malodorously over the entire nest. Finally, they drop off the shrub to pupate inconspicuously in vegetation on the ground.

## THE BLACK-VEINED WHITE IN BRITAIN

The story of the Black-veined White in Britain has been one of extreme fluctuations, with periods when it was locally common, punctuated by decades when it was rare. It was largely restricted to England, with the most northerly record coming from Yorkshire. It was absent from Ireland, and only penetrated the borders and southeast of Wales, where, however, it was quite common from time to time.

Comprehensive records begin early in the nineteenth century. There were probably three major strongholds – eastern Kent, the New Forest, and a wide swathe of wooded, hilly land extending from the Cotswolds southwards into Somerset and westwards through the Forest of Dean and Glamorgan. The occasional colony was also found in most other southern counties, but these colonies were temporary and few and far between, suggesting that this was nothing like so mobile a species as is popularly supposed. There is, for example, just one reliable record for Dorset, in 1815, despite the presence of huge populations in the New Forest 50 years later. It was also rare in other counties bordering the strongholds, such as Surrey and the whole of East Anglia, which had about half-a-dozen colonies between them.

Colonies disappeared one by one throughout the first 40 years of the nineteenth century, until the butterfly was restricted to the three strongholds and a few sites elsewhere. There was then an extraordinary resurgence, followed by an equally dramatic demise. Thus it occurred "in thousands" in several parts of the New Forest in 1860-70, but the colonies had collapsed three years later, and the last Hampshire specimen was taken in 1883. The great Kent populations went through the same cycles, but hung on longer. The butterfly had been recorded throughout the county in the first half of the century, and occurred in "phenomenal numbers" in the mid-1850s. At Wye it was the commonest butterfly on the wing in midsummer, and yet had disappeared altogether within four years.

So extensive was the decline that the butterfly was not seen at all in Kent from 1875-82. This caused great concern, and hundreds of continental specimens were imported and released, to the fury of some English entomologists. These attempts at reintroduction appear to have failed, and the small resurgence of Black-veined Whites in the extreme northeast corner of Kent is generally believed to stem from an overlooked pocket of native insects. Whatever their origin, these experienced a temporary recovery along the Stour Valley, and were common between 1902 and 1906. However, another decline set in, and the last reliable Kentish record was from Herne Bay, in 1922. The last authentic British colony died out a year later at Craycombe, Worcestershire, and the butterfly has only occasionally been seen as an adult since then, and never, so far as I know, as a caterpillar.

## THE PUZZLE OF POPULATION CHANGE

Black-veined White populations show the same kind of fluctuations in Europe as they did in Britain, at least in the north and west. For example, they crashed in Scandinavia in the 1950s, only to increase enormously after 1965. There have been many attempts to re-establish the butterfly in Britain, and although these seldom lasted more than a year or two, deliberate releases are probably responsible for all of the very occasional sightings that have been made since 1923. Vast numbers were released in Winston Churchill's grounds at Chartwell in Kent, only to disappear without trace, and hundreds were released on Holmwood Common in Surrey in the 1970s.

Why these attempts failed, and why the butterfly disappeared in the first place, is almost entirely unknown. Its habitat, so far as this is known, does not appear to have changed, and the only plausible lead is that declines often occurred in years that had been preceded by a wet September. This, however, has not always been the case. We must clearly await further studies of fluctuating populations by butterfly ecologists before we obtain the full story of its mysterious collapse.

# BLACK-VEINED WHITE · *Aporia crataegi*

LIFE-CYCLE

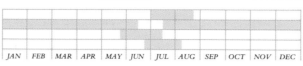

|  | JAN | FEB | MAR | APR | MAY | JUN | JUL | AUG | SEP | OCT | NOV | DEC |
|---|---|---|---|---|---|---|---|---|---|---|---|---|
| EGG |  |  |  |  |  |  |  |  |  |  |  |  |
| CATERPILLAR |  |  |  |  |  |  |  |  |  |  |  |  |
| CHRYSALIS |  |  |  |  |  |  |  |  |  |  |  |  |
| ADULT |  |  |  |  |  |  |  |  |  |  |  |  |

**Male upperside**
Grey, triangular patches at end of
wing-veins are sometimes absent.

**Male underside**
Undersides of both sexes are similar,
although male forewings are whiter.

**Female**
Scales lost during mating give the
forewings a translucent appearance.

**Chrysalis [x1½]**
As with other Whites, the
colour varies considerably.

**Egg [x15]**
Laid in batches of 50 to
200 on the underside of
leaves, hatching after
two weeks.

**Caterpillar on twig**
Mature caterpillar rests with
its body pressed against the
bark of a tree-trunk or twig.

**Mating**
Mating Black-veined Whites on blackthorn, with male grasped tightly
between the wings of the female.

**Caterpillar [x1½]**
Gregarious at first, living
within webs, but later solitary.

203

# BATH WHITE

## *Pontia daplidice*

Tнis ʟᴏᴠᴇʟʏ, dappled White has a curious pattern of immigration. Excessively rare in most years, it was nevertheless known and named by the earliest entomologists and had a brief resurgence in the 1940s when, in one year alone, over 700 individuals were reported. It has been virtually absent ever since, yet is common enough in southern Europe. I well remember the thrill of my first sighting – in the Colosseum in Rome – where scores of Bath Whites were fluttering around the scrubby vegetation surrounding the monuments.

The Bath White's true home is the Mediterranean and North Africa. As with so many Whites, the adults migrate north each spring, breed for two or three generations, and their offspring return south in autumn. But migrants seldom penetrate very far north, and the species is generally killed by British winters, despite some circumstantial evidence that a few successfully hibernated after the extraordinary influx of 1945.

Like the Orange Tip, whose female this somewhat resembles *(see p.53)*, the Bath White lays its eggs on Crucifers, although in this case the leaves, rather than the flowerheads, are the caterpillars' food. Another difference – in Sweden at least – is that the Bath White has a penchant for laying on seedlings and low-growing rosettes, and deliberately avoids large, mature Crucifers. This has little to do with the nutritional value of the leaves, but reflects the fact that the caterpillar needs to lie in the warmest spots available when living near the northern limit of its range.

### RECORDS FROM THE PAST

The first British record of a Bath White came from Gamlingay, near Cambridge. It was possibly a temporary resident, for specimens appear to have been caught in more than one year by William Vernon in the late seventeenth century. "Vernon's Half Mourner", as it was soon universally known, was thereafter extraordinarily rare and hardly featured at all among the patchy butterfly records from the eighteenth century. It did, however,

*Distribution Most sightings occur in southern England, close to the coast. Numbers are erratic, with large numbers being seen in some years.*

appear in an embroidery by a young lady of Bath, and Vernon's name was supplanted from 1795 onwards.

Records continued to be few and far between during the next 150 years. The butterfly was often entirely absent, and under 400 specimens were reported from between 1826 and 1944. Moreover, half of these stem from an unsatisfactory record by W. W. Collins who, in 1906, reported seeing over 200 Bath Whites on the Dorset Cliffs, west of Durdle Door. Unfortunately Collins' account was written some 30 years later, when just a single specimen survived to verify his memory.

### A YEAR WITHOUT PARALLEL

The year 1945 was the most extraordinary known for many of our rarer immigrants. It started, for the Bath White, on 14 July when, in less than an hour, J. Blaythwayt netted 38 specimens in a Cornish field, just exceeding Bernard Kettlewell, who took 37 in Cornwall that day. Together, they had collected more than the total number seen in Britain over the previous 50 years!

This was clearly part of a freak migration that embraced the whole of southern England and even reached Ireland. Between July and late October, over 700 specimens were reported. Most were probably immigrants, but numerous observations were made of egg-laying on sea radish *(Raphanus maritimus)*, wild mignonette *(Reseda lutea)*, and, especially, on hedge mustard *(Sysymbrium officinale)*, and many caterpillars, chrysalises, and emerging adults were found.

The phenomenon was, alas, short-lived. Although sightings were more frequent than usual in 1946-51, there has since been a very lean period indeed, with only 12 reported in the past 37 years, similar to the poorest stretches of the nineteenth century. It is, however, one of the fascinations of butterfly-watching that there remain a few erratic rarities that can yet be seen on British soil. Mid-July to late August is when the majority are reported, almost all from the southern English counties.

# BATH WHITE · *Pontia daplidice*

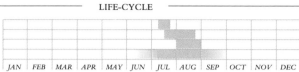

| | JAN | FEB | MAR | APR | MAY | JUN | JUL | AUG | SEP | OCT | NOV | DEC |
|---|---|---|---|---|---|---|---|---|---|---|---|---|
| EGG | | | | | | | | | | | | |
| CATERPILLAR | | | | | | | | | | | | |
| CHRYSALIS | | | | | | | | | | | | |
| ADULT | | | | | | | | | | | | |

**Male, second brood**
Underside hindwings yellow-green; first (spring) brood undersides are greener, but these rarely occur in Britain.

**Female, second brood**
Similar to the male, but more heavily marked with black; first-brood females are rarely seen in Britain.

GREEN FORM    BROWN FORM

**Feeding adult**
In Britain, adults lay their eggs on wild mignonette, and also feed on its nectar.

**Egg [*x15*]**
Laid singly; very similar to egg of the Orange Tip *(see p.53)*.

**Chrysalis [*x1½*]**
Attached to the foodplant; ground-colour is variable, as in other Whites.

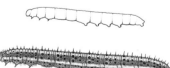

**Caterpillar [*x1½*]**
Feeds on the leaves of a wide variety of Crucifers.

# MAZARINE BLUE

*Cyaniris semiargus*

OF THE FOUR British butterflies to have become extinct since the mid-nineteenth century, the Mazarine Blue is the least spectacular and has attracted the least attention. To my knowledge, there has been no serious attempt to reintroduce it, in contrast to the considerable efforts made over the Large Copper, Black-veined White, and Large Blue. Occasional records of single specimens do still crop up, suggesting that a few surreptitious attempts may have been made. On the other hand, it is equally likely that twentieth-century records stem from accidental releases, for the eggs of this butterfly are easy to find on the Continent, and I know several naturalists who have brought them back to rear in captivity. Some of the resultant adults are then photographed on wild flowers, and a few will inevitably escape.

*Distribution A grassland species, extinct for over 100 years. Its main strongholds were Dorset, southeast Wales, and Gloucestershire.*

pale bases of firm, young tubes formed by the petals. In central France, the butterfly is particularly attracted to the clovers that regenerate in steamy, warm hay meadows, about three or four weeks after the first crop has been cut. The eggs are quite easy to find if you part the petals of the youngest, tightest clover buds. The egg hatches after one to two weeks.

The caterpillar lives first in the flowerheads, boring into the flowers with an ugly little head on an extensible neck, rather like a young Holly, Small, or Large Blue. Pupation, in northern Europe, takes a further nine months, for the caterpillar hibernates when half-grown, and resumes feeding on sprouting clover shoots the following spring. In its later stages, it possesses all the ant-attracting organs described on p.99, and is probably tended by ants as it feeds, although I have no first-hand knowledge of this. The chrysalis, too, attracts ants, and is probably buried by them in the same way as other Blues.

## HABITAT AND FOODPLANTS

This is an attractive, medium-sized Blue, looking rather like a large Silver-studded Blue *(see p.85)* from above, with lovely, cinnamon-coloured underwings spotted more like those of a Small or Holly Blue *(see pp. 81 and 103)*. It lives in small, discrete colonies on the Continent, as it clearly once did in Britain. Our populations, like those in northern Europe, had one generation a year, with the main adult period lasting from mid-June to mid-July. My experience of the species in Scandinavia, central France, the Pyrenees, and the Alps, suggests that it lives mainly in flowery meadows on damp soils, and again this appears to have been the case in Britain, or at least in its stronghold of Dorset, where most recorded colonies were on the heavy clays of the Blackmoor Vale, with just a few on sandstone and chalk.

The British foodplant of the Mazarine Blue is unknown, but was probably red clover *(Trifolium pratense),* for some of its sites were clover meadows and this is its principal food on the Continent. Kidney vetch *(Anthyllis vulneraria)* is also eaten on drier limestone sites. The females lay their eggs on flowers, fluttering around clovers, and often laying three or four on the

## COLONIES IN BRITAIN

In Britain, the Mazarine Blue has always been one of the rarest butterflies known. It was first recorded in 1710, and was subsequently found in 22 counties during the next 150 years, mainly in the south, but with a few records extending to Yorkshire. It is impossible to say how widespread it really was, for butterfly records were then extremely patchy, and travel was often difficult before the second half of the nineteenth century. On the other hand, some old records may be false, for frauds were quite common among certain Victorian dealers, and continental Mazarine Blues were imported and sold as British from as early as 1860.

There are three main areas where colonies definitely occurred. The most famous is Dorset, where the butterfly was "formerly widely distributed and locally common" according to E. R. Bankes, one of the leading local entomologists of that era. Almost everything known about these populations comes from

# MAZARINE BLUE · *Cyaniris semiargus*

## LIFE-CYCLE

| | JAN | FEB | MAR | APR | MAY | JUN | JUL | AUG | SEP | OCT | NOV | DEC |
|---|---|---|---|---|---|---|---|---|---|---|---|---|
| EGG | | | | | | | | | | | | |
| CATERPILLAR | | | | | | | | | | | | |
| CHRYSALIS | | | | | | | | | | | | |
| ADULT | | | | | | | | | | | | |

**Male**
Deep blue coloration of upperwings
is distinctive; underwing markings
resemble those of the Small Blue.

**Female**
Upperwings have a bronze sheen
shortly after emergence from
the chrysalis.

**Colour variants**
Two aberrant forms, with
extremes of spotting, caught
in the nineteenth century at
Glanvilles Wootton, Dorset.

**Feeding female**
Both adults and caterpillars
feed on red clover.

**Egg [x22]**
Pale blue-green when laid,
hatching after about 10 days.

**Feeding male**
Kidney vetch is used as a source
of nectar by the adults and as a
foodplant by the caterpillars.

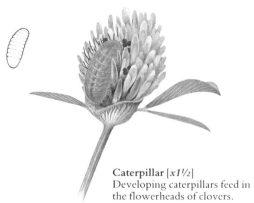

**Caterpillar [x1½]**
Developing caterpillars feed in
the flowerheads of clovers.

the collection and diaries of J. C. Dale, squire of Glanvilles Wootton. Dale's most famous colony was in a meadow near his home, where he collected or recorded the butterfly in 27 of the summers between 1808 and 1847. It was clearly common in at least 10 of those years, including 1808, when the 17-year-old Dale began his famous diaries. Nearly 300 adults were seen or collected from this colony; a few still survive in mint condition in the Hope Museum at Oxford, where I have had the pleasure of examining them. Three are included in the famous first plate of E. B. Ford's classic work, *Butterflies,* and others were loaned to Richard Lewington for the illustrations in this book.

There were at least eight other colonies in Dorset at that time, but these, although mainly in the Blackmoor Vale, were further afield and seldom visited. When and why they disappeared is unknown. The Glanvilles Wootton population "suddenly disappeared" in about 1841, and no colony has been reported from Dorset since then.

The other localities in which the butterfly was seen regularly and often were near Hereford, in Gloucestershire, and in Glamorgan. In Gloucestershire, it was found in various places up to 1865, and survived 12 years longer in Glamorgan, where it had previously been known "in plenty" near Merthyr between 1835 and 1837. The last authentic British colonies were at Penarth and Llantrisant, near Cardiff, where the butterfly was seen from 1871 to 1877. These became quite famous as a source of specimens. A local entomologist, Evan John, "took it every year and once saw about twenty in a field". He invited collector friends from Bristol to come and watch the butterflies at the sites, and had the edges of the hay meadow scythed so as not to impede their progress. This colony also disappeared, however, and there have been only a few single sightings since, although there is rumoured to have been a colony on the north Lincolnshire border that survived as late as 1903.

## AN UNEXPLAINED DISAPPEARANCE

Nobody can say why this attractive Blue disappeared from its scattered sites in the nineteenth century. One suggestion is that it was the victim of changes in haymaking, which resulted in clover being cut at a time when the eggs and caterpillars were still present. This is pure speculation, but is plausible: the single-brooded northern colonies of Mazarine Blue must be much more vulnerable than the southern ones, which develop more quickly. In central France, the colonies appear to move between the patchwork of little hay meadows that are still mown over a range of dates.

Today, most former British sites are greatly altered – at least in the Blackmoor Vale where I live – although there are still a few unfertilized, moist meadows where clover grows luxuriantly and is seldom cut. It would be interesting to try a reintroduction at some time in the future, perhaps using Scandinavian individuals, which have proved so suitable in the case of the Large Blue. Indeed, this may become a legal necessity if, as is likely, Britain signs the Berne Convention for the Conservation of European Wildlife. For, hidden among the small print is an obligation for all signatory nations to re-establish extinct species in their country. In the case of the Mazarine Blue, this would make a pleasant and harmless experiment, which could restore a delightful butterfly.

# LONG-TAILED BLUE *and*
# BLOXWORTH OR SHORT-TAILED BLUE

*Lampides boeticus* and *Everes argiades*

O N THIS and the following two pages, we deal with two of the daintiest vagrants to reach the British Isles. The Long-tailed Blue is one of the most widely distributed and common of the 6,000 species of Lycaenid butterfly known throughout the world. It occurs over the whole of Africa, in southern Asia, and Australia, and through the entire southern half of Europe. But in Britain it is a rare immigrant, causing understandable excitement when it does arrive. The silvery little Bloxworth or Short-tailed Blue is also a widespread species, being found from France to Japan. Despite this, it is the rarest vagrant illustrated in this book, and would scarcely merit inclusion were it a less attractive species.

## THE LONG-TAILED BLUE

The Long-tailed Blue is a lovely little insect, with a rapid, jerky flight more reminiscent of a Hairstreak than of a Blue. It also resembles our Hairstreaks in possessing long, delicate wing-tails, with an eye-spot where each joins the wing. It, too, has a curious way of slowly rotating each hindwing in unsynchronized circles. This makes the tails wave, thereby distracting the attention of predators from the more vulnerable parts of the body. One often sees the butterfly with a beak-mark where a bird has attacked the "wrong" end.

Unfortunately, this charming butterfly cannot withstand our winters, and in Europe is probably a permanent resident only in the Mediterranean region. There it can be extremely common; I have often watched Long-tailed Blues buzzing around the flowerheads of brooms *(Cytisus* spp.*)* and bladder senna *(Colutea arborescens)*, which are the principal leguminous plants on which they lay. The egg is a small white disc, similar to those of most other Blues, and the tiny caterpillar feeds first among the flowers before boring into the broom and senna pods. It grows quickly on this unappetizing medium, and the plump green caterpillars will be found munching away, by splitting open any pods that have a hole bored in their sides.

*Distribution* Long-tailed Blue: a *rare immigrant from southern Europe; Bloxworth Blue: a rare immigrant, recorded in Dorset, Hampshire, and Somerset.*

## LONG-TAILED BLUES IN BRITAIN

I have yet to see the Long-tailed Blue in Britain. This is scarcely surprising, for only about 120 have been reported since two were caught near Brighton, and one at Christchurch, in 1859. The species has been a scarce and irregular visitor ever since, with just 30 adults spotted in the following 80 years. Others have undoubtedly been overlooked, for this is one of our less conspicuous immigrants, especially when tattered, and it has at times been mistaken for the Common Blue *(see p.93)*.

The records for this species show an abrupt change in that extraordinary year of 1945, when an unprecedented number of Bath Whites, Queen of Spain Fritillaries, and other immigrants arrived. This wave of visitors included 38 Long-tailed Blues about a quarter of all British sightings of this species. Unfortunately, the butterfly subsequently settled down once again to the former pattern of immigration, and although six individuals were reported in the 1980s, the Long-tailed Blue belongs firmly to that group of butterflies that the naturalist in Britain may see once in a lifetime, if at all.

## BREEDING AND MIGRATION

The earliest British sighting of a Long-tailed Blue was in June, but most are seen in August and especially September, with a few in October and November. Nearly all have been evenly divided between the southern coastal counties, from Devon to Kent, with the remaining reaching the Midlands and north Wales. They are particularly attracted to gardens, probably because of the large, pod-bearing leguminous plants that are grown there.

In captivity, the Long-tailed Blue will breed on a wide range of legumes, and was known as the "Pea-pod Argus" to Victorian naturalists. There is clear evidence that it breeds in the wild in Britain. In 1952, a Mr. Chevalier found 26 eggs on an everlasting pea in Dorking, Surrey, where a female had been seen the week before; at Torquay in Devon, three were once caught together in one garden, and another six sightings made over the next few days. Caterpillars have also been found in broom pods at Bexhill in Sussex, and in 1945, eight emerged from senna pods that had been brought indoors as a flower arrangement. Caterpillars are occasionally imported in beans, but it is uncertain whether many wild adults result from these.

The Long-tailed Blue is certainly a powerful flier, given to annual migrations throughout the world, and regularly crossing large seas. These have been little studied in Europe, but a southerly migration definitely occurs through the Pyrenees each autumn, suggesting that there is a northerly movement from southern Spain in spring; our Long-tailed Blues are possibly the offspring of these migrants. It is surprising how few do arrive here, or penetrate northern Europe as a whole, given their migrations in Asia. There, they regularly ascend the foothills of the Himalayas in the dry season, and have been recorded in large numbers, still climbing, as high as 3,650 m. (12,000 ft.) in Nepal. The butterfly then follows this by a return to the lowlands in the wet season.

### THE BLOXWORTH BLUE

The Bloxworth or Short-tailed Blue was first reported in Britain by the Rev. Octavius Pickard Cambridge, the Victorian spider expert, whose sons took a female on 18 August 1885, while butterfly collecting on Bloxworth Heath. Two days later, they caught a male on the same heath, and the next day another schoolboy, Philip Tudor, took a third about 16 km. (10 miles) away, near Bournemouth.

1885 was one of the great years for immigrant Lepidoptera and this clearly included a small band of Bloxworth Blues, as they were promptly christened. Entomologists were few and far between in east Dorset a century ago, and the fact that three of these butterflies were found within three days suggests that a good many more may have been present. Unlike the Monarch, the Bloxworth Blue is not the sort of rarity one spots from afar. On the contrary, it can easily be mistaken for a Small, Silver-studded, or even Common Blue when on the wing.

These, in fact, were not the first British Bloxworth Blues to be caught. Two specimens of this rare species had already been netted 11 years earlier in a small quarry near Frome, and one, more dubiously, was taken at Blackpool in 1860. They remained unidentified, however, until Pickard Cambridge published the beautifully illustrated account of his findings in the *Proceedings of the Dorset Field Club* in 1886.

The next 55 years were very sparse indeed, with only three more records of what was increasingly being called the "Short-tailed Blue", after the minuscule wisps on the hindwings. Then,

in 1945, four specimens were seen. Since then there have been two records of the Bloxworth Blue in east Dorset in 1952 and two from Sussex, in 1958 and 1977.

### IMMIGRANTS AND OFFSPRING

It is interesting that 11 of the 17 British Bloxworth Blues were from a comparatively small area of central southern England, comprising east Dorset, west Hampshire, and south Somerset. This led the entomologist R. F. Bretherton to suggest that our specimens may originate from the heaths of Brittany, where the butterfly is still locally abundant.

Breeding has never been verified in Britain, but it is likely that some sightings were of the offspring of earlier immigrants. The butterfly has two broods a year in north Europe, the first emerging in May and June, the second in July to September, when all 17 British records were made. Although immigrant butterflies often arrive in bands, it would be extraordinary if two had stayed together as far inland as Frome, or even Bloxworth. It is much more likely that each pair was the offspring of an earlier immigrant. There would certainly have been an abundance of the caterpillar's foodplants present – clover *(Trifolium pratense)*, lucerne *(Medicago sativa)*, various trefoils *(Lotus* spp.*)*, tufted vetch *(Vicia cracca)* and, reputedly, gorse *(Ulex* spp.*)*.

There is therefore very little chance of seeing this butterfly in Britain, although it is common enough in central and southern Europe, where I have watched it many times. It does not appear to be a particularly strong flier, and is seldom mentioned among the true migrants of Europe. No one to my knowledge has studied its flight patterns, and it remains possible that it is more of a local wanderer than a migrant, akin to our own Holly Blue.

The male Bloxworth Blue, in particular, is attractive in flight, producing alternate flashes of deep blue and silver as the upper and underwings catch the sun. It has a jerky fluttering flight and, like most butterflies, is on the wing during the morning in central southern Europe, then resting during the heat of the day. There follows a second short period of activity in the late afternoon. On the Continent, it can often be seen along the edges of woods, in wasteland, and flying around the edges of scrub. Females frequently flutter over moist hay meadows a week or two after the first cut, laying profusely on sprouting clumps of clover as these regenerate from rootstocks in the warm damp soil.

This butterfly is an easy species to rear in captivity, and worth attempting, for the chrysalis is attractive, with long white hairs and black spots and lines on a pale green background. The caterpillar is pleasant but unexceptional – fleshy, slug-like, and a uniform pale green.

# LONG-TAILED BLUE
*Lampides boeticus*

# BLOXWORTH BLUE
*Everes argiades*

LIFE-CYCLE

|  | JAN | FEB | MAR | APR | MAY | JUN | JUL | AUG | SEP | OCT | NOV | DEC |
|---|---|---|---|---|---|---|---|---|---|---|---|---|
| EGG |  |  |  |  |  |  |  |  |  |  |  |  |
| CATERPILLAR |  |  |  |  |  |  |  |  |  |  |  |  |
| CHRYSALIS |  |  |  |  |  |  |  |  |  |  |  |  |
| ADULT |  |  |  |  |  |  |  |  |  |  |  |  |

ADULT

**Male**
Rarely seen in Britain; flight
rapid and jerky, like a Hairstreak's.

**Male**
Tiny wing-tails and twin orange spots
on undersides distinguish this from
other Blues.

**Female**
Amount of purple on the uppersides
varies; the undersides are constant
in both sexes.

**Female**
Purple coloration is variable, and almost
absent on some specimens.

**Chrysalis [*x2¼*]**
Formed inside a dry, curled
leaf, loosely attached by
silken threads.

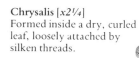

**Chrysalis [*x2¼*]**
Formed on the caterpillar
foodplant; adult emerges
after two weeks.

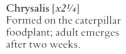

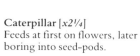

**Caterpillar [*x2¼*]**
Feeds at first on flowers, later
boring into seed-pods.

**Caterpillar [*x2¼*]**
Feeds on leguminous plants;
caterpillars are sometimes
cannibalistic.

# CAMBERWELL BEAUTY
## *Nymphalis antiopa*

THE CAMBERWELL BEAUTY is one of the most spectacular butterflies to be seen in the British countryside, and one that has always elicited great excitement. It is, in fact, a scarce and irregular immigrant from northern Europe, but for about 150 years the belief prevailed that it was native. "True British" specimens came to be regarded as the greatest of all prizes among early collectors. Fierce debates raged about their distinguishing features. For over a century, it was held that British Camberwell Beauties had whiter wing borders than their counterparts on the Continent. Cream-bordered specimens were considered to be foreign and valueless, with the result that at least one "British" specimen in the Natural History Museum was found to have had its borders painted white.

Although the Camberwell Beauty has a reputation for excessive rarity in Britain, roughly 1,500 sightings have been reported since the first two adults were seen in 1748, flying around willow trees along Cold Arbour Lane near Camberwell, which was then a village rather than the busy urban area of today. It has been a regular visitor ever since, with at least one sighting in nine-tenths of the years since 1850. Nevertheless, it is unusual for this butterfly to occur in any numbers. The great *"antiopa* years" of 1846, 1872, 1947, and 1976 caused a sensation, partly because they were so unexpected. In 1976, roughly 300 butterflies were seen.

### CLIMATE AND BREEDING
Despite being the second most frequent of the rarities included in this section, the Camberwell Beauty is the only species for which there is not even circumstantial evidence of breeding in the British Isles. This is puzzling, for adult Camberwell Beauties hibernate in far colder localities in Scandinavia than we experience in Britain.

It may be that our winters are too mild and wet for more than a handful of individuals to survive, although there is evidence that some achieve this in certain years. For example, although

***Distribution*** *Most sightings are in late summer, on the east coast of England and Scotland. Seen far inland in exceptional years.*

the vast majority of British sightings are made in August and September, small numbers are usually seen in April following an *antiopa* year. An exacerbating factor may well be that, like all species which hibernate as adults, the Camberwell Beauty does not pair until the following spring. Thus there may not be enough survivors within a particular region for any to find a mate.

There appears, at first sight, to be an abundance of suitable breeding sites for the Camberwell Beauty in Britain. The butterfly lays its eggs in large clusters around twigs, like its close relative the Large Tortoiseshell. Grey willow *(Salix cinerea)* is the main foodplant in Scandinavia, although other willows, poplars *(Populus* spp.), elms *(Ulmus* spp.), and birches *(Betula* spp.) are also used. The caterpillars are gregarious and highly conspicuous.

Caterpillars wander to form solitary chrysalises in late July, and the adult emerges about three weeks later. It is both the latest and largest of the northern European Tortoiseshells to appear, and loops among the trees in a bold, flitting flight, similar to that of a Peacock. Most of the butterflies enter hibernation quite early, and although they roam over the entire countryside the following spring, numbers fluctuate enormously even in Scandinavia.

### ARRIVALS IN BRITAIN
British immigrations are probably no more than an extension of these periodic buildups, wanderings, and expansions. Records in the British Isles were certainly few and far between 1954 and 1972, when Camberwell Beauties were absent from Denmark. Sometimes they have been introduced.

Most sightings of genuine immigrants are made in eastern counties. These cover the entire coastline, including Scotland, but most are from Kent and East Anglia, with Norfolk possessing the highest tally. The Camberwell Beauty does, however, wander inland more than most other rare immigrants.

# CAMBERWELL BEAUTY · *Nymphalis antiopa*

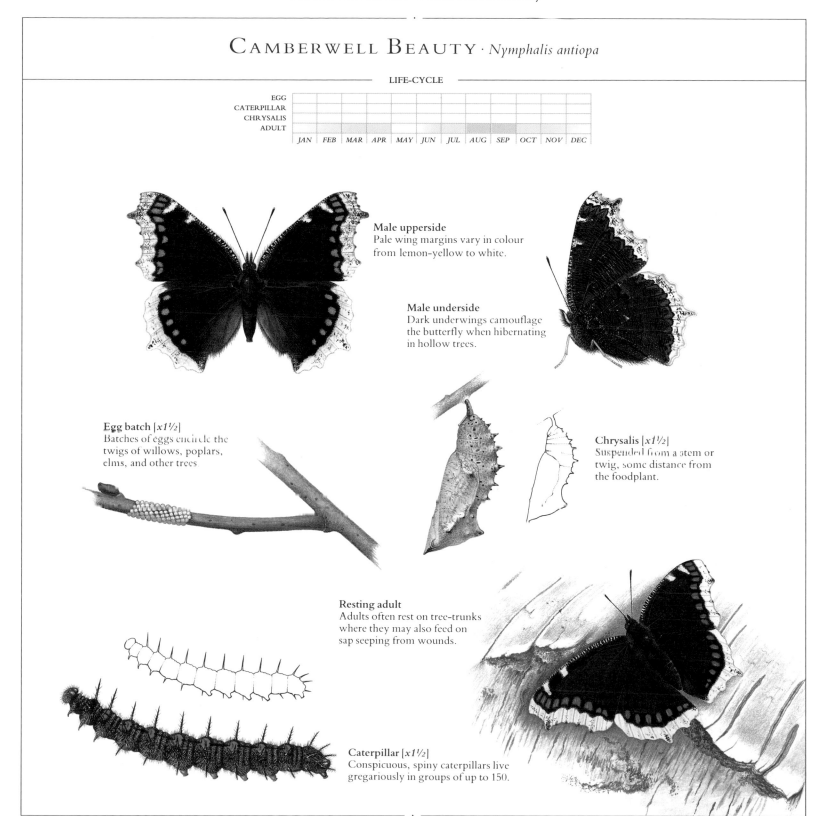

LIFE-CYCLE

| | JAN | FEB | MAR | APR | MAY | JUN | JUL | AUG | SEP | OCT | NOV | DEC |
|---|---|---|---|---|---|---|---|---|---|---|---|---|
| EGG | | | | | | | | | | | | |
| CATERPILLAR | | | | | | | | | | | | |
| CHRYSALIS | | | | | | | | | | | | |
| ADULT | | | | | | | | | | | | |

**Male upperside**
Pale wing margins vary in colour
from lemon-yellow to white.

**Male underside**
Dark underwings camouflage
the butterfly when hibernating
in hollow trees.

**Egg batch [x1½]**
Batches of eggs encircle the
twigs of willows, poplars,
elms, and other trees.

**Chrysalis [x1½]**
Suspended from a stem or
twig, some distance from
the foodplant.

**Resting adult**
Adults often rest on tree-trunks
where they may also feed on
sap seeping from wounds.

**Caterpillar [x1½]**
Conspicuous, spiny caterpillars live
gregariously in groups of up to 150.

213

# QUEEN OF SPAIN FRITILLARY

*Argynnis lathonia*

THE QUEEN OF SPAIN FRITILLARY was first recorded in Cambridgeshire nearly 300 years ago. It is unable to survive our winters, and all British sightings are of immigrants or their immediate offspring. Although an attractive – even spectacular – species, it has been reported no more than 380 times since its discovery, with over half the records being from the nineteenth century. It was, indeed, sufficiently well known to early English collectors to have acquired a range of names, including the "Scalloped Winged Fritillary" and the "Lesser Silver-spotted Fritillary".

In this century, however, the Queen of Spain Fritillary has been one of the scarcest of all immigrants. It is not, however, particularly rare on the Continent, nor is it especially associated with Spain. It is a butterfly that lives in a patchwork of apparently residential populations from which migrants spread every spring, and there is some evidence that their offspring return south in the autumn. Despite this, some permanent populations occur quite far north, for example on dry limestone pavement, beaches, and heaths in southern Scandinavia, and among the dunes along the Dutch coast. Here it breeds, apparently exclusively, on field pansy *(Viola arvensis)* and the beautiful tricolor pansy *(Viola tricolor),* although violets are also eaten in southern Europe. This may partly explain the absence of colonies in Britain, for neither of these pansies is particularly common in the dry southern grasslands where summer temperatures are warm enough for this species.

***Distribution*** *An extremely rare immigrant, seen about 380 times in the past 300 years, mainly near the south coast.*

## SHORT-RANGE MIGRATIONS

In northern Europe, the sites known to harbour this Fritillary are generally hot, dry localities where the adults fly in strong, zig-zagging flights between flowers. They frequently alight to bask on bare patches of ground, sitting with wings held open in a V towards the sun, so that the beautiful silver patches on the undersides are often half-visible. The caterpillars, too, spend much time basking, allowing their dark, velvety bodies to absorb the maximum heat from the sun's rays. Although the Queen of Spain Fritillary is a powerful flier, and makes genuine migrations every year, the distances covered appear to be much shorter than those achieved by its close relatives, the Painted Lady and Red Admiral. Thus, having arrived in Britain, it is seldom seen north of the southern coastal counties, and there are just three records from Ireland. There was a strong predominance of nineteenth-century records from the extreme southeast, mainly from the cliffs around Dover. This may merely reflect the distribution of naturalists in those days, but F. W. Frohawk, writing in the early 1930s, attributed it to the presence of strong permanent breeding colonies just across the Channel on the coast near Calais. These had already been destroyed by the time Frohawk was studying the butterfly, and he considered that the marked drop in immigrations in the present century was due to the loss of this source.

## FUTURE PROSPECTS

There has been a considerable decline in sightings of this beautiful Fritillary; most are made in September and early October, with some in July and a very few in June and May. Some of the late records are probably the offspring of single early immigrants, for the butterfly has two or three broods on the Continent, and egg-laying has been noticed in Britain. The discovery in early September 1945 of 25 individuals flying together at Portreath, Cornwall, strongly suggests that this is so.

The greatest years for the Queen of Spain Fritillary were 1868 (46 records), 1872 (50), and 1882 (25). There was then a long gap in which none was seen at all until the great immigration year of 1945 when 37 were reported, including the group at Portreath.

Unfortunately, Queen of Spain Fritillaries have been extremely scarce since 1950. The outlook is gloomy if our immigrant butterflies truly depend on making short flights from northern France, for flowery fields of pansies are now a great rarity there.

# QUEEN OF SPAIN FRITILLARY · *Argynnis lathonia*

### LIFE-CYCLE

| | JAN | FEB | MAR | APR | MAY | JUN | JUL | AUG | SEP | OCT | NOV | DEC |
|---|---|---|---|---|---|---|---|---|---|---|---|---|
| EGG | | | | | | | | | | | | |
| CATERPILLAR | | | | | | | | | | | | |
| CHRYSALIS | | | | | | | | | | | | |
| ADULT | | | | | | | | | | | | |

**Male**
Large silver patches of the undersides of the hindwings characterize this rare species.

**Female**
Larger than the male, with more green at the wing-bases; silver underwing patches similar to male's.

**Chrysalis [*x1½*]**
Suspended in low vegetation and camouflaged as a bird-dropping.

**Egg [*x22*]**
Laid singly; the tiny caterpillar emerges after about 10 days.

SIDE VIEW          VIEW FROM ABOVE

**Resting adult**
Male resting with forewings almost concealed by the hindwings.

**Basking adult**
Adults bask frequently on bare ground, with wings held open in a V towards the sun.

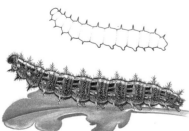

**Caterpillar [*x1½*]**
Coloration variable; some specimens may be almost black.

215

# MONARCH

## *Danaus plexippus*

THE MONARCH, or Milkweed, is the largest and most spectacular of the world's great migratory butterflies. It dwarfs every other species seen in Britain, and like most really large butterflies, looks very different from them on the wing. Instead of launching into the air in the fluttery or darting way to which we are accustomed, it flaps its black and tawny wings slowly and deliberately, like a lumbering bird of prey. However, once aloft, it soars and glides as gracefully as any species. It is a wonderful sight, one that is commonly seen in North America, whence most, if not all, our Monarchs originate.

After the many declines chronicled in this book, it is pleasant to report that Monarchs are being seen with increasing frequency in the British Isles, with over one quarter of all sightings being made in the single year 1981. Although this was something of a freak, the trend has also improved. It is little more than a century since the first British sighting was made, at Neath in south Wales on 6 September 1876. Three more were seen that year – two in Sussex and one in Dorset – and by the turn of the century, a total of 39 Monarchs had been reported. There was then a lull for about 30 years, when just the occasional individual was spotted, followed by a gradual, if erratic, increase ever since.

To date, about 400 specimens have been seen in the British Isles, with roughly 300 during in the past 50 years. There was even a period in the autumn of 1981 when you could more or less guarantee to see a Monarch in Cornwall and, especially, the Scilly Isles.

*Distribution A rare immigrant from America, mainly seen in the West Country and Isles of Scilly. Seen more frequently in recent years.*

beautiful striped caterpillars are also conspicuous as they chew the poisonous leaves of milkweeds *(Asclepia* spp.*)*. They strip and devour whole plants, impervious to the milky latex that deters other herbivores.

This immunity is responsible for the striking colours of the butterfly. The cocktail of chemicals, including heart-stopping agents and emetics, that is found in milkweed leaves is absorbed by the caterpillar and passed on to the adult, making both unpalatable to potential enemies. A few species of Mexican mice can apparently eat Monarchs, and some birds have learned to strip off the more poisonous parts, but by and large the butterfly is highly obnoxious, causing immediate vomiting and distress to anything eating it. The warning colours are soon learned by predators, and for every one Monarch killed, many others are later spared.

## THE MONARCH IN AMERICA

To appreciate this butterfly properly, you must visit America. Each continent has its own subspecies, but those seen in Britain are invariably the North American form. There the Monarch is one of the commonest and most spectacular of butterflies, breeding in weedy meadows, damp pasture, and wasteland almost everywhere as far north as the Hudson Bay. The

## MIGRATIONS AND MASS ROOSTS

The Monarch is a feature of the American countryside throughout spring and summer, yet this is essentially a tropical butterfly that is unable to withstand intense winter cold. In September, adults start to fly south, first in groups of two and threes, gradually gathering numbers all the way and finally culminating in gigantic swarms. One awed observer in the 1880s wrote that these were "almost beyond belief... millions is feebly expressive... miles of them is no exaggeration".

Migrating Monarchs fly mainly by day, resting at night by the thousand on trees. Two major streams soon develop, divided by the Rocky Mountains. Western Monarchs settle in California, where they hibernate in many different places, mainly near the sea. Thousands roost together in groves or on individual trees, dangling below the branches with their wings closed, as if the tree itself were a gigantic butterfly and they the scales. These wonderful roosts have long been a feature of Californian culture, celebrated in statues, children's parades, and Beach Boys' songs. Needless to say, not everyone is as

# MONARCH · *Danaus plexippus*

## LIFE-CYCLE

| | JAN | FEB | MAR | APR | MAY | JUN | JUL | AUG | SEP | OCT | NOV | DEC |
|---|---|---|---|---|---|---|---|---|---|---|---|---|
| EGG | | | | | | | | | | | | |
| CATERPILLAR | | | | | | | | | | | | |
| CHRYSALIS | | | | | | | | | | | | |
| ADULT | | | | | | | | | | | | |

**Male upperside**
Male has a small scent patch (sex-brand)
on each hindwing.

**Male underside**
Markings similar to those of upperside,
but hindwing paler.

**Egg [x15]**
Laid singly on the
leaves of milkweeds.

**Chrysalis**
Wing patterns are visible
just before emergence.

**Female**
Similar to male; veins often more heavily
marked with black.

**Caterpillar**
Poisons obtained from the
foodplant protect the caterpillar
from predators.

appreciative as might be hoped, and there are heavy fines for anyone who interferes with a roost.

## A MYSTERY SOLVED

Californian Monarch roosts are one of the natural wonders of the world, but even they are surpassed by the almost unbelievable wintering site of the east and central American populations. Their destination had always been a mystery, and it was not until 1975 that this was solved by Fred Urquhart, following a lifetime's pioneering research on this species. Urquhart traced the migrations to the Sierra Madre, and the mountain forests of middle Mexico. Here, in contrast to California, the entire east continental swarm hibernates in just one (or possibly two) small patches. Many millions of Monarchs gather together annually, smothering everything that can be perched upon. Bob Pyle, author of the *Audubon Handbook for Butterfly Watchers,* has visited the roost, and eloquently describes the extraordinary spectacle:

"Imagine yourself basking… on a Mexican mountainside… it is snowing, snowing butterflies. Monarch butterflies fill the sky and eclipse the sun; Monarchs falling, drifting, sailing, and gliding; Monarchs every shade of orange, as the sun backlights or falls full upon them: pumpkin, salmon, or flame. They alight on every surface, and every purple *Senecio* supports a dozen drinkers, every bough a hundred baskers. Monarchs alight on your boots, your belly, your face, give you a physical and mental massage of softly beating wings. So many butterflies flutter that a soft, rushing whir fills the mountain air – yes, you can actually hear the Monarchs.

"The rustle keeps up, unabated for a second, until the sun begins to fall below the Firs. Only then do the millions of migrants start to settle back onto the Oyamels for the night, clinging to every needle so thickly that they form a pelage like reddest fox fur. Then it becomes a still world of orange butterflies – walls of Monarchs, curtains, solid tree trunks, boughs, and the whole forest groves of Monarchs, with scarcely a green needle showing through. The sun goes down and a chill rises. Having caught the last beams… the masses close their wings and become ashen scales against the dark foliage of Firs."

Monarchs remain in their roosts until spring, before embarking on a return flight of up to 1,600 km. (1,000 miles) north to breed. In fact, few retrace their steps completely: the first wave usually lays eggs in the central southern states, and these develop within three or four weeks to form a second generation that in turn progresses north. This sequence continues until southern Canada is colonized in June, where Monarchs breed for three months before the great trek southwards is resumed.

## TRANSATLANTIC VISITORS

The current belief is that our British immigrants stem from these southward autumnal migrations, and represent individuals that are blown out over the Atlantic in years of strong easterly winds. About 350 of 440 dated British records have been in September or October, and peak years have coincided with unusually high numbers of immigrant birds from America. There is some evidence that Monarchs also arrive as stowaways on ships, but these are almost certainly a small minority, as are the recent escapes from butterfly houses. A few might also come from the Azores, Canary Islands, and Spain. The first two archipelagos were colonized by Monarchs in the 1860s, as part of a worldwide expansion that took the species to several Pacific islands, Australia, New Zealand, and the East Indies. The butterfly has colonized Spain in the last decade, with breeding recorded on introduced milkweeds in many localities.

The signs are, therefore, that we can expect an increasing number of Monarchs to reach Britain in future years. Most sightings have been in Cornwall and the Scilly Isles, with a gradual reduction as one progresses east and north. Nevertheless, the occasional individual penetrates very much further, and there are scattered records for almost the whole of the British Isles, including one from the Shetlands.

Unfortunately, this lovely immigrant is unable to establish itself here. In the first place, the autumn arrivals cannot survive our winters, and any that did would be unable to breed, for milkweeds are not indigenous, and are found only in a few sheltered gardens. It is interesting to note, however, that one record of a sort for British breeding exists for this species. This occurred in 1981, when a female escaped from a south London butterfly farm and laid on the milkweeds of Kew Gardens. The eggs were reared indoors, and successfully produced the only known example of home-bred Monarchs.

# FURTHER READING

Readers wishing to unearth further information on different aspects of butterfly natural history will find much of interest in the publications listed below. Many statements in this book are drawn from these, as well as from continental books, or from others that have long been out of print. The last include the influential works of J. Petiver, M. Harris, A. H. Haworth, H. N. Humphries and J. O. Westwood, F. O. Morris, E. Newman, J. W. Tutt, R. South, F. W. Frohawk, E. B. Ford, and C. B. Williams.

## FIELD AND IDENTIFICATION GUIDES

### BRITISH ISLES

Brooks, M. and Knight, C., *A Complete Guide to British Butterflies*, Jonathan Cape, London, 1982
Thomas, J. A., *Hamlyn Guide to the Butterflies of the British Isles*, Hamlyn, London, 1989 (2nd edition)

### EUROPE

Chinery, M., *Collins New Generation Guide to the Butterflies and Day-flying Moths of Britain and Europe*, Collins, London, 1989
Geiger, W. (ed.) *Die Tagfalter und ihr Lebensraum*, Schweizerisches Bund fur Naturschutz, Basel, 1987
Henriksen, H. J. (ed.), *The Butterflies of Scandinavia*, Skandinavisk Bogforlag, Odense, 1982
Higgins, L. G. and Riley, N. D., *A Field Guide to the Butterflies of Britain and Europe*, Collins, London, 1980 (4th edition)
Whalley, P., *The Mitchell Beazley Pocket Guide to Butterflies*, Mitchell Beazley, London, 1981

## DISTRIBUTION AND STATUS

Heath, J., Pollard, E., and Thomas, J. A., *Atlas of Butterflies in Britain and Ireland*, Viking, Harmondsworth, 1984

## GENERAL REFERENCE

Maitland Emmet, A. and Heath, J., *The Moths and Butterflies of Great Britain and Ireland*, Harley Books, Colchester, 1989
Williams, C. B., *Insect Migration*, Collins, London, 1958

## BIOLOGY AND NATURAL HISTORY

Dennis, R. L. H., *The British Butterflies: their Origin and Distribution*, Classey, Faringdon, 1977
Feltwell, J., *The Natural History of Butterflies*, Croom Helm, London, 1986
Ford, E. B., *Butterflies*, Collins, London, 1957 (3rd edition)
Vane-Wright, R. J., and Ackery, P. (eds.), *The Biology of Butterflies*, Academic Press, London, 1984
Whalley, P., *Butterfly Watching*, Severn House, London, 1980

## GARDENING FOR BUTTERFLIES

Oates, M., *Garden Plants for Butterflies*, Masterton, Fareham, 1985
Payne, M., *Gardening for Butterflies*, British Butterfly Conservation Society, Loughborough, 1987
Rothschild, M. and Farrell, C., *The Butterfly Gardener*, Michael Joseph, London, 1983

## ART PUBLICATIONS

Beningfield, G. and Goodden, R., *Beningfield's Butterflies*, Chatto & Windus, London, 1981

## SCIENTIFIC JOURNALS

Many learned papers on the biology of European butterflies have been published in scientific journals, particularly the following: *Biological Conservation, Biological Journal of the Linnean Society, Ecological Entomology, Entomologist's Gazette, Entomologist's Monthly Magazine, Entomologist's Record, Entomologist, Journal of Animal Ecology, Journal of Applied Ecology, Oecologia, Oikos*. The bulletins of both the British Butterfly Conservation Society and Amateur Entomological Society contain original accounts of butterflies of particular appeal to the lay naturalist.

## LOCAL PUBLICATIONS

### AVON

Manning, S., *The Common Butterfly Survey 1986*, Bristol Regional Environmental Records Centre, 1986

### BEDFORDSHIRE

Nau, B. S., Boon, C. A., and Knowles, J. P., *Bedfordshire Wildlife*, Castlemead Publications, 1987

### BERKSHIRE AND BUCKINGHAMSHIRE
*see also* Oxfordshire

Steel, C. and Steel, D., *Butterflies of Berkshire, Buckinghamshire and Oxfordshire*, Pisces Publications, Oxford, 1985

### CHESHIRE

Rutherford, C. I., *Butterflies in Cheshire 1961 to 1982*, Supplement to the *Proceedings of the Lancashire and Cheshire Entomological Society* 1983

### CLEVELAND

Smith, J. K. and Smith, H., *Butterflies in Cleveland*, Cleveland Nature Conservation Trust, 1984

### CORNWALL AND THE ISLES OF SCILLY

Agassiz, D., *Lepidoptera of the Isles of Scilly*, Isles of Scilly Museum Association, 1981
Smith, F. H. N., *A List of Cornish Butterflies and Moths*, Cornish Trust for Nature Conservation, 1984

## DERBYSHIRE

Harrison, F. and Sterling, M. J., *Butterflies and Moths of Derbyshire, Part 1,* Derbyshire Entomological Society, 1985

## DEVON

Bristow, R. and Bolton, D., *Devon Butterflies – Provisional Atlas 1989,* Exeter City Council, 1989

## DORSET

Thomas, J. A. and Webb, N., *Butterflies of Dorset,* Dorset Natural History and Archaelogical Society, 1984

## ESSEX

Emmett, A. M., Pyman, G. A., and Corke, D., *The Larger Moths and Butterflies of Essex,* Essex Field Club, 1985

Payne, R.G. and Skinner, J. F., *Butterflies of Essex – Provisional Maps,* Essex Biological Records Centre, 1982

## GLOUCESTERSHIRE

Meredith, G. H. J., *Butterfly Distribution in Gloucestershire 1975-1988,* The Gloucester Naturalist No. 4, 1989

## HAMPSHIRE

Hoskins, A. (ed.), *Hampshire Butterfly Report 1989,* British Butterfly Conservation Society (Hampshire), 1990

## HERTFORDSHIRE

Sawford, B., *The Butterflies of Hertfordshire,* Castlemead Publications, 1987

## KENT

Chalmers-Hunt, J. M., *The Butterflies and Moths of Kent 3: Heterocera and supplement,* Supplement to Entomologists' Record and Journal of Variation, 1981

## LINCOLNSHIRE

Duddington, J. and Johnson, R., *The Butterflies and Larger Moths of Lincolnshire and South Humberside,* Lincolnshire Naturalists' Union, 1983

## LONDON

Plant, C. W., *The Butterflies of the London Area,* London Natural History Society, 1987

## MERSEYSIDE

British Butterfly Conservation Society (Merseyside), *Butterflies of Merseyside,* BBCS Merseyside, 1987

## NORFOLK

Ellis, E. A., *Butterflies of Norfolk in the 19th and 20th Centuries,* Transactions of the Norfolk and Norwich Naturalists' Society 26 (5): pp.321-334, 1984

## NORTHUMBERLAND

Dunn, T. C. and Parrack, J. D., *The Moths and Butterflies of Northumberland and Durham,* Northern Naturalists' Union: *The Vasculum,* supplement No. 2 (1986)

## OXFORDSHIRE *see also* Berkshire and Buckinghamshire

Knight, R. and Campbell, J. M., *An Atlas of Oxfordshire Butterflies,* Oxford County Council, 1986

## STAFFORDSHIRE

Warren, R. G., *Atlas of Lepidoptera of Staffordshire – Part 1: Butterflies,* Staffordshire Biological Recording Scheme, 1984

## SUFFOLK

Mendel, H. and Piotrowski, S. H., *The Butterflies of Suffolk – an Atlas and History,* Suffolk Naturalists' Society, 1986

## SURREY

Collins, G. A., *Butterflies of Surrey – Provisional Maps 1970-1987,* Croydon Natural History and Scientific Society Ltd.,1988

## SUSSEX

Pratt, C., *A History of the Butterflies and Moths of Sussex,* Borough of Brighton, 1981

## WARWICKSHIRE

Smith, R. and Brown, D., *The Lepidoptera of Warwickshire, Parts 1 and 2,* Warwickshire Museum Service, 1987

## WORCESTERSHIRE

Green, J., *A Practical Guide to the Butterflies of Worcestershire,* Worcestershire Nature Conservation Trust, 1982

## YORKSHIRE

Sutton, S. L. and Beaumont, H. E., *Butterflies and Moths of Yorkshire – Distribution and Conservation,* Yorkshire Naturalists' Union, 1989

## WALES

Morgan, I. K., *A Provisional Review of the Butterflies of Carmarthenshire,* Nature Conservancy Council, 1989

## SCOTLAND

Lorimer, R. I., *The Lepidoptera of the Orkney Islands,* Classey, Faringdon, 1983

Thomson, G., *The Butterflies of Scotland – a Natural History,* Croom Helm, London,1980

## SOCIETIES TO JOIN

The Amateur Entomologists' Society, c/o 355 Hounslow Road, Hanworth, Feltham, Middlesex.

The British Butterfly Conservation Society, Tudor House, Quorn, near Loughborough, Leicestershire LE12 8AD.

The National Trust, 36 Queen Anne's Gate, London SW1H 9AS.

The Woodland Trust, Westgate, Grantham, Lincolnshire NG31 6LL.

# Index

Page numbers in *italic* refer to illustrations

# ACKNOWLEDGMENTS

Much of the information given in this book is based on the research or first-hand observations of the author and artist. However, we have obviously drawn heavily on the published and unpublished accounts of many other scientists and naturalists, past and present. Although, for reasons of space, we have not been able to mention all sources throughout the text, it is our wish to acknowledge our very great debt and gratitude to those who have knowingly or unwittingly contributed to this book.

We would like to record our particular thanks to the following, whose work has been of great assistance in the preparation of this book:

*Chequered Skipper* R. V. Collier; N. Ravenscroft *Large Skipper* R. L. H. Dennis *Silver-spotted Skipper* D. J. Simcox; C. D. Thomas *Dingy Skipper* C. D. Thomas *Swallowtail* J. P. Dempster; M. L. Hall; C. Wiklund *Wood White* M. S. Warren; C. Wiklund; E. Pollard *Brimstone* T. J. Bibby; J. Forsberg; E. Pollard *Large White* J. S. E. Feltwell; M. Rothschild; R. R. Baker; M. A. Zaher *Small White* O. W. Richards; J. P. Dempster; M. Rothschild; R. R. Baker; J. E. Moss; J. H. Myers; T. W. Gossard *Green-veined White* J. Forsberg; T. G. Shreeves; S. Yata; H. A. Leeds *Orange Tip* S. P. Courtney; C. Wiklund; J. Forsberg; R. L. H. Dennis; J. P. Dempster; C. D. Thomas *White-letter Hairstreak* M. Davies *Small Copper* J. P. Dempster *Large Copper* E. Duffey; F. Bink *Small Blue* A. C. Morton *Silver-studded Blue* C. D. Thomas; M. J. Read; D. Jordano; N. Ravenscroft; R. L. H. Dennis *Brown Argus* N. Bourn; F. V. L. Jarvis; O. Hoegh-Guldberg *Northern Brown Argus* F. V. L. Jarvis; O. Hoegh-Guldberg; B. J. Selman *Common Blue* R. L. H. Dennis; J. F. D. Frazer *Chalkhill Blue* J. F. D. Frazer *Holly Blue* K. J. Willmott *Large Blue* T. A. Chapman; E. B. Purefoy; G. M. Spooner; J. C. Wardlaw; D. J. Simcox *Duke of Burgundy* M. Oates; K. J. Porter; K. J. Willmott *White Admiral* E. Pollard *Purple Emperor* K. J. Willmott; I. R. P. Heslop; G. E. Hyde; R. E. Stockley *Painted Lady* E. Pollard *Small Tortoiseshell* R. R. Baker; R. L. H. Dennis; A. S. Pullin *Peacock* R. R. Baker *Comma* S. Nylen; C. R. Pratt *Fritillaries (violet-feeding)* R. G. Snazell; I. L. Moy *Silver-washed Fritillary* D. B. E. Magnus; W. Vielmetter *High Brown Fritillary*

M. Oates; D. J. Simcox *Marsh Fritillary* K. J. Porter; M. S. Warren; A. Fowles; D. J. Simcox *Glanville Fritillary* D. J. Simcox; C. R. Pope; K. J. Willmott *Heath Fritillary* M. S. Warren *Speckled Wood* T. G. Shreeve; N. B. Davies; P-O. Wickman; H. A. Leeds; M. J. Goddard *Wall* R. L. H. Dennis; P-O. Wickman *Mountain Ringlet* K. J. Porter *Scotch Argus* R. L. H. Dennis; J. E. H. Blackie *Marbled White* A. Wilson; A. R. Paul *Grayling* N. Tinbergen; R. Findlay; J. A. Findlay; M. R. Young; R. L. H. Dennis *Gatekeeper* P. M. Brakefield *Meadow Brown* P. M. Brakefield; W. H. Dowdeswell; M. L. Munguira; E. Pollard *Small Heath* P-O. Wickman; H. A. Leeds *Large Heath* T. Melling; J. R. G. Turner; R. L. H. Dennis; K. J. Porter *Bath White* J. Forsberg; H. B. D. Kettlewell *Black-veined White* C. R. Pratt *Camberwell Beauty* L. H. Newman *Monarch* P. Ackery; R. M. Pyle; R. I. Vane-Wright; M. Rothschild *Migrants* C. B. Williams; R. F. Bretherton; R. R. Baker.

We are also extremely grateful to colleagues for commenting on parts or all of the text, and for providing additional information. These include M. Davies, R. L. H. Dennis, M. L. Hall, T. Melling, M. L. Munguira, M. Oates, K. J. Porter, N. Ravenscroft, D. J. Simcox, M. S. Warren, I. West, and M. R. Young.

It is also a pleasure to thank G. McGavin and D. Carter, respectively, for access to specimens in the Hope Entomological Collections of Oxford, and those of the British Museum. Livestock was very kindly supplied by K. Bailey, S. Bradley, S. Foster, A. Gardner, M. Hoare, R. Lilley, J. McFeely, C. Rivers, F. Rayner, J. Tucker, M. Wilkins, K. Willmott, and C. Wiskin.

Finally, we are extremely grateful to the long-suffering team at Dorling Kindersley who produced this book. In particular, we would like to thank David Burnie, Philip Lord, Derek Coombes, Jemima Dunne, and Krystyna Mayer.

DORLING KINDERSLEY would like to thank Iain Harper of Suripace Ltd (typesetting), Guy Poltock (preparation of paste-up), Amanda Ronan and Alison Melvin (editorial assistance), and Hilary Stephens (production).